Revolt of the Rednecks

harper ✦ torchbooks

A reference-list of Harper Torchbooks, classified
by subjects, is printed at the end of this volume.

SUPPLEMENT TO

Winston County Journal

Friday, July 23, 1915.

LIEUTENANT-GOVERNOR THEO G. BILBO
THE PROGRESSIVE AND CONSTRUCTIVE STATESMAN

Revolt of the Rednecks

MISSISSIPPI POLITICS:
1876-1925

by
Albert D. Kirwan

HARPER TORCHBOOKS ♦ The Academy Library
Harper & Row, Publishers / New York, Evanston and London

To Betty

THE REVOLT OF THE REDNECKS
Copyright, 1951
University of Kentucky Press
Printed in the United States of America.

*This book was originally published in 1951 by
the University of Kentucky Press. It is here
reprinted by arrangement.*

First HARPER TORCHBOOK *edition published 1965 by
Harper & Row, Publishers, Incorporated
49 East 33rd Street
New York, New York 10016.*

CONTENTS

CONTENTS

MAPS AND ILLUSTRATIONS

Lieutenant-Governor Bilbo   *Frontispiece*

The following illustrations will be found in a group following page 162

Racial Distribution of Mississippi

Soil Map of Mississippi

James Z. George and L. Q. C. Lamar

E. C. Walthall, A. J. McLaurin, and John Sharp Williams

The "White Chief" Visits Kosciusko in the Senatorial
Election of 1911

Campaign Propaganda for Theodore G. Bilbo

With the end of Radical Reconstruction in Mississippi in the winter of 1875-1876 the whites came once more into complete control of the state government. The agency through which the whites governed was the Democratic party, and save for one or two occasions, their control was undisputed by the Republicans, whose organization rapidly disintegrated. Thereafter, all political issues had to be settled within the councils of the Democratic party, and control of the party machinery was, therefore, of paramount importance. In the early decades after the "revolution" this party machinery was in the hands of those who had led the revolt, and these leaders were, in general, sympathetic to and influenced by the new corporate and financial interests in the state—the railroads, the banks, the merchants.

In post-Civil War years agriculture in Mississippi, as elsewhere, was in a depressed condition. The price of cotton steadily declined, and the farmer was hard put to meet the payments on his mortgage. At the same time the corporate and banking interests of the state seemed to prosper. There were reasons for this beyond the ken of the poor hill farmer—the redneck, as he was popularly termed. But the redneck came to regard this situation—chronic depression for him while his mercantile neighbor prospered—as a conspiracy against him, a conspiracy which was aided and abetted by the leaders of his party.

This history is a study of the struggle of the redneck to gain control of the Democratic party in order to effect reforms which would improve his lot. He was to be led into many bypaths and sluggish streams before he was to realize his aim in the election of Vardaman to the governorship in 1903. For almost two decades thereafter the rednecks were to hold undisputed control of the state government. The period was marked by many reforms and by some improvement in the economic plight of the farmer—an improvement largely owing to factors which were uninfluenced by state politics. The period closes in 1925 with the repudiation and defeat at the polls of the farmers' trusted leaders, Vardaman and Bilbo.

I wish to express appreciation to Professor Charles S. Sydnor of the history department of Duke University, whose kindly advice and wisdom have done much to bring out whatever merit this study may have. He is, of course, in no way responsible for errors which the work may have.

I acknowledge with gratitude a grant from the University of Kentucky Research Fund Committee which aided in the publication of the study.

The staffs in the Manuscripts and Newspaper divisions of the Library of Congress gave kindly and courteous assistance to me in my research there. The staff of the Mississippi Department of Archives and History was most helpful. To them, especially to Mrs. William Harrell, I wish to express my thanks. I am also indebted to the staffs of the Duke University Library and the University of North Carolina Library.

My wife, Betty Kirwan, has aided me throughout the research, composition, and revision of the work. Her suggestions and criticisms have been invaluable aids to me. More than this, she has borne the drudgery of numerous typings and retypings. Without her assistance the study could not have been completed.

A. D. Kirwan

Lexington, Kentucky
September 6, 1950

CHAPTER I

THE STRUGGLE FOR THE
NEGRO VOTE

MISSISSIPPI politics in the period from 1875 to 1890 is a tale of almost ceaseless intraparty struggle. To be sure this is characteristic of politics in many places and in many periods. But whereas in sections blessed with a two-party system the struggles climaxed in interparty contests, the main struggle in Mississippi was for control of the Democracy. When Radical Governor Adelbert Ames resigned in 1876 while undergoing impeachment trial, he left the opposition in complete control. To many whites this recapture of the state government by the Democrats seemed like a return to ante-bellum political conditions. But new factors were present in the post-Reconstruction period that were to negate this semblance. In the first place the old party leaders had been discredited by the events of the war and Reconstruction, and the new leaders were to be men of little prominence in governmental affairs in the earlier period. Secondly, and far more important, the six years of Radical rule had left as a heritage a bitter racial antipathy which was to becloud all issues in the later period.

For a time after this overthrow in 1876 the Republican party lingered on as a threat—albeit a constantly diminishing one—to Democratic supremacy. The Democrats were determined, by hook or by crook, to retain control, and it soon became apparent that one could obtain political power only within that party. The struggle was complicated by many factors—personal ambitions, peculiar sectional needs, economic distress, and the presence of the Negro.

In 1875 Mississippians had "defied the federal laws and overthrown the government of the state without any regard for statutory law or the constitution."[1] The revolution was organized by two men—J. Z. George and L. Q. C. Lamar. George, as chairman of the state Democratic executive committee, was the guiding genius of the political battle in the field; while Lamar, from his seat in Congress, won the sympathy of the country for the plight of the southern whites. Lamar's task was a difficult one. Elected to Congress in 1873, the only representative of the Democratic party from the state, he was enveloped in the suspicion and distrust which northern congressmen held for the ante-bellum southern leaders.

[1] Statement by Dr. F. L. Fulgham, quoted in Jackson *Issue*, Aug. 12, 1910.

His earnest efforts at reconciliation between the sections first gained the respect and confidence of his northern colleagues. His astute eulogy of Senator Charles Sumner won their admiration without offending his own people.[2] By supporting the Electoral Commission in the disputed presidential election in 1876 he helped win for his section noninterference by the federal government in state affairs. His contribution to the revolution was a diplomatic one in that it helped break down sectional antagonism and made George's path less rough. Lamar's achievement has been termed "the most brilliant and successful defensive campaign ever fought by a Southerner."[3]

Lamar was chosen by the legislature of 1876 to succeed Hiram R. Revels, Negro, in the United States Senate. From this vantage point he continued to be the confidant and collaborator of George in the struggle against the Mississippi Republicans, with their "large majority of blacks so well drilled."[4] In the autumn of 1876 he returned to Mississippi to aid his party in the election. Victory seemed a good prospect, but no efforts were spared to make it doubly sure.

With the establishment of Democratic control in Mississippi, Lamar was in a position of pre-eminent political influence. The fate of candidates for office seemed to rest in his hands; his approval was almost sufficient to guarantee election—his disapproval, to insure defeat.[5]

To maintain the supremacy won in the election of 1875 the whites resorted to all sorts of stratagems. On election mornings in many towns a sunrise cannonade gave warning to the voters that a "fair election" would be held. When Negroes came to the polls, a sham battle between whites was fought, at which Negroes were terrified and fled. Generally one strongbox in each county was held in reserve and was stuffed with the required number of ballots when it was learned from headquarters how many were needed. Election victories were secured not only by intimidation and force, but also by social and business ostracism, by a drawing of the color

[2]J. Z. George to L. Q. C. Lamar, May 3, 1874, Lamar Letterbooks, Department of Archives and History, Jackson, Miss.

[3]Gerald W. Johnson, "Live Demagogues or Dead Gentlemen," in *Virginia Quarterly Review*, XII (1936), 8.

[4]George to Lamar, Sept. 11, 1876, Lamar Letterbooks.

[5]Lamar to John Allen, Mar. 18, 1878, in Willie D. Halsell (ed.), "Democratic Dissensions in Mississippi, 1878-1882," in *Journal of Mississippi History*, II (1940), 124n.

line, by discharge from employment and forced resignations, and by a certain amount of vote-buying.[6] "White violence and fraud were pitted against black ignorance and corruption, and the former won."[7]

At first the Negro was intimidated and frightened from the polls. In the congressional election of 1876 practices which produced the victory of 1875 were repeated. As a result all six Democratic congressional candidates were elected, and Tilden carried the state by more than 50,000. All but four counties which bordered on the Mississippi River gave Democratic majorities. But the Negroes' determination to vote for the Republicans, Independents, or Greenbackers was embarrassing to the Democrats if not dangerous.[8] They "never entered into any election," complained a Democrat, "in other than partizan spirit." As political partisans they were "the most consistent voting machines ever invested with the right of suffrage." They would gladly and readily, it was charged, espouse the cause of "any man who appeals to them for their votes on the sole ground of opposition to the . . . [Democratic] party."[9]

At the 1876 election, when the vast majority of whites were united in the Democratic party and when factionalism had not yet reared its head, it was necessary to keep Republican leaders from getting out the Negro vote. All methods were employed to achieve this result. Before they learned the dangers of doing so, white Republicans resisted the intimidation of their black followers. At a joint political speaking at Starkville the audience, Democrat and Republican, came armed and mounted, and the Democrats even had a fieldpiece. So tense became the atmosphere before the time for the speeches that the candidates were asked not to talk and the audience was prevailed upon to go home.[10] Such a stalemate was not often achieved by the Republicans, however, and their press carried letter after letter of protest against the intimidating practices of the Democrats. They denounced the leaders of the Democratic party who "sit back and organize and direct and encourage" young

[6]J. S. McNeily, "War and Reconstruction in Mississippi, 1863-1890," in Mississippi Historical Society, Publications, Centenary Series, II (1918), 165-535; Macon Beacon, Nov. 20, 1875.

[7]Statement by Dr. F. L. Fulgham, Jackson Issue, Aug. 12, 1910.

[8]Vernon L. Wharton, The Negro in Mississippi, 1865-1890 (Chapel Hill, 1947), 201; Natchez Democrat, Apr. 5, 1876.

[9]Aberdeen Examiner, Mar. 8, 1883.   [10]Jackson Daily Times, Nov. 1, 1876.

men of their party to "rudeness, indecencies, barbarisms . . . and deeds of desperation" in order to carry elections. A Republican editor estimated that a third of all Democrats had been coerced into joining that party "through fear . . . and intimidation."[11]

The Democrats denied that they were the originators of the color line in Mississippi politics. According to them it had been initiated by "carpetbaggers," who had, with its aid, "misruled" Mississippi for six years; only when driven to desperation had the Democrats "accepted the color line" and driven the "carpetbaggers" from power. They claimed they "did not seek the aid of Negroes but accepted the cooperation of the few who voluntarily" acted with them, and "protected them from violence from those of their own race."[12] Whether this was true or not, the Democrats soon went beyond the mere "protection" of Negroes who supported them. A white lawyer of Bolivar County complained in 1876 that he was ordered by the Democratic club of Rosedale, on threat of violence, to leave the county. He had resided there only three months and denied that he had participated in politics. Nevertheless, in fear of his life, he departed hastily, leaving all of his property behind.[13] In neighboring Washington County, four Negroes complained that they had been driven from their homes and had "lain in the woods for weeks." They had "committed no crime," but had been persecuted "because of our political opinions." Another Negro had received notice from the "Ku Klux" to leave home within twenty-four hours.[14] After a Negro riot at an election at Artesia the Democratic Jackson *Clarion*, probably the most influential paper in the state, sent out a call to all Mississippians to "quench in blood" the Negro's "lust for blood." The "unconquerable Anglo-Saxons," it said, must have in every riot "an eye for an eye and a tooth for a tooth."[15]

As long as there was complete unity among Democrats the threat of a Republican victory could be successfully withstood. Soon after 1876, however, factional fights began to appear within Democratic ranks. Such divisions might serve to resuscitate the expiring Republicans, and strong measures were taken to restore unity. In July the Clay County convention had several such con-

[11]*Ibid.*, Oct. 28, Nov. 1, 1876.

[12]Ben. G. Humphreys to Lamar, Jan. 3, 1875, Lamar Letterbooks.

[13]J. L. Murphy to J. M. Stone, Oct. 29, Nov. 1, 1876, Letters of Governors, Series E, 129A, Department of Archives and History, Jackson, Miss.

[14]Joshua Page *et al.* to Stone, Dec. 26, 1876; George Doig to Stone, June 4, 1877, *ibid.*

[15]Jackson *Weekly Clarion*, Nov. 8, 1876.

flicting elements and succeeded only in making a ticket that was unpopular. Opposing elements then put up a slate said to be composed of men of high standing in the Democratic party. When it became known that Negroes were going to support the Independent ticket a meeting was called at West Point, where violent speakers openly stated that if the Independents were elected they should not serve. The same night, under the guise of going foxhunting, a mob led by civil officers went night riding through the country, "visiting negro churches, calling for certain leading negroes." The night raids kept up until election day, and all who associated with the Independent candidates were ostracized and denounced in harsh terms. Negroes were kept from the polls by force or threats of force, and many whites dreading violence stayed away also. Negroes who went to the polls were compelled to show their tickets to the voting officials, who would tear the certificates to pieces. "Never in Radical times," said an observer, "was more fraud and intimidation practiced." The election was a "complete farce," but even so, it was said, "enough votes were put in to elect the Independents but by some means were not counted."[16]

Not only were Negroes prevented from voting Republican in 1876, but also dissatisfaction within that party was driving many of them over to the Democrats. At the Republican state nominating convention in the spring of that year the Negroes were refused places on the ticket, and a split occurred between them and their white leaders. As a result, the Democrats polled nearly 60,000 majority, although the votes of all the whites and a fourth of the Negroes would only have given them about 20,000 majority. The Republicans claimed at least 5,000 white votes in their own party. Ballot-box stuffing may have been the explanation for the Democratic majority, but the Democrats claimed it was due to the great numbers of colored voters who had joined them.[17] In April a Democratic paper stated that many Negroes were aligning themselves with the party and predicted that more would do so. By August Negro Democratic clubs were being formed all over the state and all Negroes were invited to join.[18] Discredited by their failure to rally the Negroes to their support in the election, the white managers of the Republican party allowed their organization to disintegrate

16W. W. Graham to Stone, Dec. 6, 1877, Letters of Governors, Series E, 135A.
17Jackson *Daily Times*, Jan. 16, 1877; Jackson *Weekly Clarion*, Nov. 29, 1876.
18Natchez *Democrat*, Apr. 5, Aug. 12, Nov. 10, 1876.

and in July, 1877, actually disbanded it.[19] Negro leaders thereupon revived the organization, and in some localities, notably in the city of Jackson where they maintained control until 1887, they were very strong.[20]

After their abandonment by their white leaders, the Negroes had for a time undisputed control of the Republican party machinery, deciding nominations and receiving federal patronage. Nevertheless the white wing of the party was standing by, ready at all times to ally itself with any revolting Democratic faction. The situation in 1881 presented it with such an opportunity, and although the alliance did not achieve victory, that year marked the high tide of white Republican effort. In some counties Greenbackers and Independents had got control. These groups united with the Republicans in a fusion ticket behind Benjamin King, on a platform demanding fair elections and an elective judiciary. The election was marked by fraud and violence. Lamar sanctimoniously attributed all this to the opposition, but other Democratic leaders admitted that they used "repression, intimidation, and other . . . illegal devices . . . to overcome the negro majority." The Democrats polled 47,960 votes, while 31,256 were cast for King.[21] It was the strongest opposition since 1875.

The group of men who came into power with the overthrow of the Radical government in 1875-1876 are frequently referred to as "Bourbons." Bourbons were supposed to be those who "never forgave and never forgot"; who refused to accept the results of the war and the war amendments; and who "stubbornly hold to the past and refuse to adapt themselves to a changing world."[22] They were few in Mississippi politics and they exercised little influence in the Democratic party. The new leaders after the Democrats regained

[19]Jackson Daily Times, July 10, 1877.

[20]Wharton, The Negro in Mississippi, 201; Alf W. Garner, "Public Services of E. C. Walthall," in Mississippi Historical Society, Publications, IX (1905), 245.

[21]Lamar to R. H. Henry, quoted in Edward Mayes, Lucius Q. C. Lamar: His Life, Times, and Speeches (Nashville, 1896), 435-36; also ibid., 438, quoting Kemper Herald and Yazoo Sentinel; Jackson Weekly Clarion, Nov. 22, 1882; Halsell, "Democratic Dissensions in Mississippi," loc. cit., 123-35; Frank Johnston, "Suffrage and Reconstruction in Mississippi," in Mississippi Historical Society, Publications, VI (1902), 218-19; Frank Johnston, "Public Services of Senator George," in Mississippi Historical Society, Publications, VIII (1904), 210.

[22]Willie D. Halsell, "The Bourbon Period in Mississippi Politics, 1875-1890," in Journal of Southern History, XI (1945), 521.

power in 1875 were, on the whole, men who had exerted little or no effect on state policy in ante-bellum days. Of the few who had been influential, none refused to accept the reality of Reconstruction, and they all set about adjusting the state to face the new conditions.

A battle early began for control of the party and resulted in the ascendancy of the men who had led the revolution. These new leaders entrenched themselves in power; and although classing themselves as "liberals" because of their policy of resisting the "color line" in party affairs, they were given the name "Bourbons" by their political opponents. The appellation soon became so loosely tossed around that it lost all meaning.[23] It was applied indiscriminately by all classes of politicians to anybody who differed from them and became a convenient though empty name of reproach. A Vicksburg editor, in 1882, observed that "Every politician insists that his party is the party of progress, of improvement . . . and he is of course entitled to stigmatize his opponents as Bourbons."[24]

An economic and class significance was given to the term "Bourbon" when many of the new political leaders began turning to merchandising, railroad promotion, and other business activities, and "turning deaf ears to the farmers." The agricultural distress of the period was calling for measures which the new leaders' commercial interests could not sanction, and those who had been "liberal" in 1875 became, as a rule, "conservative" by 1890. There were many things for which the new leaders stood, and few stood together on everything. Most were friendly to railroads and corporate enterprises. They wished to effect a speedy reconciliation with the rest of the nation. They all agreed in their determination to "control . . . the Negro vote to insure the continuation of white supremacy."[25]

The most spectacular threat to Democratic unity came in the early 1880's in the desertion from the party of James R. Chalmers. Chalmers had been a slaveholder and aristocrat, a general in the Confederate army, a Democrat of long standing, and a leader in the overthrow of the "carpetbag" government. He had been chosen to Congress as a Democrat from the sixth or Delta district in 1880, but his election had been successfully contested by John R. Lynch, Negro Republican, on the grounds of fraud. Chalmers thought

[23]*Ibid.,* 521-22.

[24]Vicksburg *Daily Commercial,* Jan. 31, 1882.

[25]Halsell, "The Bourbon Period," *loc. cit.,* 522-33.

Lamar failed to give him the support he deserved in the contest, and when the "Lamar legislature" of 1880 changed his district in a grotesque manner to punish him for insubordination, he went into open revolt and joined the Republicans. As a personal affront to Lamar he moved from Vicksburg to Holly Springs, in Lamar's district, and ran for Congress in 1882.[26]

Chalmers was supported by James L. Alcorn, a wealthy planter of the Delta; George C. McKee, postmaster at Jackson; Jason Niles and his son Henry of Kosciusko; Green R. Chandler, United States district attorney for north Mississippi; George R. Buchanan of Holly Springs; and Judges Luke Lea and Harvey R. Ware of Jackson. These men were denounced by the Democrats as "degenerates," "moral lepers," and "traitors to their race," but it is well established that some of them had ability, character, and some means.

According to a Negro leader who fought against the white Republicans for control of the party, they were "typical representatives of the best blood and the finest manhood of the South." Writing many years after the bitter struggles of the 1880's John R. Lynch compared the white Republicans with their brother Democrats. The Democrats had, he said, a slight advantage in experience and intelligence, "but in point of honesty and integrity . . . the advantage was with the [white] Republicans." He denied that they were "carpetbaggers," or merely "a few worthless" southern white men, but claimed that they were "the better element of native whites."[27] Although these men "elevated the general Republican standard in the state," they were slighted in patronage by the Republicans in Washington, who favored the Negro wing of the party.[28] But Lynch was writing years later when both he and they had passed from the scene of conflict.

Throughout the years 1882-1884 Chalmers and his backers grappled with both black Republicans and white Democrats for political supremacy in sections of the state. The white Republicans

[26]Willie D. Halsell, "James R. Chalmers and 'Mahoneism' in Mississippi," in *Journal of Southern History*, X (1944), 38-39, 41; John R. Lynch to Stone, Dec. 2, 1880, Letters of Governors, Series E, 165A; statement by Chalmers in Brookhaven *Leader*, June 1, 1882, quoted in Willie D. Halsell (ed.), "Republican Factionalism in Mississippi, 1882-1884," in *Journal of Southern History*, VII (1941), 87n; W. E. B. Du Bois, *Black Reconstruction* (New York, 1935), 441.

[27]John R. Lynch, "Some Historical Errors of James Ford Rhodes," in *Journal of Negro History*, II (1917), 350-52.

[28]Halsell, "Chalmers and 'Mahoneism,'" *loc. cit.*, 41.

charged that an alliance existed between the Negro Republican leaders and Lamar and George to perpetuate Democratic control. Specifically, they charged that the Negro leaders, John R. Lynch, James Hill, and Blanche K. Bruce, influenced by Lamar and George, persuaded their followers to support Democrats in state and local elections, and in exchange Lamar and George worked in Washington for patronage for Mississippi Negroes. The purpose of the Democrats in forming the alliance was twofold. It would exclude the leadership of able white men from the Republican party, and thus reduce "to a minimum the danger of the Republican party." At the same time the Democrats could point out that the Republican party in the state was controlled by Negroes, and thus use the old battle cry of the color line to rally all whites to them.[29]

White Republicans claimed that both Democrats and Negro Republican leaders worked to preserve the color line in politics; the former because "they know Such Polacy [*sic*] will bring to its Standard an Anglo-Saxon following who will demand and enforce their Rights." The Negro leaders' "*personal interests* lay in parallel lines" with the Democrats. They "reason with themselves," said Judge Ware, "that if too much worth, merit, and Character, Congregates in a Party to which they are attached in the Same ratio will their chances for Federal appointment and other advancements lessen." Hence these two groups "while Seeming in Antipodes are found running in parallel lines" and were allies. Hill, Negro collector of internal revenue for Mississippi, Ware charged, used his office to thwart and stifle "every effort in the State to broaden the guage [*sic*] and gather effective recruits for the fight against Bourbonism." Judge Ware thought the Republican party could "easily" elect "some man of broad national views" to Congress from the seventh district, but that Hill was planning "to give [it] to his Allies the Bourbons, by having himself intrigued by his various Deputies" into accepting the nomination himself. Even though it was a Republican district, Ware said, Hill knew that he would be overwhelmingly defeated, "for even with the rank and file of his own Race he is extremely unpopular." By "giving" the district to the Democrats, Hill would retain his office "and use it in the future as he has in the past for the good of himself, and for the perpetuity of Bourbon rule in the State." Ware said that

[29]Halsell, "Republican Factionalism," *loc. cit.*, 86; H. C. Niles to [George C. McKee], June 30, 1882, *ibid.*, 93-94.

the "Anti-Bourbon" whites of the state recognized Hill as the "ally of the Bourbons."[30]

Lamar and George, another Republican said, favored Hill's retaining his office as collector, since a Democrat could not get it anyway and since he was of decided benefit to them. Hill was reported to have divulged party secrets to the Democrats in the "close and intimate" consultations which he was seen to hold with them during the preceding campaign, and he was openly accused by the Republicans, Independents, and Greenbackers of being "a regular Judas Iscariot."[31] "He is in league with the Democrats," complained another white Republican, "and at every election plays into their hands." If Hill were removed and General George C. McKee put in his place, said still another white Republican, "we can organize an independent movement" of all elements "opposed to ballot box stuffing," a group which could carry three districts "without a doubt."[32]

The plight of the white Republicans was indeed a hard one. An open accusation and proof of the alliance between Democrats and Negro Republicans "would add Negro recruits to the party, while the Democrats could then point that the Republican party was dominated by Negroes and thus repel white recruits."[33] "Between the upper millstone [of] Southern folly," lamented McKee, "and the lower millstone of Southern crime we are ground to powder, useful only for the purpose of sending . . . delegates from rotten borough constituencies to National Republican Conventions."[34] "If Lamar can keep the Negro on top," said Henry Niles, "—the 'race issue' will be the cry in every contest—and we will be the sufferers."

When Hill succeeded in getting the nomination from the seventh congressional district the white Republicans resolved they would "never raise one arm to aid a band of drunken negroes." If the Republican party was to concentrate on "a miserable scramble for Federal patronage," it could not gain respectable recruits. "The differ-

---

[30]H. R. Ware to W. E. Chandler, May 15, 28, June 14, 1882, *ibid.*, 87-89; George M. Buchanan to Chandler, July 11, 1883, *ibid.*, 99-100.

[31]Niles to Chandler, June 7, 1882, *ibid.*, 90.

[32]J. L. Morphis to Chandler, June 15, 1882, *ibid.*, 91-92.

[33]Niles to [McKee], June 30, 1882, *ibid.*, 93-94; McKee to Chandler, July 6, 1882, *ibid.*, 93.

[34]McKee to Chandler, July 6, 1882, *ibid.*, 93.

ence between Jim Hill's crowd and Democracy," said Henry Niles, "is scarcely worth fighting for."[35]

The Republican patronage bestowers in Washington were well aware of the schism within the party in Mississippi. But there were revolts brewing against the national Republican administration in other states. It was important that the administration have the support of the Mississippi delegation in the next national convention, and Hill, at least, had promised to obey orders. He was the boss of the Negroes. He had the political machinery in his hands, and it would not do "to remove him while both armies are in motion."[36] Nevertheless, by the fall of 1882 Chalmers' prospects were so fair that the Washington Republican leaders could not ignore him, and jobs and some money were placed at his disposal.[37]

Chalmers used the patronage to advantage. His Democratic opponent in the second congressional district was Van Manning. Chalmers was victorious but charges of fraud were made by both sides. Since Manning was defeated his cries were louder and more prolonged. Chalmers was reported to have personally led United States marshals who took possession of the polls in Marshall County, "dictated the conduct of the election," and attempted to "awe and intimidate [the voters] with threats of Federal prosecution." The marshals were reported to have threatened personal violence to Manning's followers. Consequently "many of his supporters . . . either did not vote at all or voted for Chalmers." At Hudsonville, after the balloting was over, a United States marshal, on pretense of fearing a riot, took the ballot box and jumped on a train with it. At Byhalia, John Watson, the Democratic election officer, was arrested on election morning by a United States marshal. Since no one else could open the polls, "the legal voters of Byhalia were . . . disfranchised." More votes were found in the ballot box at Red Banks, a strong Greenback precinct, than there were legal voters. "Everywhere," said an irate editor, "the United States Deputy Marshals proved by their acts that they regarded Chalmers' election to

[35]Niles to Chandler, Nov. 25, 1882, *ibid.*, 96-97.

[36][David B.] Henderson to My Dear Secretary [Chandler], July 4, 1882, *ibid.*, 92.

[37]Chalmers to Chandler, Oct. 24, 1882, *ibid.*, 94-95.

be their chief and only duty."[38] The incongruity of Republican federal officials using such tactics to elect a man whom their party had recently turned out of Congress "on the ground of force and fraud practised against it by himself" did not pass unnoticed. Now, it was said, the Republican party had turned to Chalmers "on his promise to use the same means in its favor."[39]

Hill's district, the seventh, went Republican by more than 10,000, but Hill was beaten by more than 7,000. It was reported that 5,000 white Independents in the district refused to support Hill because he "year after year . . . had been bitter in . . . denunciation of Independents" and had repeatedly betrayed both Republicans and Independents.[40] In their effort to prevent the election of Chalmers, Hill and Lynch openly urged fusion of their own organization with the Democrats. Hill was reported to have sent instructions to his henchmen in Chalmers' district to go to the polls early and "tell every colored man you know and have influence with, that there is no Republican candidate in the field. . . . Tell him that the other candidate is a Greenbacker, who was formerly a Democrat, and that he acknowledges no sympathy with Republicanism."[41] Whether or not Hill actually gave such instructions, it seems likely that he would have preferred Democratic success in Mississippi to any division of his power over federal patronage. His own defeat and Chalmers' victory intensified the feud between them.

Despite Hill and Lynch's open advocacy of fusion with the Democrats, they were still allowed federal patronage and used it in fighting the Chalmers group. Chalmers charged that two years later Hill "manipulated the convention" in the third, fourth, and fifth districts to secure the nomination of his henchmen for Congress. Hill knew, said Chalmers, that even if elected his candidates, being Negroes, would be counted out. When Chalmers won the nomination in his district again in 1884, Hill and his deputies traveled "all over

---

[38]Aberdeen *Examiner*, Nov. 16, 23, 1882. For evidence of Democratic fraud see M. B. Collins and W. W. Mathes to Stone, Nov. 12, 1882, Letters of Governors, Series E, 165A; Wharton, *The Negro in Mississippi*, 200; Buchanan to Chandler, July 11, 1883, in Halsell, "Republican Factionalism," *loc. cit.*, 99-100.

[39]Holly Springs *South*, quoted in Aberdeen *Examiner*, Nov. 23, 1882.

[40]H. R. Ware to [Chandler], [November], 1882, in Halsell, "Chalmers and 'Mahoneism,'" *loc. cit.*, 95-96.

[41]Macon *Beacon*, Nov. 4, 1882; Hinds County *Gazette*, Aug. 11, 1883, quoted in Halsell, "Republican Factionalism," *loc. cit.*, 99n.

the State on this work of breaking down the only dangerous opposition to the democrats."[42]

Hill's efforts against Chalmers were rewarded. In the general election of 1884 the Democrats won every district, and Chalmers, who carried only one county, lost by more than 4,000 votes. The third district, which had an estimated Republican majority of 20,000, elected a Democrat by more than 5,000.[43] Chalmers' failure was probably due also to the absence of any liberal program in his platform and to his failure to work for the small farmer's vote. His revolt, it seems, was simply that of a rebellious personality fighting against the dictatorship which Lamar and his associates exercised over the party.

That there was an alliance between the Negro leaders and the Democrats there can be little doubt. From 1876 on the Democratic press courted the Negro vote. The Jackson *Clarion* became an enthusiastic supporter of the principle of Negro suffrage. It pointed to the increased representation in Congress and in the Electoral College which had come to the South as a result of emancipation and enfranchisement. It had no fear of being unable to control the Negro vote, in the absence of federal troops, and said the Democratic party would continue to be the "protector" of the Negro's right of suffrage. It called the Negro's attention to the "improved" educational system which the Democrats were providing him. Pointing out, too, that the party had actually placed several Negroes on the Democratic ticket in some Delta counties, it urged all Negroes to vote for the party.[44] The Aberdeen *Examiner* lauded the "gallant colored men who at so much of personal sacrifice come to us, and who were won . . . by a canvass . . . involving . . . months of sleepless labor, and expenditures . . . of thousands of dollars."[45]

In the state Democratic convention in 1877 John D. Webster, Negro, was placed in nomination for secretary of state and actually received 46 votes before withdrawing on the fourth ballot. Many Democrats approved of Webster as a candidate and thought he would have been nominated but for the convention's surprise at his candidacy.[46]

[42]Chalmers to Chandler, July 16, 1864, in Halsell, "Republican Factionalism," *loc. cit.*, 100-101.

[43]Halsell, "Chalmers and 'Mahoneism,'" *loc. cit.*, 56.

[44]Jackson *Weekly Clarion*, Oct. 25, 1876, July 25, Oct. 31, 1877.

[45]Aberdeen *Examiner*, Oct. 25, 1883.

[46]Natchez *Democrat*, Aug. 7, 1877.

Almost invariably Democratic county committees insisted on the appointment of a Negro as the Republican member of the local election commission.[47] Also the readiness with which Mississippi Negro appointees to federal offices were confirmed in the Senate was remarkable. Blanche K. Bruce was "unanimously" confirmed as Register of the Treasury, upon Lamar's motion, and without the customary reference to a committee.[48]

In some of the counties with large Negro majorities, the fusion tickets between Democrats and the black wing of the Republican party led by Hill and Lynch came to be openly recognized. Such tickets were formed by agreements between county Democratic executive committees and Negro leaders. Each party would name its candidates on a joint ticket previously agreed upon, but the Negro candidates were subject to "review and approval or disapproval by the Democratic committee." Generally the Negroes were given "a minority on the county board of supervisors, a few other county offices of low pay and responsibility, and one membership in the legislature."[49] In Hinds County in the election of 1883 the fusion ticket gave the Democrats the sheriff, the chancery and circuit clerks, the treasurer, the state senator, three representatives, four supervisors, and an equal number of magistrates and constables with the Republicans. Negro Republicans were given the offices of county assessor, coroner, one representative, one supervisor, and their quota of magistrates and constables.[50] The system worked well for the outnumbered Democrats. The whites kept all important offices, but the Negroes "continued to vote with much freedom and . . . gained valuable political education and experience."[51]

[47]L. P. Yerger to George, Aug. 14, 1876; T. C. Catchings to Stone, Apr. 22, 1876; and many others in the Letters of Governors Collection.

[48]Memphis *Appeal*, May 20, 1881.

[49]Wharton, *The Negro in Mississippi*, 202.

[50]Aberdeen *Examiner*, Aug. 9, 1883.

[51]Wharton, *The Negro in Mississippi*, 203. See also Natchez *Democrat*, Oct. 23, 1879. Eventually the Negro leaders gained undisputed control of the Republican party, but they did not have the solid backing of their race. A Negro paper published in Vicksburg complained in 1900 that "a dozen or less of Republicans" had met and agreed as to delegates to the next national convention. This same group, it said, would meet again shortly and decide the membership of the next state committee. All of them, it was alleged, were officeholders and merely wished "to fix things so that they may continue in office." The Negro leaders made no effort to build up the party in the state by getting Republicans to pay the poll tax, but were content to poll the "smallest Republican vote of any state in the whole Union." Vicksburg *Light*, Jan. 18, 1900.

The fusion plan was not without opposition among Democrats. Minor politicians wanted the small offices held by the Negroes. Then, too, the whites in other sections of the state felt that the "redemption should be complete." The practice in the river counties was encouraging Negroes in other counties "to have similar ambitions." Moreover, it was believed that the Negroes were accepting the plan only until they gained such strength as would permit them to vote as a party. Worst of all, in case of disagreement among the white supervisors, "a Negro sometimes cast the deciding vote."[52]

[52]Wharton, *The Negro in Mississippi*, 203.

CHAPTER II

SUPPRESSION OF INDEPENDENTS

A PARTY composed of such "incongruous and unsympathetic elements" as the Mississippi Democrats could be held together only by an appeal to some sentiment which would transcend all lesser motives of individual interest. Such an appeal was found in "white supremacy." White Democrats who sought to contest policies fixed by leaders of the party were cried down as dangers to the state and traitors to their race. It was pointed out again and again that the Radicals who had controlled the state only a few years before were still trying to organize the Negroes and vote them as formerly. Disunion of the whites might give them the chance once more to seize control. "The safety of Mississippi," said Lamar, "lies in the maintenance of the Democratic organization and in its wise direction by conservative leaders."[1]

Independent political factions developed in a number of counties soon after the triumphs of 1875-1876. Differences of opinion and clashes of ambition were fed by the impossibility of rewarding everyone to the degree that his self-valuation merited. One asked office of the governor because he was "very poor and [had] a wife and six children to support and need[ed] the emoluments of the office."[2] Another thought he should be state superintendent of education because he was "both honest and competent," because he had been engaged for some time in "teaching the young to shoot," and because he "had done his best for [Governor Stone] on two [previous] occasions."[3] Still others sought pardons for erring relatives who had run afoul of the law. All promised their unqualified support to the governor in future campaigns; but the implication was clear that the degree of their support might depend upon the satisfaction which their petitions received. To humor all but a few was impossible, and unsuccessful suitors swelled the ranks of discontent which hard times produced.

[1]L. Q. C. Lamar to C. E. Wright, Feb. 21, 1879, quoted in Mayes, *Lamar*, 395-97; also *ibid.*, 394-95.

[2]W. C. Bromley to J. M. Stone, Mar. 25, 1876, Letters of Governors, Series E, 126A.

[3]F. M. Shields to Stone, May 6, 1877, *ibid.*, 135A.

Within a year after overthrow of the Radicals a Republican paper in Jackson reported "serious trouble brewing" in the Democratic party. "When it comes to a division of the spoils," said the Jackson *Times*, " 'reformers' even will fall out. . . . They are denouncing each other now in almost as bitter terms as they are wont to denounce the much hated . . . carpetbaggers."[4]

The first general election under the new regime was to be held in 1877. Months before the nominating convention the Democratic press was loud in its praise of the new order and the virtues of its leading candidates for the gubernatorial nomination. Relating the venality which had accompanied Republican political ascendancy the Democrats said that all this was now changed and that "the office was seeking the man." Such self-glorification brought from a Republican editor the cryptic observation that "instead of candidates running for office, we now see them running and dodging to get out of the way." General Robert Lowry, he observed, was a possible victim, but he was young, active, and vigorous, and his friends hoped that the gubernatorial office would not be able to catch him. Another candidate was somewhat advanced in years, not as lithe of limb or light of foot as Lowry, and was therefore in imminent danger of being victimized. His one hope of escape was in Governor Stone, "who though in the prime of life and able bodied, is understood to be rather slow. His excellency may, therefore, not succeed in escaping."[5]

The 1875 upheaval had been a united action by an overwhelming majority of the white people motivated by a feeling of necessity. With that motivation removed the danger of discord loomed. Differences might be created by personal ambition, by a minor question of policy, or by "a natural and almost invincible tendency of the masses to divide into opposing parties." Division took shape in the form of the Independent party movement. It grew with the struggle to combat the ironclad Democratic state and county rings. It was looked upon with distrust as an entering wedge of a new Radical party and was accordingly discouraged. Soon the Independent movements sought the support of the Negroes, who "followed the advice of some of their leaders in voting for any Independent ticket that threatened Democratic solidity."[6]

[4]Jackson *Daily Times*, Feb. 5, 1877.
[5]*Ibid.*, June 27, 1877.
[6]Wharton, *The Negro in Mississippi*, 204; Mayes, *Lamar*, 319-21.

In addressing the Democratic state convention of 1877, J. Z. George warned that while the party was temporarily supreme, undisputed supremacy would lead to division on minor matters and eventually to disintegration and political death. There must, he said, be no division. The white men must settle their disputes among themselves. Nothing would be so harmful as "the victory of one section of the party over another, secured by the aid of the common enemy of both." Their aim must be, he urged, to elevate the condition of the people and not to advance the fortunes of any class.[7]

Following George's address the convention resolved that unity and harmony were essential to victory; that all Independent movements were "dangerous to the integrity of the party organization"; that all Independent candidates were "inspired solely by lust for office"; and that they should be treated as "common enemies to the welfare of the people and avowed enemies of the Democratic party of Mississippi."[8]

At first the Democratic press scoffed at the possibility of a serious rift within the party.[9] But the Jackson *Times* early saw the inevitability of such a separation. In August, 1877, it reported that the division had already come. A convention of farmers had just resolved "to secure to the farmers that recognition in the political affairs of this state which their services, their sacrifices, their numerical strength and their intelligence so much entitled them." The *Times* thought this resolution responsible for the action taken by the Democratic convention.[10] Soon the Democrats recognized the seriousness of the situation. The *Clarion*, by October, was denouncing the Independents as Republicans in disguise. Warning all good Democrats to shun them the *Clarion* said they but "sing the song that leads you . . . to destruction." "The snake," it added, "is only scotched, not killed." Another Democratic organ which had felt secure in August was warning in October that the Independent movement was an attempt of "the old Radical party for a new lease of power." It saw the movement as "an effort to foist upon the

[7]Jackson *Weekly Clarion*, Aug. 1, 1877; Vicksburg *Democrat-Commercial*, Aug. 16, 1877.

[8]Jackson *Daily Times*, Aug. 8, 1877; Jackson *Weekly Clarion*, Aug. 8, 1877.

[9]Vicksburg *Democrat-Commercial*, Aug. 16, 1877; Aberdeen *Examiner*, Sept. 6, 1877; Jackson *Weekly Clarion*, June 16, 1877.

[10]Jackson *Daily Times*, Aug. 8, 1877.

people again, men who have heretofore been extremely obnoxious."[11] The New York *Tribune* reported that Mississippi Independents were developing such strength that the "Bourbon" was wildly alarmed and that the "Solid South is quaking." "The trouble is," said the *Tribune,* "that so soon as an opposition ticket takes the field the negro vote becomes of great importance, for both parties seek it."[12]

Any national third-party movement was apt to gain a receptive hearing in agriculturally depressed Mississippi. The Greenback party was the first of these movements whose program seemed so enticing to the desperate Mississippi farmers. The Toledo platform (1878) advocated the suppression of bank notes and the issue of all legal tender money by the federal government in sufficient quantity "to insure the full employment of labor" and to effect a reduction in the interest rate. It also advocated free coinage of silver, reservation of public lands for actual settlers, reduction of the hours of labor, abolition of convict-leasing, and suppression of Chinese immigration.[13] It was more of a labor program than agrarian, but certain of its features, notably that which promised more money and lower interest rates, had a strong appeal to the farmers. A convention in Hinds County in 1877 urged repeal of the resumption act and the issuance of greenbacks. It expressed its belief that the "taxed laborer should be protected from the ravages of the untaxed bond-holder," and favored capital legislation in order "to build up our internal improvements."[14]

The Greenback movement reached its peak nationally in 1878, and by 1879 there were signs that its influence was waning in Mississippi. The Greenback state convention in August was reported "a failure," only a dozen of the seventy counties being represented. By October the Democrats were confident of carrying the election but were resentful of the fright the Greenbackers had given them. The Greenback candidates had made appeals to the Negroes for their votes and had told them that the Democrats were depriving them of their privileges. This brought bitter denouncements from the Democrats, who charged that the Greenbackers were "warming the viper, Radicalism," back to life and threatening to engulf the state.[15]

[11]Jackson *Weekly Clarion,* Sept. 26, Oct. 10, 1877; Vicksburg *Democrat-Commercial,* Aug. 16, Oct. 29, 1877.

[12]New York *Tribune,* quoted in Jackson *Daily Times,* Oct. 29, 1877.

[13]Solon J. Buck, *The Agrarian Crusade* (New Haven, 1921), 89-90.

[14]Jackson *Daily Times,* Oct. 18, 1877.

[15]Jackson *Weekly Clarion,* July 23, Aug. 20, Oct. 15, 29, 1879.

The Independent movement was a many-headed monster. The Greenback head might be severed from its body, as it was by 1880, but like the mythological dragon, another grew in its place. If no national issue was present to which the Mississippi malcontents could ally themselves, they were able to survive on local discontents. Only infrequently did they put state-wide tickets in the field, but again and again they contested county elections.

Independents themselves did not often represent a large following of whites and alone would have been no threat to Democratic control. But there was the inevitable danger of a union between them and local Republican leaders who could command a large Negro support. It was charged that 95 per cent of the membership of such fusion parties was Negro and that the blacks would have to be recognized in the distribution of offices. Election of such a ticket, it was warned, would result in "mismanagement, extravagance, and all the evils . . . of government" by those who were incompetent.[16] An Independent convention in Monroe County in 1883 was said to have been composed of about 50 Independents, 50 Republicans, "12 or 15 Radicals," and about 75 "kicking Democrats."[17]

The Independents denied that they were carpetbaggers, Republicans, or Negroes. The Memphis *Avalanche,* an out-of-state paper, said that in general they were "men who for ten years have fought under the Democratic-Conservative banner," who had "shed their blood for the Confederate cause" during the war. They had merely grown tired of selfish politicians who kept urging the color line in politics in order to perpetuate their control of the partisan organization. In reality, said the *Avalanche,* they were the liberal, progressive elements.[18] In view of the common conception of the terms "liberal" and "progressive," some justification existed for this claim. Among the programs urged by Independent conventions were: "free schools, free suffrage, and equal rights"; "equal and exact justice for all classes, no class legislation, no sectional lines, no proscription for opinion['s] sake"; the breaking of "present political bonds which bind us; refusal to be partisans of any class or party; and refusal to vote for men simply because they . . . be in accord

[16]Statement by Governor Robert Lowry, quoted in Vicksburg *Democrat-Commercial,* Feb. 28, 1882.

[17]Aberdeen *Examiner,* Sept. 6, 1883.

[18]Memphis *Avalanche,* quoted in Jackson *Daily Times,* Aug. 6, 1877.

with . . . any convention."[19] At the same time some Democratic stalwarts were urging such undemocratic measures as literacy tests for voters and the poll tax for both whites and Negroes as a method of curbing "radical" legislation.[20]

But the Democratic machines did not stop at considerations of legal disfranchisement. They used violence, intimidation, and fraud in counteracting Independent movements, and in some cases they even solicited, bought, or bargained for the Negro vote.[21] Tactics known as "bulldozing" were employed against those who showed an inclination to contest the supremacy of the Democratic organization. Stalwart Democrats who did not defend "bulldozing" contended that it had "no political significance whatever"; that Negroes were whipped, "not because they were radicals or voters," but because a class of men—the leaders of whom were themselves Radicals when it paid to be—undertook to supersede the administration of law "so far as it applied to the colored population."[22] No doubt this was true in some instances, for it is difficult to make hoodlumism conform to any set pattern. Frequently, however, those whipped were not Negroes but whites who would not accept the dictates of the Democratic oligarchs. A Republican editor pointed out the remarkable coincidence between the crusade of the Democratic leaders against the Independent movement and the revival of "bulldozing" tactics.[23]

Nor were white victims of the "bulldozers" always Republicans or carpetbaggers. Colonel R. H. Truly, who had been indicted by a federal grand jury in 1875 for intimidating Negroes to vote Democratic, announced two years later as an Independent candidate for state senator from Jefferson County. Several weeks later he announced his withdrawal. "I *thought*," he said, "I had a *legal* and *constitutional* right to run for office, but subsequent events in this county have *convinced* me that *possibly* I have no such . . . rights. I therefore withdraw."[24] Two years later an Independent movement

[19]Jackson *Daily Times*, Oct. 18, 1877; Vicksburg *Democrat-Commercial*, Oct. 1, 1877; Memphis *Avalanche*, quoted in Jackson *Daily Times*, Aug. 6, 1877.

[20]Vicksburg *Herald*, quoted in Vicksburg *Democrat-Commercial*, Oct. 1, 1877.

[21]Wharton, *The Negro in Mississippi*, 204.

[22]J. B. Chrisman to Stone, Apr. 2, 1879, Letters of Governors, Series E, 143A.

[23]Jackson *Daily Times*, Oct. 16, 1877.

[24]*Ibid.*, Sept. 18, 1877.

sprang up in Yazoo County which threatened the defeat of the "straight-outs." It became so formidable that "the best men of the county—the merchants, the planters, the farmers"—gathered together and appointed a committee to call on Captain H. M. Dixon, the head of the movement, "and request him to retire from the canvass." At first he refused, but eventually he decided to comply "for the sake of peace and harmony . . . and for the love I bear my family." He insisted, as a provision of his withdrawal, that he "be protected in [his] rights as any other citizen," and that his friend, R. A. Flanagan, be "unmolested in his rights." In jubilation over this victory a Democratic editor wrote: "The Democratic flag now waves over this glorious old county; and long may it wave."[25]

Despite Dixon's withdrawal the election in Yazoo did not go off without incident. "Peaceable blood" was shed, and a respected Democrat reported that qualified voters had been refused admission at the polls by "a lawless band and by force." Other voters had had tickets "contrary to their wishes" forced upon them. "More outrageous and unlawful conduct at the polls and around them," he reported, "I never witnessed or read of in all my life." The election, he said, was a "farce and a sham." It could not stand judicial scrutiny. "A greater fraud and cheat than our sheriff under whose nose these things are allowed and smiled upon, never existed."[26]

A most sensational incident of violence occurred in Kemper County in the spring of 1877. Political differences of long standing there had created bad blood between John Gully, Democrat, and Judge W. W. Chisholm, an Independent who had been a Republican. When Gully was ambushed and murdered, Chisholm was imprisoned in the county jail, under suspicion that he had conspired with the Negro who confessed to firing the fatal shot. Alarmed for the safety of his family Chisholm obtained permission for them to accompany him in his incarceration. There at daybreak on a Sunday morning a mob, variously estimated at from one hundred to three hundred armed men, rode into town and demanded that the jailer surrender Chisholm to them. The jailer and his deputy fled in terror. Chisholm and two loyal friends, arming themselves from the jail arsenal, proposed to sell their lives dearly. Several of the attackers fell mortally

[25]Yazoo City *Herald*, quoted in Vicksburg *Democrat-Commercial*, July 29, 1879; Jackson *Clarion-Ledger*, quoted in Vicksburg *Democrat-Commercial*, July 31, 1879.
[26]Robert S. Hudson to Stone, Nov. 4, 1879, Letters of Governors, Series E, 156A.

wounded before the besieged were forced from their stronghold by the firing of the building. Chisholm, his fourteen-year-old son, his fifteen-year-old daughter, and one of his friends, a British national, were shot down as they ran from the building.

The massacre did not receive the universal condemnation which it merited. The Meridian *Mercury,* Jackson *Clarion,* and Vicksburg *Herald* openly approved Chisholm's liquidation, and other papers were halfhearted in their criticism. The state nominating convention was only a few months off, and Governor Stone was in a quandary. Strong action on his part in prosecuting the criminals might result in his defeat and in Robert Lowry's nomination; for Lowry's followers, if not approving of the crime, opposed prosecution of the criminals. Stone vacillated, and no convictions were obtained. The Lowry press, which originally had criticized Stone when it thought he would take action, now criticized him for not doing so. "Stone knows," said the Brookhaven *Comet,* "that a vigorous effort to prosecute the Kemper County murderers would insure his certain defeat" because nine-tenths of his party sympathized with the mob. "The judges are Democrats, the prosecuting attorney is a Democrat," said the Republican *Times,* "and all have to be reelected next fall. The 'white-liners' . . . run the state, its courts, Governors and all." Stone's inaction did not antagonize the party leaders, for he was renominated in August by the convention.[27]

In such manner did the Democratic party maintain its supremacy in the years immediately following its ascendancy to power. "Independent voting was denounced; black solidarity was opposed by white solidarity; bigoted partisanship dominated both races." Even when no threat of Negro supremacy existed the race question was used as a pretext for a solid white vote. It was but natural that, out of such conditions, "rings and cliques should spring forth." Thus Mississippi, "sorely in need of progressive leadership," was actually in the grasp "of oligarchies that stifled freedom and hindered progress."[28]

[27]A. G. Horn to Stone, Oct. 29, 1877, Letters of Governors, Series E, 135A; Vicksburg *Democrat-Commercial,* June 1, 1877; Jackson *Daily Times,* May 12, 17, June 2, 19, 1877; *ibid.,* quoting Handsboro *Democrat,* Meridian *Mercury,* Jackson *Clarion,* Brandon *Republican,* Vicksburg *Herald,* Cincinnati (Ohio) *Times,* Brookhaven *Comet.*

[28]Clarence H. Poe, "Suffrage Restriction in the South; its Causes and Consequences," in *North American Review,* CLXXV (1902), 536.

Democratic leaders charged that Independent movements were always led by disappointed aspirants for office and that they always showed a disposition to make use of "Republican and colored elements."[29] They insisted that white supremacy was the only issue in politics; all others were dangerous and must be suppressed. Newspapers generally refused to print letters attacking the party. Such a policy, if followed, would result in the people passively receiving the candidates named by the machine-controlled nominating conventions. By the 1880's the majority of people, even if disgusted, could not fight against the party which to them meant white supremacy.

[29]Natchez *Democrat*, July 12, Aug. 6, 1879.

CHAPTER III

PARTY MACHINERY

THE highest party authority in the state was the Democratic state convention. While it was in session it exercised unlimited authority concerning party affairs. It apportioned among the counties representation within the convention and decided the admission of contesting delegations. It fixed the rules for nomination procedure, named candidates for state offices, and drew up a statement of party policy. The convention was in session, however, only a few days each year, and when it adjourned its authority devolved upon a state Democratic executive committee. This committee was the supreme governing body of the state party until its authority was in turn surrendered to the next convention.

Immediately after the revolution of 1875-1876 there were nineteen members of the committee—five chosen by the convention, and two by each of the seven congressional districts—but this number has been changed from time to time. The powers and duties of the committee were numerous. It was supposed to look to the success of the party in state elections and to aid in electing the party's candidates to Congress and to the Electoral College. It arranged meetings, raised campaign funds, prepared and distributed publicity, allocated speakers, made arrangements for and organized state conventions, and fixed qualifications for voting in the county primaries. State and federal patronage were the weapons used by the committee, and its chairman was frequently the most important political functionary of the state.

The basis of representation followed by all state conventions was double the number of representatives which each county had in the lower house of the legislature.[1] The apportionment of the legislature in the constitution of 1868 was made on the basis of total population rather than of white population. This removed control of the state from the white counties which had held it under the apportionments of the constitutions of 1836 and 1846. Thus the plantation counties, which were by far the most populous of the state, elected a majority of the legislators.[2] After 1875 comparatively few Negroes voted and

[1]Jackson *Weekly Clarion*, Aug. 1, 1887; Mississippi, *Laws*, 1892, Chap. LXIX, 150-51.

[2]Mississippi Constitution, 1868, Art. XI, Sec. 1; United States *Census of 1880*, 357-58; Wharton, *The Negro in Mississippi*, 151.

most of those who did voted Republican. Therefore this scheme of
apportionment gave the few whites in the heavily Negro populated
counties an exceedingly large voice in determining party affairs and
thus in government of the state. Everyone was aware of the situation, and voices were raised in protest and in defense of the scheme.
White counties contended that it violated fundamental democratic
principles, while black counties defended it as warranted by the
greater taxes paid by their section. The Brandon *Republican* complained that it gave representation in party affairs to Negroes who
did not vote Democratic, and suggested in 1877 basing representation on the number of Democratic votes cast in each county in the
preceding election.[3]

When this suggestion was unheeded the *Republican* renewed its
plea four years later. It pointed out that Smith County with 1,006
white voters had only two representatives in the convention, while
Warren with 2,217 had eight; Jackson County with 1,673 white
voters had two representatives, while Lowndes with only 1,430 had
six; and Harrison with 1,392 white voters had two representatives,
while Washington with 1,726 had four. Furthermore, said the
Republican, in the white counties almost all whites were Democrats,
and there being few Negro voters, they too voted Democratic. On
the other hand, in the black counties many whites belonged to the
Republican party in order to gain local office. "As long as the representation in our Conventions remains as it is now," concluded the
editor, "the few white men in the negro counties will name our candidates, and the white counties will have to elect them."[4] This was
no idle complaint, for the five members of the executive committee
chosen by the state convention from the state at large in 1877 were
from the five black counties of Hinds, Yazoo, Lowndes, Washington,
and Marshall.[5]

The county executive committee exercised the same powers in
regard to party affairs in the county that the state executive committee wielded in state affairs. It was the undisputed authority in
theory and fact save for the brief period when the county convention was in session. In theory it surrendered its authority when the

[3]Brandon *Republican*, quoted in Vicksburg *Democrat-Commercial*, Aug. 10, 1877.
[4]Brandon *Republican*, quoted in Jackson *Clarion*, Aug. 4, 1881.
[5]Jackson *Weekly Clarion*, Aug. 1, 1877.

convention met; in practice it controlled the convention and in most cases dictated the disposition of business there. Actually, therefore, the committee and its chairman ruled the county through their control of county patronage. Its approval was indispensable for those seeking office and frequently was all that was necessary. County committees were uniform in number throughout the state. Each county was divided into five supervisors' districts, and each district chose in a mass meeting a member of the county committee.[6] As a rule these meetings were perfunctory affairs, attended only by a few party regulars and run by the district boss. Occasionally, however, the meetings were revolts from boss rule and several hundred might attend.[7]

Within each supervisor's district one or more Democratic clubs held regular meetings, arranged to challenge doubtful voters at the polls, inspected registration lists, and made active canvasses in election campaigns. A regular chain of command descended from the state executive committee to the supervisors' district clubs. The clubs made regular reports to the county committee, and the county committee kept the state committee informed of all important matters within the county.

The county committee determined the method of choosing county nominees and of delegates to county, district, and state conventions.[8] Since 1902 all nominations have been made by primary, but before then the committee ordered nominations by primary or convention and fixed the time and place. It could order preferential primaries for nomination of United States senators. This choice was binding in theory, but not always in fact, upon the county's representatives in the legislature which ultimately elected the senators. In theory, the fixing of qualifications for voting in county primaries was the province of the state committee, but frequently this authority was usurped by the county committee.[9] The county committee prorated expenses of the primary among candidates, and

[6]After 1892 county committees were enlarged by law to thirteen, two chosen from each district and three from the county at large. They could be chosen "as the party may determine." Mississippi, Laws, 1892, Chap. LXIX, 149.

[7]Jackson Weekly Clarion, Aug. 22, 1887; Aberdeen Examiner, Oct. 18, 1883; Macon Beacon, Dec. 10, 1887, May 23, 1891.

[8]Mississippi, Laws, 1892, Chap. LXIX, 149-50.

[9]After 1892 the county committee was authorized by law to fix qualifications. Ibid., 152.

decided all disputed elections. It canvassed returns of the county primary, announced the names of victorious candidates, and in case of a tie, made provision for a second primary between the two highest candidates.[10]

Whether nomination for county offices was by primary or convention, a county convention was held to ratify the decision of the primary, to choose a new executive committee, and to transact other business. If the committee feared the convention might reject the decision of the primary, however, it ordered the returns to be made directly to it instead of to the convention. Occasionally the county committee let the voters decide by ballot whether to hold a nominating primary or convention. Where nominations for county offices were made by primary, the county convention still retained the privilege of choosing delegates to the state convention.[11]

In case no county primary was held, and as frequently as not this seems to have been the case, the county convention was preceded by district or "beat" conventions or mass meetings. These district meetings chose delegates to the county convention, and frequently agreed upon certain candidates whose cause they proposed to further in the county convention. The delegates to the county assembly were then instructed "to vote as a unit for the nominees of this Convention as long as there is a possible hope of success."[12]

One cause for the numerous intracounty quarrels with which the state was constantly plagued was the method of representation in county conventions. The Negro population in a county generally settled together in a local community, and this "black" district consequently had very few whites. Representation in county conventions was apportioned equally among the five supervisors' districts or else in proportion to total population. This gave the few whites in the "black" districts the same advantage in county conventions which the delegates from the black counties enjoyed in the state convention. As a rule, the Negroes did not vote Democratic, or if they did, their vote was controlled by the few white men in the district. Thus these white men had influence in the county conven-

[10]In case of a tie vote in the second primary the county committee was empowered to decide the nomination by lot. Macon *Beacon*, May 23, 1891, Dec. 10, 1887; Aberdeen *Examiner*, Oct. 18, 1883; Jackson *Weekly Clarion*, Aug. 22, 1877; Jackson *Clarion-Ledger*, Apr. 20, 1899; Mississippi, *Laws*, 1892, Chap. LXIX, 151-52.

[11]Macon *Beacon*, Dec. 10, 1887; Chickasaw *Messenger*, Feb. 24, Mar. 10, 1887; Jackson *Clarion-Ledger*, Apr. 20, 1899.

[12]Aberdeen *Examiner*, Oct. 25, 1883.

tion many times that of the whites in the white districts. Where representation in the county convention was based on total population, the heavily populated Negro districts made the disparity even greater. This frequently led disgruntled candidates who did not have the support of the "black" districts to clamor for cutting down the representation of those districts in the convention.[13] Yazoo, one of the black Delta counties, gave equal representation in its convention to each of its five beats. Beat 5 there had only 78 registered Democratic voters, but it had 30 delegates in the county convention just as did Beat 3, which had 534 Democratic voters. Ethelbert Barksdale, who had great strength in Beat 3 but little in Beat 5, attributed his failure to control the convention and carry the county in his race against Senator George in 1891 to this inequitable representation.[14] So great was the opposition to this system that some of the county committees yielded to pressure and apportioned representation in the convention on the basis of votes which the party had polled in each district in the preceding election.[15]

County conventions were apt to be drab affairs if the executive committee had firm control or if there was no vital issue stirring the people. Such a convention was held in Adams County in 1899. There the chairman of the committee called the "large assemblage" to order at noon on August 4 and explained the purpose of the convention as the naming of delegates to the state convention and "the consideration of such business as may legally come before it." A permanent chairman and a permanent secretary were named "by acclamation," and five men were then appointed by the chairman as a resolutions committee. A committee of five others was appointed "to select 20 delegates and 20 alternates to represent Adams County at the State Convention." "Out of respect for Honorable Ed. H. Ratliffe," the county's choice for the nomination for Congress from the fifth district, he was allowed to name the county's six delegates to the congressional district convention. While the several committees were meeting the convention was "at ease" and listened to "impromptu addresses" by such candidates "as happened to be present." The

13Aberdeen *Examiner*, Oct. 18, 25, 1883; Jackson *Clarion-Ledger*, July 11, 1891, May 25, 1899; Natchez *Democrat*, Aug. 5, 1899.

14Jackson *Clarion-Ledger*, July 11, 1891.

15The executive committee of Monroe County in 1883 awarded to each beat one delegate for "every 50 Democratic votes or fraction over half thereof polled at the preceding general county election of 1881." Aberdeen *Examiner*, Oct. 18, 1883.

committees then reported and the reports were unanimously adopted. The convention had organized, completed its business, and adjourned within the space of three hours.[16]

More frequent, however, were conventions such as that held in Noxubee County in 1881. A two-thirds majority was required for nomination and the balloting was long and furious. It required 88 ballots to nominate the candidate for sheriff, 19 for the county treasurer, and 14 for the legislative representatives. The county assessor was nominated after a "long contest." "After a most laborious session all day and all night the Convention adjourned Saturday morning at 5 o'clock."[17]

In addition to the state and county conventions there were also state senatorial district conventions, congressional district conventions, judical district conventions, and flotorial legislative representative district conventions. These district conventions were relatively unimportant. Generally only one office was at stake, and no permanent organization such as the county and state executive committees was attempted. The purpose of a flotorial convention was to nominate a candidate for the legislature who had been jointly apportioned to two counties. In such a convention one county might dominate. The rule of representation established for the state convention applied to the flotorial convention, and each county had twice as many delegates as it had representatives in the lower house of the legislature. Thus, in the Holmes-Yazoo flotorial convention, Holmes, which had two representatives of its own and a floater with Yazoo, was given five representatives. Yazoo, which had three representatives of its own in the legislature in addition to the floater, had seven delegates to the flotorial convention and could thus outvote Holmes. When the Yazoo County chairman offered equal representation to Holmes in the convention of 1881, he was taken to task by his constituents. But frequently agreements were made which permitted each county to name the flotorial candidate in alternate elections.[18] In any of the conventions a county might divide its allotted votes among as many delegates as it chose to honor.

[16]Natchez *Democrat*, Aug. 5, 1899.

[17]Macon *Beacon*, Aug. 13, 1881.

[18]Jackson *Clarion-Ledger*, Aug. 12, 13, 1881; Aberdeen *Examiner*, Aug. 23, 1883; Macon *Beacon*, July 15, 1882.

The rigid control which the leaders of the Democratic party wielded in Mississippi in the years following the revolution of 1875 produced dissatisfaction among those who were outside the magic inner circles. Throughout the period from 1876 until 1902 there was a ceaseless clamor against the evils of the convention, state and local. Many who had taken an active though subaltern part in the revolution felt that they were not adequately rewarded. It was inevitable that ambitious outsiders who could not gain admittance should think of the small central body as a corrupt ring or clique. The leading Republican paper in the state reported having heard many representatives from the "cow counties" at the Democratic state convention of 1877 speak in disgust of the "Jackson Clique" which "dictated" Stone's nomination for governor. "The Democrats are united in only one thing—to get office—and this union becomes the source of the bitterest and most incurable division of all." A large number, it thought, had come to the convention "for office," but had gone home "in disgust."[19]

There was plenty of evidence in the Democratic press of discontent with this convention. The Raymond *Gazette* concluded after the convention that the party showed no disposition "to reward . . . those who have performed valuable services in overthrowing the Radicals." If a man wished position in the party, he must "be always on the alert for himself." The Forest *Register* condemned the platform adopted as "cut and dried," and called it "the most arrant clap-trap and machinery ever thrust down the throats of the people." Both the *Register* and the Canton *Mail* condemned the "dictatorial methods" of Lamar at the convention. "Col. Lamar has demonstrated to the people of Mississippi," said the *Mail* editor, "that he's more concerned about himself and his own success than he is about the affairs of the State. He is for Lamar first and Mississippi next."[20]

The party leaders had early mastered the technique of convention control and were reluctant to change. The dissatisfied elements, rebuffed at conventions, sought to better their chances by changing the rules of the game by making primaries mandatory. Throughout the period the convention-primary controversy raged. One "progres-

[19]Jackson *Daily Times*, Aug. 3, 4, 1877.

[20]Raymond *Gazette* and Forest *Register*, quoted in Jackson *Daily Times*, Aug. 10, 1877; Canton *Mail*, quoted in Jackson *Daily Times*, Sept. 4, 1877.

sive" editor in 1879 noted that all "bourbon journals" were attempting to "whip the various Democratic county committees into line"
for conventions. The editor admitted that conventions and "strict
party organzation" were all right in the past when it was deemed
necessary that "Mississippians should rule Mississippi." Now that
that condition existed he thought that the party should be run de-
mocratically, without "the dictates of a few . . . self-interested
politicians."[21]

A specific charge made against the convention was that nominations were frequently the result of barter. The Natchez *Democrat*
admitted that trading was a common practice at conventions, and
the Aberdeen *Examiner* blandly published an account of a trade
between Monroe and Yazoo counties in the state convention of 1885.
"Our candidate for Auditor," said the *Examiner*, "received the 7
votes of Yazoo . . . on every ballot, and when the nomination for
attorney-general was reached Monroe supported her candidate until
he was withdrawn."[22] A Republican paper reported widespread
dissatisfaction among Hinds County Democrats with their county
convention in 1877. The charge was freely made, said the editor,
that nominations were "the result of bargain and sale among the
delegates."[23]

Dissatisfaction led to revolt. The disgruntled voters of Hinds in
1877 called a rump convention and nominated a new ticket of county
officers; and reports came into Jackson of Independent tickets complete from governor to beat officers in other parts of the state. The
movement, however, proved abortive; the Independents met the fate
of most third parties, and the regular tickets had their own way in
the election.[24] As time went on the practice of revolt spread and
Independent tickets were formed in many sections. A group of
Democrats met at Athens Camp Ground in Monroe County on
September 4, 1883, in protest against the "combinations and tricks"
and "glaring frauds" in the county primary held on July 21 and ratified by the county convention of July 28. The meeting declared
nine of the nominees to have been illegally and fraudulently chosen.
It nominated nine others in opposition, acceded to the other nomina-

[21]Vicksburg *Democrat-Commercial*, June 4, 1879; Macon *Beacon*, July 30, 1881.
[22]Natchez *Democrat*, Aug. 27, 1885; *ibid.*, quoting Aberdeen *Examiner*.
[23]Jackson *Daily Times*, Nov. 2, 1877.
[24]*Ibid.*, Nov. 2, 6, 8, 1877.

tions made by the primary, and appointed a committee of fifteen, three from each district, as an executive committee to manage the campaign. This movement, too, proved futile; three of the men nominated by the meeting declined the honor, and the other six were defeated.[25]

A revolt against the action of the county convention in Noxubee in 1889 was barely averted. There a county primary had been held, but the county committee had highhandedly refused to confirm the nomination of the candidate for sheriff who had polled the highest vote. When the state executive committee refused to order another primary in the county the charge was made that it was partisan. Later the state committee reversed itself and ordered a second primary, at which time the original victor won again. This produced a kind of harmony, but wounds remained.[26]

Even the advocates of reform in the practices of nominating conventions to eliminate "machine politics" admitted that the system "with all its . . . evils" had given good officials. But fears were expressed that if party dissension continued to grow, the Republicans would "quietly step into office."[27]

In the political machinery of the state, election officials were only slightly less important than party officials. A state board of election commissioners, composed of the governor, secretary of state, and attorney-general, appointed county boards, consisting of "three discreet persons" not all of the same party. The state board also appointed a registrar in each county to register the names of the voters. County election commissioners were appointed two months before each congressional election and held office for two years unless removed. The registrar was appointed for a four-year term. The county election commissioners appointed three managers for each election district, not all of the same party, and they also had appellate jurisdiction from decisions made by the registrar. The managers were to see that the election was conducted "fairly and agreeably to law," and were to be the judges of the qualifications of electors presenting themselves at the polls.[28] After 1875 two of the commis-

[25]Aberdeen *Examiner*, Sept. 13, 20, Nov. 12, 1883.

[26]Macon *Beacon*, Oct. 5, 12, 26, 1889.

[27]*Ibid.*, May 7, 1881, March 31, 1883.

[28]Mississippi, *Laws*, 1876, Chap. LXVII; *ibid.*, 1880, Chap. LVI; *Code*, 1880, Secs. 121, 124, 128, 133, 138-140.

sioners were always Democrats and the other a Republican. As a general practice the state board named the Democratic members to the county boards upon the recommendation of their respective county committees. But where a county committee was hostile to the state administration, its recommendation was frequently disregarded. Also, the Republican member was supposed to be appointed upon the recommendation of the Republican county committee. But if the Republican recommendation did not meet the approval of the Democratic county committee, it had little chance of acceptance.[29]

The local election officials occupied positions of great power. By encouraging some to register and by discouraging others they could influence elections. They could also exercise influence by locating voting places close to certain groups of voters and distant from others.[30] The choice of the election commissioners by Democratic state officials "made all things possible." Thousands of opposition votes were thrown out on technicalities, fraudulent returns were frequently made, and, if necessary, ballot boxes were stuffed.[31] Since Independent movements were widespread it was thought that any methods which would insure victory were justifiable.

With so much at stake there was certain to be great interest in securing "proper" parties for election officials in the several counties. In 1876 Warren Cowan wrote Governor Stone from Vicksburg protesting against the appointment of the Republican member of the county board who had been recommended by Thomas C. Catchings, Democratic congressman from the district. According to Cowan the man had served on the old Republican board during Reconstruction, had then switched to the Democratic party, but had recently rejoined the Republicans. "He is utterly unreliable," wrote Cowan, "and keeps a small drinking saloon." He had no "permanent property interests" in the county, and his appointment would "produce dis-

[29]Charles A. Stovall to J. Z. George, June 27, 1876; Stovall to J. M. Stone, Sept. 18, 1877; Warren Cowan to Stone, Apr. 19, 1876; T. C. Catchings to Stone, Apr. 22, 1876; L. P. Yerger to George, Aug. 14, 1876; J. L. Lake to Stone *et al.*, Aug. 7, 1876; Robert Lowry to Kinloch Faulconer, Nov. 3, 1877, Letters of Governors, Series E, 128A, 136A, 126A, 135A; Jackson *Clarion*, Aug. 18, 1881; Wharton, *The Negro in Mississippi*, 201; Macon *Beacon*, Mar. 12, 1881; Chickasaw *Messenger*, Sept. 1, 8, 15, 29, Oct. 20, 1887.

[30]Stovall to George, June 27, 1876, Letters of Governors, Series E, 128A.

[31]Wharton, *The Negro in Mississippi*, 204.

satisfaction and create distrust among the better classes."[32] In Leflore County the Radicals were attempting to have Sam McRae, Negro, removed as Republican member of the election commission, but the Democrats were insisting that he be retained. "By his fair dealings, his conservative views, and his gentlemanly deportment," wrote L. P. Yerger, he had made friends "among his political enemies, the Democrats." Frequently complaint had been made that Republican members of the county commissions were illiterate, but Yerger pointed out that McRae was not, since "he can sign his own name." Invariably the Democrats recommended a Negro as the Republican election commissioner.[33]

Within a few years after the overthrow of the Radicals fear of the Republican party in itself disappeared, but danger of a fusion of dissident groups of Democrats with Republicans remained. Independent factions were striving to secure representation on the election boards, and frequently there was danger they might succeed. Learning that a vacancy was about to occur on the Clarke County board in 1877 and "knowing the importance to the Democratic party of maintaining a proper control of the registration," Charles Stovall wrote Governor Stone urging the appointment of W. C. McDonald. "We have much to contend with in this county," wrote Stovall, "to maintain the party conquests recently made. We have local complications and broils which must be delicately handled." The Independent spirit was abroad in the county and had to be dealt with. It was "vital to the party to see that [the] Board of Registrars are 'Sound on the Goose'."[34]

Unfairness on the part of election officials was repeatedly charged, not only by Republicans and Independents but, in the few cases where the opposition had gained local control, by regular Democrats. During the campaign of 1876 the secretary of the Republican state central committee charged that in Washington County, where there were over 6,000 registered voters, the election commissioners had reduced the voting precincts to seven and had "determined to remain only *two days*" at each precinct to conduct registration. In one district with 250 voters two voting precincts

[32]Cowan to Stone, Apr. 19, 1876; W. H. McCardle to Stone, Apr. 17, 1876, Letters of Governors, Series E, 126A.

[33]Yerger to George, Aug. 14, 1876; Catchings to Stone, Apr. 22, 1876, *ibid.*

[34]Stovall to Stone, Sept. 18, 1877, *ibid.*, Series E, 136A.

were established, while in another with 1,700 voters "provision has been made for only one polling place. It is obvious," he wrote, "that such arrangements are well calculated to deprive many citizens of an opportunity to register and vote." Election under such circumstances would be a "farce." He urged the removal of the Washington board and the choice of another.[35] The following year a prominent Democrat of Hinds County charged R. H. Reeves, the Hinds registrar, with "fraudulent action" in registering unqualified voters and in refusing to register some who were qualified.[36]

By 1887 agrarian factions had gained control in some counties and were engaged in a bitter duel with the administration of Governor Lowry. After a nominating convention in Chickasaw the successful candidates requested the county executive committee to recommend to the state board of election commissioners three men to serve on the county election board. But the county executive committee was split by factionalism, and while nine of the fifteen members made the requested recommendation, the other six refused to do so and started a petition for the appointment of three other men. The nominees thereupon addressed a letter to the public charging the six dissident committeemen with being "unfriendly to . . . the Democratic ticket and in sympathy with an opposition movement, which means the antagonism of the races in this county." When the state board appointed the opposition men the nominees published compromising letters of the dissident committeemen to the governor plotting the defeat of the Democratic nominees.

A correspondent from Holmes County reported a similar occurrence there. The state board had given two of the three commissionerships to the opposition—one to the regular Republican organization and one to the Independent Democrats—while giving only one to the regular Democratic organization. The correspondent attributed the action to the fact that Holmes had gone against Lowry in the preceding election, as had Chickasaw, and that the administration was simply "settling old scores." In both instances Lowry was thus in the position of supporting Independents, some of whom had been Republicans in the past and were suspected of being allied with them now. The Fayette *Chronicle* openly charged that Lowry was trying to beat Frank Burkitt, agrarian leader of Chicka-

[35]Lake to Stone *et al.*, Aug. 7, 1876; W. A. Percy to State Board of Registrars, Aug. 14, 1876, *ibid.*, Series E, 128A.

[36]Lowry to Faulconer, Nov. 3, 1877, *ibid.*, Series E, 135A.

saw, with an Independent because Burkitt was an "anti-Lowry Democrat." The Kosciusko *Star* echoed the charge, and the Jackson *New Mississippian* added that Lowry had done the same thing in his own county of Rankin, which had opposed his renomination.[37]

At the same time the Bolivar County Democratic executive committee was protesting the reappointment of the election board in Bolivar, charging it was dominated by George Y. Scott, the "political boss" of the county. One of the commissioners, it was claimed, was the brother of the chancery clerk who was a candidate for re-election, and was also the attorney for the Negro county treasurer who was a candidate for re-election. Another of the commissioners was a brother-in-law of the chancery clerk and "a close relation" of George Scott.[38]

Thus the struggle went on. Where the interests of the faction in control of the state administration coincided with those of the group in charge of local affairs, things moved on a comparatively even keel. Complaints there were to be sure, but frequently these were the complaints of Republicans and Independents, often a discredited set among the more substantial folk. But where state and local leaders were at variance, the struggle was of more consequence to the state party organization. When the local respected leaders broke with the authority at Jackson trouble was sure to follow. Generally such revolts were not confined to one area, and there was danger not only that such factions might unite, but also that they might ally themselves with Republican leaders who had influence with the great potential voting masses of Negroes. Any and all factions made use of these black "pawns" where it was necessary and it suited their purpose to do so. This bidding for the Negro vote, it was felt, was damaging to the prestige and morals of the whites and, more important still, was a threat to "white supremacy."

[37]Chickasaw *Messenger*, Sept. 1, 8, 15, 29, Oct. 6, 1887; *ibid.*, Sept. 29, 1887, quoting Fayette *Chronicle* and Kosciusko *Star; ibid.*, Oct. 6, 1887, quoting Jackson *New Mississippian*.

[38]Chickasaw *Messenger*, Oct. 20, 1887.

CHAPTER IV

AGRARIAN DISCONTENT

ONE cannot view the politics of Mississippi without seeing that sectional interests within the state produced political issues. In the northwest corner of the state, in a region formed by the confluence of the Mississippi and Yazoo rivers, is the Delta. Here centuries of inundations have built up an alluvial soil thirty feet deep. It is a region of large plantations heavily populated by Negro tenants, and the rich soil is almost exclusively devoted to the production of long-staple cotton. Fifteen hundred pounds to the acre is not an unusual yield in the Delta, whereas in other parts of the state six hundred pounds is considered good. Twelve of Mississippi's eighty-two counties are entirely within the Delta region and half a dozen more are partly so. In all of these counties the population is predominately Negro, varying in ratio from 3 to 1 in some, to 8, 10, and even 15 to 1 in others.[1] The Delta was by far the wealthiest region of the state, and should therefore have borne a considerable portion of the tax burden. It did not always do so, however, and attempts to redistribute tax loads were resisted as strongly in the Delta and other rich counties as they were urged by less fortunate sections. Then, too, the constitutional machinery, inherited from Reconstruction days and preserved for more than a dozen years thereafter, gave the same wealthy counties an influence in politics far beyond that warranted by the number of their voters. Efforts to reform this inequity were marked by the same sectional cleavages as was the struggle over finances. Indeed the two movements converged in one and it was impossible at times to distinguish them.

Nor when political reforms were finally effected—they were begun in 1890 and consummated twelve years later—did the sectional struggle cease. Thereafter the Delta counties felt that their taxes were out of all proportion to their political influence, and the hill counties and Piney Woods section were dissatisfied because they felt that the political influence of the Delta was still greater than its voting population warranted.

[1]This and succeeding paragraphs concerning geography and population are based on E. N. Lowe, *A Preliminary Study of Soils of Mississippi* (Nashville, 1911), 61-67; United States *Census of 1890*, I, 770-71.

The hill counties are those at the northeast corner of the state bordering the Tennessee River. Here the land is rough, unproductive, and ill-suited for profitable agriculture. At the same time failure of nature to provide the essential ingredients of industry—coal and water power—has relegated the inhabitants to subsistence farming. It is a region of small farms where the whites outnumber the Negroes as greatly as the Negroes outnumber the whites in the most densely populated Delta counties.

The Piney Woods is a region including approximately the southeast quarter of the state. Here the soil is sandy and unproductive, but the region is heavily timbered with pine. This timber was to furnish the Piney Woods with its one brief period of prosperity in the early years of the twentieth century. But that time was not yet, and in the period before 1890 the region was one of small farms where cotton growing and truck gardening were carried on at a subsistence level. Both here and to the south in the sandy Coastal Plain the population is overwhelmingly white.

In general, the richest counties of the state are in the Delta and the poorest are in south Mississippi. Next to the Delta in wealth is the strip of brown loess counties on its eastern border, with scattered here and there a county in the prairie region. Next in poverty to the Piney Woods region of the south is the Tennessee River Hills area to the north and east. In the assessment valuations in 1888 the thirteen counties of the first class were all Delta counties, and the fifteen counties of the fourth and last class were all located either in south Mississippi or in the northeastern area.[2]

The variance of economic advantages in the different sections was reflected in the political struggles within the state, although not with perfect consistency and unanimity. To classify certain regions of the state as committed entirely to this or that political philosophy would be oversimplification. It must be borne in mind that there were rich and poor, educated and uneducated, cultured and uncultured in all regions, and as often as not class interests did not follow sectional lines.

It would be too simple to think of Mississippi as divided into merely the large landowners of the Delta in an area that is predominantly Negro, and the small landowners of the hill country where

[2]Macon *Beacon*, Dec. 22, 1888.

the population is predominantly white. Yet these two classes do exist and there is little love between them. The small hill farmers, who work their farms with their own hands, dislike and distrust the plantation owners, whose lands are worked almost entirely by Negroes. The whites beyond the Delta greatly exceed those within, and frequently the two groups are in opposing political factions. On the other hand, the whites within the Delta thought that the white counties had abandoned them to the Negroes in the congressional redistricting after the overthrow of the Radical regime in 1876, and their pride in their self-salvation was rivaled only by their resentment against the white counties who had left them to their fate.[3] "The river counties will certainly be represented on the next State ticket," wrote a Delta editor in 1887, "or the little Shoe-String District will have a ticket of its own." The district might divide on political and race issues but would "be solid" on a sectional fight and "all lump in together, Republican and Democrats, white and black, and poll such a vote" as would make the political aspirants of "north Mississippi and of the Cow Counties open their eyes in astonishment."[4]

Peculiar sectional needs were a source of irritation. In the 1880's sheep raising was a considerable industry in northeast Mississippi, and the people of that region were resentful when they could not persuade the state legislature to instruct the congressmen and senators to vote for a tariff on wool.[5] South Mississippi and the white counties in general could not provide adequate schooling for their children, and their pleas for a redistribution of school funds persisted for half a century. The particular need of the Delta was levees to protect it from the annual overflows of the Mississippi and the Yazoo. But levees cost money and the rest of the state was slow to see any advantage it could derive from taxing itself to protect the property of the plantation owners. In their extremity the Delta farmers actually considered allying themselves with the Republican party in an effort to get federal aid for levee construction. "If we of the Delta are subjected to the annual floods of the river," wrote a farmer to Governor Lowry, "our country is not

[3]Natchez *Democrat*, Jan. 26, 1877.

[4]Vicksburg *Daily Commercial*, Mar. 23, 1877.

[5]Aberdeen *Examiner*, July 19, 1883. Said the *Examiner*, "the wool tariff is the farmer's tariff."

habitable, and the character of the government that may prevail over it becomes a minor question."[6]

Although Mississippi was and has remained predominantly an agricultural state, industry began to develop in the period after the Civil War. Lacking water power and coal, industry never flourished to the extent it did in other southern states; yet in the decade of the 1880's it increased threefold. The depression in cotton prices impressed the need of a more varied industry. In his message to the legislature in 1882 Governor Lowry urged industrial encouragement, and the legislature responded by an act exempting new industries from taxation for a period of ten years after starting operation.[7] Much was expected as a result of this measure, but the deficiency in coal and water power restricted development. In 1890 lumber, textiles, oil, and railroads were Mississippi's leading industries. Most of this industry was located in southern Mississippi, but even there it took second place to agriculture whose products were valued at four times those of industry.[8]

Industry was gaining an importance, however, not indicated by statistics. Before the war agriculture had dominated southern thought and society. The clergy, press, bar, and other opinion-forming agencies reflected its views and represented its interests. Despite differences in wealth and social status the small farmer's interests were in many cases tied closely to those of the planters. While the Civil War brought "desolation and ruin to the farmer and planter, it wrought a revolution within the towns." Many were turning from agriculture to merchandising, banking, railroading, manufacturing, and other occupations. Reconstruction transferred social and economic power from the farms to the towns. The store usurped the prestige of the plantation, and towns grew in population and importance. By the 1880's agriculture was no longer the dominant influence it had been. The farmer's social pre-eminence had been taken by the merchant, the banker, and the lawyer who found he could get fatter fees from this new clientele than from the old.[9]

[6]A. J. Paxton to Robert Lowry, July 9, 1882, in Letters of Governors, Series E, 176A; also Green Clay to Lowry, July 6, 1882, ibid.

[7]Mississippi, Laws, 1882, Chap. XLIX, Sec. 1.

[8]Halsell, "The Bourbon Period," loc. cit., 534-35.

[9]Benjamin B. Kendrick, "Agrarian Discontent in the South: 1880-1890," in American Historical Association, Annual Report (1920), 271-72, 274; Daniel M. Robison, "From Tillman to Long: Some Striking Leaders of the Rural South," in Journal of Southern History, III (1937), 294-95.

A divergence was evolving between the economic interests of farm and town that was to effect a change in politics. "The unanimity with which the spokesmen of the people had championed the cause of agriculture was no more."[10] The farmers realized that they had lost their leaders, and resentment against them and against political "machines" and "rings" grew up.[11] Economic distress was upon them, and they felt they must have new leaders to replace the old.

One particular grievance of the farmer in the 1870's and 1880's was the lien law. This was a mortgage on the crop to be planted and was originally designed to give the landlord security for supplies furnished his tenants. But soon it began to be used by the merchants to the disadvantage of the landlord. If the landlord had had the capital to finance his tenants, all would have been well. But he did not, and he had to borrow it either directly from the banks or indirectly through the merchants who furnished supplies to both him and his tenants. Because of the low value of land after the war, merchant and banker had suffered losses on real security, and when the lien law was passed they quickly took advantage of it to demand one of these ironclad mortgages of any farmer desiring credit. In return for the credit extended him, and through him to his tenants, the farmer mortgaged his crop, stock, and agricultural implements to the merchant. The contract usually provided that the merchant's accounts were incontestable. The crops when sold frequently brought less than these accounts, so that the farmer "continued from year to year in debt to the same merchant under the same galling conditions." Because of the monopoly which the merchant enjoyed, as well as the uncertainty of the investment, the prices charged the farmer were generally from 25 to 50 per cent above the cash price. Better to secure himself and to increase his sale of supplies, the merchant insisted that the farmer plant most of his land in cotton. Frequently, under the prevailing low price of cotton, the farmer failed to make both ends meet, and "the land began to go piece-meal to the merchant." The merchant then cropped it with Negro tenants. The Negroes preferred to crop with

[10]Robison, "From Tillman to Long," *loc. cit.*, 294.
[11]See Memorial of State Farmer's Alliance to legislature, in Mississippi, *House Journal*, 1890, pp. 145-48.

merchants because they gave less supervision, and thus the merchants were able to obtain the better tenants.[12]

During the 1880's recorded mortgages increased from less than five thousand to more than eleven thousand. Cotton prices continued low and farm tenantry was increasing, but the "lien merchant rose in prosperity [while] the farmer sank further into the slough of economic despondency."[13] The farmer sought by devious means, some legal and some violent, to extricate himself from this depressed condition. A meeting of farmers in Brookhaven in the fall of 1877 demanded a price of fifteen cents for cotton, and denounced merchants who by "usurious rates and enormous profits supped the life blood from the farmers."[14] In many places the rougher element organized into gangs of "bulldozers" and took direct action against farmers who rented land from merchants. In Amite, Wilkinson, Franklin, and Pike counties in the southwest corner of the state, the most diabolical crimes were secretly committed. Whippings, mutilations, robberies, rapes, and murders by bands of men under the guise of "Bulldozers or protective clubs" were common occurrences. When good men denounced these practices, they too were mysteriously threatened with violence.[15] But the lawlessness was not altogether unpopular even among the "good citizens." A correspondent from Amite reported that reputable men were publicly applauding the "bulldozers" and that politicians were making capital of the farmer's grievances. Indeed it was commonly thought there, he wrote, that the "bulldozers" were authorized agents of the Farmers' Alliance. In any event, prominent farmers were openly repudiating contracts made with merchants, and the latter were desperate as they realized that in the present state of feeling they could not collect. So bad did "bulldozing" become that the governor

[12]Kendrick, "Agrarian Discontent," loc. cit., 274-76. Both Negroes and whites made up the tenant population of Mississippi, but the Negro tenants greatly outnumbered the whites. The planter had found in the years after the war that the Negro was an agricultural worker far superior and more easily controlled than the white, and thus the Negro became a victim of the share-cropper system. In seventeen counties in 1880 not one Negro in a hundred owned the land he worked. In twelve counties the proportion was less than one in twenty; in many other counties it was less than one in fifty. According to Vernon L. Wharton these ratios had undergone some change by 1890 when, of the 87,819 Negro farm homes, 10,032 were owned by their occupants. Wharton, The Negro in Mississippi, 61-62.

[13]Halsell, "The Bourbon Period," loc. cit., 533.

[14]Jackson Daily Times, Sept. 19, 1877.

[15]Brookhaven Ledger, Vicksburg Herald, and Holly Springs South, quoted in Jackson Daily Times, Aug. 29, 1877.

asked and the legislature granted funds to suppress the lawlessness.[16]

Violence was not the only attack made by the farmers on the lien law. For months preceding and during the legislative session of 1878 active propaganda for repeal of the law was carried on. Most of the rural papers advocated outright repeal, while the journals of the larger towns joined in the defense of the law. The Jackson *Daily Times*, a Republican paper, took a middle-of-the-road attitude and suggested making the lien legal only for necessities.[17] The Vicksburg *Democrat-Commercial* violently attacked the law because of its injustice to tenants by protecting the usurious rates charged by the merchants.[18] The *Democrat* called on the legislature to "do something practical" for the farmers, pointing out that all other classes were aided in some way by the government—mechanics could obtain patents, vending taxes protected the merchant from outside competition, and the lawyer's license guaranteed exclusive privileges to the members of that profession. "But the farmers," said the editor, ". . . are left to struggle alone and unassisted in their laborious efforts to contribute to the wealth and prosperity of the state."[19]

The farmers traced many of their ills to middlemen whose toll of goods passing through their hands was not commensurate to the services rendered. To the farmer it seemed that the middleman was an invisible but strongly unified monopoly, and he became an inveterate foe of anything that smacked of monopolism.[20]

The greatest of all monopolies, as the farmer saw it, was the railroad. It was the main highway which furnished him with an outlet to a market for his produce. Only in rare instances did the farmer have the benefit of competing lines, and even here he frequently suspected that the competitors were in secret agreement against him. The railroad problem most closely affected the farmer on the question of rates. It was believed that the tariffs were too high and that "gross discrimination was practiced in fixing them." In the days before the Interstate Commerce Commission, clamor

[16]Jackson *Daily Times*, Sept. 20, 1877, Feb. 4, 1878.

[17]*Ibid.*, Jan. 10, 1878.

[18]Vicksburg *Democrat-Commercial*, Jan. 18, 1878.

[19]*Ibid.*, Jan. 2, 1882.

[20]James S. Ferguson, "Cooperative Activity in the Grange in Mississippi," in *Journal of Mississippi History*, IV (1942), 5-19.

began for state regulation.[21] There was much agitation about the inequalities, discriminations, and extortions of the railroads, particularly the Mobile and Ohio.[22] So strong was the feeling that a prominent Democratic paper urged the defeat of any legislative candidate, "even if beaten by a Radical," who did not favor federal aid to the Texas-Pacific which, it was hoped, would break the monopoly.[23]

Frequently the farmer's animosity toward the carriers sprang from an even more personal grievance than that of discriminatory and oppressive rates. Quite often he had invested in stock of a proposed road in order to gain access to market. In addition counties and towns furnished loans and rights of way, and purchased stock. Because of corrupt construction rings, unscrupulous directors, or inefficiency, many of the roads went through receivership before the undertaking was completed, sometimes before it was begun. When the stock failed to pay dividends, the farmer who had frequently mortgaged his land to buy it suffered. When his taxes were increased to pay the county's or town's gift to the road a blind antagonism grew up in him against railroads in general.[24] He might not understand just what the situation was or where the trouble really lay, but that did not lessen his antagonism. When his government failed to protect him against the predatory practices of the "monster," he denounced the government as an ally of the "interests." When the legislature of 1882 passed legislation favorable to railroads and industrial enterprises, the Macon *Beacon* and the Enterprise *Courier* were outspoken in their criticism. The *Courier* charged the legislature with "class legislation in favor of capital and corporations" and predicted that its actions would be a heavy weight for the Democratic party to carry in the next campaign. The editor foresaw a revolution within the party against the monopolists and the money power, and the *Beacon* echoed the sentiment.[25]

That the farmer's grievance was real there has long ceased to be any doubt. The railway corporation's power was growing "and

21Solon J. Buck, *The Granger Movement, A Study of Agricultural Organizations and its Political, Economic, and Social Manifestations, 1870-1880* (Cambridge, 1933), 13-14.

22Jackson *Weekly Clarion,* most issues through the winter and spring of 1878.

23Vicksburg *Democrat-Commercial,* Oct. 5, 1877.

24Buck, *The Granger Movement,* 10-11.

25Enterprise *Courier,* quoted in Macon *Beacon,* Mar. 18, 1882.

was being used to influence public officials." Construction systems were wasteful and corrupt; watering of stocks and securities was a common practice; and rates were "higher than was necessary for a fair return on the physical value of the road."[26] There were discriminations against shippers which injured not only them but consumers as well. The legislator's plight was not an enviable one. He was "between the devil and the deep sea" in the fear of offending the farmers, who had votes, and the railroads, who had money. Whether or not the numerous charges of bribery were true, "railroad favors were undoubtedly distributed among well disposed legislators."[27]

The farmers, however, were not without representatives during the period. The three most prominent of the new leaders—General James Z. George, Lucius Q. C. Lamar, and Edward C. Walthall—were all corporate lawyers. George, who by all odds had the largest corporate practice in the state, was not as clearly identified with corporate interests politically as were Lamar and Walthall. At times he seemed to enjoy the confidence of the small farmers, who were dubious of the other two.[28] But of the seventeen congressmen elected from 1876 to 1890, "seven . . . sympathized with, worked for, and were approved by the farmers." The lower house of the legislature "was controlled by the farmers throughout the . . . period," and there was always a large minority of farmers in the Senate.[29]

With such representation it is remarkable that the farmers were not able to secure more favorable legislation than they did. But they were not politically organized, and they lacked able leadership. Their two outstanding leaders—Putnam Darden and Frank L. Burkitt—never occupied offices of great importance, and generally the disorganized farmers "worked along with and voted for" the men in power. Until the turn of the century they "were generally content to accept the so-called Bourbon senators and representatives . . . or, if unwilling, they did not make their influence felt."[30] But agrarian journals did not join in the eulogies which were so

[26]Buck, *The Granger Movement*, 15.
[27]Buck, *The Agrarian Crusade*, 52, 53.
[28]Halsell, "The Bourbon Period," *loc. cit.*, 524-26; R. T. Wilson to L. Q. C. Lamar, Sept. 15, 1891, Lamar Letterbooks.
[29]Halsell, "The Bourbon Period," *loc. cit.*, 524-28.
[30]*Ibid.*, 531.

frequently and with such abandon showered upon officeholders by their supporting press. Grange papers were both articulate and devastating in their attacks upon politicians who did not favor agricultural interests. But for a long period their voices were unheard, or if heard were disregarded. The control of the entrenched leaders was too complete to be upset by this leaderless and disorganized opposition. When the opposition showed signs of unification, as it did in 1881, 1888, and again in 1895, the cry of "white supremacy and party regularity" sufficed to scatter its forces.

CHAPTER V

CORPORATIONS AND THE FARMERS

ONE of the Democratic leaders of the state who had contributed mightily to the victory of 1875-1876 was Ethelbert Barksdale, editor of the Jackson *Clarion*. Barksdale was frequently denounced as an "ultra-Bourbon" by editors professing to be "progressive." But Barksdale was an advocate of railroad regulation, the elimination of the convict lease system, cheap currency, free coinage of silver, the sub-treasury, and other programs not generally identified with "Bourbonism." Barksdale did not approve of Lamar's policy of conciliating northern Republicans and had taken issue with him on his eulogy of Sumner. When Lamar supported the report of the Electoral Commission in the Hayes-Tilden election of 1876, the estrangement widened between him and Barksdale. Barksdale even charged that Lamar had exchanged his vote for the commission report in return for his own admission to the United States Senate.[1]

The controversy between silver and gold was getting under way in Mississippi in the late 1870's, and political factions were forming on this issue. Barksdale, as a Farmers' Alliance man, favored the repeal of the Specie Resumption Act and the passage of the Bland bill. Lamar, on the other hand, was a "Goldbug" and sympathized with banking and railroad interests. Popular sentiment in Mississippi, however, was overwhelmingly in favor of cheap money, and in 1878 the legislature sent instructions to Lamar and Blanche K. Bruce to support the Bland bill and to vote for repeal of the Resumption Act in the Senate. Bruce did so, but Lamar, testing his hold on his people almost to the breaking point, refused. For this he was excoriated by a large part of the Mississippi press and suffered the humiliation of having the state House of Representatives pass a resolution commending the action of his Negro colleague while ignoring him.[2] The *Clarion* published a letter from Jefferson Davis expressing his belief in the obligation of a Senator to follow instruc-

[1] Jackson *Weekly Clarion*, Dec. 10, 1874, Feb. 23, 1876; Mayes, *Lamar*, 302; Vicksburg *Democrat-Commercial*, Mar. 24, 1877; Natchez *Daily Democrat*, July 14, 1881.

[2] Natchez *Democrat*, Feb. 3, 1878; Mississippi, *Senate Journal*, 1878, pp. 212, 215, 235, 236, 343; Mayes, *Lamar*, 330-48.

tions from his legislature,[3] and the Natchez *Democrat*, heretofore a loyal supporter of Lamar, said he had "destroyed his usefulness and popularity" in the state.[4]

The struggle between Lamar and Barksdale for party control came to a head in 1880 over the choice of a successor to Bruce in the Senate. Barksdale and Congressman Otho R. Singleton, both silverites, had announced themselves as candidates. Edward C. Walthall, close personal and political friend of Lamar and like him a "hard money man," had not announced, but it was known that Lamar was grooming him for the race. The choice rested with the state legislature, meeting in joint session. This body was composed overwhelmingly of regular Democrats, but there were twenty-seven "mongrel" members variously classed as Republicans, Greenbackers, and Independent Democrats. To prevent this group from promoting "geographical jealousy" among the Democrats,[5] and to prevent the "unseemly spectacle" of Lamar and Barksdale appealing to this opposition group, it was agreed that the Democratic members should decide in caucus on a candidate and then unite behind him in the legislative election.[6] This would exclude Republicans and Greenbackers but would not decide the status of Independent Democrats. Barksdale demanded that "only straight-laced Democrats" be admitted to the caucus. This would exclude the Independent Democrats, who at this time were aligned with Lamar. But Lamar won on this point and the Independents joined the caucus.[7]

Lamar, Walthall, Singleton, Barksdale, and several lesser candidates descended on Jackson for the caucus. "Button-holing and soft sawder, to say nothing of less justifiable measures are made use of to gain votes," said an observer. Lamar's activities came in for particular censure. It was thought undignified and unfair for him to use his position and influence in behalf of one of the candidates.[8]

---

[3]Jefferson Davis to Ethelbert Barksdale, Dec. 14, 1878, published in Jackson *Weekly Clarion*, Jan. 15, 1879; also in Mayes, *Lamar*, 363-64.

[4]Natchez *Democrat*, Feb. 17, 1878.

[5]Lamar, whose term did not expire for two more years, was from north Mississippi, as were Walthall and Singleton. It was argued by the Barksdale supporters that a "geographical distribution" should be made, and that Bruce's seat should go to a man from south Mississippi, that is, Barksdale.

[6]Port Gibson *Reveille*, Jan. 7, 1880; Jackson *Weekly Clarion*, Jan. 14, 1880.

[7]Halsell, "Democratic Dissensions," *loc. cit.*, 127.

[8]Vicksburg *Democrat-Commercial*, Feb. 11, 1880; Jackson *Weekly Clarion*, Jan. 7, 14, 1880.

The charge of "Bourbonism" was freely tossed back and forth by adherents of both Lamar and Barksdale.

The caucus developed into a deadlock. On the sixth ballot, Barksdale led all other candidates and was within two votes of the required majority.[9] But the Lamar forces held at that point, and the caucus dragged on. Suddenly, on the forty-ninth ballot, Barksdale threw his support to J. Z. George, who had been belatedly nominated, and George was elected.[10] Since Walthall had finally supported George too, both the Lamar and Barksdale factions claimed victory in George's nomination. Barksdale said it was evidence of Lamar's waning power, but Lamar's supporters maintained that George was of the same political school as Lamar, and that they saw eye to eye on many questions. Nevertheless, George had not been Lamar's first choice, and he had won only with Barksdale's help.[11]

Lamar's successor would be chosen by the legislature to be elected in 1881, and conventions or preferential primaries were ordered in many of the counties to indicate choices for the Democratic senatorial candidate. The legislators thus chosen would be pledged. The necessity of choosing both a senator and a governor in the same year complicated the Lamar-Barksdale feud. Lamar people said they would support none but a Lamar man for governor, and denounced as "Bourbons" all who opposed him. The Tupelo *Journal* ridiculed this "everlasting and senseless tirade against an imaginary . . . Bourbonism." It and other journals supporting Barksdale held that if a Lamar man were nominated for governor, Barksdale should replace Lamar in the Senate. Others, such as the Grenada *Sentinel*, suggested a compromise whereby Lamar would be renamed to the Senate and Barksdale chosen governor. The Natchez *Democrat*, which was again supporting Lamar, protested against such an arrangement as smacking of "bossism."[12]

The senatorial preferential primaries were bitterly fought

[9]Halsell, "Democratic Dissensions," *loc. cit.*, 127.

[10]Jackson *Weekly Clarion*, Jan. 28, Feb. 4, 11, 1880; Mayes, *Lamar*, 411-12; Halsell, "Democratic Dissensions," *loc. cit.*, 128.

[11]Halsell, "Democratic Dissensions," *loc. cit.*, 128; Mayes, *Lamar*, 412; Jackson *Weekly Clarion*, Feb. 11, 1880.

[12]Grenada *Sentinel* and Vicksburg *Herald*, quoted in Mayes, *Lamar*, 431-33; Jackson *Weekly Clarion*, June 2, 1881, quoting Vicksburg *Herald*, Holly Springs *South*, Yazoo *Sentinel*, and Tupelo *Journal*; Natchez *Daily Democrat*, June 18, July 8, 1881.

through the spring and early summer. The Lamar press charged that Barksdale's course was dictated by resentment over his defeat for the Senate in 1880. They tried to link him with the numerous Independent movements in the state, despite the fact that no one was as straightforward in his denunciation of party irregularity as was Barksdale, and despite the fact that it was Lamar's alliance with Independents which had prevented Barksdale's election by the caucus the year before. [13] By the end of July, county conventions and primaries had indicated their choice of Lamar, and his election was conceded. Attention then centered on the gubernatorial race in which Lamar's enemy, Barksdale, was opposing Lamar's friend, Stone, running for a third term. The convention met on August 3, and a stalemate again developed between the two factions of the party. After the twenty-ninth ballot, Barksdale called a caucus of all anti-third termers. He announced his withdrawal and succeeded in uniting all present in support of Robert Lowry, a dark horse. When the convention reconvened the Lamar forces were thrown into consternation by the sudden announcement of Barksdale's withdrawal, and the placing of Lowry's name in nomination. They were granted an hour's recess by the Barksdale faction, which now that Barksdale was out of the race had control of the convention. The hour's respite served no useful purpose for the Lamar forces, and Lowry was chosen on the next ballot.[14]

Again Barksdale had failed to reach his goal, but again he had stopped Lamar. Lowry's nomination was undoubtedly a blow to Lamar. On the other hand, Barksdale's failure to win the gubernatorial nomination for himself angered and disappointed his followers, and a movement was started to contest in the legislature the election of Lamar, but this did not materialize.[15] As an indication of the control which the black counties had over the convention, it may be noted that from them came all candidates but one. The press of other parts of the state said that their people did not feel "very amiable over this persistent neglect" of their sections.[16]

[13]Natchez *Daily Democrat*, July 8, 1881; Jackson *Weekly Clarion*, all issues during May, June, and July, 1881; Vicksburg *Herald*, quoted in Jackson *Clarion*, June 30, 1881; Macon *Beacon*, March 12, 1881.

[14]Mayes, *Lamar*, 433-34; Jackson *Weekly Clarion*, Aug. 4, 1881; Macon *Beacon*, Aug. 13, 1881; Lexington *Advertiser* and Port Gibson *Reveille*, quoted in Jackson *Clarion*, Aug. 18, 1881; Halsell, "Democratic Dissensions," *loc. cit.*, 134.

[15]Mayes, *Lamar*, 434; Halsell, "Democratic Dissensions," *loc. cit.*, 134.

[16]Jackson *Weekly Clarion*, Aug. 4, 1881; Macon *Beacon*, Aug. 13, 1881.

The reaction to Lowry's nomination was as varied as might have been expected. He had had some dealings with the Republicans during Reconstruction days, and was classed by some as a "ring" politician.[17] Some hoped his nomination would have a harmonizing influence on the factions; others branded him as "a representative of the Bourbons"; most saw in it a Barksdale victory. The Lamar press was bitter over Barksdale's strategy in calling the caucus, charging that it resulted in a "minority" nomination and hinting that a deal was made whereby Lowry promised support for Barksdale against Lamar in the coming senatorial election.[18] Perhaps the Natchez *Democrat and Courier* summed up the popular reaction in its prediction that "Some will support it [the ticket] because Stone is not on it; some because Barksdale's name does not appear in the list, some because neither Stone nor Barksdale were [sic] nominated."[19]

In the early 1880's opposition to corporations was not as strong as it later became, and there were many rural areas that feared a regulatory commission would discourage railroad building. The Aberdeen *Examiner,* a rural paper, opposed regulation as a matter of policy and reported that all east Mississippians—Democrats, Republicans, Greenbacks, and Independents—did also, as they wanted to encourage, not discourage, more railroad building in their section.[20] The *Examiner* thought it would be well for Mississippians, instead of listening to the abuse of railroads by demagogic aspirants for office, to consider how important railroads were to them. Across the state in the Delta the Democratic convention in Washington County declared against railroad regulation "for the present" as "especially hurtful."[21]

Within a few years, however, a different tune was heard. Frank Burkitt, a leader in the state Grange and Farmers' Alliance, and later a Populist leader, became the most outspoken critic of corporate

[17]Jackson *Daily Times,* July 15, 1877; Vicksburg *Democrat-Commercial,* May 15, 1877.

[18]Vicksburg *Democrat-Commercial,* Louisville (Ky.) *Courier-Journal,* New Orleans *States,* New Orleans *Democrat,* Meridian *Mercury,* and Vicksburg *Herald,* quoted in Jackson *Weekly Clarion,* Aug. 11, 1881; Natchez *Democrat and Courier,* Aug. 9, 1881; *ibid.,* quoting Chickasaw *Messenger* and Columbus *Dispatch.*

[19]Natchez *Democrat and Courier,* Aug. 16, 1881.

[20]Aberdeen *Examiner,* May 17, 1883.

[21]*Ibid.,* June 21, 1883, quoting Columbus *South;* Aberdeen *Examiner,* Sept. 20, 1883.

interests. In issue after issue of his Chickasaw *Messenger* he exposed
their venality, as well as that of the "corrupt political rings" which
formed the basis of their control. He charged that this unholy union
of politicians and corporate interests, backed by money "extorted
from the people" and by "the corrupt use of the election machinery,"
resulted in the choice of officials unsympathetic with the farmer's
interests. He saw the political rings in the black counties joining
hands with the monopolists to corral the Negro vote.[22]

In the early years after the war the Memphis, Birmingham, and
Atlantic Railroad had received a charter from the state government.
According to Burkitt, Nathan Bedford Forrest, the organizer of the
company, had gone over the proposed route taking subscriptions
for capital stock from counties, towns, and individuals. Years had
passed without the line having been completed, and when the coal
and iron fields of north Alabama were opened the promoters of
the road sought an amendment to their charter which would permit
it to deviate from its proposed line through Chickasaw, Pontotoc,
and Lowndes counties. Burkitt opposed the bill authorizing the
changed route, and when he saw that its passage was inevitable he
offered an amendment requiring the railroad to repay the subscriptions with interest. But the amendment, too, had been defeated,
Burkitt thought, "through the conivance [*sic*] of members" of the
legislature who were interested in the new route.[23]

At the same time Burkitt was leveling his attack on the Gulf and
Ship Island Railroad, a line proposed through east Mississippi to
the Gulf. Hamilton, Hoskins and Company, lessees of the state's
convicts, were some seventy-five or eighty thousand dollars in
arrears in payments to the state, and their lease was to expire in
1888. They "hatched a scheme" to transfer the convicts to the Gulf
and Ship Island and to extend the lease to 1892. In order to do so
they secured from the attorney-general, Thomas C. Catchings, a
certificate which he later repudiated as "an error," stating that
their arrears to the state had been paid. Burkitt charged that Governor Lowry and Catchings were in this conspiracy. The move, he
said, was "intended more to control and concentrate influences than
to build railroads." Support for the scheme was obtained by "shrewd
lobbyists" telling people the road would run by their property. Their

[22]Chickasaw *Messenger*, Mar. 20, 1884.

[23]Signed statement by Frank Burkitt published in Chickasaw *Messenger*, Jan. 18,
1877.

real purpose, according to Burkitt, was to pass a bill "to relieve them of the payment of money they owed the state on the present lease."[24]

The farmers linked Lowry with their oppressors, the corporations, and in the spring of 1885 a movement was started in the hill counties to prevent his renomination. It was even reported that there was strong opposition to him in the river counties, but this was stoutly denied by one of the leading papers there.[25] An energetic campaign was waged by Putnam Darden, head of the state Grange and the farmer's idol, and by S. S. Calhoon, a wealthy lawyer and planter of Hinds County. But the Lowry machine was too well oiled and he was nominated in the convention on the first ballot. Besides, the apathy of the farmers toward ring-selected candidates was growing. The farmers had come to feel that their aims were popular with a vast majority of the voters, but that the rings, through bribery and other unfair means at primaries, nominating conventions, and even in the halls of the legislature, were preventing their attainment.

To the farmers had come disillusionment and distrust of their old leaders. Lowry, as present head of the administration, became the target of most of their invective. When Lamar resigned from the Senate in 1885 to enter the Cleveland cabinet, they saw little chance of preventing Lowry's succeeding to his seat. Even though his administration had been "weak and wicked," said the Chickasaw *Messenger*, his chances were good. The appointing power which he could bring to bear at the next session of the legislature, the aid which he could expect from the Gulf and Ship Island Railroad, and the numerous vetoes which he could hold over the heads of the state institutions, would be hard to overcome.[26] The *Messenger* charged, and the *Clarion*, a supporter of Lowry, was forced to admit, that the state debt had increased by more than $650,000 during the six years of Lowry's incumbency.[27] It was after this exposure that Lowry invaded Chickasaw in the interest of Independent legislative candidates and in an effort to defeat Burkitt. The Independents,

[24]For an account of the penitentiary controversy see *Report of the Senate Standing Committee on Penitentiary and Prisons*, in Mississippi, *Senate Journal*, 1886, Appendix; also signed statement by Frank Burkitt published in Chickasaw *Messenger*, May 6, 1887; *ibid.*, July 7, 14, 1887.

[25]Natchez *Democrat*, June 26, 1885; *ibid.*, quoting Memphis *Avalanche*.

[26]Chickasaw *Messenger*, Mar. 31, 1887.

[27]*Ibid.*, Aug. 11, 25, 1887, quoting Jackson *Weekly Clarion*.

said Burkitt, would not, if elected, favor an investigation of the administration's connection with the penitentiary scandal and the Gulf and Ship Island. When Lowry canvassed the state in an attempt to refute the charge of corruption, he only convinced many farmers that he himself "is a thief and guilty as charged."[28]

Even the great Lamar did not escape the suspicion with which the farmers were coming to regard their leaders. The Brookhaven *Leader* recalled the incongruity of Lamar's "exceedingly liberal and conciliatory utterances at Washington" closely followed by a series of speeches in Mississippi "which caused the heart of every bull-dozer and ballot-box stuffer in the state to leap for joy." "Can it be," the *Leader* pondered, "that our Lucius Quintus Cincinnatus is only a selfish demagogue after all—deeper and shrewder than the rest of his class?" The editor concluded that he was, and that "so long as he himself holds a fat office and is floating upon the flowing stream of popular adulation," his attitude would be "the people be d——d." The Woodville *Republican* echoed the *Leader's* sentiment.[29]

The regular Democratic press defended its idols and charged their critics with fostering division within the party in order to expedite the return of the "Republican gang with all their vileness and infamy." Burkitt and the *Messenger* were termed "Republicans in disguise" by the Vicksburg *Herald*, but both denied any connection with the Republican party.[30] For better or worse the farmers of Mississippi were on the march. They were fed up with a condition where party affairs were dictated by a small oligarchy whose great power rested on the narrow base of a small group of whites in the heavily populated Negro counties. They were tired of having these oligarchs name their candidates and then call upon them to elect the candidates in the face of a violent and popular opposition. They would change this set of conditions by rewriting the fundamental law.

[28]*Ibid.;* Greenville *Daily Review,* quoted in Chickasaw *Messenger,* Sept. 1, 1887.

[29]Brookhaven *Leader* and Woodville *Republican,* quoted in Chickasaw *Messenger,* Apr. 7, 14, 1887.

[30]Chickasaw *Messenger,* Mar. 10, Sept. 22, 1887.

CHAPTER VI

CALLING THE CONSTITUTIONAL CONVENTION

B Y THE late 1880's it had become apparent to many leaders in Mississippi that the body politic was unable either to assimilate or to eliminate "the unholy African leaven." With the growth of class and factional divisions within the white man's party, there was a growing tendency for both factions to compete for the Negro vote. Negro domination once more seemed possible when all that stood between the Negro majority and control were "election methods and contrivances, . . . not sanctioned by law, and which were in themselves harmful to the cause of public morals."[1] "With each succeeding election after 1875," said a contemporary, "restiveness and revolt against the party bonds became more menacing." Moreover, it was a serious matter to suppress or count out the lawful Negro vote polled by a white candidate with a considerable white following. Riot and bloodshed generally threatened and were sometimes involved in such an undertaking. In the decade of the 1880's "it became apparent that the 'Mississippi' plan of dealing with black majorities would, unless checked, pollute the very sources of representative government."[2] The tremendous internal struggles in the Democratic party, of which those led by Barksdale and Chalmers were only the most publicized, convinced many of a need for permanent disfranchisement of the Negro.

While specific charges of corruption were naturally denied by the participants at the time, it was commonly known that illegal tactics were the general rule at elections. This was freely confessed by Democratic leaders. Judge J. J. Chrisman, a prominent Democrat, said on the floor of the Constitutional Convention of 1890:

. . . it is no secret that there has not been a full vote and a fair count in Mississippi since 1875—that we have been preserving the ascendency of the white people by revolutionary methods. In plain words we have been stuffing the ballot boxes, committing perjury, and here and there in the state carrying the elections by *fraud* and violence until the whole machinery for election was about to rot down.[3]

---

[1]Johnston, "Public Services of Senator George," *loc. cit.,* 211; McNeily, "War and Reconstruction," *loc. cit.,* 531.

[2]McNeily, "War and Reconstruction," *loc. cit.,* 531-33.

[3]Jackson *Daily Clarion-Ledger,* Sept. 11, 1890.

Equally incriminating was a statement in an address by S. S. Cal-hoon, president of the convention: "Besides the exercise of force, there was also brought into use fraud in the manipulation of ballot boxes, . . . and it, unfortunately became chronic. It began to be used even as between the whites themselves, and following this, came a train of political juggling."[4]

These practices were putting "too great a strain on the public conscience,"[5] and one of the causes for the calling of the Constitu-tional Convention was a desire to revise the franchise law so as legally to eliminate the Negro vote. But there were other reasons. One was the gaining of control of both houses of Congress by the Republicans in the election of 1888, and the growing fear that fed-eral control of elections might result. It was noted that the Negroes were "more aroused" after returns had shown the Republican ma-jority in the national legislature. They were demanding more offices in counties where fusion tickets were customary and were even re-fusing to pay taxes until the right to vote was guaranteed. In July, 1889, a Negro convention in Jackson asked the Democrats for a state fusion ticket. When this was refused, a Republican convention nominated a complete ticket for the first time since 1876.[6]

In June, 1890, Henry Cabot Lodge moved in Congress to institute federal supervision of congressional elections. The bill passed the House but was defeated in the Senate. This threat of federal inter-vention argued the necessity of substituting legal for illegal tactics in disfranchising the Negro. It was thought by some that the elec-torate should be restricted before a federal "Force Bill" should pass. Even the *Clarion-Ledger*, which had been opposed to the conven-tion, saw virtue in such a policy and thought it might render the Lodge bill "largely nugatory and deprive it of much of its power for evil."[7]

[4]*Ibid.*, Nov. 1, 1890.

[5]Walter C. Hamm, "Three Phases of Colored Suffrage," in *North American Re-view*, CLXVIII (1899), 290; Wharton, *The Negro in Mississippi*, 207.

[6]Wharton, *The Negro in Mississippi*, 209. In 1881 the Republicans had staged a state-wide campaign in an attempt to elect Ben King, but they did not have a complete ticket.

[7]Jackson *Daily Clarion-Ledger*, Aug. 7, 1890; William A. Mabry, "Disfranchise-ment of the Negro in Mississippi," in *Journal of Southern History*, IV (1938), 322; McNeily, "War and Reconstruction," *loc. cit.*, 534.

There were other motives, however, for the calling of the convention. These were disconnected from the desire of eliminating the Negro vote—or at least sought it for reasons different from those expressed by the *Clarion*. Voters in the white counties believed that a corrupt ring was kept in office by "the power and fraud of the Democratic cliques in the black counties." The cry of white supremacy was to them merely a blind to hide the politicians' debauchery of the ballot box, enabling them to maintain control of the state "through the instrumentality of the stolen negro vote." On the other hand, there was no urgency for suffrage restriction insofar as affairs in the white counties themselves were concerned. In fact there was a repugnance to any scheme for disfranchising the Negro which might also disfranchise some whites. Quite aside from the franchise question there was considerable sentiment in white counties for genuine democratic reforms—amendment of the judiciary system to make judges elective, elimination of convict leasing, more equitable distribution of public school funds, and restriction of the powers of corporations.[8]

The question of calling a constitutional convention first came up in 1877. Many state papers advocated it, but the two most influential, the *Clarion* and the Vicksburg *Herald*, were opposed, as were Democratic leaders generally. Bills were introduced in both houses of the legislature the following year, but they did not pass. Frank Burkitt introduced a bill in 1886 submitting the question to the voters at the next election. It passed the House but was defeated in the Senate "by sharp practice on the part of the machine crowd," so Burkitt charged. A bill passed both houses in 1888, but was vetoed by Governor Lowry.[9] The following year the legislature passed a resolution urging that the question be made an issue in the election that year.

Although Frank Burkitt and the Farmers' Alliance were the early advocates of the convention, they were suddenly joined by Senator George, who took the leadership of the movement from Burkitt. George's conversion was due, he said, to his fear of the Lodge "Force

[8]Chickasaw *Messenger*, Jan. 27, Mar. 24, 1887; Wharton, *The Negro in Mississippi*, 207-208; McNeily, "War and Reconstruction," *loc. cit.*, 535.

[9]Mississippi, *Senate Journal*, 1878, p. 17; *Senate Journal*, 1886, pp. 66, 536; *Senate Journal*, 1888, p. 146; McNeily, "War and Reconstruction," *loc. cit.*, 531-33; Chickasaw *Messenger*, Mar. 24, 1887; Macon *Beacon*, Jan. 8, 1888, Oct. 15, 1892; W. H. Hardy to Robert Lowry, Mar. 18, 1888, Letters of Governors, Series E, 195A.

Bill."[10] Another powerful advocate was the Prohibition organization. This group had succeeded in carrying local option elections in forty of the seventy-five counties of the state. The thirty-five wet counties were mostly in the black belt and it was held that they "are kept wet by the negro vote."[11]

In general the "conservative" press and leaders in the black counties were opposed to the calling of a convention, and Senator Walthall was their spokesman. In a speech at Macon, in October, 1889, he argued that disfranchisement of the Negro was "impossible without disqualifying tens of thousands of white men."[12] In a later speech in Jackson he leveled the heaviest guns of his oratory against it. He called it "an unnecessary, expensive, and dangerous experiment." He pointed out that the greatest objection to the existing constitution was sentimental, being based on the fact that it had been framed by "aliens" during Reconstruction. The Negroes, he said, were now quiet, but their interest in politics would be revived by the excitement of a convention called to make their disfranchisement legal and permanent. Why arouse them? Evil whites, he said, were lying in wait for some serious division among the Democrats, when they would "rally the disorganized negro and attack us . . . weakened by divided counsels." Why give them the opportunity? Disfranchisement, which would necessarily include tens of thousands of the best white Democrats in Mississippi, would create such a division.[13]

Walthall's views were given strong support. Writing in the *Clarion* "Prudentia" opposed the convention. He pointed out the similarity of the present constitution with that of 1832. The appointive judiciary, he said, was the greatest difference, and this was a worthy departure because of the inexperience of the newly enfranchised freedmen. Any attempt to change the suffrage laws to

[10]Speech by J. Z. George in Jackson, Oct. 21, 1889, quoted in Jackson *Daily Clarion-Ledger*, Oct. 24, 1889; *ibid.*, Nov. 28, 1889.

[11]Memorial of J. B. Gambrell, Chairman of the Executive Committee of the Prohibition State Convention, to the Mississippi Constitutional Convention of 1890, in *Journal of the Proceedings of the Constitutional Convention of the State of Mississippi Begun at the City of Jackson on August 12, 1890 and Concluded November 1, 1890* (Jackson, 1890), 94; Wharton, *The Negro in Mississippi*, 207.

[12]Natchez *Daily Democrat*, Oct. 25, 1889.

[13]Speech of E. C. Walthall delivered in Mississippi House of Representatives, Oct. 28, 1889, quoted in Jackson *Daily Clarion-Ledger*, Oct. 31, 1889; Natchez *Daily Democrat*, Oct. 29, 1889; Wharton, *The Negro in Mississippi*, 209.

exclude the Negro would, he thought, bring federal intervention.[14] Others thought after the failure of the Force Bill to pass that it had only been intended to frighten the Democrats into support of the tariff bill.[15]

The most influential papers of the state were opposed to the convention and gave strong support to Walthall. Pitted against them were the comparatively feeble voices of the Okolona *Times* and the Chickasaw *Messenger*.[16]

The Natchez *Democrat* criticized George for raising "this deep and most delicate question" without advancing a solution. It cited the unprecedented peace and prosperity in Mississippi and thought the move to foist a convention on the people was without reason and "springs from individual motives." It condemned the various plans suggested for disfranchising the Negro as proposals "to remove the temptation by legalizing the fraud." It denounced George's expressed fears of Negro supremacy as "hypothetical and imaginary dangers" and said need of a convention had not been established, nor had the will of the people expressed itself in favor of it. On the contrary, it thought, "every indication points to an overwhelming opposition to it." White domination was "as complete as the superior race chooses to make it."[17]

The *Clarion-Ledger*, though not as vocal as the *Democrat*, was also opposed to the convention. It denied that an additional guarantee of white supremacy was needed by the state or could be provided by the convention.[18] The Columbus *Index*, even more than the *Democrat*, questioned "the sincerity of Senator George when he favors a constitutional convention."[19] "Conservative," writing in the Raymond *Gazette*, said the charges against Negro suffrage made by the advocates of the convention were unfounded, and that actually the Negro co-operated with the "better class of whites" in supporting the public interests.[20]

[14]Jackson *Daily Clarion-Ledger*, Oct. 24, 1889.

[15]New Orleans *Daily States*, Aug. 13, 1890.

[16]Excerpts quoted in Jackson *Daily Clarion-Ledger*, Nov. 14, 1889.

[17]Natchez *Daily Democrat*, Oct. 22, 25, 29, 1889, Jan. 4, 21, 30, Aug. 24, Oct. 21, 1890.

[18]Jackson *Daily Clarion-Ledger*, Jan. 26, 1888, Oct. 31, 1889.

[19]Columbus *Index*, quoted in Natchez *Daily Democrat*, Oct. 29, 1889.

[20]Raymond *Gazette*, Apr. 26, 1890, quoted in Wharton, *The Negro in Mississippi*, 211.

It is difficult to say which of the several motives gave greatest impetus to the convention movement. Governor Lowry, in vetoing the convention bill in 1888, said: "Quiet reigns throughout our borders. . . . The colored people are content and happy. . . . Why disturb society. . . ? Why agitate and convulse the country?"[21] The legislature in debating the veto message failed to mention the need of disfranchising the Negroes, but discussed the desirability of limiting the governor to one term, of making the judiciary elective, and of arranging a more equitable scheme of representation in the legislature.[22] Undoubtedly there was greater support for the convention in the white counties than in the black; more support from the rural than from the urban areas; and the farmers favored it more than did the mercantile, banking, and corporate classes. It is not so clear, however, that all those who favored the convention were as pleased with the result as were some of those who had opposed it.

It has been suggested that the convention movement was sponsored by the "intrenched ruling class" and the commercial and industrial interests in an effort to prevent the growing radicalism of the strong agrarian movement. If this is true, it was indeed subtly done. The political powers of the state, with the exception of George and Stone, were strong in their vocal opposition, and their voices had a sincere ring. On the other hand such agrarian leaders as Burkitt and Putnam Darden were consistent in their advocacy of a convention, and most of the farmers' journals supported them. At the same time the control of the state was so completely in the hands of the "intrenched ruling class" that it is difficult to see how the farmers could have forced through a convention bill against their united opposition. The conclusion is inescapable that there was a division on the question within the ranks of those in power. Though on the whole they opposed the convention, the tremendous influence of several of their number who favored it—particularly that of George—was sufficient to swing the balance to the agrarians.

Several candidates were early in the field for the gubernatorial nomination in 1889, but by the time of the Democratic convention former Governor Stone was in a commanding position. Barksdale

[21]Mississippi, *Senate Journal*, 1888, p. 148.

[22]Excerpts from the debate in the Jackson *Daily Clarion-Ledger*, Jan. 26, 1888; Vicksburg *Herald*, Feb. 2, 1888.

had withdrawn,[23] as also had General W. S. Featherstone,[24] and Stone was nominated on the first ballot. It was known that he would approve a convention bill if it were passed, but the Democratic platform did not commit the party to such a bill. Instead it recommended that the calling of a convention be made an issue in the election of legislators that fall.[25]

During the fall campaign, however, the convention question seems to have had little consideration. The Republicans again had a full ticket in the field, but like the Democrats they were not committed either way.[26]

When the legislature met the following January, however, both the Farmers' Alliance and the state Grange memorialized it in favor of the convention.[27] The legislature responded and passed a bill calling for a convention to meet in Jackson on August 12.[28]

[23]When Barksdale announced his withdrawal in late June, Lamar, now Secretary of the Interior, issued a statement calling his withdrawal "a public calamity." Possibly this indicates a closing of the breach between Lamar and Barksdale. More likely it was a gesture to secure Barksdale's support for Lamar's candidate, Stone. Natchez *Democrat*, June 27, 1889. The *Democrat* suspected the withdrawal was a "political trick" putting Barksdale in the position of a "dark horse" in case of a deadlock.

[24]Featherstone withdrew in protest against the action of several county conventions which resolved that "no one but . . . a member of the Farmers' Alliance would be a suitable . . . governor." *Ibid.*, July 12, 1889.

[25]Jackson *Daily Clarion-Ledger*, July 18, 26, 1889.

[26]Natchez *Daily Democrat*, July 2, 12, 17, 18, 26, 1889, Jan. 21, 1890.

[27]Mississippi, *House Journal*, 1890, p. 148; Natchez *Daily Democrat*, Jan. 21, 1890; Jackson *Daily Clarion-Ledger*, Jan. 30, 1890; Macon *Beacon*, Oct. 15, 1892.

[28]Mississippi, *House Journal*, 1890, p. 300.

CHAPTER VII

FRANCHISE AND APPORTIONMENT

AFTER the passage of the convention bill, opposition to the movement seemed to fade out. However, there were fewer votes cast in the election of delegates to the convention than in any election since the war. Under the constitution of 1868 practically all adult males, Negro and white, were qualified electors. Of the 262,000[1] qualified electors, only 40,000 votes were cast for the delegates from the state at large. In Hinds, the largest county in the state with 8,500 electors, only 540 votes were cast, and in Sharkey County which had 1,600 qualified electors, only four votes were cast.[2] Of the 134 delegates chosen, 130 were Democrats, one a Republican, one a "National Republican," one a "Conservative," and one a Greenbacker. Fifty-two of the delegates were lawyers, 7 classed themselves as "planters," while 42 gave their occupation as farmers. The one Republican, Isaiah T. Montgomery, a Negro from Bolivar, was seated after a contest with a Democrat. He was reported to have promised support to Senator George's faction before he was voted admittance.[3]

In the organization of the convention, S. S. Calhoon was chosen president over R. C. Patty by a majority of one vote. Though both were from black counties, Patty was leader of the Alliance in Noxubee, while Calhoon was a well-to-do lawyer and planter of Hinds.[4] Calhoon proceeded to appoint committees, the most important of which was that on Elective Franchise, Apportionment, and Elections. To this committee he named a majority of lawyers, as it was charged he did to all committees.[5]

[1]See United States *Census of 1890*, I, 786.

[2]Jackson *Daily Clarion-Ledger*, Aug. 8, 14, 1890.

[3]*Journal of the Constitutional Convention, 1890*, pp. 704-708, 390; Jackson *Daily Clarion-Ledger*, Aug. 14, 1890.

[4]It is claimed by Wharton that Isaiah Montgomery's vote enabled the George faction to elect Calhoon and thus gain control of the organization of the convention (*The Negro in Mississippi*, 211). On the other hand, Monroe McClurg, twenty-five years after the event, stated that George told him that he (George) voted for Patty for president, rather than for his friend Calhoon, in order "to secure Patty's support for the understanding clause." Vicksburg *Daily Herald*, Aug. 8, 1915.

[5]*Journal of the Constitutional Convention, 1890*, p. 21; Jackson *Daily Clarion-Ledger*, July 21, 1891.

Regardless of the various incentives for calling the convention, once that body assembled it was evident that a majority of its members was primarily concerned with devising some scheme to insure white supremacy. Had it not been for the hope of accomplishing this, the *Clarion* thought, the convention would not have assembled.[6] "All understood and desired," said one delegate, "that some scheme would be evolved which would effectually remove from the sphere of politics in the State the ignorant and unpatriotic negro."[7]

The schemes proposed for effecting Negro disfranchisement may be divided into two general categories. One urged educational qualifications for voters, while the other proposed a poll tax, payable some months in advance of an election, as a prerequisite of voting. Property qualifications were also urged, but advocates of this plan were not so numerous.

Throughout the convention there was a bitter struggle between black and white counties, the former wanting educational or property qualifications, the latter opposing them. The delegates from the white counties in general attacked the proposals because they feared they would disfranchise too many whites. T. S. Ford, a white county resident, perhaps best expressed the white county view. He argued against such qualifications as a threat to white unity. He feared that white men thus disfranchised might, if they later qualified, "retaliate." He argued against the substitution of a white problem. Judge J. J. Chrisman petulantly expressed the black county view when he said, "To avoid the disfranchisement of a lot of white ignoramuses we can't have an educational qualification, and to pander to the prejudices of those who have no property we cannot have a property qualification."[8]

To eliminate the Negro vote without violating the Fourteenth and Fifteenth amendments to the federal Constitution required some

[6]Jackson *Daily Clarion-Ledger*, Oct. 24, 1889, Dec. 22, 1890; speech of Mayre Dabney, in *Proceedings of the Reunion of the Survivors of the Constitutional Convention of 1890 on the Twentieth Anniversary of the Adoption of the Constitution, held in the Senate Chamber of the Capitol at Jackson, Mississippi, November 1st, 1910* (Jackson, n. d.), 12; New Orleans *Daily States*, Aug. 13, 1890; *Journal of the Constitutional Convention, 1890*, especially President S. S. Calhoon's address, 10; *ibid.*, 64; S. S. Calhoon, "Causes and Events that Led to the Constitutional Convention of 1890," in Mississippi Historical Society, *Publications*, VI (1902), 110.

[7]Dabney, in *Reunion of Survivors*, 12.

[8]Jackson *Daily Clarion-Ledger*, Sept. 17, 18, 1890.

skill. Furthermore, a provision of the act of Congress which readmitted Mississippi into the Union in 1870 had prohibited the state from later limiting the suffrage in any way beyond the provisions fixed in the state constitution of 1868. Under the liberal franchise provisions of that constitution, practically every male adult who had resided in the state six months and in the county one month prior to an election was entitled to vote.[9] It was estimated that under this provision there were seventy thousand more qualified Negro voters than white.[10] This problem was referred to the Judiciary Committee, of which Wiley P. Harris, George's law partner and an outstanding member of the Mississippi bar, was chairman. The committee report held that Congress had exceeded its power in attempting to regulate the franchise of the state. Mississippi, as a sovereign state, was empowered to fix such restrictions as she saw fit, provided "the regulations which it prescribes shall apply alike to both races." A poll tax, property or educational qualification, longer residence, or a combination of all these would be legal, reported the committee, if they were impartially applied to both races.

In spite of this report A. J. Paxton proposed that "No negro, or person having as much as one-eighth negro blood, shall hold office in the state." Mayre Dabney offered a resolution requesting Congress to submit to the states an amendment repealing the Fifteenth Amendment. D. S. Johnson proposed that "No person who has not an occupation or profession shall be entitled to vote in any election." W. C. Wilkinson submitted a declaration of principles relative to the franchise, "Preferring a less representation in Congress or the Electoral College" in lieu of federal consent to disfranchisement of the Negro.[11] A more subtle project was that of Judge H. F. Simrall who urged the requirement of one year's residence in the precinct as a prerequisite for voting. He frankly explained that the reason for his proposal was "the disposition of young negroes . . . to change their homes and precincts every year."[12] Judge J. A. P. Campbell,

[9]Mississippi Constitution, 1868, Art. VII, Sec. 2; Mississippi, *Laws*, 1874, Secs. 117, 118.

[10]Statement of W. S. Eskridge before the convention, reported in Jackson *Daily Clarion-Ledger*, Sept. 18, 1890. This figure seems somewhat excessive. According to the United States census the Negro voting majority should have been in the neighborhood of 42,000. See United States *Census of 1890*, I, 786.

[11]*Journal of the Constitutional Convention, 1890*, pp. 65, 83-87, 113, 109-10, 191.

[12]Jackson *Daily Clarion-Ledger*, Sept. 18, 1890.

whose fertile brain brought forth a new plan almost weekly, suggested the granting of a multiple vote to property owners on a basis of one vote for each forty acres of land owned.[13] J. W. Fewell proposed a qualified scheme of woman suffrage. He would give the vote to every woman who owned, or whose husband owned, real estate in the value of $300.[14]

A few voices were raised in behalf of the Negro. Ethelbert Barksdale, although not a delegate, warned against discriminating against him,[15] and Irvin Miller and W. J. Lacey, white county delegates, said Negroes gave no trouble in their districts. J. E. Gore, another white county delegate, "would not vote for any plan that would take from any citizen rights that he now enjoyed." He did not share the fears that "the black man would ever dominate the country."[16] But there can be no doubt that many of the delegates were of the mind of a prominent editor who wrote that Mississippians did not object to the Negro's voting "on account of ignorance but on account of color." He published and approved a statement of the Charleston (S. C.) *News and Courier*: "If every colored man in Mississippi were a graduate of Yale College the two races would remain just as widely separated as they are now in all political and social matters."[17]

The leaders of the black counties were eventually able to persuade the convention that educational and property qualifications, with the addition of a poll tax, would be the best means of eliminating the Negro vote. The white county delegates acquiesced, having been unable to unite on any program save that of reducing the representation of the black counties in the legislature. Besides, they were not as ably led as their opposition, and eventually they submitted to the latter's superior influence.[18]

After more than two months' deliberation, the Committee on Elective Franchise, Apportionment, and Elections reported, and the convention adopted several provisions which were to have a marked effect on the future political structure of the state. Section 241 pro-

13*Ibid.*, Apr. 3, 1890.
14*Ibid.*, Aug. 28, 1890.
15*Ibid.*, March 20, 1890.
16*Ibid.*, Sept. 18, 1890.
17Quoted, *ibid.*, Oct. 18, 1890.
18Wharton, *The Negro in Mississippi*, 214.

vided for a residence requirement of two years in the state and one year in the election district. It further provided that a voter must be "duly registered"; that he be untainted by certain crimes; and that he must "produce to the officers holding the election satisfactory evidence that he has paid" by February 1 of the year in which he sought to vote "all the taxes which may have been legally required of him, . . . for the two preceding years."

Section 243 provided that "A uniform poll tax of two dollars, to be used in aid of common schools, and for no other purpose," must be paid by all male inhabitants between the ages of twenty-one and sixty. Men over sixty, as well as certain unfortunates—the deaf, dumb, or those who had lost a hand or a foot—were exempt from the poll tax. The board of supervisors of any county was empowered, at its discretion, to increase the poll tax in its county, but in no case was the tax to exceed three dollars for any one year. No criminal proceedings were to be allowed to enforce the collection of the poll tax. Sections 249 and 251 provided for registration of all voters at least four months prior to the election at which they offered to vote.

The "infamous section five"[19] of the committee report became Section 244 of the state constitution. It provided that after January 1, 1896,[20] every voter must be able to read any section of the state constitution, or "be able to understand the same when read to him, or give a reasonable interpretation thereof." There was a "general understanding" that any white illiterate would be passed by the registrars while no Negro would be.[21]

In brief the conditions of the franchise were: "mental capacity, age of majority; residence of two years in the state and one year in the election district . . .; freedom from a criminal record (crimes specified); non-delinquency in payment of [a poll] tax for two years; and ability to read or comprehend the Constitution."[22]

There is some uncertainty as to the authorship of the several franchise clauses. The *Clarion* credited the poll tax to President

[19]Natchez *Daily Democrat*, Oct. 4, 1890.

[20]This was amended on the floor of the convention to read 1892.

[21]Mississippi Constitution, 1890, Secs. 241, 243, 244, 249, 251; Wharton, *The Negro in Mississippi*, 215.

[22]Dunbar Rowland, *History of Mississippi, the Heart of the South*, 2 vols. (Chicago and Jackson, 1925), II, 255.

Calhoon and the "understanding clause" to Senator George, as also
did J. S. McNeily, a delegate to the convention.[23] Another delegate,
however, attributed the authorship of the "understanding clause"
to Wiley P. Harris, and said that George merely used it to secure
the support of the white county delegates to the rest of the franchise
provision. James K. Vardaman believed that George was really out
of sympathy with the understanding clause and only consented to
it to forestall possible attacks on the constitution in the United States
Senate.[24] Still another eyewitness of the convention and a close
associate of Harris states that Harris actually opposed the clause and
only consented to it to mollify George.[25]

George was the "dominating figure of the Convention and . . .
the Constitution . . . was largely his work."[26] Without his presence,
some of the delegates later admitted, the convention would have
been a failure.[27] Though a resident of a black county, he was chosen
from the state at large and took a position between the extreme
views of the two factions. He was opposed to all property qualifications and hoped to eliminate Negro voting without touching the
illiterate whites. Whether or not George was the author of the franchise clauses, he defended them from beginning to end, and prevented by a point of order reconsideration of them after their
adoption.[28]

According to the proponents of the "understanding" provision
it was not intended to be a disfranchising clause, but was designed
to furnish a loophole to qualify illiterate whites who would otherwise
be disfranchised by the literacy requirement. It was, of course,

[23]McNeily, however, was writing many years after the convention. Vicksburg
Daily Herald, Aug. 10, 1915.

[24]Vardaman, too, expressed this opinion some seventeen years after the convention. Jackson *Issue*, Feb. 22, 1908.

[25]Statement of Alfred Holt Stone, Jackson, Mississippi, to author, Sept. 2, 1945.
For other opinions on the authorship of the clauses see: Jackson *Daily Clarion-Ledger*,
Sept. 18, Oct. 25, 1890, Sept. 16, 1897, Aug. 12, 1915; Macon *Beacon*, Mar. 10,
1894; Johnston, "Suffrage and Reconstruction," *loc. cit.*, 229; James W. Garner,
"Senatorial Career of J. Z. George," in Mississippi Historical Society, *Publications*,
VII (1903), 256.

[26]Garner, "Senatorial Career of J. Z. George," *loc. cit.*, 256.

[27]Statements by J. S. McNeily and Monroe McClurg, Vicksburg *Daily Herald*,
July 18, Aug. 8, 1915.

[28]Garner, "Senatorial Career of J. Z. George," *loc. cit.*, 256; Jackson *Daily Clarion-
Ledger*, Oct. 25, 1890.

urged by the white county delegates, and bitterly opposed by those from the black counties. Most black county papers denounced it as a "fraud."[29] The Natchez *Democrat* called it "an absurdity . . . a subterfuge . . . and a temptation to corruption." It pointed out the danger of having votes rejected for political reasons. If the provision should be honestly enforced, it said, it would disfranchise "a large majority of the voting population of the state, including a considerable number of white citizens." But that was not the intention nor the desire, it said, of those who favored it. It foresaw that the clause would make it easy to "suppress any necessary quantity of votes, and to let only such ballots go into the box as will serve the interests of a certain party."[30]

The *Democrat's* point was well taken. The "understanding clause" did provide a sure and regularized means of disfranchising Negroes as well as illiterate whites, if the group in power chose to disfranchise them. Obviously the test could be as easily interpreted to admit illiterates, Negro or white, as to reject them. It merely depended on whether the "machine" wished to admit or reject their votes. The clause would prevent the participation of a large Negro vote sponsored by an opposition group, but it could also prevent the votes of a considerable number of opposition whites. Certainly despite the constitutional restrictions, illiterate voters could be easily brought into the primaries by the faction in control. It would be almost impossible for an opposition to bring them in.

The franchise provisions did not specifically exclude the Negro from the polls. "Every provision in the Mississippi Constitution," said Frank Johnston, "applies equally and without any discrimination whatever, to both the white and negro races."[31] In theory this was true, but in practice it was not. The several suffrage requirements combined, while not discriminating against the Negro explicitly, did legislate against his "peculiar racial characteristics" and his limitations. In the words of the United States Supreme Court, the builders of the Mississippi franchise provisions "swept the hori-

[29]Port Gibson *Reveille*, Vicksburg *Post*, Lexington *Advertiser*, Aberdeen *Weekly*, Columbus *Index*, Natchez *Banner*, Natchez *Democrat*, Brandon *Republican*, Grenada *Sentinel*, Yazoo City *Herald*, Aberdeen *Examiner*, Scooba *Herald*, quoted in Jackson *Daily Clarion-Ledger*, Oct. 9, 1890.

[30]Natchez *Daily Democrat*, Sept. 23, Oct. 4, 1890.

[31]Johnston, "Suffrage and Reconstruction," *loc. cit.*, 228.

zon of expediency to find a way around the Negro amendments to the Federal Constitution."[32] Nevertheless the Supreme Court held that neither the poll tax nor the literacy clause violated the federal Constitution.

For a time it was feared that the new requirements were having exactly the opposite effect on the Negroes from that desired. It was reported in December, 1890, that 230 Negro names had been added to the voting lists in the first district of Hinds County.[33] But when the new rolls were published in 1892, of the 76,742 voters only 8,615 were Negroes.[34]

From 1890 the legal Negro voter, and consequently the Republican party, has been a negligible factor in state-wide elections. The Republican party, which had polled more than 52,000 votes for Hayes in 1876 and more than 43,000 for Blaine as late as 1884, cast less than 1,500 votes for Harrison in 1892. In no election thereafter until 1920 did the party poll as many as 6,000 votes. Since 1920, because of the Woman's Suffrage Amendment, there has been a proportionate increase of the Republican vote, but it is still too slight to have any influence.[35]

But for a dozen years after 1890 the Negro continued to be of considerable influence in black county elections. Some of the river counties maintained their fusion tickets and continued to send Negroes to the state legislature until the turn of the century.[36] A few Negroes participated in the Democratic primaries and in some instances may have been a deciding factor in such primaries. But in these cases they were not voting for a Negro ticket. They were simply being exploited by factional groups of white men.

If the Negro ceased to be a direct influence on politics after 1890, indirectly his influence has been incalculable. His mere presence has had an intangible but tremendous influence on the behavior of

[32]*Williams* v. *Mississippi,* 170 U. S. 213; J. S. McNeily, "History of the Measures Submitted to the Committee on Elective Franchise, Apportionment, and Elections in the Constitutional Convention of 1890," in Mississippi Historical Society, *Publications,* VI (1902), 137; Mabry, "Disfranchisement of the Negro in Mississippi," *loc. cit.,* 333; *Vardaman's Weekly,* Oct. 21, 1920.

[33]Jackson *Daily Clarion-Ledger,* Dec. 18, 1890.

[34]*Appleton's Cyclopedia,* 1892, p. 472; Wharton, *The Negro in Mississippi,* 215.

[35]*Mississippi Official and Statistical Register 1924-1928* (New York, n.d.), 312-13.

[36]Wharton, *The Negro in Mississippi,* 215.

Mississippi's white electorate. More tangible has been his influence on the composition of that electorate. It may be that the framers of the 1890 constitution were aiming only at the Negro, but their multiple-loaded franchise laws struck from the voting lists tens of thousands of white men. The *Farmer's Democrat* estimated in 1892 that the new registration would find "no less than fifty-thousand white voters" disfranchised.[37] The estimate was not far wrong. There had been approximately 120,000 qualified white voters in Mississippi in 1890.[38] After the 1892 registration this figure slipped to slightly more than 68,000.[39] True, all of the 120,000 qualified voters had not exercised their privilege of voting before 1890, yet there were more than 85,000 votes cast for Cleveland in the state in 1888. Two years after the poll tax requirement went into effect, and the very year the educational requirement became effective, Cleveland polled only 40,237 votes in Mississippi.[40]

Instead of improving, this condition seemed to grow worse with the years. The press of the state repeatedly complained of the dwindling electorate, and the editors agreed that the cause was the poll tax. The *Clarion* in 1901 estimated the eligible white voters of Mississippi at 140,000 but thought that not more than 30,000 would pay their poll taxes for that year. It estimated the delinquent list in Hinds County alone at 5,000. The following year the sheriff's office in Hinds reported indications that a larger number of Hinds citizens than ever before had failed to pay the poll tax. The *Clarion* pleaded with delinquents to "walk around to the city hall and settle up," or the vote that year would be "the smallest ever recorded."[41]

In 1896 the attorney-general ruled that the collection of the tax could be enforced by legal levy. Such an interpretation was discouraged, however, when Senator George addressed a letter to the public explaining that the purpose of the tax was to limit the franchise and that this object would be defeated by such action.[42]

[37]*Farmer's Democrat*, quoted in Macon *Beacon*, Oct. 15, 1892.

[38]United States *Census of 1890*, I, 786.

[39]*Appleton's Cyclopedia*, 1892, p. 472.

[40]*Ibid*. James B. Weaver, Populist candidate for President in 1892, received 10,256 Mississippi votes. *Ibid*. Probably many of these were cast by Negroes. Whether this be true or not the conclusion is not essentially changed. *Mississippi Official and Statistical Register 1912*, pp. 113-14.

[41]Jackson *Daily Clarion-Ledger*, Jan. 26, Feb. 14, 1901, Jan. 30, 1902.

[42]*Ibid*., June 18, 1896.

The reduced electorate seems to have been caused more by the poll tax than by the educational qualification. In an attempt to find out which of the two methods was working more effectively to disfranchise the Negro, Mayre Dabney in 1896 visited each county in the third congressional district, examining records in the circuit clerks' offices, the poll books, and tax lists. It was a rare occurrence, he was told, for any person, white or Negro, to be denied registration when he applied. One clerk said he had refused to register only one man on account of the literacy requirement. Others said they had refused "very few for any cause"; and still others said they had never refused one "because he could not read or write or could not understand a clause of the Constitution when read to him." However, Dabney found that a very small per cent of the Negroes had paid their taxes. The Washington County records showed 1,280 white and 338 Negro registered voters, but 8,834 delinquent in poll tax payments.[43] It was estimated that the ratio of whites to Negroes on the delinquent rolls was about one to eighteen. It must be borne in mind, however, that in these counties examined the ratio of white to Negro population was almost as unequal. Dabney concluded that the educational requirement was "of but little effect or value, and constituted but a small factor, if any at all, in precluding the Negro from voting."[44] These conclusions seem to be borne out by statistics. The avowed intent of the "understanding clause" was to permit illiterate whites to qualify despite their illiteracy. But in the first registation after the literacy clause went into effect only 1,307 whites and 1,085 Negroes were registered under it.[45] In the following year only 2,672 illiterates, both white and Negro, had registered under the understanding clause. It was thought that more Negroes than whites had taken advantage of it in most counties. This was attributed to the white man's reluctance to "advertise his incapacity."[46]

Although the poll tax disfranchised nearly all Negroes, the "political apathy" which it seemed to create among the whites gave

[43]Dabney, in *Reunion of Survivors*, 13-14.

[44]*Ibid.*, 14.

[45]*Appleton's Cyclopedia*, 1892, p. 472; Dunbar Rowland, *Encyclopedia of Mississippi History*, 2 vols. (Madison, Wis., 1907), I, 541.

[46]R. H. Thompson, "Suffrage in Mississippi," in Mississippi Historical Society, *Publications*, I (1898), 43.

concern to some thinkers. It was feared that it would tend to form a "small voting class and . . . government by an oligarchy."[47]

That the poll tax requirement would have a discouraging effect on many white as well as Negro voters is not difficult to see. The cash income of many farm families in Mississippi is very low, in some years not more than a few hundred dollars. In 1899, for instance, the average income of all Mississippi farms was $411.[48] Many farmers were tenants and got only a share of the income. From this share the storekeeper who had given credit for the year's supplies had to be paid before the tenant received any cash at all. Poll receipts for the two years previous are required before registration. Thus if a voter falls behind one year the cost becomes excessive. Besides, the tax must be paid on or before February 1 of the year in which the election is to be held. This, according to one critic of the system, was "like buying a ticket to a show nine months ahead of time, and before you know who is playing or really what the thing is all about. It is easy to forget to do."[49]

There is conclusive evidence that politicians have paid poll taxes for voters, and it may be assumed in such cases that there was an understanding as to how the ballot should be marked. No evidence is available, however, as to the extent of this practice.

It is evident, however, that voting in Mississippi has been greatly reduced since 1890 and that the agency which has been most effectual in accomplishing this has been the poll tax. The complicated franchise requirements of the new constitution discouraged many voters from attempting to register. Failure to register barred them from both primary and general elections. But this ineligibility could be waived by party officials whose interests might be served thereby. The restricted franchise thus could be a weapon to defeat revolts against the party's discipline.

The franchise clauses did not, however, seem to cause a decline in balloting on all occasions. On the contrary, an examination of the returns from some of the black counties in the Democratic primary of 1903 reveals startling excess of votes cast over eligible voters. The Democratic primary was by law that year restricted to white men.

[47]Hamm, "Three Phases," loc. cit., 294.
[48]United States Census of 1900, V, cxxiii.
[49]George S. Stoney, "Suffrage in the South, Part I, The Poll Tax," in Survey Graphic, XXIX (1940), 4, 8-9.

Yet Washington County, which three years before had only 1,728 white men, cast 1,917 Democratic votes. This excess of voters over eligibles in Washington might be accounted for by an influx of voters there between 1900 when the census was taken and 1903 when the primary was held. Yet the census figures for 1910 showed only 2,032 white men in the county—115 more than the vote cast seven years before.[50] If there is doubt that election officials in Washington permitted illegal votes to be counted in the Democratic primary of 1903, there can be none that Yazoo officials did so. In the primary that year Yazoo reported 3,698 Democratic votes. Yet Yazoo had only 2,489 white men in 1900, and only 2,794 in 1910.[51]

But these are rare instances of high voting percentages and must be attributed to dishonest election officials. Undoubtedly, and to a shocking degree, the ratio of voters to population has declined in Mississippi since 1890. The reduced electorate has had the result of enhancing the Mississippi voter's influence in Congress and in the Electoral College. Mississippi's 76,742 registered voters in 1892 chose nine representatives to Congress and to the Electoral College, while Massachusetts' 335,747 voters chose only fifteen. In a sense, therefore, a Mississippi voter had almost three times as much influence in national affairs as had the Massachusetts voter. Furthermore there has seemed to be a tendency on the part of Mississippi and other poll tax states to keep their congressmen in office for longer periods than do non-poll tax states. Under the seniority rules of Congress this gives a preponderant number of important committee chairmanships to the congressmen and senators from the poll tax states, thus increasing the national influence of such states.

A further effect of the poll tax was its influence on the age distribution of the Mississippi voters. The law exempted from the tax, in addition to the blind, the deaf, and the halt, all men over sixty years of age. While no records were kept of the ages of those who cast ballots, it would be strange indeed if the proportion of those above that age was not much larger than that of other age groups.

There were other effects of the poll tax on the white voter, but

[50]For population statistics see United States *Census of 1900*, II, 190-91, *Census of 1910*, II, 1044-59. For voting statistics see *Mississippi Official and Statistical Register*, 1908, p. 248.

[51]*Mississippi Official and Statistical Register*, 1908, p. 248; United States *Census of 1900*, II, 190-91, *Census of 1910*, II, 1044-59.

they will be dealt with in subsequent chapters. That it greatly reduced the electorate, both white and Negro, is clearly established. That it "redeemed" the state from Negro rule and made it impossible for the Negro ever again to assert his influence, as is frequently claimed, is debatable. Writing in 1897, Judge J. A. P. Campbell, one of the delegates of the convention, said it was a fallacy "to ascribe the political quiet we have enjoyed since 1890 . . . to anything done by the . . . convention." The same conditions would have existed, he said, if the convention had not met. That the Negro had already "dropped out of politics" was shown, he said, "by the fact that there was only one negro in the . . . convention." To impute to the convention such a motive in imposing the franchise restrictions was, he thought, "to charge it with folly, no less than fraud." Taxes would be no barrier to Negro voting. When the Negro felt sufficient interest in politics he would "as surely pay his taxes" as he would "raise money for a circus." If he did not, "campaign funds would pay for him, if interest was felt in his vote."[52]

It had been the expressed hope of the proponents of the restrictive franchise clauses that better government would result. A review of events in the years following the convention will raise serious doubts of the fulfillment of this hope. Writing of the deplorable conditions in Mississippi's government in 1898, the *Nation*, which had earlier hailed the franchise clauses as "a forward step,"[53] was forced to ponder. Taxes, it said, were "higher than since the black vampires of radicalism." The administration, it charged, was responsible for the lack of public improvements; the issuance of $400,000 of interest-bearing bonds "in times of profound peace"; the appropriation of $200,000 to feed a depleted treasury and to pay current expenses; the imminent closing of state institutions for lack of funds, or the calling of an extra session of the legislature to keep them open; and the spending of thousands of dollars to investigate official drunkenness in high places. "This is certainly a pretty bad showing," it concluded, "for that 'Caucasian rule' from which so much was promised."[54]

Mississippi thus became the first of the southern states to solve

[52]Speech of Judge J. A. Campbell at Jackson, Feb. 8, 1897, quoted in Jackson *Daily Clarion-Ledger*, Feb. 11, 1897.

[53]"The Ballot in Mississippi," editorial in *The Nation*, LV (1892), 139.

[54]*Ibid.*, LXVI (1898), 398.

the problem of legally disfranchising the Negro. The success of the "Mississippi Plan" was eagerly watched in neighboring states where potential Negro voters were proving embarrassing to white political leaders, and within a dozen years most states in the deep South had drawn restrictions of a similar nature around their Negro citizens.

Another problem with which the Constitutional Convention of 1890 had to deal was that of apportionment of the state legislature. The constitution of 1868 had apportioned legislators among the several counties "according to the number of qualified electors," both white and Negro.[55] The provision was not unfair under the conditions which then prevailed. Black counties were much more heavily populated than white, and since the Negro at that time was a voter he was clearly entitled to this representation. But when the Negro vote was curbed after the revolution of 1875 a different condition existed. There were comparatively few white men in the black counties, yet these few whites continued to elect the same majority of legislators which their counties had enjoyed when the Negro was an independent voter. As time went on and the Negro's voting privileges were further curtailed, the white counties felt that the affairs of the state were being dominated by a small oligarchy in the black counties. The feeling was not unwarranted. According to the census of 1890 there were approximately 44,500 eligible white voters in the black counties and more than 71,000 in the white counties.[56] Yet the black counties sent 68 representatives to the lower house of the legislature, while the white counties sent only 52.[57]

The inequality was not confined to differences between white and black counties. Of two white counties, the one with fewer white voters might have a larger representation because of a larger nonvoting Negro minority. Similarly a black county might have larger representation than another black county because of a larger nonvoting Negro majority. This was true in the case of De Soto and Lowndes counties. De Soto had 1,640 eligible white voters and Lowndes 1,437. But Lowndes had 1,000 more eligible Negro

[55]Mississippi Constitution, 1868, Art. IV, Sec. 34. As has already been pointed out, the apportionment provision of the constitution of 1868 enabled the black counties to control both the legislature and Democratic state conventions.

[56]United States *Census of 1890*, I, 770-71.

[57]Mississippi, *House Journal*, 1890, pp. 3-5.

voters than De Soto and was given three representatives to De Soto's two.[58]

The injustice did not stop with representation in the legislature. The same system was extended into the state Democratic nominating conventions, where each county was given twice the number of votes it had in the lower house of the legislature. Thus the black counties were able to control the state nominating conventions and to name the candidates in August who would win practically by default in November. Furthermore, the governor appointed all judges and many lesser officials. Thus there was some justification for the feeling in the white counties that they were in the grasp of a small oligarchy in the black counties. It was largely to eliminate this inequity, and not so much to eliminate the threat of "Negro supremacy"—which, indeed, had already been eliminated—that the white counties urged the calling of the convention.

Apportionment was as bitterly debated in the convention as were the clauses restricting the franchise, for the black county delegates were as reluctant to give up their control as the white county delegates were eager to wrest it from them. Many proposals were made, but that of Senator George prevailed and was adopted by the convention. According to George, his plan was based on "voting population" rather than on total population.[59] It purported to create a majority of white constituencies by increasing the number of representatives in the legislature by thirteen and allotting the increase to the white counties. In addition, several legislative districts were carved out of white sections of black counties.[60] Another provision created an electoral system of choosing the governor, each county being allotted electoral votes corresponding to its number of representatives. The unit system was established, and the candidate who carried a county received the electoral vote of that county. To be elected, however, a candidate must receive both a majority of the popular vote and a majority of the electoral vote.[61] In case no candidate should receive both, the election was to be decided by the House of Representatives, which was to choose between the two

[58]United States *Census of 1890*, I, 770-71; Mississippi, *House Journal*, 1890, pp. 3-5.

[59]Johnston, "Suffrage and Reconstruction," *loc. cit.*, 237.

[60]Mississippi, *Journal of Constitutional Convention, 1890*, pp. 677-78.

[61]Mississippi Constitution, 1890, Sec. 140.

candidates receiving the highest popular vote.[62] The professed object of this apportionment was the erection of "an impregnable barrier to any possible organization of the Negro majority, by extraneous force or internal faction for political dominance."[63]

George's plan was bitterly attacked by the press of the black counties.[64] The Jackson *Clarion* outdid all others in its opposition. It called the legislative apportionment a "visionary, impracticable, arbitrary, unjust, and unequal scheme" and thought the electoral college plan "the very worst" of all possible ways of choosing a governor. The apportionment scheme was unnecessary, it said, because the fear of Negro domination was only "a phantasm, a dream." It chided the convention for proposing thus to reward the white counties, many of which in the past had been the seats of the strongest Independent movements. On the other hand, no black county had ever "been unfaithful in its allegiance to white rule." The *Clarion* found no validity in the proposition that it was necessary to "lodge power in white counties to guarantee Democratic control" of future legislatures. Black counties were "as reliably Democratic as . . . the white counties" and would remain so "with or without any changes in the suffrage." The *Clarion* thought the scheme "was designed to advance the political fortunes of certain persons, who . . . were willing to sacrifice every other idea" for it.[65] So great was the opposition to the scheme in the Delta that there was actually talk of secession from the state. A supplemental report of the legislative committee of the convention provided that "the Legislature may consent to the creation of another State or territory . . . out of a portion of this State whenever the consent of the Congress of the United States shall be given thereto." But this clause was stricken out by the convention.[66]

Had apportionment been carried out in a fair and impartial manner there would have been less room for criticism. It was pointed out at the time, however, that some of the white counties which received additional representation did not have a population to war-

62*Ibid.*, Sec. 141.

63McNeily, "History of Measures," *loc. cit.*, 133-35.

64Yazoo *Sentinel*, Brandon *Republican*, Natchez *Democrat*, Aberdeen *Examiner*, Greenville *Democrat*, Lexington *Bulletin*, Forest *Register*, Grenada *Sentinel*, and Water Valley *Progress*, quoted in Jackson *Daily Clarion-Ledger*, July 10, 1890.

65Jackson *Daily Clarion-Ledger*, July 10, Aug. 27, Sept. 2, 3, 16, 18, 1890.

66*Ibid.*, Oct. 2, 1890.

rant the increase, while others which did were passed over.[67] It was feared that the plan would divide the white people of the state sectionally. It was denounced because of the "politics in it" and "the demagoguery behind it." The Natchez *Democrat* charged that George had fostered the scheme to further his selfish political ambition. He had, it said, led the people of the state "into a contest, the white against the black counties." He had caused a break in the peace which the state had enjoyed and was driving a wedge of discord between the whites of the state.[68]

The Birmingham (Ala.) *Age-Herald* thought it was strange "that a sensible man . . . like Senator George" should lend his influence to the plan. "It is a gerrymander . . . and will be productive of discontent and local jealousies." The Greenville *Democrat* thought George had not measured up to expectations "and has lost strength before the people by his advocacy of the Convention and failure to furnish a plan" that could overcome the difficulties. The Natchez *Democrat,* attributing the calling of. the convention to George, failed to see in his conduct at the convention "anything which commends itself as the thought or work of a statesman." It thought George's motive in the apportionment was "due to the fact that [his] Senatorial term expires in 1893 and that perhaps on this account the apportionment scheme appears [to him] to be judicious." The Vicksburg *Post* thought the scheme the greatest "juggelry" which had ever been "placed in the organic law of a state."[69]

Most delegates from the black counties were opposed to the plan.[70] The black counties had a slight majority on the Committee on Elective Franchise, Apportionment, and Elections, however, and it was necessary to gain support from some of them in order to get the plan before the convention. Such support came from H. J. McLaurin of Sharkey, William G. Yerger of Washington, W. C. Richards of Lowndes, and Isaiah T. Montgomery of Bolivar. Mc-

[67]*Ibid.,* Sept. 16, 18, 1890.

[68]Natchez *Daily Democrat,* Sept. 21, 1890.

[69]Birmingham *Age-Herald,* Yazoo *Sentinel,* Shaw *Utopian,* Greenville *Democrat,* quoted in Jackson *Daily Clarion-Ledger,* Sept. 25, 1890; Natchez *Daily Democrat,* Sept. 20, 1890; Vicksburg *Post,* Oct. 1, 1890.

[70]Chrisman, Muldrow, Martin, Calhoon, Taylor, Featherstone, Alcorn, Campbell, Simrall, Magruder, Fewell, Witherspoon, Hooker, Odom, Sykes, Thompson, Winchester, McLean, Eskridge, Cutrer, Farish, Ward, Love, Coffey, McGehee, Johnson, and Noland all spoke against it. Jackson *Daily Clarion-Ledger,* Sept. 25, 1890.

Laurin scoffed at the "unnecessary sympathy" which delegates from black counties were expending upon themselves, and suggested that the black counties would be "able to take care of themselves" under the proposed apportionment. Yerger expressed surprise that any delegate of the black counties should object to the plan. He regarded it as "the bulwark of safety" for both white and black counties.[71]

In a remarkable speech before the convention, Montgomery, the only Negro in the body, defended both the franchise clauses and the apportionment. He estimated that the franchise provision would disqualify more than 123,000 Negroes, but he was willing to sacrifice them "upon the burning altar of liberty" for the easing of the tension between the races. He believed that the apportionment plan would return a majority of fourteen legislators from white constituencies, but he was willing, he said, to make this sacrifice in the interest of better government.[72]

Senator George said that the proposed apportionment plan would erect an impregnable barrier to any threat of Negro dominance. He argued that the provision was necessary because the federal courts might declare the franchise restrictions unconstitutional, and because a national Republican administration might enforce Negro voting at elections. The opinion seems to have been unanimous that the apportionment would meet such a challenge and that, under it, white supremacy would be guaranteed even though all Negro

[71]*Ibid.*

[72]*Ibid.*, Sept. 18, 1890; New Orleans *States*, Oct. 26, 1890. Montgomery had been a slave of Jefferson Davis' brother, and after emancipation he acquired some property and rose to a position of wealth and influence as a planter in Bolivar County. He was popular with the white leaders and had been admitted to the convention despite the fact that he was a Republican and his seat was contested by a white Democrat. He has been charged with being a traitor to his race, but a recent study credits him with good faith, despite the fact that he must have known that "all calculations based on an honest application of the franchise provisions were meaningless." (Wharton, *The Negro in Mississippi*, 212.) Perhaps Montgomery in supporting the clauses which purported to disfranchise so many of his race and decrease their representation realized that the Negro was already disfranchised and that the constitution, by reducing the number of eligible Negro voters, might permit an actual increase in Negro voting. It is possible, too, that he knew that the apportionment would not work out as most people seemed to think it would. For a white leader's opinion of Montgomery see letter of John Sharp Williams to President Wilson, Aug. 4, 1920, Williams Papers. For Montgomery's admission to the convention see *Journal*, 7-10.

men were permitted to vote.[73] This was called by Mississippi's most prolific historian "the legal basis and bulwark of the design of white supremacy."[74]

Such authority is impressive, but an examination of the census does not justify such confidence. The apportionment was said to be based upon the "voting population" instead of the total population. If this "voting population" was comprised of all male adults, the claim that it in fact would have given a majority of legislators to districts with white majorities is questionable.

On the contrary the census of 1890 shows that if all male adults in every legislative district in Mississippi had voted, and if they had divided on race lines, Negroes would have returned 69 representatives and whites 64. In 1900, according to census figures, such a hypothetical vote would have returned the same number of whites and Negroes as in 1890, and in 1910 there would have been 71 Negroes and 66 whites. Not until 1920 would shifts of population and creation of new counties have given the whites a majority of the legislators. In that year an election by all male adults on race lines would have returned 77 whites and 63 Negroes.[75]

After 1890 there was, therefore, not only a gross inequality of legislative representation as compared to eligible white voting population, but also to the actual number of votes cast in the several counties. That delegates from the white counties should have failed to see this is almost unbelievable. There is no evidence that they protested against the apportionment clause on such grounds. The only protest came from delegates from the black counties. True, the new apportionment would slightly decrease the representation of the black counties. But it would not and did not wrest governmental control from the hands of the comparatively small number of whites in the black counties. Even when the state-wide primary

[73]Statement by James L. Alcorn in Memphis *Appeal-Avalanche,* quoted in Jackson *Daily Clarion-Ledger,* Nov. 27, 1890; statement of Isaiah T. Montgomery in New Orleans *Sunday States,* Oct. 26, 1890; McNeily, "History of Measures," *loc. cit.,* 133-35; Rowland, *Encyclopedia,* I, 540-41; Johnston, "Suffrage and Reconstruction," *loc. cit.,* 223; Alfred Holt Stone, "The Basis of White Political Control in Mississippi," in *Journal of Mississippi History,* VI (1944), 232.

[74]Rowland, *Encyclopedia,* I, 540-41.

[75]For a detailed discussion of this point, see Albert D. Kirwan, "Apportionment in the Mississippi Constitution of 1890," in *Journal of Southern History,* XIV (1948), 234-46.

was established a dozen years later the black counties remained in control of the legislature. The apportionment provision has never had to meet the test for which it was professedly designed. Negro disfranchisement, illegally effected before 1890 and legally since, has been so complete as to spare the apportionment provision the failure which it must have faced prior to 1920 had the Negro voted as freely as the white man and on race lines.

CHAPTER VIII

THE FARMERS REVOLT

IF THE farmers of Mississippi thought to improve their lot by means of a new constitution they were not long in having their illusion dispelled. Their real aim in their struggle for political control had been an improvement of their economic plight. A readjustment in the balance of political power, they thought, would effect a readjustment of economic power. They believed that their depressed economic condition was not the result of natural causes of supply and demand in a free economy. Rather it was due to the monopolistic hold which banks, railroads, manufacturers, and "middlemen" had gained over the governmental processes.[1] If they could but break this hold over government, they could effect an economic change to their own advantage.

For years economic conditions in Mississippi had been going from bad to worse. Money among the people was getting scarcer, and property was depreciating with the decline in commodity prices. The free-silver doctrine had long ago won its struggle in Mississippi, and with the passing of Lamar from the political arena to the cloistered confines of the Supreme Court, scarcely a politician failed to pay lip service, at least, to the doctrine soon to become the supreme national issue. Mississippians advocated the issue as a means of obtaining relief from an economic pressure "which for many years had been growing increasingly more odious."[2] The farmer suffered from a variety of evils. The price of cotton was low; the state taxation system placed the greatest burden of government finances on him; the poor educational system kept him and his children in ignorance; the railroads extorted excessive tariffs from him; and the national currency system, which was regulated by the banks, made it almost impossible for him to pay his debts.[3]

One of the agencies through which the farmer expressed his class views was the Farmers' Alliance. An attempt was made in the late

[1] Memorial of State Farmer's Alliance to legislature, in Mississippi, *House Journal*, 1890, pp. 145-48.

[2] James A. Barnes, "Gold Standard Democrats and the Party Conflict," in *Mississippi Valley Historical Review*, XVII (1930-1931), 422.

[3] See Farmer's Alliance Memorial, in Mississippi, *House Journal*, 1890, pp. 145-48; Kendrick, "Agrarian Discontent," *loc. cit.*, 272.

1880's to effect a union of all state Alliances, but fear of southern radicalism had caused the northern Alliances to stand aloof. Thereupon the southern branch formed a union with the Knights of Labor. In 1889 this hybrid group held a convention at Toledo. A platform was adopted advocating abolition of national banks, prohibition of speculation in futures on all agricultural and mechanical products, the free and unlimited coinage of silver, reclamation of excessive lands sold or granted to corporations, decrease of the tax burden on the masses, fractional paper currency, and government ownership and operation of transportation and communication facilities.

The Mississippi Alliance men were not advocates of a third party. They were Democrats and sought to effect the desired reforms by gaining control of the party. In their Alliance conventions they named candidates for state office and instructed their members to work for the nomination of those men in the Democratic state convention. This produced irritation among other Democrats who considered such action dictation by a minority of the party. The Alliance denied the charge. It was, it said, only recommending, and promised to support whomever the party nominated.[4]

The legislature elected in 1891 had to choose a successor to Senator George. The state Alliance was advocating the Sub-Treasury scheme, but George would not accept such a plan. He denounced it as "delusive and impracticable and . . . beyond the legitimate functions of the government." He stated frankly that he would not obey an instruction from the legislature, if it were sent him, to vote for such a bill.[5] Thereupon the Alliance put forward Barksdale in opposition to him, and the Sub-Treasury became the big issue of the campaign. A bitter canvass ensued in which even some of Barksdale's closest friends took the stump against him, so strongly did they resent what they considered a radical scheme.

The first phase of the struggle was in the state Democratic convention. Nomination by the convention was not, in the case of United States senators, tantamount to election. Senators were chosen by the legislature, and legislators were bound in theory not by the state convention but by conventions or preferential primaries in their respective counties. In many cases legislators were unin-

[4]Macon *Beacon*, Feb. 28, 1891.

[5]Garner, "Senatorial Career of J. Z. George," *loc. cit.*, 257-58; Jackson *Daily Clarion-Ledger*, Sept. 11, 1891.

structed as to senatorial candidates, in which instances they were free agents and in a position to exercise their own judgment in choosing among the several candidates. Nevertheless, nomination by the state convention gave prestige to a candidate and was eagerly sought.

When the convention met "The atmosphere was heavily laden with the usual rumors that this and that candidate had made a combination against another." The amount of "log rolling," said one observer, would have done credit to a much larger and more important body. The George forces won control and not only nominated their man but also passed a strong resolution denouncing the Sub-Treasury advocates as radicals. The *Clarion*, which was embarrassed in its opposition to the Sub-Treasury while supporting Barksdale, thought tariff reform, pensions, and free coinage should be the issues. It criticized the George faction for "offending a great army of men whose Democracy is unimpeachable" and predicted that the unnecessary resolution would prove a Pandora's box to the party. It denounced the "assumed leaders" whose intolerance would read Barksdale out of the party because of his endorsement of Alliance principles. It predicted that unless the spirit of despotism and intolerance of these leaders toward "erring members" was abated, "a division of the white people of the state at an early day may be considered an absolute certainty."[6]

Rebuffed and insulted by the "egregious folly" of the convention, the Alliance men rolled up their sleeves and went to work. With George nominated by the convention their efforts now were concentrated on electing legislators pledged to vote for Barksdale. Their movement grew rapidly, and county after county which had been regarded as safe against the Sub-Treasury became the scene of party battles. George's Senate record was scrutinized, and he was criticized for voting for pension bills for Union veterans, for favoring corporate over agrarian interests, and for being a hard-money man. The George faction was accused of bolting mass meetings which declared for Barksdale and of forming "little third parties of their own." They were accused of sending out hecklers to interrupt Barksdale's canvass speeches, and George himself was charged with using opprobrious language directed at Barksdale.

[6]Jackson *Daily Clarion-Ledger*, July 15, 16, 25, Aug. 11, 1891; Biloxi *Herald*, quoted *ibid.*, July 21, 1891.

George had the support of Senator Walthall and Congressman H. D. Money, of the second district. Walthall, a conservative on economic questions, was temperate and gentlemanly as always. He scouted the "absurd ravings" of politicians who saw the struggle as a disruption of the party. He admitted that the farmers had cause for their movement, needed relief, and ought to have it instead of being mocked in their calamity. Nevertheless he supported George as the real friend of the farmer, and his tremendous popularity was used to George's advantage. Money's participation provoked violence. In a speech at Oxford, Barksdale charged that Money, while a member of Congress, had advocated chartering Collis P. Huntington's Texas Railway and had secured a $50,000 loan from Huntington as consideration for his support. Money, who was present, arose and interrupted Barksdale. He admitted receiving the money but said that "any man who charged that the loan was in consideration of support to the Huntington road was a liar." Barksdale became enraged and threw a law book which struck Money. Pandemonium ensued for a time. Guns were drawn and blows were struck, but peace was restored without serious casualty.[7]

As the campaign progressed the bitterness of the farmers against George grew. His activities, old and new, were denounced. He was charged with having opposed the impeachment of Ames, the Radical governor, in 1876. Even his personal integrity was challenged. Enemies circulated a story that as chairman of the state Democratic executive committee in 1875 he had advised Jefferson County leaders to carry the county "at all hazards." When they did and sixteen of them were indicted for their activity, it was said that George notified them that he would defend them for fifty dollars each.[8] It was charged that a corrupt ring in Jackson owned the state and that George was a member not only of it but of every other ring in the state. Critics linked him with the penitentiary lessees, whose nefarious activities were beginning to come in for general condemnation. So bitterly did the *Clarion,* the most influential journal of the state, attack George that a group of the Senator's friends entered into a compact to boycott the paper, and so notified the editor.[9]

[7]Jackson *Daily Clarion-Ledger,* July 2, 6, 13, 14, 18, 24, Aug. 4, 8, 18, Sept. 3, 12, Nov. 14, 1891.

[8]*Ibid.,* July 27, 31, Aug. 3, 1891.

[9]*Ibid.,* July 15, 17, 1891.

But the cards were stacked against the farmers. The state Democratic executive committee yielded to pressure and recommended a division of county election managers between supporters of George and of Barksdale. But George's henchman, Stone, sat in the governor's office and controlled the state board of election commissioners. The state board disregarded the recommendation of the executive committee and appointed George men exclusively for the November election. The only recourse left by this treatment was for the Barksdale faction to appoint special committees at each voting place "to watch the polls and see that there is a free ballot and a fair count."[10]

Where county primaries were held they were conducted under rules prescribed by county executive committees which, according to Barksdale supporters, were dominated by the George machine. Numerous charges of fraud were made by the Barksdale faction. In Yalobusha County they declined to take part in the primary because of the arbitrary rules of the county committee, "clearly designed to prevent a fair expression of the will of the county." The farming element of the county, comprising two-thirds of the party, refused to submit "to the prejudiced and one-sided umpire on whose altar" the George faction had plotted to victimize them. They withdrew their candidate, but "the farce of the primary was played nevertheless, with less than a fourth of the registered voters.[11]

In the Claiborne County primary on July 4, E. H. Stiles and N. S. Walker, Barksdale candidates for the legislature, claimed majorities. The county committee, however, refused to declare them the party nominees and selected others in their stead. The Barksdale faction then called a mass meeting and passed resolutions declaring the committee's action "revolutionary, null, and void" and calling on all loyal Democrats to give "these gentlemen [Stiles and Walker] our cordial and hearty support."[12]

Charges of even greater fraud were made in the general election. In October the Pontotoc courthouse was broken into and all thirty-nine registration books were "stolen or concealed and probably burnt." Barksdale had carried the county by a large majority in the primary, and the election of Barksdale legislators was considered an

10*Ibid.*, Sept. 7, 1891.

11*Ibid.*, Aug. 29, 1891.

12Diary of G. W. Humphrey, in George Wilson Humphrey Papers, Mississippi Department of Archives and History.

assured fact. The *Clarion* called this "a monstrous crime, scarcely paralleled by any outrage of the sort in the worst days of reconstruction."[13] In Okolona the office of Frank Burkitt's Chickasaw *Messenger* was destroyed by fire. Burkitt charged that the conflagration was the outgrowth of "the bitter and unrelenting war made on me as an Alliance official and a supporter of Major Barksdale in the present canvass." "And some good people, who differ from me politically," he added, "share the opinion."[14]

The canvass was characterized as one of the meanest ever conducted in the state. Barksdale, it was said, was more savagely assailed than Ames had been in 1875. He was ridiculed, misrepresented, and slandered from one side of the state to the other. His Democracy was questioned and his honor impugned. On the other hand, even the *Clarion* admitted that "some very silly things have been said of Senator George."[15] The election returns revealed that a majority of the legislators chosen were pledged to George. His election in January, when the new legislature was to meet, was therefore almost a foregone conclusion.

It would be futile to attempt to determine which faction was more guilty of fraud and what the outcome would have been had there been "a free ballot and a fair count." Several facts, however, stand out. It was fairly demonstrated that the constitution of 1890 had not transferred power from the "oligarchs" of the black counties to the farmers of the white districts. Admittedly Barksdale was the choice of the great mass of Mississippi farmers. He was put forward by the Alliance and given its unstinted support. He was backed by Frank Burkitt and Putnam Darden, the two foremost agrarian leaders of the state. The farmers comprised an overwhelming majority of the state's population, and it is difficult to believe that in a popular election Barksdale would have failed to receive a substantial majority. Yet, because of the system of legislative apportionment as fixed in the constitution of 1890, George's faction succeeded in electing a majority of the legislature. That constitution had not broken the hold of the black counties on the state government. The contest was simply a repeat performance of elections during the previous sixteen years.

[13]Jackson *Daily Clarion-Ledger*, Oct. 5, 10, 1891.
[14]*Ibid.*, Oct. 19, 1891.
[15]*Ibid.*, Oct. 16, 1891.

Nor did the new franchise clauses succeed in preventing Negro voting. It is unlikely that many Negro votes were cast. Yet the charge was made on both sides that Negroes were brought into the primaries. The same charge had been made in every election since 1875, and there is no way of knowing whether more or fewer Negroes actually voted in 1891 than in previous years.

Equally reminiscent of the old days were incidents of violence— brawls, burnings, burgling of courthouses and poll books. The *Clarion* thought the crimes perpetrated were "scarcely paralleled by any outrage . . . in the worst days of reconstruction." The constitution, it had been said, would put an end to all such barbarities by eliminating the Negro from the electorate. The conclusion is inescapable that the Negro was not eliminated and that the framers of the franchise clauses had held in too high regard the self-restraint of the white man.

Both George and Barksdale were eminent men and rendered efficient service to their state over a long period of time. The charge was frequently made during the canvass that Barksdale was leading an "opposition" movement and was actually heading a third party. The charge was groundless. No one in the state was more loyal to the Democratic party than Barksdale, and no one denounced more violently any attempt to form a third party. He split with many of his most loyal supporters the following year when he refused to lead them into the Populist party. His contest with George was an "opposition" movement, but it was opposition merely to the leaders of the party. He tried to wrest the party from their control—a thing he had a perfect right to do without forfeiting his claim to regularity. When he failed he remained in the party and gave it his complete support throughout the rest of his career. George, too, remained steadfast in Democratic regularity. But his faction retained control until after his death so that his loyalty was never put to the test which Barksdale's was.

The election was indicative of social unrest. The farmers had shown they could unite behind a leader in an effort to assert the authority which they thought their numbers warranted. But rules of the contest were so drawn that they could not win. Remedy lay in changing the rules, but it was to be a decade before this would be accomplished. Meanwhile, the farmers were to suffer division and retardation in the Populist movement.

Lamar misinterpreted the farmer's unrest. Writing as an old man no longer actively interested in Mississippi politics, he mourned the passing of the old conservative southern farmer who had used the franchise "without any motive of personal advantage or profit" to himself. To him it seemed that the franchise was now exercised by the farmers "to make it minister to their own recently awakened cupidity and lust for office."[16]

Lamar must have forgotten his own struggle with Barksdale in the early 1880's. Or was that merely a struggle for power between ambitious individuals, with no social discontent at its core? But the economic status of the farmer had fallen even lower by 1891 than in Lamar's day. The price of cotton had dropped, and the power of the corporate interests was growing. To the farmer it seemed that his only salvation lay in political ascendancy. The movement was not peculiar to Mississippi. It was swelling at the same time in all parts of the country—North as well as South, East as well as West. If the movement in the South was marked by more bitterness and hatred than in other sections, perhaps it was due to presence of the Negro and to backwardness of educational facilities. But regardless of motive, it was clear to many besides Lamar that a change had come over the Mississippi farmer. He had become class conscious, and he saw in politics the only chance to improve himself and his class. He would not rest until he had gained control.

The new legislature met in January, 1892. Despite the fact that it was known that a majority of that body was committed to George, Burkitt and the Alliance which he headed tried to effect "combinations and schemes" to defeat George. "Every act of persuasive guile," said J. S. McNeily, "was used to have members violate instructions."[17] But it was not to be. George was elected to succeed himself,[18] and Burkitt and other dissatisfied Democrats left the party.

[16]L. Q. C. Lamar to Walter Barker, 1891, in Mayes, *Lamar*, 552-53.
[17]Vicksburg *Daily Herald*, Jan. 19, 1912.
[18]Mississippi, *House Journal*, 1892, pp. 178-81.

CHAPTER IX

POPULISM

THE ONE-PARTY system which prevailed in Mississippi after 1876 vested the power of election in the party convention and control of the convention in the hands of comparatively few men. The dissatisfaction which this one-party system produced was closely linked with economic depression. In the period 1880-1890 conditions were generally bad, but after the latter date they grew worse. In 1878 production of cotton in the South had equalled the mark set in 1860, and thereafter it steadily increased until by 1890 the production of 1860 was doubled. This increase was reflected by a drop in price. At the same time production in other parts of the world was bringing outside competition. Until 1890 the price of cotton hovered around 11 cents. By 1892 the price had dropped to 7½ cents. From there it descended, with occasional small but temporary increases, to 4.9 cents in 1898.[1] Seven-cent cotton was considered below the cost of production, and farms had to be mortgaged to raise cash to pay the lien merchant. But banks were reluctant to lend money on even good lands, and interest rates were high.

The farmer became convinced that he was the "forgotten man." To him it seemed that an enemy class—"Wall Street speculators who gambled on his crop futures; the railroad owners who evaded taxes, bought legislatures, and over-charged him with discriminate rates; the manufacturers, who taxed him with a high tariff; the trusts, that fleeced him with high prices; the middleman, who stole his profit"—had got control of the Democratic party—the party which had redeemed him from Negro-Republican rule.[2] To seek salvation in the Republican party was as useless materially as it was unthinkable morally, for to the farmer it seemed that that party was even more abandoned to the power of the trusts than was his own. The result of all this discontent was the formation of the Populist party.[3]

The membership and program of the Populist party were similar to those of the Farmers' Alliance. Its following was agrarian, par-

[1]Emory Q. Hawk, *Economic History of the South* (New York, 1934), 450-51.

[2]C. Vann Woodward, *Tom Watson, Agrarian Rebel* (New York, 1938), 132.

[3]Hawk, *Economic History*, 452; J. S. Williams to Grover Cleveland, Dec. 20, 1892, Cleveland Papers, Library of Congress.

ticularly in the South where the urban workers had not become sufficiently large to become class conscious. In general it was made up of the mass of small farmers, both tenants and owners, although it contained a surprising number of large landowners. The large landowner might be an exploiter of his tenant, but the two fought side by side in the People's party, united "by the crushing oppression of capitalist finance and industrialism."[4] Although a "radical" party, it was not revolutionary, and it accepted the capitalist system.

The farmers believed that their old leaders had abandoned them and were "just as much the tools of plutocratic opinion" as were the Republican leaders. The agricultural interest, they argued, was not regarded at heart by either of the old parties. "What they call 'vested rights' and 'business interests' will finally control them," said the Populists. The old parties were "Tools of the money power," "Cowards when it comes to any real protection of the many against the organized robberies of the few." These and other phrases were dinned into the ears of Mississippi farmers by the leaders of the new party.[5] Finally the farmers, "Oppressed, depressed, and suppressed," knowing something was wrong somewhere though they knew not precisely where, "like drowning men, were willing to catch at straws."[6]

The leader of the Mississippi Populists was Frank Burkitt, former Democratic agrarian leader and editor of the Chickasaw *Messenger*. Both he and Barksdale had accepted the principles of the Ocala platform in 1891, but both sought at first to effect reforms from within the Democratic party. With the defeat of Barksdale, Burkitt went into open revolt and began organizing the Populists to overthrow what he called the "putrid, putrescent, putrifying political moribund carcass of bourbon democracy."[7] The Mississippi Populists advocated abolition of national banks, the Sub-Treasury, 2 per cent federal loans direct to the farmer, an increase of currency to fifty dollars per capita, prohibition of speculation in farm futures, free coinage of silver, forfeiture of unearned land grants to railways and a limiting of their landholdings, a tariff favoring the producer

---

[4]Buck, *Agrarian Crusade*, 133; Woodward, *Tom Watson*, 217-19.
[5]Williams to Cleveland, Dec. 20, 1892, Cleveland Papers.
[6]*Ibid.*
[7]Chickasaw *Messenger*, quoted in Macon *Beacon*, Aug. 27, 1892.

rather than the processor, a graduated income tax, reduction of government expenditures, regulation of railroads, and election of United States senators by direct vote.[8] On this platform they nominated candidates for Congress in all districts in 1892 and sought to carry the state. They bitterly attacked the franchise clauses of the 1890 constitution. They charged that "the Bourbon Democrats" had foisted those provisions on the people in an attempt to curtail the privilege of voting.[9]

The Democrats answered the challenge with the old rallying cry of white supremacy. They accused the Populists of favoring Negro suffrage. As for the franchise restrictions, they charged that the 1890 convention had been an Alliance movement from the beginning; that the Alliance had held such a majority in the convention that no measure could be adopted without their concurrence; and that they had voted almost solidly for it. Now, they said, "a lot of contemptible demagogues" were trying to lead Alliance men out of the Democratic party for upholding the constitution.[10]

To all the clamor which the Populists made for reform, the Democrats answered that there were some things more important than reforms in the economy. A Populist victory, they warned, would result in Negro supremacy and the degradation of southern womanhood. Fear was expressed of a new Lodge Force Bill which would insure the election of Republican congressmen from all southern states. Then would follow heavy taxes, abolition of separate schools and churches for the races, and repeal of state laws against intermarriage. With this unspeakable eventuality painted in lurid colors, they called upon all white men to support the Democratic party. "If any White man . . . can encourage such doctrines," said the Natchez Democrat, "he is unworthy of recognition despite his color." The Democrats charged that Burkitt was deceiving the people and that he really favored such Republican measures as the tariff and the Lodge Force Bill.[11] When the Republican convention in Grenada County resolved not to put a ticket in the field, the decision was interpreted as evidence of a Republican-Populist alliance. "Of

---

8Macon *Beacon*, Feb. 28, 1891.
9*Ibid.*, Oct. 15, 1892.
10*Ibid.*
11Natchez *Democrat*, quoted in Macon *Beacon*, Oct. 22, 1892.

course," said the Macon *Beacon,* "they will vote for the Populist [candidate]. . . . Mr. Burkitt has sold out his whole party."[12]

The campaign, although uncertain until the end, resulted in a clean sweep for the Democrats. "Neither you nor any of the Democracy of the North and East," wrote a successful Democratic candidate to President Cleveland, "have any idea of how close many of the Congressional districts . . . were. You cannot judge by the final result." The third district, he said, had been adjudged Populist or doubtful but "finally went Democratic by the largest vote in the State. When the tide once turned it turned overwhelmingly." But the question of turning at all had been a "horrible doubt." There was, he said, a state of dissatisfaction, *"not with the avowed purposes of Democracy,"* but with its *"alleged insincerity* and *dreaded inefficiency.* It was said, and the *people believed,* that even if we got in we would do nothing."[13]

The Populists were undismayed by the election results and began laying plans for the congressional election of 1894. All the bitterness of Reconstruction days was revived. Families were split, feuds were started, and killings resulted.[14] The Populists were strongest in white counties as a rule and weakest in the Delta. Chickasaw, one of their strongholds, had a slight majority of Negroes, but Webster, Choctaw, Pontotoc, Attala, and Marion—other counties where they were strong—were white counties.[15] Their program, however, was one which had appeal for the farmer, tenant as well as owner, Negro as well as white. There was danger, therefore, that the agrarian classes might unite and enlist the aid of the Negro vote. In such case it would have been extremely difficult to defeat them.

One of the Populists' heavy guns was spiked in Mississippi by the early conversion of Mississippi Democrats to the free-silver doctrine. Senator Walthall's term did not expire until 1895, but the legislature of 1892 had elected him to a new term to begin at its expiration.[16] In poor health in the winter of 1893-1894, he resigned the remainder of the current term, thus creating a year's vacancy

[12]Macon *Beacon,* Oct. 29, 1892.

[13]Williams to Cleveland, Dec. 20, 1892, Cleveland Papers.

[14]Macon *Beacon,* Mar. 10, 24, 1894; clipping from Chicago *Blade,* in Charlton M. Clarke Papers, Mississippi Department of Archives and History.

[15]William D. McCain, "The Populist Party in Mississippi" (M. A. thesis, University of Mississippi, 1931), 24.

[16]Mississippi, *House Journal,* 1892, pp. 180-81.

which had to be filled by the legislature of 1894. Governor Stone, Chief Justice Campbell, A. J. McLaurin, Congressmen C. E. Hooker, T. C. Catchings, and John Allen, and several others were eager for the temporary appointment. But it soon became clear that none but a free-silver man need apply. The Democratic legislators met in caucus and formulated four questions which all candidates for the office must answer. Two of these had to do with the silver question, the other two with the tariff and national banks. "Few other qualifications [than being a free-silverite] appear to be demanded," complained a "gold-bug" paper. "The plum will doubtless go to him who shouts the loudest, longest, and strongest for the greatest amount of the white metal." The candidates were invited to address the caucus for thirty minutes. This created a spectacle which a "gold-bug" called "ludicrous as a circus," with all the candidates trying to outdo one another in their advocacy of free silver. Stone and Catchings, both hard-money men, withdrew from the contest, and McLaurin, who probably shouted "loudest, longest, and strongest," won out over the others.[17]

Reinforced by this strategy the Democrats prepared for the congressional elections of 1894. Walthall, in temporary retirement and formerly identified with the gold-standard faction, urged preservation of party harmony and condemned the "gold-bug" Democrats who sought to read the free-silverites out of the party on the ground that they had not backed Cleveland. The entire Mississippi delegation, including Walthall and George, had voted for free-silver legislation even over the President's veto. Despite this, said Walthall, the Mississippians were loyal to Cleveland "in all but financial matters."[18]

The Populists nominated congressional candidates in all but the Delta district, where Catchings was the incumbent. This caused a "gold-bug" editor to remark on the incongruity of an anti-free-silver man from a free-silver state being the only unopposed candidate. Odder still, thought the "gold-bug," Catchings had more influence

[17]Mississippi, *House Journal*, 1894, p. 376; Natchez *Daily Democrat*, Jan. 24, 25, Feb. 14, 1894; Jackson *Daily Clarion-Ledger*, Feb. 8, 15, 1894; Macon *Beacon*, Jan. 20, 27, Feb. 3, 1894.

[18]E. C. Walthall to editor, *Clarion-Ledger*, May 28, 1894, quoted in Jackson *Daily Clarion-Ledger*, May 31, 1894.

in the free-silver Congress than any of the free-silver representatives from Mississippi.[19]

The strategy of the Democrats proved successful. Although polling more than a third of all the votes, the Populists failed to elect a single congressman. They received substantial majorities in some white counties but were overwhelmed in the black counties.[20]

Still undismayed the Populists met in convention in the summer of 1895 and adopted a program reiterating the demands enunciated in the Ocala and Omaha platforms. Avoiding the silver question they condemned the state Democratic administration for "squandering 2,700,000 acres of public school lands," and they urged a law to prohibit the acquisition of land by nonresidents. They condemned "ring-rule" and the "oligarchy" of officials who sought only to perpetuate themselves in office. Burkitt, in an address to the convention, charged that taxes were relatively higher than under Radical government and compared the venality of the administration with that of the Ames regime. He attacked the appointive power of the governor, which made the state "anything but a republic." He pledged that the party would provide free public schools for a term of four months to "all the children of the state without regard to race, color, or condition of life."[21]

Burkitt was nominated for governor along with a full state ticket. Although the platform had taken a liberal attitude toward the Negro in general, it did not advocate Negro voting, nor did the ticket include a single Negro or Republican. All nominees were former Democrats. Even the "gold-bug" Natchez *Democrat* praised the quality of the men making up the ticket, although it warned that there might be an "understanding" between the Populists and Republicans.[22] The moderation of the *Democrat* was not copied by other Democratic papers. The *Clarion* derided Burkitt as a recent convert to Populism after he had been nestled by the Democracy. He had only left the party, it said, when "he saw his chances for promotion were not worth looking after." Day by day and week by

[19]Macon *Beacon*, May 3, 1894; Charles E. Hooker to Col. G. W. Humphrey, Sept. 25, 1894, in George Wilson Humphrey Papers.

[20]Macon *Beacon*, Nov. 17, 1894; McCain, "The Populist Party," 25.

[21]*Ibid.*, 31-40, 47-48; Jackson *Daily Clarion-Ledger*, Aug. 1, 1895.

[22]Natchez *Daily Democrat*, Aug. 2, 1895.

week its language became stronger in denunciation of Burkitt and the Populists.[23]

The Democratic convention met the week after the Populist and copied many planks of its platform, including that on silver. It condemned third parties, however, as tending "to divide or weaken our [the white] party . . . and dangerous to the welfare and happiness of both races."[24] Before the convention met, the three chief candidates were Senator McLaurin, H. C. McCabe, and James K. Vardaman, editor of the Greenwood *Enterprise*. McCabe represented the gold wing of the party. McLaurin and Vardaman, while advocates of silver and other Populist proposals, were both bitter against the "third party." Vardaman withdrew his candidacy a month before the convention met, and McCabe the week before.[25] This left McLaurin unopposed, and he was nominated by acclamation.[26].

There had been no dangerous opposition to Democratic state tickets since 1881. Democratic nomination for governor had been tantamount to election, and all serious campaigning had ceased after nominating conventions. Such was not the case in 1895. The Populists had polled more than a third of the state's ballots the year before, and it was feared that they had grown stronger since. Democratic orators were sent into all sections, but the supply never equalled the demand. McLaurin himself received pleas by the hundreds from distraught county chairmen urging him to come to save the day. The Negroes were courted by both sides and must have made capital of the confusion among the whites. "I am very uneasy about our county," wrote a local chairman to McLaurin. "We have been calculating on the negro vote which is inclined to the straight Democratic," he said, but a Democratic speaker had come in and delivered a bitter, anti-Negro tirade. "This has imperilled the negro vote," he wrote, and "our county is almost certain to go Populist this fall unless some vigorous work is done."[27]

Coahoma County seemed lost to the Democrats when the county

23Jackson *Daily Clarion-Ledger*, Sept. 12, 19, Nov. 14, 1895.

24*Ibid.*, May 2, Aug. 8, 1895; McCain, "The Populist Party," 50-53.

25Jackson *Daily Clarion-Ledger*, Nov. 1, Dec. 6, 13, 1894, July 11, Aug. 8, 1895; Natchez *Daily Democrat*, June 2, 7, 8, 11, 28, Aug. 7, 1895.

26Natchez *Daily Democrat*, Aug. 7, 1895; Jackson *Daily Clarion-Ledger*, Aug. 8, 1895.

27F. S. Ford to A. J. McLaurin, Sept. 19, 24, 1895, Letters of Governors, Series E, 99.

executive committee refused to have county candidates nominated by a primary. Dissidents held a mass meeting, denounced the committee, and decided to form a fusion ticket with the Republicans of the county. The Republicans had nominated for sheriff W. A. Alcorn, "the bitterest and most uncompromising Radical in the state," and for circuit clerk a Negro named Chatters. These were the two offices which could be most effectively used for political purposes, and it was imperative that something be done to win the Negro vote and to prevent "Radicals" from getting control. There were at the time "not exceeding 150 eligible negro voters in the county" but if Alcorn and Chatters were elected, Negroes would, within a few years, it was feared, "outvote the whites . . . *four* or *five* to one."[28]

At Brandon, in Rankin County, the Democrats felt confident of success, but even there they wanted McLaurin to speak. He was needed at Monticello to "create some enthusiasm among our folk." If he could not come himself, they begged that "some good . . . populite killer" be sent. Burkitt had been there and the section was badly tainted with Populism. DeKalb was infested with the same virus. Populists there were "making more howl" than ever before, and in addition, many Democrats were "sore and disgruntled" at the effects of the late primaries. Burkitt had spoken three times in Prentiss County, and the Populists were showing considerable strength there. The Democrats were "having a fight" to carry Attala County, and McLaurin had to speak there. He could not fill a date at Wesson and so Vardaman spoke for him; but he had his "gun well loaded" for the crowd at Meridian, where it took forty cows to feed the "ten square acres of people" in the audience. "The lies I have told this people about you," wrote one county chairman to McLaurin, "are legion."[29]

The oratorical efforts of the campaign were not without some effect. Numerous letters attested to the writers' having seen the light only after listening to a campaign orator. A typical letter was that

[28]W. H. Fitzgerald to McLaurin, Sept. 28, 1895, *ibid.*
[29]J. H. Caldwell to McLaurin, Oct. 1, 1895; P. J. Jones to McLaurin, Oct. 2, 1895; Joseph Dale to McLaurin, Oct. 3, 1895; D. A. Hopper to McLaurin, Oct. 5, 1895; Sam P. Allen to McLaurin, Oct. 12, 1895; A. A. Armistead to McLaurin, Oct. 12, 1895; James K. Vardaman to McLaurin, Oct. 15, 1895; A. M. Byrd to McLaurin, Oct. 15, 1895; W. S. Davis to McLaurin, Oct. 21, 1895; O. A. Luckett, Jr., to McLaurin, Oct. 26, 1895; Dr. M. J. Ferguson to McLaurin, Oct. 4, 1895; W. H. Hardy to McLaurin, Oct. 31, 1895, *ibid.*

of Joe Cook to McLaurin. "Four years ago," he wrote, "it would give me great pleasure to support anyone who would oppose you. I continued to feel that way until . . . I . . . heard the Hon. M. F. Smith. . . . I am now on your side."[30]

The misgivings of the Democrats about the outcome proved unwarranted. Without their knowing it the tide had turned against the Populists. While the Populists carried a county or two and elected a few legislators, Burkitt was defeated by more than 25,000 votes in a total of 60,000.[31]

The high tide of Populism had been reached, and the party was to dwindle quickly into insignificance. Although it had seemed for a time a serious threat to Democratic supremacy, the Populist party never adequately expressed the extent of the Mississippi farmer's disaffection from the Democratic party. Had it not been for the presence of the Negro the Populists might have swept the state in the early 1890's. But many Democrats who actually preferred Populist principles feared to have two parties and thus divide the white vote. They insisted that reforms should be brought about within the Democratic party, and they preferred the lesser evil of "ring control" to the greater evil of "negro domination." The result was that after a brief upsurge the party subsided and, after Bryan dealt it the deathblow in Chicago, went into oblivion. In 1897 the Democrats carried even Chickasaw County, the Populist stronghold and home of Burkitt.[32] The Populist candidate for governor in 1899, R. K. Prewitt, polled only 6,000 votes in a total of 48,000.[33] By 1900 the Populist party was breathing its last in Mississippi. That year it cast only 1,644 votes.[34]

The failure of the Populists was due to a multitude of causes. Most important was probably the race question. Other reasons were mismanagement, lack of enlightened leadership, the comparative conservatism of its program, returning prosperity, and the national split resulting from the nomination of Bryan.

[30]Joe Cook to McLaurin, Mar. 29, 1899, *ibid.*, Series E, 110A.
[31]Jackson *Daily Clarion-Ledger*, Nov. 9, 1895; Vicksburg *Herald,* Nov. 10, 1895.
[32]Greenwood *Commonwealth*, Dec. 3, 1897.
[33]Macon *Beacon,* Dec. 16, 1899.
[34]*Ibid.*, Nov. 24, 1900.

Although the party had practically expired in Mississippi by 1900, its influence was still felt in the growing hostility of rank and file Democrats to big business, particularly the lumber interests and insurance companies.[35] Its most important contribution in Mississippi was "the training of the agricultural population to independent thought and action."[36]

[35]McCain, "The Populist Party," 140-47.
[36]Buck, *Agrarian Crusade*, 199-200.

CHAPTER X

McLAURINISM

UNTIL 1895 a well-defined pattern was given to Mississippi politics by such issues as free silver and the farm revolt. By that date the silver men had triumphed. Practically all Mississippi politicians at least paid lip service to the white metal, although a few irreconcilables, such as Stone and Catchings, remained adamant. But even Walthall, who had been born a conservative on economic questions, and George who had become one with the years were converted. The farm revolt, given a sedative by the reaction to Populism, was to seethe beneath the surface for almost a decade, when it was to boil up and engulf the state in the election of 1903. Meanwhile, though preserving an outward calm, the state was to be torn by bitter factional struggles within the Democratic party. The issues were now personal ones. To be sure personal issues had been present in all other periods, but now the political scene was to be characterized by a dearth of other issues. The tale of Mississippi politics for the next eight years is essentially the story of ambitious men at grips for political power.

The most sought after offices were the two United States senatorships. The incumbents in 1895 were J. Z. George and Edward C. Walthall. George had served since he was chosen to succeed Blanche K. Bruce, Negro, in the early 1880's; and Lamar when appointed to Cleveland's cabinet had succeeded in placing his friend Walthall in his seat. Both had been last elected in 1892, Walthall for a term which did not expire until 1901, George for one which expired in 1899. In the spring of 1895 George announced his intention of retiring at the end of his term, and a wild scramble was started for his place. The most talked of candidates were Congressman H. D. Money from the fourth district and former Governor Robert Lowry. But Congressman "Private" John Allen of the first district and Anselm J. McLaurin were known to have ambitions. McLaurin had just completed Walthall's unexpired term and was relinquishing the seat to Walthall who was again prepared to take up duties which he had resigned because of ill health. In addition Congressman Hooker and W. V. Sullivan, a wealthy lawyer from Lafayette

County, were anxious to round out their careers with a term in the
Senate.

Irritated because George had not announced his retirement until
after McLaurin announced for governor, McLaurin charged that
George had timed the announcement so as to smooth the way for
his friend Money.[1] It was too late for McLaurin to retire from the
governor's race and wait for the Senate election. He continued the
campaign against Burkitt, but at the same time plotted some kind of
a *coup* which would land him in Washington. "Now something
personal and *private*," wrote one of his lieutenants at the end of a
letter, "C. B. Greaves, Senator from this county, pledges now, he has
no candidate for United States Senator except Anse McL." J. N.
Lipscomb and another legislator had "also made the same promise."
Another wrote McLaurin immediately after his election as governor,
that he could be the next Senator and insisted that he "not refuse."[2]

The game was an intricate one and had to be played deftly. Mc-
Laurin's strategy was to create a deadlock in the legislative caucus
by uniting the opposition to Money, the strongest candidate, and
then enter himself as a compromise or "dark horse." But there was
danger in this scheme. Yerger, one of the opposition candidates from
the Delta, had strong second choice backing from both the Money
and Allen factions. Charles Scott, a powerful Delta politician, was
already in Jackson working for Yerger in the caucus. "If any of the
Bolivar delegation waver," wrote McLaurin's lieutenant from that
county, "wire me and I will come down. . . . Do not let Yerger run
too high up on the scale as Money might throw him enough votes to
elect him."[3]

The task proved too difficult for McLaurin. He was unable to
unite the opposition, and Money was chosen by the legislature on
the twentieth ballot.[4] The contest, although heated, was good na-
tured, and no ill feeling was engendered. A new opportunity presented itself, however, when George's health broke and it became
apparent that he could not live out his term. Six months before

[1]*Deer Creek Pilot*, clipping in Letters of Governors, Series E, 99; J. Z. George
to A. J. McLaurin, Nov. 16, 19, 1895, *ibid.*, Series E, 110.

[2]W. B. Jones to McLaurin, Sept. 6, 1895; James M. Dop to McLaurin, Nov. 28,
1895, *ibid.*, Series E, 99.

[3]Walter Sillers to McLaurin, Jan. 11, 1896, *ibid.*

[4]Mississippi, *House Journal*, 1896, pp. 144-45.

George's death, McLaurin was urged to come to terms with Allen, appoint him to fill the unexpired term, then back him for governor in 1899 in exchange for his support in the next senatorial race.[5] The plan was too daring even for McLaurin, and when George died in August, 1897, McLaurin appointed Money to serve the remainder of the term.[6]

But fate was to place still another opportunity in McLaurin's way. Within a few months after George's death it was known that Walthall could not long survive him. Sentiment was put aside while calculations were made as to the succession. Some counselors urged McLaurin to resign the governorship at once on Walthall's death and then have the lieutenant-governor appoint him to succeed Walthall. The Meridian *Star*, its editor promised, "will stand by you."[7] But W. V. Sullivan had another plan. Two days before Walthall's death he wrote McLaurin that although "several now are figuring on his [Walthall's] place," McLaurin must take no action until Sullivan had a chance to talk to him.[8]

Sullivan's plan must have pleased McLaurin, for he appointed him to serve until the legislature's next meeting in January, 1900, at which time successors would be chosen to both the short, unexpired term and to the full term beginning in 1901. It was generally understood that McLaurin and Sullivan had agreed that McLaurin should have the long term and Sullivan the short.[9]

But Lowry's senatorial ambitions had not been appeased, and in the summer of 1899 he and Sullivan canvassed the state for the short term. Sensational charges of "debauchery" were made by each candidate. Sullivan connected the former governor with the abduction of a young girl for immoral purposes, and Lowry retorted in kind. "It seems," said the Greenwood *Commonwealth*, "that all that is necessary to elect a man to office in Mississippi, is to convict him of 'drunkenness in office,' smear his name with a filthy scandal, or prove

[5]Sillers to McLaurin, Feb. 9, 1897, Letters of Governors, Series E, 110.

[6]Jackson *Daily Clarion-Ledger,* Jan. 13, 1898.

[7]H. Sidney King to "Dear Anse," Apr. 22, 1898, Letters of Governors, Series E, 111.

[8]W. V. Sullivan to McLaurin, Apr. 19, 1898, *ibid.*

[9]Sullivan later charged that McLaurin had actually promised to support him for both long and short terms and had broken faith with him. See Vicksburg *Post*, quoted in Natchez *Democrat and Courier,* July 6, 14, 1899; Vicksburg *Herald,* Jan. 5, 1900.

that he shamefully prostituted the functions of his office . . . to pay a private debt. Most anything that unfits him for heaven seems to commend him for office holding."[10] Credit given the charges against both candidates made the issue doubtful. In the legislative caucus, however, Sullivan was chosen by a vote of 88 to 72.[11] That was "ample proof" to the Vicksburg *Herald* that the charges against Sullivan, at least, "were without foundation."[12]

Meanwhile McLaurin had entered the campaign for the long term against "Private" John Allen. Allen, a roguish clown, had acquired his nickname early in his political career. In the first decades after the end of Reconstruction there was a marked tendency among southern Democrats to choose for political preferment those who had held high military office in the Confederacy. Arrayed against one of these in joint debate, Allen had sat quietly while the former general regaled his audience with an account of his military exploits. The climax of his narrative centered about the field of Shiloh. On the night before the attack, he said, he was seated in his tent reviewing his plans for the morrow. Outside raged a fierce storm, and from time to time the general would lift the tent flap to look out. All that met his eye was the figure of a lone sentry pacing to and fro. When it came Allen's turn to speak he said he had greatly enjoyed the general's story because it brought old memories back to him. He could vouch for the story for he had been the sentry whom the general had seen. He then mischievously urged all in the audience who had been generals to support his opponent. For himself, he said, he would be content if only the privates would cast their votes for him.

Allen pitched his campaign on the theme of opposition to McLaurin's record as governor. It was commonly charged that McLaurin had used his appointive and pardoning powers to build up his political following in the state. "McLaurinism" became synonymous among the opposition with "one man government." McLaurin was a strong personality and provoked unrestrained feelings on the part of his contemporaries. They either loved or hated him. Ambitious for personal success, he was none too scrupulous as to how he

[10]Greenwood *Commonwealth*, Nov. 10, 1899.
[11]Sullivan was then unanimously elected by the legislature. See Mississippi, *House Journal*, 1900, p. 91; *Senate Journal*, 1900, p. 85.
[12]Vicksburg *Herald*, Jan. 5, 1900.

attained it. He seems to have bound his relatives and friends to him by bands of political patronage as well as affection, and he pursued his enemies not only with exclusion from patronage but with personal vindictiveness. Just what his political philosophy was, if he had any other than that of gaining and retaining office, is not clear. He probably had the affection and loyal support of the small farmers more than any governor up to his time, and he at least made a pretense of catering to their wishes. He seems to have been opposed by certain of the corporate interests.

The use of patronage to enhance political fortunes was a common practice in Mississippi. Judicious appointments to a multitude of offices, great and petty, was of tremendous consequence to one's political fortunes. Such appointments were the basis upon which present control and future success rested. Persons with local prestige could influence county conventions and were likely to be delegates at state conventions. They must be humored in the matter of local patronage if their good will was to be retained. If, despite all efforts, the local celebrity refused his support to the administration, or if his support were unreliable, what more likely than that he be supplanted and another installed in his place as dispenser of local patronage? Perhaps McLaurin practiced favoritism more than others, perhaps his success in building a state organization intensely loyal to him made it seem so, or perhaps the absence of any great issue in the period left no other point of attack. At any rate he was denounced on this score more than any other governor, before or since.

He was in constant receipt of numerous petitions and individual requests for jobs, offices, pardons, and commissions.[13] Each had to be carefully weighed as to its effect. In addition, the local leaders were sometimes pressed to make recommendations which they really did not desire, and codes had to be worked out so as to distinguish such letters from their writers' real wishes. "Whenever I want specially any favor at your hands," wrote one lieutenant to McLaurin, "I will tell you in the letter that it will be doing me personal kindness to grant the favor asked." Of course, he added, he would never recommend an "unworthy person," but "I make a great distinction in the degrees of worth."[14]

[13]See Letters of Governors, Series E, 99, 110.
[14]J. A. Orr to McLaurin, Sept. 14, 1895, *ibid.*, Series E, 99.

Much interest was attached to appointment of "proper" county election commissioners. These officers were of such direct consequence in carrying elections that they caused more concern than others of more prestige. The factional fight in Coahoma County in 1895 showed signs of carrying over to the next election, and McLaurin's lieutenant there, anxious to see "fair play in the matter," solicited McLaurin's promise not to appoint new commissioners "until I can see you." As an afterthought he also wished to advise him on the appointment of a superintendent of education.[15] From Vicksburg came complaints that two of the commissioners "are known to have in the past, assisted in fraud in elections between white people [sic] and democrats." The commissioners in De Soto, it was charged, were of notoriously bad morals. In Belen, it was said, they were chronic office hunters and gaming-table proprietors. In Alcorn County, which was "for free-silver 100-1," two "gold-bugs" had been appointed, and T. L. Lamb wanted to know why.[16]

Nepotism was repeatedly charged against McLaurin, and the state jobs and sinecures held by his numerous brothers were notorious. He was a man of great family loyalty, and too often he yielded to the pleas of some impecunious relative. The Spanish-American War gave him ample opportunity. A cousin of the governor wrote that he wanted "some good place to make money out of this war business. It don't come more than once in a lifetime." He did not care to fight, he said, but "if you see anything you think would suit me and you haven't promised it to anyone else—please help me to get it." Could the governor make him a quartermaster "or get me in with one—so I could get some of the money or stealings[?]"[17] It is not known whether this favor was granted, but the assurance and frankness with which it was sought would indicate that the petitioner felt that it would be.

The charge of drunkenness was frequently made against both the governor and his brother, Judge W. K. McLaurin of Vicksburg. Their weakness on this score was so frequently discussed in the anti-McLaurin press that finally Representative Glover proposed a legis-

[15]J. Alcorn Glover to McLaurin, Nov. 9, 1895, *ibid.*

[16]W. F. Fitzhugh and E. B. Robbins to McLaurin, May 21, 1895; A. M. N. to McLaurin, Aug. 31, 1896; L. V. Cook to McLaurin, Sept. 19, 1896; T. L. Lamb to McLaurin, Sept. 26, 1896, *ibid.*, Series E, 110.

[17]Charles McLaurin to A. J. McLaurin, June 18, 1898, Letters of Governors, Series E, 111.

lative investigation of the charges of "drunkenness in high places." The resolution, which listed eight specific instances of "disgraceful exhibitions" of the judge, exempted the governor because he had "publicly admitted his weakness" and asked forgiveness, and any investigation would only "bring shame upon the state."[18] So great was the clamor over the judge that he was not reappointed at the expiration of his term. But the opposition press was not satisfied and though it unfair to limit the specific charges to only one official. "The public press has referred to others," said the Vicksburg *Herald;* "they, too, should be included."[19]

Another charge leveled against McLaurin was that he had used the pardoning power to enhance his political ambitions. In the spring of 1899 he had pardoned a convicted murderer named Loftin, and the act had created some unfavorable comment.[20] Hardly had the effect of it worn off when he issued a pardon for another convicted murderer, Ivo Miller. It was charged that the governor had promised a pardon to Miller even before his trial. McLaurin, after some delay, denied the charge of a previous agreement but did not "directly and positively" prove his case to everyone's satisfaction.[21]

A struggle for control of the Yazoo Levee Board became an incident of the campaign. Charles Scott, Murray Smith, Leroy Percy, and W. G. Yerger, members of the board, were opposed to McLaurin; and when a huge shortage in the board's accounts was discovered, McLaurin used this occasion to oust the old board and appoint a new one. This led to a bitter factional fight within the Delta. Scott, Smith, Yerger, and Percy publicly charged that McLaurin had "desecrated" the office of governor for his personal and

[18]Mississippi, *House Journal,* 1898, p. 105. The *Journal* records that McLaurin publicly issued the following statement: "With deep sorrow and contrition I know that at times I have too much indulged an appetite for strong drink. Against this appetite I have striven and prayed to the Creator in the name of the Redeemer, who said to the poor woman: 'He that is without sin amongst you, let him cast the first stone at her.'" If later reports are to be credited, it would seem that McLaurin's prayers were unanswered.

[19]Greenwood *Commonwealth,* Jan. 14, 1898; Vicksburg *Herald,* Jan. 18, 1898, Feb. 25, 1900.

[20]A. M. Buchanan to McLaurin, May 24, 1899, Letters of Governors, Series E, 115.

[21]Memphis *Evening Scimitar,* quoted in Natchez *Democrat and Courier,* May 2, June 15, 1899; *ibid.,* June 17, 1899; Columbus *Dispatch,* quoted in Vicksburg *Herald,* June 2, 1899.

political advancement and that he had "McLaurinized" the state. They further charged that his brothers were paid lobbyists for certain corporate interests. McLaurin defended the right of his brothers to lobby, and he campaigned the state charging his opposition was organized and financed by "the old levee board ring" and by the Yazoo and Mississippi Valley Railroad.[22]

The latter charge was the outgrowth of a controversy between the administration and the Illinois Central Railroad. In the years following the Civil War the legislature had exempted newly constructed roads from state taxation for a term of years. The Yazoo and Mississippi Valley had been built through the western counties during that period and came under the exemption. Subsequently it was purchased by the Illinois Central, and the McLaurin administration, claiming that this abrogated the terms of the agreement between the state and the Yazoo and Mississippi Valley, attempted to collect the back taxes of the latter road from the Illinois Central.[23] It was thus not unnatural that the railroad should oppose his elevation to the United States Senate. Reports came to McLaurin from a Delta town that "a gentleman who occupies a high position" with the railroad was influencing "the business men of this place to indorse Allen . . . if they expected any favors shown them in the future."[24]

A somewhat larger issue than most others was the question of the building of a new capitol. For some years the old building had been deemed inadequate, and the legislature of 1896 had passed a bill for the erection of a new one. But the governor had vetoed it because the state's finances were not adequate for such a project. He was still unsympathetic with the idea the following year, when a special session of the legislature had to be called to alleviate the state's financial distress. It was estimated that a new capitol would cost $750,000, and the state already faced a deficit for the year of $184,000. The special session revived the question, however, and the issue became confused. If the capitol were to be built, McLaurin would favor a plan submitted by an architect named Weathers. He was charged at the time with lobbying for the Weathers plan by

[22]Natchez *Democrat and Courier*, Jan. 19, 20, 1899; Vicksburg *Herald*, June 16, 1899.

[23]Natchez *Democrat and Courier*, Jan. 24, 1899.

[24]J. R. Pitts to McLaurin, May 16, 1899, Letters of Governors, Series E, 115.

setting up a "free dispensary of drinks in a certain upstairs room in the capitol city—giving out pass keys to thirsty members." The legislature adopted the Weathers plan, but McLaurin again vetoed the bill, and the building of a capitol became a political issue in the succeeding years.[25] In March, 1899, an article by "Spectator" appeared in a Jackson paper urging delay on the question of a new capitol and praising the stand taken by the governor. Two months later, the former editor of the paper said that the letter had been brought to him by the governor's secretary with the governor's request that it be published. Thereupon, "Private" John Allen claimed he recognized the handwriting of McLaurin in the letter. McLaurin denied he had written or knew anything of the letter, but this became the opposition's big issue in the campaign. It branded as dishonorable the influencing of legislation by the governor in writing a newspaper article in his own praise and under a *nom de plume*. The governor's friends called it "an insignificant point."[26]

Probably as a counterattack McLaurin urged an investigation of the activities of the "School Book Trust" in the 1896 legislature. This seems to have caused a temporary panic in the councils of the opposition, and impeachment proceedings against the governor were discussed as a means of avoiding it. The 1898 legislature passed a resolution to investigate its predecessor, charging that that body had been "corrupted and debauched . . . for the benefit of school book trusts." It further charged that the schoolbook amendment "was passed by corruption and fraud and that certain members of the Senate and House were beneficiaries thereof." The committee investigated, but found no evidence of fraud.[27]

Balked in this, the governor's strategy was reduced to a rather puerile attack on Allen's innocuous congressional record. It was charged that his fifteen years in Congress had not resulted in the passage of a single bill which he had originated. It was observed that Allen, in his campaign, never referred to his congressional

[25]Mississippi, *House Journal*, 1898, p. 105; Jackson *Daily Clarion-Ledger*, Jan. 28, Apr. 29, 1897, Mar. 15, 1900; Macon *Beacon*, Mar. 6, 1897; Vicksburg *Herald*, quoted in Greenwood *Commonwealth*, June 3, 1897.

[26]Vicksburg *Herald*, June 22, 1899; *ibid.*, quoting Natchez *Bulletin*.

[27]Mississippi, *House Journal*, 1898, pp. 38, 40, 44; William S. McAllister to McLaurin, Dec. 24, 1897, Letters of Governors, Series E, 111; Vicksburg *Herald*, Jan. 6, 22, 1898; Jackson *Daily Clarion-Ledger*, Jan. 13, 1898.

career. Instead, the strategy adopted by Allen was to attack the record of the opposition, and also to tell anecdotes to amuse his listeners.[28]

By a clever bit of tactics McLaurin was able to divide his Delta opposition. It was known before Walthall's death that Leroy Percy was anxious to have his friend W. G. Yerger appointed to his unexpired term. On the other hand, McLaurin wanted to get rid of Thomas Catchings, the "gold-bug" congressman from the Delta district, and also to secure an uncontested delegation from the Delta counties to the next state convention. Friends of Percy and Yerger called on McLaurin's lieutenant, Walter Sillers, with a proposal. If Yerger were appointed, they and their friends would support McLaurin's candidate for governor, and Catchings would not run two years hence. Sillers, without giving them an answer, then looked up Percy. He proposed that "if Catchings' friends will withdraw him from the race for Congress and permit us to name his successor Governor McLaurin will appoint W. G. Yerger United States Senator. . . . They must also support our man for governor next time." Percy was willing to promise that Catchings would not run in the next election but believed that Catchings' campaign had gone too far for him to withdraw that year, and the deal did not materialize. But Sillers permitted the details of the proposal to leak out and showed that the original suggestion to sabotage Catchings had come from his friend Percy. This placed Percy in an exceedingly unfavorable light. Not only did it bring his loyalty to his friend in question, but it tended to convict him of a willingness to partake of the same "corrupt deals" for which he was so bitterly denouncing McLaurin. He defended himself feebly. He said he was only "attempting to lessen the bitterness of the . . . fight within the party in the Delta." He had reason to believe, he said, that Catchings "could not be induced to make the race for Congress again." Percy's county, Washington, had expressed no preference for governor in the next election. If Yerger were appointed Senator, Percy would induce his friends to support "silver men" for congressmen and governor next time, provided, of course, "they would name good men, not McLaurinites."[29]

[28]Pres Grooves to McLaurin, Apr. 20, 1899; William Griffin to McLaurin, Apr. 1, 1899, Letters of Governors, Series E, 115.

[29]Greenwood *Commonwealth*, May 26, June 2, 9, July 21, 1899; William Alexander Percy, *Lanterns on the Levee* (New York, 1941), 66.

When the deal fell through the McLaurin faction, without disclosing itself as such, held a "convention" at Greenville and nominated for Congress Pat Henry of Vicksburg, a free-silver man. Although Catchings later won, there were many bolters to Henry among the silver men of the Delta. So deep was the division in the opposition ranks there that by August Sillers could report to McLaurin that "We are fully organized in the Delta and your friends enthusiastic and confident."[30]

Meanwhile McLaurin's position was complicated by the uncertainty of Congressman John Sharp Williams' position. Conflicting reports that he would or would not enter the Senate race kept coming in. It was surmised that the Allen crowd was promoting Williams' candidacy, since McLaurin was counting on heavy majorities in the eastern hill counties of Williams' district. But the Baptists there, who had been somewhat alienated by McLaurin's appointment of a Catholic as adjutant-general, were devoted to Williams. "You must do everything in your power at once," wrote one of McLaurin's advisers, "to keep him [Williams] out of the race—Our people over here are perfect fools about him." Another suggested the appointment of a Baptist state superintendent of education. "It would strengthen you in the Eastern counties of Williams' district," he wrote, "besides neutralize the dissatisfaction of some of our Baptist brothers."[31]

Despite McLaurin's best efforts Williams decided to run. Allen people, however, were not unanimous in the belief that Williams would prove merely a stalking-horse. The Vicksburg *Herald,* convinced that Allen already had McLaurin whipped, feared that Williams might reap the fruits of Allen's labors and walk off with the prize himself. It called attention to the "debt" which Mississippi owed Allen for having exposed "McLaurinism."[32]

The first big rally of the campaign was held at Winona on March 16, 1899. It was an all-day affair with five candidates for governor present, together with the three senatorial aspirants. Each candidate

[30]Sillers to McLaurin, Aug. 5, 1898, Letters of Governors, Series E, 115; Greenwood *Commonwealth,* May 26, 1898, July 21, 1899.

[31]Thomas F. Pettus to McLaurin, Aug. 1, 1898; Pres Evans to McLaurin, Sept. 11, 1898; C. C. Miller to McLaurin, June 11, 1899, Letters of Governors, Series E, 112, 115.

[32]Vicksburg *Herald,* June 23, 1899; Yazoo *Sentinel,* June 15, 1899.

was given an hour in which to present his platform and twenty minutes rebuttal at the end. The platforms were much alike, with planks wide enough to hold as many followers as possible. All agreed on the Chicago platform (1896) and on all national issues. After general statements as to their aims if elected, each candidate launched an attack on his opponents. This consumed most of the time for the main addresses and all of that allowed for rebuttal. "The personal character which the debate at times assumed," observed the *Clarion*, "is not calculated to give assurance that the campaign will be conducted with that dignified tone which . . . should pervade a canvass for . . . high office."[33]

After this opening performance the campaign resolved itself into a series of joint speakings of the opponents throughout the state. Frequently the candidates traveled on the same train, were met at the station by their supporters with a band of musicians, and were conducted to different quarters where they were given final grooming by the local managers. At the appointed hour the candidates tore into one another with verbal beltings, then departed together on the next train.[34]

The purpose of the canvass was not to get votes directly for the candidates but to get votes for legislators who were pledged to support one or the other of the senatorial candidates. A legislator might be pledged as a result of a county primary, a county convention, or in case he was uninstructed by his constituents, by private agreement.

Because of the unusual interest in selecting a successor to Senator George, the holding of a state-wide primary to select a senatorial candidate had been urged. The suggestion met with conflicting reactions from the various members of the different factions. It was generally agreed that McLaurin himself would profit by such a procedure. Williams, after belatedly entering the race, had withdrawn, entered again, and dropped out finally in July. With him out, McLaurin had a much greater popular appeal with the masses than did Allen. But there were other factors to be considered. Local politicians, once in control, thought they could retain that control more easily by a county convention than by a primary. Where a

[33]Jackson *Weekly Clarion-Ledger*, Mar. 23, 30, 1899; Vicksburg *Herald*, June 6, 1899.

[34]Natchez *Daily Democrat*, July 18, 1899.

candidate's followers were not in control locally, however, the primary would offer a better chance of upsetting the group in power than would a convention. Thus supporters of either Allen or McLaurin were inclined to oppose or favor a primary according to whether they had or did not have local control. As one local politician put it, "This move for primaries originates with the old ring that ... controlled politics in this section up to a few years ago, and they now seek the opportunity to do what we have frequently begged for, and just as frequently been denied." Another factor had to be considered in this connection, however. A state-wide primary to select a senatorial candidate would be decided by the total number of votes cast. This would greatly reduce the influence of the Delta counties, and they would, therefore, be inclined to oppose it. Weighing these factors McLaurin threw his influence for a convention, and the state Democratic executive committee so ordered.[35]

Many of the county committees, however, ordered primaries for the nomination of legislators, and word was passed down by the senatorial candidates to vote for men committed to them.[36] But uncertainty developed as to who were qualified to vote in such primaries. Code Section 3269 restricted primary voting to those who were legally qualified to vote in a regular election. Since many whites were delinquent in their poll taxes they were not eligible to vote in regular elections. But it was argued that the intent of the framers of the constitution of 1890 was that all whites should vote in primaries. The Hinds County Democratic executive committee, controlled by McLaurin, announced that delinquents would be permitted to vote in the primary there, and this raised a stormy controversy. The Greenwood *Commonwealth* warned that the vote of Hinds might be contested in the state convention, and the Greenville *Times* called the committee's action "a blow at the fundamental principle underlying the franchise article of the constitution." The *Clarion* thought permitting of delinquents to vote was only a "trifling and immaterial disregard of the law." "The white men of Mississippi ... must stand together," it said, "and no scheme based upon

[35]S. C. Dulaney to McLaurin, Nov. 11, 1895; J. M. Montgomery to McLaurin, Apr. 8, 1899; J. F. Thomas to McLaurin, June 20, 1899, Letters of Governors, Series E, 99, 115; Macon *Beacon*, Apr. 15, 1899; Jackson *Weekly Clarion-Ledger*, Mar. 23, 30, 1899; Natchez *Democrat and Courier*, June 17, 1899.

[36]Vicksburg *Herald*, May 6, 1899.

taxpaying or other qualifications should separate them." Generally the Delta papers argued that only those who paid their poll taxes were eligible and called on the next state convention to make clear this requirement.[37]

When McLaurin's candidates received large majorities in the Hinds primary the opposition attributed this more to "disqualified votes" than to McLaurin's endorsement. Also they charged him with making "trades" with candidates for county offices. "All kinds of trades, combinations, and agreements," said an anti-McLaurin paper, had been made in the Hinds primary. It predicted that "county politics will cut a considerable figure in the balloting for senator in this county [Warren]." When another anti-McLaurin paper called on the circuit clerk of Hinds to "thoroughly fumigate" his poll books, he wrote on their cover, "These books have been purged, fumigated, disinfected, regenerated, and made as pure and free from taint as some of the recently defeated candidates for office in Hinds County. So don't be afraid of them."[38]

Hinds was not the only county where irregularities were charged. Two hundred Negroes were reported as having voted in the Carroll primary. Senator Money actually refused to vote there because of "the way the election was carried on." The Greenwood *Commonwealth,* which at first professed disbelief in the charges in Carroll, investigated and reported them true. It "shamedly confessed" that "responsible citizens . . . saw . . . with their own eyes, negroes in Carrollton voting," and it attributed McLaurin's victory there to the Negro vote. It reminded Carrollton citizens that they had sent J. Z. George to the constitutional convention "to settle that question." He had given Mississippi, it said, white supremacy. How could the Carrolltonians be so ungrateful to his memory now? "Had it been [only] democratic negroes," said the *Commonwealth,* "it would not have been so bad, but republican negroes" also voted.[39]

The superintendent of education in Jefferson City reported that votes had been cast for one of the candidates by men "who had been

[37]*Ibid.,* June 2, 6, 11, 1899; Greenwood *Commonwealth,* June 2, 1899; Jackson *Weekly Clarion-Ledger,* June 8, 15, 22, 1899; Greenville *Times,* quoted in Vicksburg *Herald,* June 11, 1899; Vicksburg *Dispatch,* quoted in Macon *Beacon,* Aug. 12, 1899.

[38]Greenwood *Commonwealth,* July 7, Nov. 3, 1899; Vicksburg *Herald,* July 1, 1899.

[39]Greenwood *Commonwealth,* July 14, 28, 1899; Vicksburg *Herald,* July 7, 16, 18, 1899.

residents of other districts for two years and they [the election officials] knew it." Writing some time after the election, the Vicksburg *Post* called the primary "perhaps the most unfair and the trickiest ever held in any state in the Union." It doubted if any of the officials chosen had "a really honest title to the offices which they are now holding as a result of those tricky primaries."[40]

Many of the charges of corruption in the election of 1899 were true, and McLaurin himself, if not a direct participant, had knowledge of the fraud. Writing from the home town of Lowry, who was opposed to McLaurin, one of the McLaurinites explained that because of the strength of Lowry there, "what work we did for the Senator [McLaurin] was done on the sly. You will understand the rest."[41] Walter Sillers, McLaurin's Delta lieutenant, wrote that "Edwards and I have paid the taxes of over one hundred white men. In time of peace prepare for 'wah.' "[42] One who must have been a professional ballot box stuffer, willing to sell his "skill" to either faction, wrote directly to the governor before the primary: "I will carry any box for you but you must assist me in so doing. . . . You understand what I mean you write me what you will be willing to pay to carry a box answer at once."[43] The governor's answer, if he made any, is unknown.

By late July results from county primaries showed that McLaurin was a certain winner, and when the legislature met in January he was chosen for the long term. It was at this time that his stablemate, Sullivan, was chosen over Lowry for the short term by the narrow margin of 88-72.[44] This was the last time McLaurin was to be a candidate for office, but his influence was felt in all subsequent elections until his death and for some years thereafter.

Obviously the professed aims of the constitution of 1890 had not been reached by the end of McLaurin's administration. Negroes had not been eliminated from the polls but were playing the same

[40]Greenwood *Commonwealth,* July 28, 1899; Vicksburg *Post,* quoted in Jackson *Weekly Clarion-Ledger,* Jan. 2, 1902; J. Rives Wade to McLaurin, July 26, 1899, Letters of Governors, Series E, 112.

[41]Edward Henderson to Dear Wallace [McLaurin?], Aug. 25, 1899, *ibid.,* Series E, 116.

[42]Sillers to McLaurin, Feb. 9, 1897, *ibid.,* Series E, 110.

[43]W. H. Parker to McLaurin, May 1, 1899, *ibid.,* Series E, 115.

[44]Mississippi, *Senate Journal,* 1900, p. 85; *House Journal,* 1900, pp. 91-92; Vicksburg *Herald,* July 23, 1899; Jackson *Clarion-Ledger,* Jan. 11, 1893.

part, a decade after its proclamation, that they had played for the dozen or fifteen years before its adoption. Nor were issues brought forth and discussed between the white factions any more than they had been before 1890, if as much. In the election of 1899 all candidates were in agreement on all questions of policy. The only issue seemed to be the personalities of the candidates. But McLaurin had sensed more than any other Mississippian of his time the growing political consciousness of the small farmer, and he had catered to him. It was this new factor which was soon to be seized upon by other leaders and played to its extremity in the struggle for political control.

The gubernatorial election in 1899 was to be the last in Mississippi in which the candidate was nominated by a state convention. Many candidates were early in the field, but the most prominent were James K. Vardaman, just returned from military service in Cuba; A. H. Longino, McLaurin-appointed judge of the state supreme court; Judge Frank A. Critz of Oktibbeha; Judge Robert Powell of Lincoln; and W. A. Montgomery of Hinds. Although it was generally supposed that Longino had the backing of McLaurin, it was noted as "a singular fact" that all the candidates disclaimed any connection with the McLaurins "in any shape."[45] Vardaman's hostility to the governor and his "infamous assaults" on him in the Greenwood *Commonwealth* had culminated in McLaurin's refusal to commission him in the state militia. Vardaman had thereupon joined the United States Volunteers, had been commissioned a major, and had served actively in the Spanish-American War. The hostility between him and McLaurin on his return was unabated and remained so.[46]

Vardaman's platform included a radical change in the educational system (which will be given in some detail in a later chapter), curtailment of governmental expenses, free silver, a revenue tariff, an elective judiciary, and support of "Bryanism." He said he intended to make "a clean, honest, straightforward fight for the office" and would make no pledges to gain support of any faction. He opposed the "bartering or farming out" of patronage. He pledged the people of Mississippi that he would not use the office to build up a

[45]Macon *Beacon*, Apr. 22, 1899.
[46]W. A. White to McLaurin, Nov. 1, 1898, Letters of Governors, Series E, 112.

private or political fortune. "I am opposed," he said, "to jobbing and deals of all kinds."[47]

Longino among other things advocated the building of a new capitol, a program which seemed inconsistent with his alleged alliance with McLaurin. Critz, carrying water on both shoulders, advocated the new capitol, collection of back taxes against railroads, an elective judiciary, and "correction of certain evils in the distribution of school funds."[48]

The usual amount of preconvention trading was indulged in. The Hinds County convention endorsed Montgomery and permitted him to name the county's twenty-one delegates to the convention. The delegates were then instructed to cast Hinds''seven votes for Montgomery "first, last, and all the time, and to use all honorable means to secure his nomination so long as his name may be before the convention."[49] Nothing was said about their course in case Montgomery's name should be withdrawn, which omission endowed Montgomery with seven votes to cast where he would.

Warren County, which had no candidate for governor, endorsed a native son, T. S. Lawrence, for railroad commissioner and empowered him to name Warren's delegates to the state convention. The obvious purpose of this was to give him dictatorial power over the delegation to trade for support of his candidacy. The Vicksburg *Herald*, which claimed neutrality in the gubernatorial race, called this "not only a usurpation of authority but a wrong." Criticism provoked the county committee to reverse itself and order a preferential primary for governor, permitting the candidate receiving a plurality to name the delegates. This provoked even greater criticism.[50]

Vardaman was reported to be in alliance with Critz to defeat Longino. The alliance was said to have the backing of "some of the shrewdest politicians in the state," among whom were Vardaman's cousin, Senator Money, and "Private" John Allen, still chafing at his own defeat by McLaurin.[51] Their strategy seemed to be to prevent Longino's nomination on an early ballot and then to swing the con-

[47]Greenwood *Commonwealth*, Feb. 11, 1898, Jan. 6, 1899.

[48]Magnolia *Gazette*, quoted in Macon *Beacon*, Apr. 29, 1899.

[49]Jackson *Clarion-Ledger*, July 27, 1899.

[50]Vicksburg *Herald*, June 6, 24, 1899.

[51]Monroe McClurg to McLaurin, Aug. 18, 1899, Letters of Governors, Series E, 115; Natchez *Democrat*, Aug. 23, 24, 1899.

vention to Vardaman as a second choice. The Vicksburg *Herald*, still claiming neutrality, thought Vardaman had created a "firm impression" during his short canvass. "He has grown," said Editor McNeily on the eve of the convention, "more than any other man in the state during the past month—his canvass has been clean and clear cut."[52] Longino was charged with having "formed enough trades to give him the nomination on the first ballot." District Attorney Pat Henry of Warren County was reported to have said he was backing Longino so that his friend W. K. McLaurin would be reappointed judge of the circuit. Longino denied having made such a promise, but this denial was called a "vague disavowal."[53]

On the day the convention met, Longino, as the leading candidate, received a "rush" from leaders of various delegations wanting to make terms for some favorite candidate who was trying for some other place on the ticket. Longino refused, however, to consider any proposals until he was nominated. This was reported to have "brought all the candidates [for other offices] into the Longino column." They instructed their friends "to make no trades against Longino," and this left nothing for the opposition to take hold of. On the first ballot Longino received 128½ votes, within 5½ of the necessary majority. Balloting went on throughout the night. At midnight Powell withdrew, at dawn Montgomery. New caucuses were then called to see where these votes would go. At eleven-thirty, convinced that the game was up, Critz and Vardaman withdrew, leaving Longino as the only candidate. Vardaman's good-humored speech of withdrawal was reported to have "completely captured the convention."[54]

After the nomination of Longino and the hearing of committee reports, the convention adjourned for the night, and "logrolling began for the places on the . . . ticket" not yet filled. Next day there were "rumors of things being fixed," but hard contests developed for auditor, treasurer, and railroad commissioner for the northern district. When the convention adjourned for dinner, however, the ticket was complete. Taken as a whole, said the Natchez *Democrat*,

[52]Vicksburg *Herald*, Aug. 22, 1899.

[53]Greenwood *Commonwealth*, Aug. 11, 1899; Vicksburg *Herald*, July 12, 14, 1899.

[54]Jackson *Clarion-Ledger*, Aug. 24, 1899; Natchez *Democrat*, Aug. 24, 1899; Macon *Beacon*, Aug. 26, 1899.

the convention was controlled by "the same influences that controlled the election of McLaurin." It was generally understood, it said, "that the men who did most for McLaurin were to be the nominees . . . and this was carried out." The victory meant, thought the *Democrat,* that McLaurin "will dominate the state for several years to come."[55]

A discordant note was produced in the convention when Judge Coleman of Greenwood opposed a resolution endorsing the McLaurin administration. Leroy Percy backed Coleman and even offered a substitute to the Resolutions Committee's report charging McLaurin with nepotism, intoxication, and other shortcomings. His conduct had, said Percy's resolution, "tended to lessen the respect which the people of the state are wont to accord to their chief executive." Percy's substitute resolution was voted down and McLaurin was endorsed.[56]

The *Clarion* was pleased with the results of the convention. It thought it a matter for general rejoicing that of the thirteen nominations made at the convention seven were arrived at without the taking of a single ballot.[57] The Greenville *Democrat,* although not so well pleased as the *Clarion,* denied that Mississippi politics was "decaying," as was frequently charged. Conditions might be bad, but they were no different than they had been in the 1880's. "Mud throwing . . . today is . . . the same," it said, "as during the campaign of 1885. . . . There is no more demagogism, no more shysters, no more small potatoes . . . in Mississippi . . . than usual."[58] The *Democrat* had a longer memory than some of its contemporaries.

[55]Macon *Beacon,* Aug. 26, 1899; Natchez *Democrat,* Aug. 25, 1899.

[56]Jackson *Clarion-Ledger,* Aug. 24, 1899; Macon *Beacon,* Aug. 24, 1899.

[57]Jackson *Clarion-Ledger,* Aug. 31, 1899.

[58]Greenville *Democrat,* quoted in Macon *Beacon,* Feb. 25, 1900.

CHAPTER XI

THE PRIMARY LAW OF 1902

UNTIL 1902 party nominations were almost completely under control of state and county executive committees. At times these committees made nominations with no pretense of submission to party membership. State and district officers were uniformly nominated by conventions. Sometimes county conventions nominated county officials, but there was no uniformity in this respect. In the late 1870's some of the counties began holding primaries for local offices, and the movement grew considerably during the next two decades. The decision of whether or not to hold a county primary was altogether in the hands of the county executive committee. Where county primaries were held, delegates to the county convention, as well as candidates for county offices, were generally nominated. The county convention, however, always chose the delegates from the county to the state convention. The latter body nominated all state elective officers.[1]

Complaints against the convention system were of long standing. In Bolivar County in 1878 a convention had been ordered for the purpose of making a recommendation to the governor for the appointment of a chancery clerk. One of the four candidates complained that when the other three found he had the greatest strength, "they formed a joint stock company of the office, agreed to divide the profits, and defeated me."[2] A decade later the Natchez *Democrat*, complaining of the declining quality of Mississippi's public men, attributed it to the "crowding out" of the "able men" by the convention system of nominating.[3] In 1894 it was claimed that Colonel Charles E. Hooker, the popular candidate, failed to receive the congressional nomination from the seventh district convention because of collusion and manipulation among the candidates.[4]

[1]Edmund F. Noel, "Mississippi Primary Election Laws," in Mississippi Historical Society, *Publications*, VIII (1904), 241; Vicksburg *Herald*, June 18, 1899; Jackson *Clarion-Ledger*, May 18, 1899.

[2]Alex Yerger to J. M. Stone, Apr. 1, 1878; J. C. Herndon to Stone, Nov. 5, 1878, Letters of Governors, Series E, 143A.

[3]Natchez *Democrat*, quoted in Jackson *Clarion-Ledger*, Apr. 4, 1899.

[4]Jackson *Clarion-Ledger*, Sept. 27, 1894.

The constitution of 1890 had provided that "The Legislature shall enact laws to secure fairness in party primary elections, conventions or other methods of naming candidates."[5] This gave the legislature power to require all nominations to be made by primary, but for some years it did not exercise this power. Party nominations could still be made by convention if the constituted authorities so decreed. The matter of who should vote at beat meetings for delegates to county conventions was also determined by the party authorities. This led to uncertainty as to whether the authorities could not also decide who might vote in the primaries.

The convention system survived the constitution of 1890, and complaints against it grew with the years. Primaries would give as little satisfaction to defeated candidates and their followers as had conventions, but the latter furnished a good target for those who wished to break the control of the group in power. Accordingly, the primary plan gained many advocates, and the time was looked forward to when conventions, those "stenches in the nostrils of the people," would be a thing of the past. "Nothing can be fairer than a primary election," said the *Clarion*, "and, as a rule, it is only opposed by those who imagine themselves stronger in a convention than before the people."[6] Not infrequently at conventions, it was charged, the weakest candidate would bear off the prize.[7] The prime object of the convention, said the Macon *Beacon*, was "to ignore the will and wish of the majority, and to carry into effect the designs of the few who exercise control" over the parties.[8]

The primary movement gained a great impetus after 1895. Most of the press of the state seemed to favor it, and none of the papers had the temerity to oppose it. Edmund F. Noel became the leader of the movement and started a campaign for a state law requiring all nominations to be made through primaries. He branded conventions as "prolific with schemes" whereby the most popular candidates were often defeated by others who "developed little or no strength among the masses." Denial of participation in nominations "to all who can not make the sacrifice in time and money required to par-

[5]Sec. 247.

[6]Jackson *Clarion-Ledger*, Oct. 4, 11, 1894.

[7]*Ibid.*, Oct. 18, 1894; *ibid.*, Dec. 20, 1894, quoting Terry *Headlight* and Tunica *Independent*.

[8]Macon *Beacon*, Feb. 22, 1902.

ticipate in the uncertain rangle-tangle of county mass meetings" was an imposition and was undemocratic.[9] A state primary bill was introduced in the 1896 legislature but failed of passage.[10]

Opposition to party dictatorship apparently reached high tide in 1900. The state executive committee that year ordered primary elections to select presidential electors and delegates to the Democratic national convention but failed to provide for the choice of a new state executive committee. This failure created an uproar. The state press was almost unanimous in its condemnation of the committee and of its chairman, C. C. Miller. "Barring the carpet-bag period," said the Vicksburg *Herald,* "such a lesson in ring politics was never before administered to the voters of Mississippi." The *Clarion* called it "a glaring but intentional oversight" and suggested that the committee intended to perpetuate itself in power *"ad infinitum,* so that it can pass upon party matters in 1903." When county committees revolted and refused to call primary elections, Governor Longino urged Chairman Miller to reconvene the state committee for it to reconsider its action.[11] This Miller flatly refused to do.

Excitement ran high. The *Clarion* issued a call for a crusade. It was, said Editor R. H. Henry, "a fight between the people and the bosses, and the people, who are always right . . . will win." The Vicksburg *Herald* proposed making capital against McLaurin over the dictatorial action of the committee. It pointed out that Miller was an intimate friend of the senator and had been brought forward by him for chairman of the state convention that had nominated McLaurin for governor in 1895.[12]

With the party machinery threatening to break down, James K. Vardaman proposed to the county executive committees that they hold preliminary meetings and select delegates to a state mass convention to meet in Jackson, June 5. The purpose of such a convention would be the nomination of presidential electors, delegates to the national convention, and a new state executive committee. All of

[9]Jackson *Clarion-Ledger,* Jan. 31, Feb. 7, Mar. 7, 1895, Aug. 24, Sept. 7, 1899.
[10]Mississippi, *House Journal,* 1896, p. 824.

[11]Vicksburg *Herald,* May 1, 6, 15, 25, 1900; Jackson *Weekly Clarion-Ledger,* May 3, 10, 17, 24, 1900.

[12]Jackson *Weekly Clarion-Ledger,* May 31, 1900; Vicksburg *Herald,* June 5, 1900.

the nominees, he proposed, would be voted on at a specially called state-wide primary on June 21.[13]

Twenty-nine counties sent delegates to the June 5 convention. Vardaman was chosen chairman, and the plan he had proposed was followed. The convention disclaimed any intention of bolting the party but passed resolutions denouncing the action of the executive committee and nominated its successor as well as presidential electors and national delegates.[14]

A division now occurred in the party as a result of the revolt against the old executive committee. Governor Longino and Senator Money opposed the old committee, while Senator Sullivan and Senator-elect McLaurin defended it.

A campaign was started to defeat in the special primary of June 21 the ticket named by the convention. Some of the state press now came to the defense of the committee. The Meridian *News*, claiming that the Hinds, Jackson, and Leflore delegates constituted a majority of the June convention, termed it a "rump" gathering. The *Clarion* denied this and pointed out that, in the past, state conventions had always been called to name delegates to national conventions and on such occasions had always chosen new executive committees. When the primary was held the convention ticket was successful, and the new executive committee assumed office.[15]

An even greater uproar was produced by the scandals growing out of the June 21 primary. Politicians in the Delta were reluctant to see power slipping from their hands, and hardly a county there escaped charges of fraud in the election. Election returns were sent in from Coahoma, but it was alleged, and upon investigation proved, that no election had been held there. The Coahoma Democratic executive committee itself branded the returns as a "forgery." The "old gang" in Warren was reduced to almost equally desperate straits, and there were charges of ballot box stuffing. An examination of the ballots cast in the Red Bone district in Warren revealed that sixty-six men had voted exactly alike for sixteen delegates to the national convention. Forty-one had done so in the Oak Ridge

---

[13]Jackson *Weekly Clarion-Ledger*, May 31, 1900.

[14]Vicksburg *Herald*, June 8, 1900; Jackson *Clarion-Ledger*, June 7, 1900.

[15]Jackson *Clarion-Ledger*, June 14, 21, 28, July 5, 1900; Meridian *News*, Ripley *Sentinel*, Winona *Times*, Kosciusko *Herald*, Meridian *Star*, Greenwood *Commonwealth*, Lexington *Advertiser*, Ellisville *News*, quoted, *ibid.*, June 14, July 15, 1900; Vicksburg *Herald*, July 6, 1900.

district, and at Bovina and McGinity's Store an identical vote had been cast. This coincidence was said to be "too absurd for human credulity." It was also charged by "reputable citizens" of Vicksburg that the returns from that city "were three times as large as the vote actually cast.[16] As a result of the Warren County scandals other counties started a move to get out of Warren's congressional and judicial districts.[17]

Charges of fraud equally as gross were made in Issaquena, another Delta county. In the primary there 182 votes had been reported. Since there were only 169 white registered voters in the county and only 84 votes had been cast the preceding year, fraud was conclusive. Of the 182 ballots, 178 had been cast for Senator Sullivan for national delegate and 4 for R. H. Henry. The *Clarion* called this evidence of a "steal," but the Vicksburg *Dispatch* said it was merely "zeal."[18]

As a result of the revelation of fraud a strong reaction set in against the old state executive committee and against its followers in the Delta. The Yazoo *Sentinel* suggested raising a fund of $5,000 to employ detectives to secure evidence so that the guilty individuals could be prosecuted. Even county conventions in the home districts of C. C. Miller and "Anse" McLaurin condemned the fraud and called on the new state committee to investigate. But that group, for some reason, was not eager to do so. After repeated promptings it finally, in late October, appointed an investigation committee. But it was on the eve of the presidential election, and interest in the matter had abated.[19] An examination of the files of the press of the period fails to reveal that the committee ever reported.

But reaction against "boss control" and the convention system of nominating did not abate. The "shams and frauds" of the 1900 primary had been too glaring. It had been conclusively shown that the votes returned to and counted by the old executive committee were

[16]Friar's Point *Coahomian*, quoted in Jackson *Clarion-Ledger*, July 19, 1900; *ibid.*, July 19, 26, Aug. 2, 9, 1900.

[17]Jackson *Clarion-Ledger*, July 26, Aug. 2, 1900, Mar. 7, 1901; Port Gibson *Reveille*, quoted, *ibid.*, Aug. 2, 1900; Vicksburg *Post*, quoted, *ibid.*, July 26, 1900; Vicksburg *Herald*, Aug. 2, 1900, Jan. 18, 20, 29, Feb. 1, 1902.

[18]Jackson *Clarion-Ledger*, July 26, 1900; *ibid.*, quoting Vicksburg *Dispatch*.

[19]Yazoo *Sentinel*, quoted in Jackson *Clarion-Ledger*, Sept. 20, 1900; *ibid.*, Oct. 4, 25, 1900.

largely in excess of the votes actually cast.[20] The feeling grew that political matters must be brought closer to the people and that every voter should have free opportunity to express his individual preference. Such was impossible under the convention nominating system.

Governor Longino in his message to the legislature in 1900 had urged a compulsory primary law. The white people of the state, he said, were "impatient and displeased with the dubious and devious methods of the party nominating machinery," which might differ in procedure "according to the interest and views of the party leaders in the different counties." The Senate, after some delay, passed such a law, but it reached the House too late for action before adjournment.[21]

The frauds revealed in the election the following summer had emphasized the need of reform, and before the legislature met in 1902 the press of the state was sending forth ringing appeals to that body to do something to rid the state of "the fraud and farce" of its elective process. There was nothing, said the *Clarion*, of greater importance to the state than this. The present "slip-shod" law had been "conceived in sin and born in iniquity." Under its provisions there had been created "more bad feelings, more bickerings, more resentments, more swindlings and cheatings and ballot-box stuffings than were ever before known or heard of in the state."[22] The Vicksburg *Post* agreed that a new primary law was "the most important measure" that could come before the legislature. According to the *Post,* the "trickery, frauds, and dishonesty practiced at primary elections in the state during the past few years, would disgrace even the notorious evil election practices attributed to the 'machine' in Philadelphia, and Tammany in New York City."[23]

Papers were advocating not only compulsory primaries for all nominations, but reform in the primary system itself. By fixing different primary dates in their respective counties, the executive committees were able to effect trades of candidates for district and state offices. This seems to have been only one of the offenses practiced, but advocates emphasized the necessity of holding primaries

[20]Carthage *Carthagenian*, quoted in Jackson *Clarion-Ledger*, Aug. 2, 1900; *The Baptist*, quoted, *ibid.*, Sept. 6, 1900.

[21]Mississippi, *Senate Journal*, 1900, pp. 92, 567-69; *House Journal*, 1900, p. 720.

[22]Jackson *Clarion-Ledger*, Jan. 2, 1900.

[23]Vicksburg *Post*, Dec. 12, 1901.

in 'all counties on the same day.[24] It would tax "the range and scope of the most fertile and versatile imagination," said the Crystal Springs *Meteor*, "to picture a condition of greater political rottenness than that which has grown out of the primary law of this state."[25]

Responding to popular clamor, the governor again urged the legislature to act. Pointing out that the constitution required the legislature to enact laws to secure "fairness" in the nomination of party candidates, he observed that the "existing statutes on the subject" did not meet the requirement "or amount even to a respectable makeshift."[26]

Insofar as reforming the machinery of the existing county primaries was concerned, sectionalism was not a factor. Such reforms might be favored or opposed by different elements in the several counties, depending upon how such changes might affect their fortunes. Popular sentiment, however, was so overwhelmingly in favor of these reforms that opposition to local reform melted away. But elimination of the state nominating convention was a different matter. A state-wide primary would equalize the power of the white voters in all sections of the state. Control by the black counties would be eliminated, and supremacy of the white counties would be assured. Naturally the black counties opposed such a change.

As was to be expected, therefore, opposition to a state-wide primary law centered in the Delta. On the day the legislature met a New Orleans reporter noted "a great element of friction" in the body, growing out, he thought, of fear "on the part of the Delta that that great tax-paying section" might be shorn of its power "by a primary election law which will give the white counties absolute control of all nominations."[27] It was noted during debate on the measure that "all members of the Delta counties, with the exception of Mr. Campbell, of Greenville," spoke against the bill.[28] After the bill was passed it was observed that "the primary law is very obnoxious to the people of the Delta country."[29]

The act was approved March 4, 1902. It provided that party nominations in Mississippi should thereafter be made by primary

---

[24]*Ibid.*; Jackson *Clarion-Ledger*, Jan. 2, 1902.
[25]Crystal Springs *Meteor*, quoted in Jackson *Clarion-Ledger*, Jan. 30, 1902.
[26]Mississippi, *House Journal*, 1902, p. 48.
[27]New Orleans *Picayune*, quoted in Vicksburg *Herald*, Jan. 4, 1902.
[28]*Ibid.*, Feb. 25, 1902.
[29]Jackson *Clarion-Ledger*, May 29, 1902.

election on a date to be fixed by the state executive committee but not later than August 10. If no candidate received a majority in the first primary, a second was to be held three weeks later. The old electoral college system of nominating gubernatorial candidates was preserved by a provision that a candidate must poll a majority of the popular vote, or the highest popular vote and a majority of the electoral vote,[30] but this provision has never had any effect in practice.

Party and election procedures were stipulated. Beginning in 1904 each party was to be required to hold a state convention every four years to select a state executive committee, delegates to the national convention, and nominees for presidential electors. The old plan of representation was preserved in the state convention, each county being entitled to twice the representation which it had in the lower house of the legislature. Delegates to the county convention were to be chosen by ballot. They might be apportioned equally among the supervisors' districts or in proportion to the votes cast by the party in the districts in the preceding presidential election. The county executive committees were left as before; they consisted of fifteen members each, chosen by the county convention, three from each supervisor's district. The county convention chose its committeemen for the congressional district and judicial district executive committees. Members from the state-at-large were eliminated from the state executive committee. The new law provided that each congressional district, acting separately in the state convention, should choose three of its citizens to serve on the state executive committee for four years.[31]

Rules governing general elections were to apply to primaries, thus settling the uncertainty as to the ineligibility of poll-tax delinquents. No person was eligible to participate in primary elections unless he was a qualified elector, had been identified with the party for the two preceding years, and was not excluded from the primary by party regulations. No candidate's name was to be placed on the official ballot in general elections as a party nominee who was not nominated in pursuance of the provisions of the act.[32]

---

[30]Mississippi, *Laws,* 1902, Chap. LXVI, Secs. 1, 5.
[31]*Ibid.,* Secs. 2, 3.
[32]*Ibid.,* Secs. 9, 16.

The county executive committees were to serve in primaries as did the county board of election commissioners in general elections. They were to appoint three managers for each election district. The managers were to "perform all the duties . . . required of [managers] at general elections" and were the judges of the qualifications of electors.[33] The managers were to be distributed "as far as practicable between the supporters of the candidates for those offices about which there are the leading contests."[34] Expenses of the primary were to be borne by the party, but these could be apportioned among the candidates.[35] The poll books were to be revised by the county board of election commissioners before each primary, and no one was to be permitted to vote whose name was not on the books when they were turned over to the managers.[36]

The county executive committee was to meet on the first or second day after the primary, canvass the returns, announce the names of nominees for county offices, tabulate and certify within thirty-six hours the vote by precincts for state offices to the state executive committee of the party, and make proper certification to the senatorial or other district executive committees of the returns concerning them. The state and district executive committees were to meet a week from the day of the primary, canvass the returns submitted by the county committees, and announce the nominees and the names to be submitted to the second primary. A week after the second primary the former procedure was to be repeated. When the final vote was tabulated the state executive committee was to submit it to the secretary of state.[37]

The primary law sheared most powers from the state executive committee and a few from the county committees. The state committee was restricted, practically, to receiving and compiling the primary vote submitted to it and to passing on questions of fraud. County committees were required to submit all nominations to popular vote but were given tremendous power over the local election machinery. As for the primary voter, however, he must pay his poll tax for the two years preceding the year of the primary, and not

[33]*Ibid.*, Sec. 1.
[34]Mississippi, *Laws*, 1904, Sec. 8. This was not provided in the original law but was an amendment made two years later.
[35]Mississippi, *Laws*, 1902, Chap. LXVI, Sec. 10.
[36]*Ibid.*, Sec. 22.
[37]*Ibid.*, Secs. 6, 11.

later than February 1 of that year. He must have registered not later than four months preceding the general election. He must be able to read or "understand" the constitution, must not have been convicted of certain felonies, and must not be "excluded from voting by the regulations of the party" holding the primary.[38]

The Democratic state executive committee met in Jackson on June 22, 1903, and adopted a resolution providing "that every white Democrat who will be entitled to vote at the general election in November, 1903, be permitted to vote at the primary election to be held by the order of this committee."[39] This legally excluded all Negroes from the Democratic primary, and the rule was not changed by succeeding executive committees. Since nomination by the Democratic party in Mississippi was equivalent to election in all state-wide contests and to most local offices, debarment from the primary was in effect disfranchisement. Thus an additional hurdle was placed between the Negro and the franchise. For even if he could overcome the constitutional restrictions and unconstitutional intimidations and secure the right to vote at the general election, the election, for all practical purposes, had already been decided in the Democratic primary three months before. The effect of the poll tax from that time on has been to disfranchise the white man only.

In this respect the primary law was a move away from democracy. In another sense, however, the primary law was the most democratic measure which the voters of the state had yet obtained. Henceforth in election of state officials choice rested not with a small group acting through the medium of a state convention, but with the mass of voters in the state. If thousands of white men were barred from the franchise, yet those who could vote actually had a voice in the selection of officers. Furthermore the control of the black counties over the nominating process was effectively broken. In the state-wide primary every voter was equal because the winner was determined by the total popular vote in the entire state. Thus the white counties, where the great majority of votes had always been cast, could dominate. On the other hand, the primary law did not diminish the dominance of the black counties in the legislature.

It may be asked why the black counties, if they had this control, permitted the passage of the primary law. The explanation is not

[38]*Ibid.*, Sec. 9.
[39]Natchez *Democrat*, June 23, 1903; Jackson *Clarion-Ledger*, June 23, 1903.

simple. Undoubtedly they could have prevented it had they voted solidly against it. A majority of them opposed its passage, but they did not vote with complete unanimity. Popular resentment against the convention frauds of recent years was too strong, and some black county legislators joined those from the white counties in support of the bill.

The primary law was to work some profound changes in Mississippi politics. The technique of campaigning was revolutionized. Prior to its passage candidates for state offices did engage in extensive canvasses throughout the state. But their appeal was made not to the mass of voters directly, but to a special group—to prospective legislators, county executive committeemen, and those who were likely to be chosen delegates to the state convention. It mattered little whether they impressed the mass of voters, although such popularity might have its advantages. If they could gain the ear of the small group who controlled affairs locally, there was little effective protest which the ordinary voter could make. He might stay away from the polls on election day; in which case the unpopular nominee would win by default anyway. With the passage of the primary law the situation was changed. Support from local leaders was still important and was eagerly sought, since they were influential in the community. But their aid was not indispensable, while support of the masses was. Successful candidates in the future were to be those who could rally the masses to them. Since these masses were likely to respond to a different type of appeal from that to which the local leaders had been responsive, it was to be expected that programs would be presented to them strikingly different from the cut and dried aphorisms which had heretofore been the politician's stock in trade.

It was soon to become apparent that the primary while removing some ills was to bring forth others. It was discovered that politicians had ways of getting around some of its provisions. For instance, the Warren County executive committee named two of its members to the congressional district executive committee. Since the latter body was empowered to review appeals from decisions of the county committee, this presented the ludicrous spectacle of the congressional district committeemen sitting in judgment over their own actions done in their capacity as county committeemen.[40] Furthermore, requiring all nominations to be made by primary resulted in a complicated ballot. Within a few years after the law went into effect the Adams County election officials had to find accommodations on the ticket for 31 candidates for state offices, 3 for district offices, 11 for county offices, and "a long raft of names" for justices of the peace and beat offices.[41] Candidates who wanted their names on the ballot had to file petitions two weeks before the primary with the proper number of names subscribed and deposit the necessary fee. The committee was then hurried to prepare the ballot, appoint managers, see that they were paid, and tabulate results. Doubtless many a harrassed committeeman working late at night at his new chores had nostalgic memories of convention days when the machinery was thoroughly lubricated weeks or even months before.

The average fees assessed candidates were not excessive. A different scale was worked out for state, district, and county candidates. The Hinds executive committee in 1903 fixed assessments for state candidates at $1.50, county candidates at $2.50, and county district candidates at $2.00. Of course the state candidate had to pay a fee in every county. This varied from $1.50 in Hinds to $15.00 in Yazoo —the average was $2.50. The total assessment of a state candidate that year was "between three and four hundred dollars."[42] But this was a small part of the candidate's total expenses. State headquarters had to be opened and maintained, and in many places local headquarters as well.

The new technique required a state-wide organization. The initial step in forming such an organization was the selection of a state chairman. The chairman would then set up state headquarters. Headquarters would then carefully select a prominent citizen in each county to form county organizations. In counties where a candidate was unusually strong even precinct organizations might be formed to get out as large a vote as possible. Generally the county chairman would be well-to-do, or have contacts which would enable him to raise money by local subscription. Clerical help, stationery and stamps, calls for charitable donations, paid advertisements in the press, and traveling expenses, when added together, made the cost

[40]Jackson *Clarion-Ledger*, June 12, 1902.
[41]Natchez *Democrat*, July 14, 1907.
[42]Vicksburg *Herald*, July 1, 2, 1903; Macon *Beacon*, Feb. 28, 1903.

of a campaign large indeed. After withholding enough to defray local expenditures the county chairmen would forward subscriptions to state headquarters. The size of county contributions varied, naturally, with the size and wealth of the county and with the strength of the candidate in each. In the early days of the primary it was estimated that they ranged between $100 and $500. In recent years, however, they are said to be larger. In 1903 it was estimated that the campaign would cost each state candidate a minimum of $10,000.[43]

After the county organization was perfected, rallies were held in the courthouse with the best local speakers to whip up enthusiasm. The highlight of the county campaign was the appearance of the candidate himself. Generally he would attempt to speak at least once in each of the seventy-five or eighty counties. Frequently such occasions would be joint speakings between opposing candidates, and a holiday atmosphere would permeate the community. Farmers would flock into town from the neighboring county, business would be at a standstill, and oratory, sometimes lasting eight or more hours, would reign supreme. Oratorical ability and personality in candidates were important and unless some issue deeply stirred the people might be decisive. "Generally speaking," said one editor after a life-time of political observing, "the men who can shake hands best, wear the broadest smile, know the most people, and tell the funniest stories, have the best chance to win in this state."[44] Perhaps he was disillusioned, or perhaps he was looking to a near election where his candidate faced a dismal prospect, but there is no reason to doubt that such qualities as he described were valuable in politics.

After the main actor made his appearance and departure, the local committee continued its tub thumping until the election. Then like the Arabs, and regardless of the outcome, it would fold its tents and disband. The county campaign committees were not permanent. A candidate might have one chairman one year and a different one the next.

Such was the organization which the primary law brought about. Perhaps, in theory, it was not greatly different from that of the convention period. But in practice the new organizations had to do

---

[43]Vicksburg *Herald*, July 1, 2, 1903; Macon *Beacon*, Feb. 28, 1903.
[44]Jackson *Clarion-Ledger*, Nov. 17, 1910.

work of a different nature and greater volume than had the old.

Reflecting on the inconsistency of a law "devised and perfected" to give every man a chance to express his choice and the "red tape business" and expense which would tend to restrict officeholding to the wealthy, one of the proponents of the law came seriously to question its wisdom. The poor man could afford neither the time nor the money which such a campaign would entail. Therefore the office-seeking class would be confined to "those who have money, or those who are already entrenched and use this lever to prolong their tenure." The critic could not defend the old system. It had become too odious to the masses "owing to the features that permitted the real wishes of the voters to be set aside" and let men be nominated "who ordinarily would not be the choice of the people." Yet he could not but reflect that with all its evils "the system gave us good officials."[45]

The reasoning was not bad, even if events were to disprove some of the conclusions. Poor men were to become successful candidates and yet die paupers. It was true that the old system had produced able men. Lamar, Stone, George, Walthall, and a host of lesser men would perhaps have been able to hold their own in any society. Furthermore they could claim gentility, and some of them were scholarly. But like all successful politicians, they had been responsive to the wishes of the dominant group in their community; and that dominant group had not been the overwhelming majority of the state's electorate—the poor white farmers of the hill counties. With the primary law that class had come into its own. It gave them their opportunity, and they would have no more of the old system. A country editor issued a prophetic warning some months before the first primary. "There will be a state primary . . . next year," he said, "and the old time convention manipulators will find that their fine . . . hands have lost their cunning."[46]

[45]Ibid., July 30, 1903.
[46]Macon Beacon, Oct. 4, 1902.

CHAPTER XII

NEW SECTIONAL ALIGNMENTS

IN ADDITION to the time-worn conflict between Delta and hill country, new issues were developing which were to confound an already confused geographic-political division within the state. Since these new issues were to have considerable influence in the outcome of the first primary election it is necessary to trace their development.

The first uniform school system in Mississippi was established in 1870 under Radical Republican rule.[1] Each county and each city of five thousand population was made a school district, and free schools were to be maintained for a period of four months each year. Normal schools for training Negro teachers were established at Holly Springs and Tougaloo. Despite the burdensome taxation which this system brought to an impoverished land, the Democrats continued it after they came into power in 1876.[2] Mississippi paid a larger proportion of her wealth to education than such eastern states as New York and Pennsylvania, but the rural predominance of her population together with the comparative paucity of taxable wealth within her borders made her per capita expenditure for education only a fraction of the national average.[3]

The school funds consisted largely of license fees and fines. These funds were divided among the counties on a basis of total number of educable children, white and Negro, in each. This would have been fair enough save for the fact that a smaller percentage of Negro children attended school than did white children, and the facilities provided the Negroes were inferior to those provided the whites. In the first year after the Democrats regained control there were

[1] Miss Elsie Timberlake tries to make a case for the pre-Civil War school system, but it is not a strong case. Timberlake, "Did the Reconstruction Regime Give Mississippi Her Public School?," in Mississippi Historical Society, *Publications,* XII (1902), 72-93.

[2] Report of Superintendent of Education, 1876, in Letters of Governors, Series E, 129A; Edgar Gardner Murphy, *Problems of the Present South* (New York, 1904), 42-46; *Mississippi,* compiled and written by the Federal Writers' Project of the Works Progress Administration (New York, 1938), 120-21.

[3] Murphy, *Problems of the South,* 44.

164,000 white educable children in the state and 190,000 Negroes. Yet the average monthly attendance of the white children was 65,000, while the average Negro attendance was 68,000. Both figures were shockingly low, but the Negro truancy was greater than the white. To make matters worse there were approximately half as many Negro as white teachers. Thus, while the average student load for a white teacher was twenty-nine, it was fifty-six for the Negro teacher.[4] This simply meant that the black counties were spending a considerably larger proportion of state funds on their white children than were the white counties. This fact seems to have gone unnoticed for a time, and the only controversy on the subject was between the counties with large urban populations and those largely rural. Since the towns paid a large proportion of the fines and license fees that went into the school fund, they urged the retention of all fines and fees in the counties where they were paid.[5] Nothing came of their pleas.

Small as were the sums spent for education, many thought that they were too large. There were many complaints until 1885 when the legislature undertook a retrenching program. Thereafter there were fewer complaints, but there seems to have been little improvement in the state school system. Enrollment increased but the number of teachers did not. The average Negro teacher in 1899 taught sixty-three children, still twice as many as the white teacher. Had it not been for irregular daily attendance, his task would have been formidable indeed. City schools were showing considerable improvement in the length of the school term. Some of them, through local taxation, were able to keep open a total of 150 or more days a year. But only a small proportion of the children of the state lived in towns comprising separate school districts, and most of the county schools could barely last the four months required by law. Nor could the quality of education have improved much. For the state superintendent reported in 1903 that 90 per cent of Mississippi teachers had no professional training and that 75 per cent had no higher educational opportunities than the rural school afforded.[6]

[4]Report of Superintendent of Education, 1876, in Letters of Governors, Series E, 129A.

[5]Natchez *Democrat*, Jan. 24, 1877; Vicksburg *Democrat-Commercial*, Mar. 3, 1878.

[6]Stuart G. Noble, *Forty Years of the Public Schools in Mississippi* (New York, 1918), 73-75, 82.

Despite such depressing statistics, there seems to have been a delusion on the part of some that the school system was creditable. The Macon *Beacon* in 1894, lauding the "progress" that was being made, pointed with pride to the $615,677 of school funds to be distributed among the schools that year. Although on a per capita basis this was only $1.11 per child, it was hoped that it would enable the county schools to remain open a minimum of four months in all counties, and even eight months in some.[7] Illiteracy among native whites was 8 per cent in 1900, but it was believed that this as well as the number of Negro illiterates was being reduced.[8]

Meanwhile there had arisen a movement in opposition to the expenditure of the white man's money to educate the Negro. This seems to have had no sectional basis. In the constitutional convention of 1890 a delegate from Attala, a white county, offered a resolution prorating the school fund "among the children of white and colored races, according to the amount [of taxes] paid by each race." When the committee on education refused to adopt this provision, a delegate from Adams, a black county, submitted a minority report objecting to the "large sums" which it was proposed to spend on "a race which contributes but a small part of the moneys called for."[9]

The Negroes did receive more funds than they paid in taxes, but, as has been shown, they did not share equally with the whites. This was due not only to the lower average attendance, but also to the fact that fewer Negroes than whites went beyond the lower grades, where the cost of education was much less than in the higher grades.[10]

The constitution of 1890 provided that the poll tax receipts should be used to augment the common school fund. It further provided that the common school fund was to continue to be prorated among the counties on the basis of the total number of educable children.[11] It did not, however, make it clear whether only the state fund was to be distributed on the basis of the number of educable children—the poll tax being retained in the county where

[7]Macon *Beacon*, June 30, 1894.

[8]Murphy, *Problems of the South*, 46.

[9]*Journal of the Constitutional Convention, 1890*, pp. 132, 190-91.

[10]Holland Thompson, "The New South, Economic and Social," in *Studies in Southern History and Politics* (New York, 1914), 313.

[11]Mississippi Constitution, 1890, Sec. 206.

paid—or whether the poll tax and state fund combined were to be divided on the basis of the number of educable children. The latter method, however, was followed.[12]

This method of distribution favored the black counties. Poll tax receipts accounted for a considerable share of the total school fund. Since black counties paid few polls they paid little toward the support of schools in proportion to their wealth.[13] But the black counties were heavily populated and therefore received relatively large amounts from the state fund. This enabled them to maintain a longer term and pay higher salaries to their teachers. There was also discrimination in the salaries paid white and Negro teachers in the black counties. During the decade of the 1890's the average annual salary for white teachers in black counties was $288, and $112 for Negroes. In many instances, however, the salary of the Negro teachers in black counties was higher than that of white teachers in white counties, although as a rule the Negro teacher was not as well trained.[14] Washington County, where the Negroes outnumbered the whites more than eight to one, maintained schools for seven months in 1893 and paid its teachers an average monthly salary of $37. In the same year Jones and Smith counties, both having a seven to one majority of whites over Negroes, were able to maintain terms of little more than three months and paid their teachers an average monthly salary of $16.[15]

By the latter years of the decade the white counties became aware of this inequity, and they began clamoring for a constitutional amendment which would leave the poll tax receipts in the counties where they were collected. This was opposed, of course, by representatives of the black counties, who argued that the division of poll tax receipts among the counties was the consideration which had won black county consent to the legislative apportionment of 1890.[16] One black county editor, however, admitted that the scheme of distribution was manifestly inequitable and unjust. He pointed out that

12Noble, *Forty Years*, 91.
13According to Noble three-fourths of all school funds came from poll-tax receipts, license fees, and fines, and about 14 per cent from local taxation. *Forty Years*, 77-81.
14*Ibid.*, 77-81, 93.
15Report of State Superintendent of Education, 1893, quoted, *ibid.*, 92.
16Vicksburg *Herald*, Jan. 19, 1898; Natchez *Democrat*, Feb. 2, 1898; Macon *Beacon*, Jan. 6, Feb. 10, 1900.

his country, Noxubee, had only 4,300 children attending school but collected funds for 15,300, almost 12,000 of whom were Negroes. The attendance was about a fourth of the educable children, but the funds received enabled Noxubee to maintain a 5½-month term, and to pay its white teachers an average monthly salary of $40.04, and Negro teachers $19.67. "This is about the way it runs," said Editor Ferris, "in all the counties where the population, by race, is similarly proportioned."[17]

In his inaugural message in 1900 Governor Longino pointed out the unfairness to white counties of the existing scheme. The black counties, he said, were able to provide much better schools than the white counties because they used the funds allotted to them for their Negro children who did not attend school for the benefit of whites who did. He urged division of the funds among counties on a basis of actual school attendance. He called upon the legislature to submit such an amendment to the state constitution to the voters at the next election.[18]

The white counties thought this "the best part" of the governor's message, "more important than the new capitol" which Longino also advocated. It was not well received in the Delta, however, and the legislators from the section opposed the resolution almost unanimously.[19]

The amendment resolution, however, passed the legislature. For ratification a majority of those voting on the amendment as well as a majority of the total number of votes cast in the election was necessary. Ratification was fought quite bitterly by the Delta, where not one Negro in five hundred paid a poll tax. At the same time it was estimated that of the whites who would go to the polls in the state, not 10 per cent understood the meaning of the issue.[20] Nevertheless, in the general election the amendment received 42,931 votes as against only 7,522. This was also a majority of the votes cast in the general election, and the amendment therefore became part of the constitution. Only Adams, Lowndes, Noxubee, Tunica, Warren,

[17]Macon *Beacon*, Nov. 18, 1899.
[18]Mississippi, *House Journal*, 1900, pp. 100-101.
[19]Macon *Beacon*, Jan. 20, July 28, 1900; Vicksburg *Herald*, Feb. 11, 1900.
[20]Macon *Beacon*, Sept. 29, 1900.

Washington, and Yazoo counties gave adverse votes.[21] All of these were black counties, and all but Noxubee and Lowndes were in the Delta.

Meanwhile a movement had been growing in south Mississippi for a number of years for a reapportionment of legislative representatives. Population there had increased notably in the decade after the constitution of 1890 was adopted, largely as a result of the development of the lumbering industry. It was overwhelmingly a white population, and there was a feeling within the section that it was being discriminated against to the advantage of the black counties in the west and the mixture of black and white counties in the northeast and central parts of the state. Agitation for reapportionment was growing in the south, and there was danger that that section might gain the support of individual counties in other sections which thought that they too were not adequately represented. This was a threat to black county predominance and, combined with the school fund controversy, placed the white counties of the north in an advantageous position. They might join with the western counties in opposing a reappointment in consideration for black county support for the school fund amendment. Accordingly, in the same election at which the school fund amendment was ratified, Section 256 of the constitution—that which fixed the apportionment—was also amended. This amendment divided the state into three sections—west, northeast, and southeast. The legislature was to retain the power to reapportion after each decennial census, but none of the sections was ever to have more than forty-four representatives. Thus, any additional representatives which a county received must be drawn from other counties in the same section.[22] This did not affect the white-black county ratio of representation in any respect. It simply made it impossible for the southern counties to attain legislative parity with those of the other sections.

Thus the feeling of sectionalism in the state was being complicated by the emergence of a third section—the southeast—having its own peculiar interests. Heretofore the rivalry had been largely one of white versus black counties, with the latter having dominant political influence. But the emergence of south Mississippi with a large and growing population, combined with the innovation of the state-

[21]*Biennial Report of the Secretary of State to the Legislature, October 1, 1899-October 1, 1901* (Jackson, 1901); Macon *Beacon,* Nov. 24, 1900.

[22]*Report of Secretary of State, 1899-1901.*

wide primary, was to break that stranglehold. There had never been a time when the white counties of the east could not outvote the black counties of the west in any popular election restricted to whites. The trouble was that until the institution of the state primary there had been no opportunity for them to do so. Also, in legislative matters the western counties, when supported by the few black counties in the east, had been able to attain their will. Now a combination of the two eastern sections could exact concessions from the west. The passage of the school fund resolution by the legislature indicated this.[23] At the same time it could not be expected that the interests of the two white sections would always coincide. This was the case in regard to the apportionment amendment which was passed by a coalition of northeast with west.

A third factor that was to influence the political trend in the next decade was the exposure of scandal in the state's fiscal affairs. The legislature of 1900, responding to Governor Longino's request, had passed a bill for the construction of a new capitol.[24] Suddenly, in the late fall the governor swore out a warrant against an Indiana contractor, J. E. Gibson, charging him with an attempt to get the construction contract through bribing state officials. Gibson at first denied the charge but later pleaded guilty and paid a fine of a thousand dollars. The first reaction to the exposure had been one of enthusiastic praise for the governor's stand, but shortly sentiment began to be expressed that some kind of a "deal" had been made and that the governor was trying to make too much political capital of his righteousness. Even the *Clarion*, which was and continued to be an admirer of the governor, expressed doubt as to whether all the facts had been revealed. The same sentiment was expressed by many other papers, although an equal number continued to extol the governor's stand.[25]

[23]Nineteen black county representatives joined with fifty-two white county representatives to pass the school-fund amendment resolution in the House. Of the thirty-one representatives who voted against the resolution, all were from black counties. See Mississippi, *House Journal*, 1900, pp. 466-67.

[24]Mississippi, *Senate Journal*, 1900, pp. 296-335.

[25]Vicksburg *Herald*, Jan. 26, 31, 1891; Meridian *Star*, Summit *Sentinel*, Terry *Highlight*, *Holmes County Progress*, Port Gibson *Reveille*, and Raymond *Gazette* were critical of Longino. See quotations in Jackson *Clarion-Ledger*, Jan. 29, 1901. Hazelhurst *Courier*, McComb *Enterprise*, and Aberdeen *Weekly* supported him. *Ibid.* See also *Clarion-Ledger*, Nov. 29, 1900, Jan. 29, 1901, Mar. 17, 1910.

The following year a more shocking incident occurred. A shortage of $100,000 of state funds was discovered in State Treasurer J. R. Stower's office. Upon investigation it was found that the money had been "lent" to a Memphis banker, John Armistead, who in turn lent it to the Memphis Street Railway Company. Stowers, Armistead, F. T. Raiford, chief clerk in the treasurer's office, and Phil A. Rush, a capitol commissioner, were indicted. Raiford turned state's evidence, pleaded guilty to the charge of embezzlement, and involved the others in the conspiracy with him. Stowers was tried and convicted. Rush was released after a mistrial, and the governor of Tennessee refused to grant extradition on Armistead.[26] Longino was charged with trying to protect the confederates but denied the charge.

Six months after the Stowers scandal, a forgery was discovered in the office of the new treasurer, G. W. Carlisle. A bill which had passed the legislature and been enrolled had had three words added to it while it was in custody of the treasurer's office. The addition created a liability of thousands of dollars against the state in favor of heirs of the Weineman estate. Everyone connected with the treasurer's office denied committing the forgery and the guilty person was never ascertained.[27]

Exposure of these frauds, one coming so close upon the other, caused a reaction against the old crowd of politicians who had been running the state. Criticism did not centralize on any particular figure. McLaurin was recognized as the political "boss" of the state, but no one linked him directly with the crimes. Likewise Longino was linked in most minds with the McLaurin "machine," and it was members of his administration about whom the charges centered. But Longino enjoyed an excellent reputation for honesty, and no one charged him with direct complicity in the frauds, although it was believed by some that he was not as diligent as he might be in pursuing the wicked. Rather the reaction was against an intangible "old crowd," who it was thought had run the state too long and to their own personal advantage. It was argued that new blood was needed. The people were ready for a new leader with a new program.

26Vicksburg *Herald*, July 2, 10, 1902; Macon *Beacon*, July 12, 19, 1902; Jackson *Clarion-Ledger*, July 10, 1902.
27Vicksburg *Herald*, Feb. 26, 1903; Jackson *Clarion-Ledger*, Feb. 25, 28, 1903.

CHAPTER XIII

THE FIRST PRIMARY ELECTION

THE NEW leader was James K. Vardaman, editor of the Greenwood *Commonwealth*. He was no newcomer to state politics, having served two terms in the state legislature and having twice attempted to win the Democratic nomination for governor. Both times he had failed—once defeated by McLaurin himself, the second time by Longino with McLaurin's backing.[1] These defeats, however, were at the hands of the convention bosses. He had never had a chance to carry his cause to the people. The passage of the primary law in 1902 gave him this chance.

Vardaman always claimed to be "a scholar of George" and a "friend of the people."[2] He had belonged to the Barksdale-Burkitt wing of the party in the late 1880's and early 1890's. He was a champion of the farmer against the "predatory" corporate interests, but like Barksdale he refused to leave the party to gain his ends. He had always advocated, however, the reforms embodied in the Populist program. Money interests, he believed, ruled the world for their own selfish ends. Banks and railroads he saw as locusts, devouring the farmer by their usurious rates and exorbitant tariffs. He would curb the one by a reduction of the interest rate. For the other he advocated commissions, both state and federal, co-operating in the regulation of all railroad activities. The only alternative he saw to such regulation was government ownership. "When competition is no more," he said, "then the strong arm of the government will be invoked, and government ownership will follow." Such ownership would not come in a vindictive spirit, but "in a spirit of self preservation." Throughout the world "the wealth producers are growing restless and weary carrying the burden of the nations." Wealth, on the other hand, was "conscienceless and insatiate. It never gets enough . . . and knows not the correcting pangs of remorse." Trusts, if left unhindered, would themselves be "the evangelist[s] who will ultimately convert the world to communism."[3]

[1] Walter Sillers to A. J. McLaurin, Feb. 9, 1897, Letters of Governors, Series E, 110.

[2] Greenwood *Commonwealth*, Mar. 17, 1899.

[3] *Ibid.*, Feb. 18, 1898, Mar. 17, 1899.

There was nothing new about this program in Mississippi. It had been advocated by Barksdale, Burkitt, and many of the Independents. But Vardaman, with his "majestic stature, his massive head, his long black hair, his deep brown intelligent eyes,"[4] and immaculate white suit, must have somehow given it a different ring.

There was, however, something new in Vardaman's program—his blunt attack on the Negro problem. Studying the deplorable condition of Mississippi's school system, he came to the simple and logical conclusion that there were too many people to educate and not enough money to go around. Under the law as it stood, the bulk of the school funds, he reasoned, went to the thickly settled Delta counties. Those counties had "plenty of schools—well paid teachers." In the sparsely settled hill counties where the whites predominated, there were "only a few schools—poorly paid teachers." The result of this, he thought, was that the Negro children were getting educated while the whites were not. At the same time, he said, the Negroes were paying less than 5 per cent of school funds. This led him to advocate division of the funds, not according to school attendance, but on the more extreme basis of division between the races according to the amounts paid by each. "I am making my campaign almost entirely on that issue," he announced in 1899.[5]

If the Negro were situated in a land of his own where government would devolve upon him, Vardaman said he would favor compulsory education. Situated as he was, however, he could see nothing but harm resulting from it.[6] No white man in Mississippi, he asserted in 1897, was willing for the Negro to reach a higher social, economic, or political plane than he then enjoyed. The state was ostensibly paying half a million dollars a year for the Negro's education in order to fit him for the "higher duties of citizenship." But, said Vardaman, when several millions would have been spent, the Negro taught to read and write, and he should then offer to vote, he would not be permitted to do so. "His vote will be either cast aside or Sambo will vote as directed by the white folks." "There is no use multiplying words about it," he said, "the negro . . . will not be

[4]Henry V. Watkins, Address, May 17, 1936, presenting to Mississippi Hall of Fame a portrait of James K. Vardaman, Mississippi Department of Archives and History.

[5]Greenwood *Commonwealth*, June 30, 1899.

[6]*Ibid.*, July 25, 1897.

permitted to rise above the station which he now fills." The question of Negroes voting was not solely a question of fitness, "but rather a matter of race prejudice—as deep-seated and ineradicable as the Anglo-Saxon genius for self-government." Prejudice, he thought, increased in proportion to the Negro's education. Under such conditions, would all the money which was being spent on the Negro's education improve him, "make him a better, happier, and more useful citizen?" On the contrary, it would only make him dissatisfied. Therefore, he argued, "we cannot avoid the conclusion" that all the money spent for Negro education is "a positive unkindness" to him. "It simply renders him unfit for the work which the white man has prescribed, and which he will be forced to perform."[7]

The Negro was receiving only a small portion of the money that was going to the black counties for his education. Everyone knew it and, after Vardaman raised the issue, many defended the practice. Nor did such education as he was getting seem to improve the Negro's economic and social status. As one editor wrote in 1890, "if every colored man in Mississippi were a graduate of Yale college, the two races would remain just as widely separated as they are now in all political and social matters."[8] This probably expressed the attitude of a vast majority of the white men in Mississippi.

But Vardaman did not stop with this calm and comparatively mild statement of his position. He launched into an impassioned attack upon the entire black race. The Negro, he said, was a curse to the country and had cost it more than "all the wars it has waged, added to the ruin wrought by flood and fire." He was an industrial stumbling block, a political ulcer, a social scab, " a lazy, lying, lustful animal which no conceivable amount of training can transform into a tolerable citizen." His nature, said Vardaman, was unlike the white man's but "resembles the hog's." He exaggerated the Negro's lust for white women and said the only way to curb it was by counterviolence. The statute punishing rape by death, he said, was "impuissant" without a "six-shooter." He would not be deterred if lynch law occasionally resulted in the punishment of an innocent Negro. "We would be justified," he said, "in slaughtering every Ethiop on the earth to preserve unsullied the honor of one Caucasian

[7]Ibid., July 1, 1897.
[8]Charleston News and Courier, quoted in Jackson Daily Clarion-Ledger, Oct. 18, 1890.

home." After all, the Negro was a predatory animal. "We do not stop when we see a wolf," he said, "to find if it will kill sheep before disposing of it, but assume that it will." He admitted that this was cruel. But, he said, "I am . . . writing . . . to present the cold truth however cruel it may be."[9]

Vardaman admitted that there were some good Negroes. It would be unfortunate if in ridding the land of the bad Negroes the good should suffer. But "the good are few, the bad are many, and it is impossible to tell what ones are . . . dangerous to the honor of the dominant race until the damage is done." Vardaman denied that there was anything personal or vindictive in his attitude toward the Negro. There was no one, he said, who had kindlier feelings for the Negro than he. He wished him well and wanted to see him prosper and grow better. He was simply opposed to "doing that which dissatifies him and then killing him if he undertakes to enjoy the prerogatives of citizenship." The only way for the Negro to prosper was "to avoid politics and maintain the relation which he now occupies to the white folks." Vardaman admitted that the Negro's position was full of pathos and that he was the victim of circumstances over which he had no control. He was here because of the white man's cupidity and had the right to expect "such treatment as will best promote his moral and material interest."[10]

Such were the views of Vardaman on the race question. In all his political career he did not deviate from them. For three decades he campaigned for political office in Mississippi, and in every speech in every campaign he played upon the same theme. Much has been said in condemnation of him. It was merited, for doubtless his impassioned appeals emphasized, if they did not increase, the tension and bitter feeling that existed between the Negro and those whites at the bottom of the economic and social orders. Something, however, might be said in amelioration, if not in defense, of Vardaman's views. As might be expected from the Negro's depressed condition, he was responsible for an overwhelming majority of crimes in Mississippi, and the number of criminals had more than tripled in the past two decades. Moreover, this increase was in crime against the

[9]Greenwood *Commonwealth*, July 15, 25, 27, Aug. 26, 1897, Mar. 29, Dec. 6, 1901.
[10]*Ibid.*, Mar. 29, Dec. 6, 1901.

person. Negro crime against property was on the decline.[11] Furthermore, no white man in public life in Mississippi proposed doing anything constructive for the Negro. All were as determined as Vardaman that he should remain in his lowly place.

As the election of 1903 approached, the various leaders began aligning themselves with the different candidates. Governor Longino announced that he would contest the re-election of H. D. Money to the United States Senate. A coolness had developed between Longino and McLaurin in the early years of Longino's administration, but as the election approached there were convincing signs of "hatchet-burying" between them.[12] There were four candidates for governor—Vardaman, Frank A. Critz, A. Fuller Fox, and Edmund F. Noel, author of the primary law. The combinations which they were attempting to make with the senatorial candidates, Longino and Money, were complicating the system of alliances. Several months before the primary one editor announced that there was "no alignment on the gubernatorial and senatorial question, and none is possible under present circumstances." Too many supporters of the gubernatorial candidates were divided in their choice for senator and vice versa. This editor could see nothing but a "mixup and blending of incongruous and inharmonious elements, a uniting of forces in many instances on common ground that has caused surprise."[13]

Vardaman and Money were cousins and had always been political allies. Congressman J. S. Doxey was a Vardaman supporter, but he disliked Money, and besides he was friendly to McLaurin who was backing Longino. Congressman John Sharp Williams disapproved of Vardaman's "radical" views, but he had to support Money because he "is the most competent and best informed Mississippian in the public service today." Longino would have preferred Fox among the gubernatorial candidates, but McLaurin had made commitments to Critz.[14]

Some of the newspapers were in like predicament. The Vicksburg *Herald* was a champion of railroads and objected to any form

[11]Noble, *Forty Years*, 124-25.

[12]Jackson *Clarion-Ledger*, Mar. 2, June 3, 1901, May 15, 1902.

[13]*Ibid.*, Apr. 2, 1903.

[14]*Ibid.*, Mar. 30, 1903; Natchez *Democrat*, July 5, 9, 1903; Vicksburg *Herald*, July 3, Aug. 16, 1903.

of regulatory legislation. Yet, it said, it had to support Vardaman "for his unquestioned political integrity, and the manly candor of his position on all public questions." The *Herald* was also an inveterate enemy of the McLaurin machine, and its backing of Vardaman was likely due as much to "his antagonism to the shabby hybrid state political machine" as to his "political integrity" and his "manly candor." Even Vardaman's "unsound views on the negro" did not lose him Editor McNeily's strong support. Vardaman was also supported by other McLaurin opponents, including "Private" John Allen and the old Delta crowd—Charles Scott, Leroy Percy, and Murray Smith. None of these, it was said by a neutral editor, subscribed to his platform. They were merely trying to hit at McLaurin and Longino, who were supporting Critz.[15]

Such was the confusion in the alignment of Mississippi political leaders on the eve of the first state-wide primary. Despite the number of prominent men who for one reason or another were supporting Money and Vardaman, the preponderance of influence seemed to be with Longino and Critz. They had the backing of the McLaurin "machine," and that organization had rolled smoothly over all opposition for almost a decade. As to how much the primary was to change the former influences, few seemed to suspect. Neither McLaurin nor Vardaman had been enthusiastic advocates of a primary in 1895 or in 1899.[16] Even now the Vicksburg *Herald*, perhaps Vardaman's most enthusiastic supporter, was dubious as to its merits. It predicted that after a few years it would be discarded and replaced by the old nominating convention. Five months later, after both its candidates had won, it was converted. "As a tutelage in the exercise of the right and the trust of self-government," it said, "the primary is unequalled."[17]

In the spring of 1903 the farmers of the state, busy with the spring plowing, were reported to be paying little attention to the campaign. Candidates in some counties were unable to gain audiences in their house-to-house canvasses.[18] But with the swinging of the big guns into action they awoke from their lethargy. Vardaman

15Vicksburg *Herald*, spring and summer of 1903, especially June 6; Jackson *Clarion-Ledger*, Aug. 27, 1903.

16New Orleans *Times-Picayune*, quoted in Jackson *Clarion-Ledger*, Jan. 10, 1895; *ibid.*, June 5, 1899.

17Vicksburg *Herald*, Aug. 28, 1903, Jan. 20, 1904.

18Macon *Beacon*, Mar. 21, 1903.

was again making the race question and the school funds the issues. He argued that the current method of dividing school funds was working an injustice on the mass of white children in the state for the benefit of a few. Such of the funds as were spent for Negro education he considered worse than useless. "We spent $150,000 [in 1890] disfranchising the negro," he said, "and $6,000,000 since to bring him back to the polls." Negro education would thus tend to defeat the purposes of the constitutional convention of 1890, the franchise clauses of which all white Mississipians still extolled.[19]

Vardaman's argument was attacked by all the other gubernatorial candidates. Noel lumped the poll tax with the ad valorem tax and showed that the black counties paid more into the state treasury than they received while some of the white counties received more than they paid. This was due to higher assessments in general in the black counties, and this was not denied. But it still did not dispose of Vardaman's argument. Nor did Noel attempt to. Proper schools for white children in black counties could be maintained, he said, only "by so dividing the money . . . as to give very little of it to the negro schools, through low salaries and numerous pupils to a teacher." He did not explain how counties without large Negro populations could maintain "proper schools." He scoffed at Vardaman's contention that too much was being squandered on Negro education to the neglect of white children. "White officials," he said, "chosen by white people, regulate the number and size of the districts for negro schools . . . and . . . they can give the negro only such a part of their school fund as may be just and right."[20]

Much the same stand on the race question was taken by Critz and Fox. Fox claimed to have "a rational intellectual platform on the Negro educational issue." He attacked Vardaman's plan as likely to destroy the good relationship of the races established by the wisdom of Senator George. "Under the present system," he said, "we [select] their teachers, [make] our own contracts with them, [and prescribe] the textbooks studied." Under such conditions talk of education as raising a threat to white supremacy was absurd. Fox won the approval of many conservatives. He was backed by many

[19]Speech at Winona, Apr. 6, 1903, quoted in Jackson Clarion-Ledger, Apr. 9, 1903; Macon Beacon, Jan. 31, 1903.

[20]Macon Beacon, Feb. 14, 1903; Jackson Clarion-Ledger, Apr. 9, 1903.

of the influential political personalities of the state and by the leading daily paper, the *Clarion*. A wave of racial hatred arising out of an incident at Indianola in the Delta, however, inundated his "rational" policy, and shortly thereafter he withdrew from the contest.[21]

Critz, who inherited most of Fox's following, had as little feeling for the Negro's plight as did the others, including Vardaman. He sympathized with Vardaman's plan for abolishing Negro education but thought it was both unnecessary and unconstitutional. Besides, it would drive hundreds of Negro laborers from the state. He favored, he said, repeal of both the Fourteenth and Fifteenth amendments to the federal Constitution, but he feared that if Negro schools were not preserved, the federal government might require that Negroes be admitted to white schools. On the corporation question, both Noel and Critz favored "inducements" and a "liberal policy" toward corporate interests, while Vardaman opposed any such policy.[22]

Critz was accused by Vardaman's supporters of using large sums of money in the campaign. Critz emphatically denied the charge, but the Meridian *Press,* which was supporting him, admitted that Critz was paying his canvassers $125 a month. The *Press* defended this as the "pay as you go plan" and thought it much superior to the "deferred payment plan," wherein offices were promised.[23]

The charge was frequently made that Vardaman was not genuinely sincere in his stand on the Negro question. His former legislative record was exhumed and examined to discover inconsistencies. It was shown that as chairman of the Appropriations Committee of the House of Representatives in 1892 he had reported favorably and voted for the appropriation for the Negro Agriculture and Mechanical College.[24] Again in 1894 as speaker he had voted for the appropriation and had also voted for the appropriation for the Negro State Normal School at Holly Springs.[25] Because of his position as chairman of the Appropriations Committee and later as speaker he had had unusual influence in shaping legislation and appropriating money. Because he had not blocked such appropriations it was

21Jackson *Clarion-Ledger,* Apr. 2, 30, 1903.

22*Ibid.,* Apr. 9, 30, 1903.

23Vicksburg *Herald,* June 14, 18, 1903; *ibid.,* quoting Meridian *Press;* Natchez *Democrat,* July 9, 1903; *ibid.,* quoting New Orleans *States.*

24Mississippi, *House Journal,* 1892, p. 758; Natchez *Democrat,* June 30, 1903.

25Mississippi, *House Journal,* 1894, pp. 247, 345; Natchez *Democrat,* June 30, 1903.

charged that he was now "exploiting a bubble . . . to attract that class of voters . . . who are ready to adopt any ism which satisfies their petty prejudices against the weaker class."[26]

Thus the question of Vardaman's intellectual and political honesty was raised early in his career. In succeeding campaigns it was to be raised again and again. Vardaman was accused by his enemies of demagogy. He denied it. One might reach any conclusion on the question according to one's inclination. Certainly nothing can be said in defense of Vardaman's vicious diatribes against the Negro.

But if there is question as to Vardaman's sincerity, there can be none as to his opponents'. Critz, Noel, and Fox by their own admissions had no concern with efforts to improve the Negro's condition. Admitting sympathy in principle with Vardaman's objective, they argued for a pretense of Negro education on the ground of expediency. They feared federal intervention if discrimination were openly and flagrantly practiced. That and danger of disrupting the labor market formed the burden of their protest against Vardaman's scheme.

Had Vardaman restrained himself in the campaign to a calm and dispassionate discussion of the "folly" of Negro education he might well have escaped the charge of demagoguery. Such a position, while not an enlightened or liberal one, might well, under the circumstances, be stamped with sincerity. But he did not so restrain himself. Carried away by the force of his own oratory, or shrewdly calculating the effect of his words on his audience, one knows not which, he launched into a defense of lynching. "If I were the sheriff," he said, "and a negro fiend fell into my hands, I would run him out of the county. If I were governor and were asked for troops to protect him I would send them. But if I were a private citizen I would head the mob to string the brute up."[27] The Vicksburg *Herald*, which a few months before had termed Vardaman's position on the Negro question "unsound" and was to do so again within a few years, praised his "courage" for making the statement and dared Noel and Critz to challenge it.[28] Neither of them did.

Vardaman could not find language too strong nor too indelicate to use in condemning President Theodore Roosevelt's appointment

[26]Natchez *Democrat*, June 30, 1903.
[27]Jackson *Clarion-Ledger*, July 30, 1903; Vicksburg *Herald*, June 30, 1903.
[28]Vicksburg *Herald*, June 30, 1903.

of Negro officeholders in Mississippi. One particular incident provoked such an outburst. "It is said that men follow the bent of their genius," he said, "and that prenatal influences are often potent in shaping thoughts and ideas of after life. Probably old lady Roosevelt, during the period of gestation, was frightened by a dog and that fact may account for the qualities of the male pup which are so prominent in Teddy." He did not wish, he said, to do either an injustice, "but I am disposed to apologize to the dog for mentioning it."[29] The anti-Vardaman press professed to be shocked by the remark. The Natchez *Democrat* thought it "beyond the pale of human conception" that any one could vote for Vardaman after reading it. The Jackson *Evening News* played up the southern origin of Roosevelt's mother and apologized to the country for the insult. The Meridian *News* thought the remark "inexcusable," which it was.[30]

The urban press was almost unanimous in its condemnation of Vardaman's program. Its opposition had the same utilitarian flavor expressed by Critz and Noel. The Biloxi *Herald* regarded Vardaman as "the most dangerous man that ever aspired to the governorship of Mississippi." It was unwise, the editor thought, to excite irrational prejudice against the Negro farm laborer. "Anything that disturbs this labor disturbs values and begets stagnation."[31] "Every white farmer knows," said the Hazelhurst *Courier*, "that negro labor is the best that can be had." Vardaman's agitation, it feared, was calculated to disorganize this labor "who are [now] docile and contented." Then the farms in both the hills and the Delta would be abandoned and land values would drop and taxation would begin to increase.[32]

Vardaman's opponents derided his warning that the state was threatened with "mongrelization." "What home is threatened," asked the Natchez *Democrat*, "with social equality with the negro? Let every voter ask himself, is the negro obtaining social equality at his home?" All this "hubbub" was "something conjured up by its

<hr/>

[29]Affidavits charged that the quotation was published in Vardaman's paper, the Greenwood *Commonwealth*, Jan. 10, 1903. See Jackson *Clarion-Ledger*, Aug. 27, 1903.

[30]Jackson *Evening News*, July 27, 1903; Natchez *Democrat*, Aug. 1, 1903; and *ibid.*, quoting Meridian *Press*.

[31]Biloxi *Herald*, quoted in Natchez *Democrat*, June 16, 1903.

[32]Hazelhurst *Courier*, quoted, *ibid.*, May 17, 1903.

agitator upon which to ride into office."[33] Bishop Charles B. Galloway, an eminent Methodist, joined in the attack. He canvassed the
state in an effort to discredit Vardaman. "With every executive,
judicial and legislative office of the state in the hands of the white
people," he said, "and with suffrage qualifications that have practically eliminated the negro from political affairs, the old slogan
[of Negro domination] is the emptiest of cant."[34]

There were reports that several papers which had begun the
campaign supporting Vardaman and Money were "cooling off"
because of the racial issue. By late June the Hattiesburg *Progress*
had turned completely over and was predicting defeat for both
Money and Vardaman. The *Progress* attributed this to "Vardaman's
negro issue" which had pulled him down, and "he has pulled down
Mr. Money along with him." The Vicksburg *American* and the Jackson *News* were also reported to have left Vardaman-Money ranks.[35]

If the editors were leaving Vardaman, the people did not seem to
be doing so. Great and enthusiastic crowds were flocking to hear
him speak. This was admitted by his enemies, but it did not seem to
give them much concern. The crowds were made up, they said, of
poor whites who were "disqualified [from voting] by the same clause
which disqualifies the negro."[36] Let the rabble howl its head off.
Only votes would count in the end.

The Vicksburg *Herald* was one of the few urban papers to support Vardaman throughout the campaign. Its editor, J. S. McNeily,
himself a member of the franchise committee of the 1890 convention,
said the plan of dividing school funds between the races according
to the amounts each paid barely escaped adoption in the convention.
According to him, S. S. Calhoon, W. T. Martin, Anselm McLaurin,
and many other conservatives voted for it. The *Herald* denied that
recent outrages against Negroes were caused by Vardaman's incendiary speeches. Rather were they due to Governor Longino's failure
to take action to check them. It quoted from a Chicago paper showing that Mississippi had had six Negro lynchings during Longino's

[33]Natchez *Democrat*, July 14, 1903.

[34]Charles B. Galloway, *Great Men and Great Movements* (Nashville, 1914), 127.

[35]Natchez *Democrat*, May 14, June 16, 20, 1903; *ibid.*, quoting Meridian *Press*,
Hazelhurst *Courier*, Biloxi *Herald*, and Hattiesburg *Progress*.

[36]Natchez *Democrat*, July 2, 1903; *ibid.*, quoting Biloxi *Herald*.

administration, none of which evoked one word of condemnation from the governor.[37]

Under the new primary law a candidate who obtained a plurality of votes in any county was entitled to the electoral vote of that county. If he could get a majority of electoral votes, even by a plurality of popular votes, he would win the nomination. Thus, with three or more candidates in the field, it was theoretically possible for a candidate to win the nomination without receiving a majority vote in any county. The possibility of this was foreseen by the candidates and figured in their plans. Critz and Noel feared that Vardaman might win the nomination in this way, and they made an arrangement to prevent it. Vardaman's committee in Hinds County got hold of and published a letter from Critz's headquarters urging Critz supporters in Hinds to throw their votes to Noel there in order to keep Vardaman from carrying the county's electoral vote by plurality.[38]

Although Vardaman received a plurality of the total state vote, he did not have a majority of either popular or electoral votes, and a second primary was necessary. Noel, the low man of the three, was eliminated.[39]

The racial issue was carried into the senatorial campaign. Longino was endorsed by most of the Negro politicians of the state, and he also had, as governor, more pleasant relations with President Roosevelt than his opponents deemed proper. His brother-in-law, Edgar S. Wilson, was a Republican, and Roosevelt had appointed him referee in bankruptcy for Mississippi. During Longino's administration a controversy arose over the post office at Indianola, a small settlement in the Delta. Roosevelt had appointed a Negro woman postmistress there, and the residents had boycotted the office, refusing to accept their mail from her. Finally the federal government had closed the office, and the residents were put to the inconvenience of journeying a dozen or so miles to a neighboring village for their mail. As a result of all this, Longino and McLaurin were charged with

[37]Vicksburg *Herald*, June 27, July 1, 31, 1903; *ibid.,* quoting Chicago *Inter-Ocean.*

[38]Vicksburg *Herald,* July 30, 1903; Natchez *Democrat,* Aug. 1, 1903; Macon *Beacon,* Aug. 8, 1903.

[39]*Biennial Report of the Secretary of State to the Legislature, October 1, 1901 to October 1, 1903* (Nashville, 1904), 119-20.

attempting to found a white man's Republican party, based on Negro suffrage. Longino was accused of appointing Negroes to office, and a circular charged that he had Negro blood in his veins. Longino ignored the latter charge but admitted appointing certain Negroes notaries public. He explained, however, that in all cases they were recommended by "representative citizens" and that he did not find out they were Negroes until after he had made the appointments. He refused to admit that the racial question was an issue and said he would not appeal to race prejudice to obtain office. The Negro's status, he said, had been settled by the constitution, the constitution had been sustained by the courts, and the Negro had acquiesced in the settlement.[40]

Longino did not abide by his promise to avoid appeals to race prejudice but later, in a speech at Natchez, taunted Senator Money with having voted for confirmation of Negro appointees in Mississippi. He quoted a press report of a Senate speech in which Money was alleged to have said that he had never voted against the nomination of anybody, white or black, for any office in any state. Money denied having made the statement and a week later produced the *Congressional Record* for the date in question. The *Record* quoted him as saying that "if every colored man in the South twenty-one years of age had been graduated from the finest university in Europe or America he would not be fit for the obligation or duties of American citizenship."[41]

The old charge which Barksdale had made against Money a dozen years before was revived. He was accused of having accepted, while chairman of the House Committee on Post Offices and Post-Roads, a gift of $60,000 from the Pan-Electric Telephone Company to "persuade" Congress to invalidate the Bell patent. Money again admitted receiving the "loan" but denied that it was a bribe.[42] The Money faction countered with the charge that judges appointed by McLaurin and Longino were openly campaigning for Longino and Critz and cited this as evidence of the need for an elective judiciary.

[40]Vicksburg *Golden Rule*, Jan. 27, 1900; Vicksburg *Herald*, July 22, 30, 1903; Jackson *Clarion-Ledger*, Apr. 16, 25, 1901, Apr. 16, May 21, July 16, 1903.

[41]Natchez *Democrat*, June 24, 30, 1903.

[42]Vicksburg *Herald*, July 22, 1903; Hattiesburg *Progress*, quoted in Jackson *Clarion-Ledger*, July 30, 1903.

The present system, it said, was dragging the bench down into the lowest depths of political corruption.[43]

Longino lauded his administration for building and paying for the new $1,000,000 state capitol and in addition for retiring $400,000 of state bonds.[44]

A pusillanimous effort was made to raise class feeling against Money. He had had a controversy with a streetcar conductor in Washington over the payment of his fare, and Longino's friends used this as proof that "his sympathy is not with the laboring people." They called upon all workers to oppose him because of his caning of the "poor street car conductor, who was simply doing his duty—collecting the fare from the rich and poor alike."[45]

In answer to the opposition's charges of ring control, the McLaurin-Longino faction exposed alleged plans of the Money-Vardaman crowd. Money was Vardaman's cousin and the father-in-law of Congressman Hill, who was supporting them both. Hill's law partner, Session, was a candidate for district-attorney. "With Money re-elected to the . . . Senate, Hill in Congress, Session district-attorney, and Vardaman Governor," said the Delta *Democrat*, "there would be an oligarchy 'to beat the band'." But this was not all. Vardaman and Money planned, it said, "that Hill is to succeed Vardaman as Governor and that Vardaman is to succeed Money as Senator and that Session is to succeed Hill in Congress."[46]

Money received a majority of the votes cast for senator in the first primary[47] and thus did not have to enter the second primary.

Those who had expected the primary to prevent trading in the old convention style were disappointed. "It is a matter of record," said the Natchez *Democrat*, "that constableships and other minor offices had been traded for governorship and senatorial votes." The *Democrat* did not condemn the practice, for it had "been done openly and above board."[48]

In the second gubernatorial canvass, that between Vardaman and Critz, the air was filled with "rumors . . . of combinations and deals

---

[43]Vicksburg *Herald*, spring and summer, 1903; *Sea Coast Beacon*, quoted, *ibid.*, July 14, 1903.

[44]Macon *Beacon*, July 18, Aug. 1, 1903.

[45]McComb City *Enterprise*, quoted in Natchez *Democrat*, July 2, 1903.

[46]Delta *Democrat*, quoted in Natchez *Democrat*, June 9, 1903.

[47]*Report of Secretary of State, 1901-1903*, pp. 119-20.

[48]Natchez *Democrat*, Aug. 7, 1903.

of all sorts and kinds." There was a sensational rumor, shortly after the first primary, that Noel's forces had gone over to Vardaman "horse, foot, and dragoon," but this was denied by Noel and discredited by Critz. "My vote shall go," said Noel, "to the candidate who best represents conservatism and who would be least willing to tear down the racial safeguards of our present constitution." Vardaman's plurality over Critz in the first primary had been only four thousand and was almost twenty thousand short of a majority. If Noel could swing three-fourths of his following to Critz, Vardaman would be defeated. The Critz forces were confident that this could be done.[49]

Vardaman's hopes rested on the chance that Noel and Longino, who had been defeated by Money, could not swing their supporters to Critz. On the other hand, the Critz people claimed that Vardaman was the issue in the first primary and had then polled all his possible votes. Their candidate had Longino's and McLaurin's support in the first primary, and they proposed to keep it. McLaurin had again announced for Critz, but Longino was maintaining an unexplained silence. Still, Critz's backers were confident he would come around and with Noel's forces, which were really voting against Vardaman rather than for Noel in the first primary, throw the balance in Critz's favor.[50]

One daily paper, the Vicksburg *Herald,* and most of the weeklies backed Vardaman. The Natchez *Democrat,* Greenville *Democrat,* Meridian *Press,* Vicksburg *American,* Holly Springs *South,* and West Point *Leader* supported Critz. The *Clarion,* which found it difficult to choose between Noel and Critz after its own candidate, Fox, had withdrawn from the first canvass, now took off its wraps and went to work for Critz.[51]

According to the *Clarion* it was a struggle between the radical and conservative elements of the state. It made urgent appeals to Noel's following to back Critz solidly. In the first primary the anti-Vardaman forces had been divided. If they now united, as the in-

[49]*Ibid.,* Aug. 4, 9, 11, 12, 16, 1903; Macon *Beacon,* Aug. 15, 1903; Jackson *Clarion-Ledger,* June 25, Aug. 13, 20, 1903; *ibid.,* June 25, 1903, quoting Meridian *Press* and Yazoo City *Herald.*

[50]Natchez *Democrat,* Aug. 4, 11, 16, 1903; Macon *Beacon,* Aug. 13, 1903; Jackson *Clarion-Ledger,* Aug. 20, 1903.

[51]Jackson *Clarion-Ledger,* Aug. 13, 20, 1903.

exorable logic of the situation called for them to do, the conservative cause would triumph. Editor R. H. Henry urged every friend and advocate of safe, conservative government to bestir himself. "See that the voters are organized in every county, district, and election precinct," he said, "and that on election day they cast their ballots for Judge Critz." Critz, he said, stood for the conservative business element of the state. Unlike Vardaman, he was a gallant old Confederate soldier and would make a model governor.[52]

The Vardaman press denied that the struggle was one between conservatism and radicalism. "No fallacy could be more palpable," said the Vicksburg *Herald,* "than that conservatism is for Critz, while radicalism is for Vardaman." It pointed out that Vardaman had the support of wealthy planters such as Charles Scott in Bolivar County and Leroy Percy in Washington and that Vardaman had carried both those conservative counties in the first primary. It condemned the inconsistency of Critz's position on the Negro, who was already eliminated from Mississippi politics. "Judge Critz," it said, "is no more disposed to change this state of affairs than would be Major Vardaman."[53]

The *Clarion* answered with a denunciation of the extreme and increasing appeals to race prejudice made by Vardaman. It expressed fear that Negroes would move out of the state, leaving the Delta plantations and the lumber districts of south Mississippi without an adequate labor supply. Like its candidate, it urged no change in the Negro's status. On the contrary it exulted over the fact that the Negro was so repressed that Vardaman's program was unnecessary. The Negro, it said, was practically excluded from the ballot box and the jury box; he was separated from the whites at hotels, theaters, and all public conveyances; and he was given only "a small proportion of the school funds, less than what he pays himself, and even this is administered by the whites."[54] Not one word of disapproval had the *Clarion* or any other anti-Vardaman paper for such conditions. Instead of joining issue with Vardaman and demanding more money for Negro education, they contented themselves with calling Vardaman "demagogue" because he argued that spending

[52]*Ibid.,* Aug. 13, 20, 1903; *ibid.,* quoting New Orleans *Times-Democrat.*

[53]Vicksburg *Herald,* Aug. 14, 15, 1903; *ibid.,* quoting Memphis *Commercial Appeal.*

[54]Jackson *Clarion-Ledger,* Aug. 20, 1903.

money for Negro education in Mississippi was useless and harmful.

Certain Negro leaders added fuel to Vardaman's fire by foolishly addressing circulars to members of their race urging them to "call on some white friend, in a nice and polite way, and ask him to vote for Judge Critz." The Vicksburg *Herald* rather incongruously branded this as an attempt at intimidation of the white voter by the Negro. Word was spread that Negroes were for Critz and had agreed that "now is the time for us to act." This was viewed by the Natchez *Democrat* as a very smooth scheme of Vardaman's to garner more votes. "What act is the negro expected to perform," it asked, "in an election for the nomination of the Democratic candidate for Governor?" A report also was spread by the Vardaman camp that President Roosevelt, who was not popular in Mississippi, had said he would give a year's salary to defeat "that man Vardaman down in Mississippi."[55]

On the eve of the election the *Clarion* suddenly realized that many extraneous issues had been lugged into the campaign that had no business there. "The negro, Roosevelt, his southern appointees, imaginery rings, etc., have been called upon to do service, and they have been used to great advantage." A half-dozen years later it felt that these "extraneous issues" were the deciding factor in the result. They stirred up feeling, it said, "appealing . . . to the passion, prejudice, and ignorance of man."[56]

The election was a victory for Vardaman. It was generally agreed by the opposition that his election was due to the revival of the white supremacy question. Critz thought that it was, although he denied that such an issue actually existed between him and Vardaman. "Everybody knows," he said, "that I believe in the divine right of the white man to rule, to do all the voting, and to hold all the offices, both state and federal."[57] Others thought that "things supposed to have been said and done by President Roosevelt" had influenced the result.[58]

What does seem obvious is that the primary itself was the new factor in Mississippi politics and in this election. Previous nominations had been won by wirepulling within the party hierarchy. Can-

---

[55]Vicksburg *Herald*, Aug. 25, 1903; Natchez *Democrat*, Aug. 20, 25, 1903.
[56]Jackson *Clarion-Ledger*, Sept. 3, 1903, Mar. 17, 1910.
[57]*Ibid.*, Sept. 10, 1903.
[58]*Review of Reviews*, editorial, XXVIII (1903), 403.

didates had, as a rule, to follow the dictates of the party chieftains, and the best manipulator generally won. Vardaman seems not to have been adept at that art. He had failed twice to win the nomination from the convention, and it was almost assured that he would have lost it under such a system in 1903. But it was a different story when he got before an audience of ordinary men. His magnetism and his oratory drew them to his support. While his opponents were addressing their hundreds, he was speaking to thousands at county fairs and church festivals. Even in the opposition stronghold, Jackson, his audiences were said to be greater than the combined audiences of his opponents. It may have been that the racial issue drew some of his hearers, but more likely they came because he made them feel that he was one of them. He was simply a better actor and gave a better show than his adversaries.

One other factor in the election was indicated by the returns. The Populist party had been strongest in the rural areas and weakest in the cities. In the election of 1903, and in all later ones in which he was a candidate, Vardaman's strongest support came from the country districts. Moreover, he carried most of the counties where the Populists had been strongest a decade before.[59] The fact that the Populists instead of being hostile to Negro suffrage had encouraged it makes it difficult to explain Vardaman's election as a result merely of the anti-Negro portion of his platform. Perhaps his social reform program had as much to do with it.

[59]McCain, "The Populist Party," 144-47.

CHAPTER XIV

SOCIAL REFORM

WRITING on the eve of the election some anti-Vardaman papers admitted that they had overplayed the racial feature of Vardaman's program. "Whether Critz or Vardaman attains suzerainty today," said the Port Gibson *Reveille*, "the negroes of Mississippi are perfectly safe and assured of good government and protection." The sentiment was echoed by the Vardaman press a few days later. "The victory," they said, ". . . conveys no menace to any class or color of good citizens. Now that the election clamor is over no more will be heard of this."[1]

In his inaugural Vardaman's views on the Negro received less attention than many had expected after the radical tone of his campaign utterances. Admitting that "little can be done to relieve the present most undesirable conditions . . . while the Constitution remains as it is," he recommended that a constitutional amendment be submitted to the people vesting all control of education in the legislature. But the problem would "ultimately be settled and settled justly, protecting alike the interests of the negro and the white man." Forty years experience, he said, had proved that the Negro was unsuited for the same type of education the white man received. Literate Negroes were criminally inclined, and it was folly for the whites to tax themselves to create criminals.[2]

But a majority of the legislature was not in sympathy with Vardaman[3] and refused to act on his suggestion. When it reconvened in 1906 he repeated his former request. "It is your function," he told them, "to put a stop to the worse than wasting a half million dollars annually—money taken from the toiling white men and women of Mississippi—and devoted to the vain purpose of trying to make something of the negro which the Great Architect . . . failed to provide for in the original plan of creation." Since the supply of money was not unlimited, he said, every dollar invested for Negro education, under the present system, was an "indefensible

[1]Port Gibson *Reveille*, quoted in Vicksburg *Herald*, Sept. 1, 1903.
[2]Mississippi, *House Journal*, 1904, pp. 151-53.
[3]A. S. Coody, *Biographical Sketches of James Kimble Vardaman* (Jackson, 1922), 23.

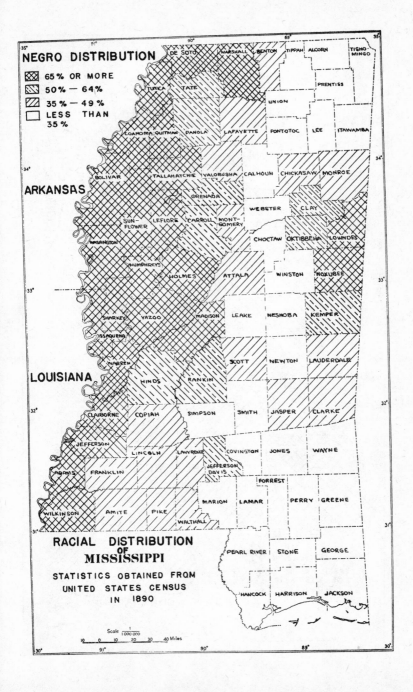

NEGRO DISTRIBUTION

⊠ 65% OR MORE
⧄ 50% — 64%
⧄ 35% — 49%
☐ LESS THAN
   35%

RACIAL DISTRIBUTION
OF
MISSISSIPPI

STATISTICS OBTAINED FROM
UNITED STATES CENSUS
IN 1890

Scale $\frac{1}{1,000,000}$

10   0   10   20   30   40 Miles

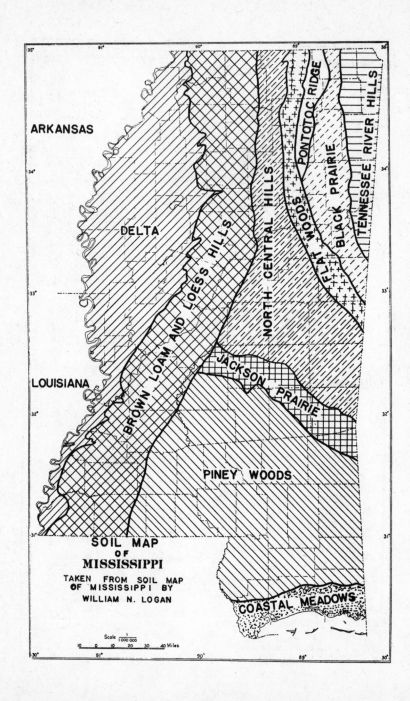

SOIL MAP
OF
MISSISSIPPI

TAKEN FROM SOIL MAP
OF MISSISSIPPI BY
WILLIAM N. LOGAN

Scale $\frac{1}{1000000}$

10 0 10 20 30   40 Miles

LUCIUS QUINTUS
CINCINNATUS LAMAR

Lamar was the patron saint and ambassador of the Mississippi Democratic Party in Washington during the so-called "Bourbon" period.

JAMES ZACHARIAH GEORGE

George was the organizing genius behind the successful political revolution in 1875-76 when the Radical government was overthrown in Mississippi.

EDWARD CARY WALTHALL

Corporation lawyer and U. S. Senator from Mississippi, Walthall was
the close friend and disciple of
Lamar.

ANSELM J. McLAURIN

Elected governor in 1895, McLaurin served also as U. S. Senator
from 1899 until his death in 1910.

JOHN SHARP WILLIAMS

A member of the Delta aristocracy,
Williams served a quarter of a
century in Congress.

The "White Chief" visits Kosciusko in the senatorial election of 1911.
James K. Vardaman is standing bare-headed in the ox-drawn wagon.

Bilbo, the People's Champion.

By W. C. Pittman.

IN EVERY period of the world's history whoever had the temerity to teach to the populace the freedom of thought and speech in politics or the Christian virtues following the free exercise of their own conscience in religious matters, has brought himself under condemnation of the aristocratic element of his time; his character maligned and blackened by character assassins, and often leading to his death by the assassin's knife or bullet. Socrates, the great Grecian philosopher, though belonging to the artitocratic element when he began teaching the moral virtues and the immortality of the soul to the populace, the sophists, who were the aristocrats and ruling element, persecuted him and eventually secured a death sentence against him. and he was forced to drink the deadly hyssop. Tiberius and Caius Gracchus were assassinated because they were political champions of the Roman plebians against the patricians. Julius Caesar excited the jealousy of the Roman senate because he was a popular idol of the people, and they had him assassinated. Martin Luther opposed the sale of indulgences and other corrupt practices in his church and was excommunicated, and only escaped death by the rivalry and jealousy of the ruling powers. John Calvin, Peter Waldo, the great French merchant prince, became a social outcast and suffered great persecution at the hands of the ruling classes because he opposed corrupt practices in the church and taught the Christian virtues to the populace. John Calvin offended the ruling classes by his austere religious views, and was forced to expatriate himself, and remained an exile in Switzerland the remainder of his life.

The early colonists of America sought a home among savages and wild beasts of the jungle that they might be permitted to worship God as their conscience dictated.

Roger Williams, assistant curate in the established church of England at Dover, Massachusetts, took the high ground that the civil authorities should not have jurisdiction in matters purely of conscience and he was ordered by the authorities to return to England, but preferred to go alone among savages; hence he settled at Providence, R. I.

When Patrick Henry defended the people against the oppressive tobacco tax fixed by the established church of Eng, land, he was characterized as a dangerous demagogue.

Sam Adams, Benjamin Franklin and Patrick Henry opposed the right of the home government to tax the colonies without representation, and advocated the rights of men above those of kings, and, for this, would have been hung for sedition if the English authorities could have laid hands upon them.

Thomas Jefferson was severely denounced by his political enemies as a demagogue and dangerous to American institutions, because he advocated a democratic government.

Abraham Lincoln was considered by the Southern people as the agent by which the institution of African slavery was destroyed, and he was assassinated. William Goebel, in his canvass for the office of Governor of Kentucky, antagonized a corrupt political machine, backed by a strong corporate influence, which led to his being assassinated. The same combination of influences brought about the death of E. W. Carmack of Tennessee. The rulers of the invisible empire have so far succeeded in keeping W. J. Bryan out of the presidency; and if Thomas Jefferson were alive in this day of corporate power and influence they would destroy him. There are very few American statesmen that have the courage to openly espouse the cause of the toiling masses against the classes. If one succeeds in running the gauntlet the agents of the invisible empire either buy him, as they did Joe Baily, or kill him, as they did E. W. Carmack.

Albert Cummins, of Iowa, and Robert Lafollette of Wisconsin, fought the big railroads and succeeded in break- and Robert Lafollette of Wisconsin, fought the big railroads and succeeded in breaking into the U. S. Senate; but they are both protectionists, consequently are only half-baked champions of the masses. Jeff Davis of Arkansas, fought his way into the U. S. Senate, but his enemies never lost his trail. There is not a chief executive of any State in the Union today, that has the temerity to stand out openly against the legislation favoring the classes that is now a part of the statute laws or is being spread upon the statute books of the different states. Many of them succeed in "fooling" the people with the kind of dope handed out by our own Earl Brewer.

James K. Vardaman is the only governor in the late history of Mississippi whose sympathies were with the masses, and stood out openly as their friend against the powers that be; and today the sleuths of this invisible power behind the throne are shadowing his every footstep; and if they could have succeeded in their efforts to get him into a series of joint debates in 1911, it would have been a miracle if he had escaped the knife or bullet at the hands of some of the bravo's that they would have placed at his heels.

Bilbo, if possible, is more intensely hated by the agencies of special interests than is Vardaman, because Bilbo laid bare their rotten political methods in the secret caucus, and since that time has been indefatigable in making other exposures and in holding up to public gaze the various traps that have been laid to ensnare him; but he has been too wary to be caught, which has intensified the malignancy of his enemies.

Brewer's proposition of forming a coalition with Bilbo was an effort to corrupt and to buy his splendid talent, which is always the first move made by the corruptionist in politics, and too often succeeds. But when Bilbo turned down this proposition, the governor began to scheme for his destruction and every failure to ensnare him has increased the activity of the character assassin, and if he could be induced to engage in a series of joint debates he would never live to finish the campaign. His enemies will repeat a slanderous statement which may be denied and proven to be untrue, but only stops long enough to reach the next willing listener when the same falsehood will be reiterated as though undeniable evidence of its correctness was too potent to be denied. It has required the greatest courage to stand out openly as a champion of the burdened tax payers as Bilbo has done. It has required the highest order of intelligence, backed by a store house of konwledge and information, to defend his position against the shrewd attorneys who are the paid agents of the community of interests which seek to exploit the people and the fruits of their toil; and it has required great astuteness of mind to correctly understand and checkmate every move of his enemies in their efforts to destroy his usefulness. As Lieutenant Governor and presiding officer of the senate he stands without a peer in the history of the State; his rulings were just and fair to those who opposed him, his great talent in constructive statesmanship always stood out brightly in the interest of the great body of the people, which fact is borne out by the Senate Journal; and were it not so, his enemies would not be pushed to the extremity of peddling falsehoods against him. He favored the antiland corporation law which will save the State from the curse of absentee landlordism. He favored the elective judiciary, and to him is due largely the credit that it is a part of our statute laws. He favored the reduction of the contract rate interest, which saves to the poor man many thousands of dollars each year.

He favored the guaranteeing of bank deposits, and the enactment of this law is due in a great measure to his constructive ability as a legislator and his power as an advocate. He favored a more equal adjustment of the burdens of taxation on the rich and the poor and succeeded in requiring, by statute, that the large land holding corporations pay taxes on their holding which had before been merely nominal. In fact, every act of his official life, so far as my association has been or my knowledge extends, has been as the unswerving friend of the common people; and during his labors in their interests he has had to wend his way through the snares that would have caught less wary feet in their toils.

These are some of the reasons why the people of the State of Mississippi are devoted to Bilbo and why they are going to elect him by an avalanche of ballots on the 3rd day of August, that will send such a shock up the spinal columns of his adversaries that they will be affected with temporary paresis, and, for a time, will paralize the corrupt machinery that is now operating against him. The people love him for the enemies he has made, using his magnificent talent in their behalf. Calumny and the assassin have been the instruments used by the favored classes against every friend and advocate of the masses, as against the classes, in every period of the world's history, whether he be priest or statesman, and the only thing that saves Bilbo from destruction, either by slander or by assassination, is the bulwark of public sentiment in the minds and hearts of an inlightened electorate, who have learned some things in duplicity and demagogy from the present administration.

In the interest of true democracy and the perpetuation of our democratic institutions let every man who loves his home and fireside go to the polls on the 3rd day of August and tell his neighbor on the way, that he's going to vote for Bilbo.

Campaign propaganda for Theodore G. Bilbo, taken from the supplement to the Winston County *Journal*, July 23, 1915.

and unwarranted prodigality of cash. It is a crime against the white man who furnishes the dollar, and a disadvantage to the negro upon whom it is spent."[4]

Vardaman was not content with the restriction placed on Negro voting by the 1890 constitution and urged outright repeal of the Fourteenth and Fifteenth amendments to the federal Constitution. The Negro, he said, was congenitally unqualified to exercise this responsible duty. He was physically, mentally, morally, racially, and eternally inferior to the white man. There was nothing in the history of his race, "nothing in his individual character, nothing in his achievements of the past nor his promise of the future" which would entitle him "to stand, side by side with the white man at the ballot box."[5]

It was charged that Vardaman's incendiary utterances were responsible for outbreaks of violence against the Negroes. During the 1903 campaign two Negroes were burned at the stake in Sunflower County, and Vardaman was accused of being an accessory, through his speeches, to the horrible deed. The Vardaman press condemned the atrocity and, after the election, pointed to the fact that the county went heavily against Vardaman and that he had little influence there. Vardaman, it said, was responsible only in the sense that every citizen of Mississippi was responsible.[6]

After his inauguration Vardaman continued his attacks on the "criminal tendencies" of the Negro. In an address to the peace officers of the state in 1905 he warned them of impending trouble. The great number of "criminal negroes" who were drifting into the cities, he said, "seeking a way to live without honest toil," had become a "menace to the safety of the white man's home."[7] Never before had the whites been confronted with such a problem.

Despite Vardaman's tirades against the Negro there is no evidence that lynching increased during his administration. He had given a "quasi-defense" of lynching during the campaign, and later called it "the natural product of unnatural conditions."[8] Yet, during his first year as governor, he called out the militia, at a cost of

[4]Mississippi, *House Journal*, 1906, pp. 23-25.
[5]*Ibid.*, 26-27.
[6]Vicksburg *Herald*, Feb. 17, 1904.
[7]Jackson *Clarion-Ledger*, Mar. 16, 1905.
[8]Jackson *Issue*, Nov. 14, 1908.

$250,000, ordered special trains, took personal command, and rushed to Washington County to protect two Negroes threatened with mob action. It was later admitted by the Natchez *Democrat* that at the time "almost every white man in the state indulged the hope that the mobs would do their work."[9] His action in this case drew the unstinted praise of the national press.[10]

Aside from one instance of alleged brutality toward a trusty convict servant, which Vardaman denied, no charges of animus toward individual Negroes were made against Vardaman. A friendly writer reported that he noted not a whit of difference in the governor's attitude toward "the negro and an influential white man." "All negroes who know him," he added, "admire him devotedly. . . . His colored servants are intensely loyal to him."[11] Vardaman vetoed an appropriation of $2,200 for the Negro school at Holly Springs,[12] but in general it seems that little was done to change the status of the Mississippi Negro during his administration.

Of much greater importance was his social reform program. In his first message to the legislature he recommended higher pay for judges; equalization of tax assessments; establishment of state depositories for state funds; abolition of the penitentiary Board of Control and entrustment of the management of the penitentiary to a separate department under one man; abolition of the "school book trust"; and the sale of the governor's mansion, the governor to furnish his own home.[13] The legislature responded but lukewarmly to most of these reforms and adjourned without accomplishing anything "radical." It was still dominated by the black counties and was not a "reform" legislature. Vardaman apparently did not exert much pressure upon it. Measures were passed easing restrictions on insurance companies and permitting a merger of the Mobile and Ohio with the Southern Railroad, but Vardaman vetoed both of these. Throughout the first session of the legislature

[9]Vicksburg *Herald*, Mar. 1, 1904; *National Cyclopedia*, XIII, 495; Natchez *Democrat*, July 4, 1911.

[10]New York *Times*, Brooklyn *Eagle*, Chicago *Tribune*, and others, quoted in Vicksburg *Herald*, Mar. 1, 1904.

[11]Garrard Harris, "A Defense of Governor Vardaman," in *Harper's Weekly*, XLIX (1905), 238.

[12]Mississippi, *House Journal*, 1904, pp. 840-43.

[13]*Ibid.*, 142-55.

the Vicksburg *Herald*, Vardaman's conservative backer, exulted over the fact that the governor had failed to exhibit much radicalism, which was as it had predicted.[14]

For some time it had been charged that the American Book Company had a monopoly of the schoolbook business. Selection of books had been left to the state superintendent of education, and changes were frequent. Responding to the governor's request, the legislature of 1904 created a state textbook commission with power to contract for books by competitive bid. The commission went to work immediately, and within a year the control of the American Book Company was broken. It had sold 80 per cent of the school books in Mississippi in 1903, but in 1905 it drew only 20 per cent of the contracts. Moreover the new books were considerably cheaper and were adopted for a five-year period, whereas former adoptions had been subject to change annually. Commenting on the work of the commission, the *Clarion*, an anti-administration paper, admitted that there had been "no suspicion here, no intimation of crooked business." "Of course," it added, "the firms that lost out heavily are badly disappointed and their representatives . . . have been beefing considerably."[15]

During Vardaman's administration Frank Burkitt, who had returned to the Democratic fold, was leading a fight in the legislature for more funds for common schools and less for higher education. Vardaman, while not openly siding with Burkitt, seems to have sympathized with his view.[16] Burkitt submitted figures showing that per capita cost at the state agricultural college and at the state university was from four to eight times as great as in the state's private colleges and forty times greater than the common school per capita. The common schools, he said, were the poor man's only university. The sons of the rich were the only ones who were able to take advantage of the higher educational facilities, and it was unjust to tax the poor to support them. Moreover, he said, the agricultural college was failing to improve Mississippi agriculture. According to him, only 95 graduates of the college at Starkville were actively engaged in agriculture, and 41 of those were em-

[14]Vicksburg *Herald*, Jan.-Mar., 1904, Jan. 3, 4, 1906; Mississippi, *House Journal*, 1906, pp. 45-50.

[15]Jackson *Clarion-Ledger*, June 15, 1905.

[16]See Biennial Message in Mississippi, *House Journal*, 1906, p. 24.

ployed at the college.[17] In Vardaman's last legislature Burkitt
secured the adoption of a rider to the appropriation bill reducing
the salary of the president of the college from $5,000 to $3,500. The
trustees ignored the rider as unconstitutional. This action by the
trustees drew Vardaman's condemnation, and he predicted that the
next legislature would greatly reduce the college's appropriation.[18]

In his 1906 message to the legislature Vardaman again pointed
out the inequity of the tax system. He urged taxation of money,
notes, and similar forms of property. Railroads, factories, telegraph
and telephone lines, he thought, should be taxed upon their "real
value . . . just as the farmer's home is taxed." He also urged creation
of the office of bank examiner to insure proper care of depositors'
interests.[19] At this session a bill was passed permitting corporations
to own ten million dollars worth of real estate. The existing law
restricted them to one tenth of this, and the new bill had been
passed at the behest of companies who were engaged in exploiting
the timber forests of south Mississippi. Vardaman vetoed the bill.
In his veto message he said that the greatest need of Mississippi
was more landlords and fewer tenants. He would like to see "the
great delta plantations cut up into small farms and owned by white
men who till the soil." He had no objection, he said, to large
lumber mill investments, but he did object to their owning the
land. That, he said, would result in a monopoly not only of lumber
but of land after the lumber was cut. "If the Legislature had undertaken in definite terms to create a lumber trust," he said, he could
not conceive of a more effective method than this measure. Its
result would be "to close the door of opportunity and hope in the
face of the struggling youth of the state, and make of them toilers
of the favored rich." He urged that land remain in the hands of
the farmers and that they sell only the lumber rights to the corporations.[20]

Vardaman took a humanitarian attitude toward the state's wards.
In an age when the insane and feeble-minded were still callously
regarded by many, his pleas for their better care were quite unusual. Although unable to get from the legislature sufficient funds

[17]Jackson *Issue*, Mar. 7, 1908.
[18]Mississippi, *House Journal*, 1908, pp. 700-701; Jackson *Issue*, May 2, 1908.
[19]Mississippi, *House Journal*, 1906, pp. 27-28, 35.
[20]Mississippi, *Senate Journal*, 1906, p. 1091.

to carry out the building program which he urged, he instituted reforms in the treatment of inmates at the state asylum. In the words of one of his admirers, "He found the asylum a mad house and converted it into an institution for the treatment of the mentally sick."[21] In his 1908 message he urged greatly increased appropriations to institutions for the insane, the blind, and the deaf and dumb. When the legislature failed to meet the request he attributed its inaction to "a disposition to magnify the importance and value of the dollar and minimize the value of a human soul." In this message he also called attention to the ravages of tuberculosis among the poor of the state and recommended building a tuberculosis hospital. He also recommended building a school for the benefit of the state's feeble-minded children.[22] Not for several years were such recommendations to be carried into execution, but Vardaman was the first politician vividly to call attention to the needs of the unfortunates.

The most striking of Vardaman's reforms pertained to the penitentiary. In ante-bellum days crime had been no great social problem. Slaves, comprising considerably more than half the state's population, were under their masters' supervision and rarely had to be dealt with by the courts. With the freeing of the slaves and the growth of towns in the postwar period, there was a great increase in petty thievery and violence, and means had to be found to deal with it. The state penitentiary was far from adequate for the growing number of convicts, and an act of 1876 authorized the Penitentiary Board to lease the convicts as laborers to individuals. The lessee was to furnish the convicts with food, clothing, and medicines and to pay the state for them at the monthly rate of $1.10 a person.[23] Under this act the firm of French and Jobes acted as a general broker, leasing all the state's convicts and subleasing them to others at increased rates. Within a year they had 321 convicts stationed on ten plantations in Washington, Coahoma, Issaquena, and Bolivar counties.[24] Ten years later French and Jobes had been succeeded by Hamilton and Hoskins, and then by Hamilton and Company, who continued to lease convicts from the state and sub-

[21]Watkins, Address, May 17, 1936, p. 14, in Mississippi Department of Archives and History.

[22]Mississippi, *Senate Journal*, 1908, pp. 29, 47-49, 50, 53.

[23]Mississippi, *Senate Journal*, 1876, p. 602; *House Journal*, 1876, p. 613.

[24]Jackson *Weekly Clarion*, Jan. 3, 1877.

lease them to plantation owners and railroad contractors. Vast sums of money were made out of these leases, but it is doubtful if the state always received its pittance. In 1887 it was charged and proved that Hamilton and Company was indebted to the state some $80,000, although Attorney-General T. C. Catchings had certified that they had paid all their dues. When Governor Lowry, too, denied that the lessee owed the state for the convicts, he, Catchings, and Hamilton were charged by the Chickasaw *Messenger* with conspiracy to defraud the state.[25]

Compared to the treatment accorded these convicts, an overwhelming majority of whom were Negroes, slavery was a mild and humane institution. Even in cases where no personal affection existed between the master and his slave, the latter had been a valuable chattel whose welfare coincided with the owner's interest. The death or incapacity of the slave resulted in considerable loss to the master. Under the convict-lease system no such conditions existed. The fact that the convict was a pariah precluded any likelihood of personal affection between him and the lessee. The absence of any property interest in the convict discouraged the lessee's interest in his welfare. If he were sick or disabled, he was replaced by a healthy substitute. Were he to die, there seemed an inexhaustible supply always available. Under such a system economy would call for the greatest exaction of labor from the convict in return for the least expenditure for his welfare, and such seems to have been the practice.

In the summer of 1887 the grand jury of Hinds County inspected the penitentiary hospital in Jackson. It found there twenty-six inmates lately returned from farms and railroads, some with consumption, some with their backs cut in "great wales, scars, and blisters." Some had frostbitten hands and feet, and all had "the stamp of manhood almost blotted out of their faces." The jury was convinced that the convicts had been more cruelly treated than "a nation of savages ought to permit." "They are lying there dying," said the report, "some of them on bare boards, so poor and emaciated that their bones almost come through their skin." The jurymen reported seeing live vermin crawling over their faces and said the little bedding and clothing furnished them was in tatters and stiff with filth. The report closed with a condemnation of a

[25]Chickasaw *Messenger*, July 7, 14, 1887; Jackson *Weekly Clarion*, July 16, 1887.

system which "takes a poor creature's liberty and [turns] him over to one whose interest it is to coin his blood into money."[26]

The exposure by the Hinds jury caused a temporary revulsion against the leasing system. The Chickasaw *Messenger* called it "a stain upon our manhood, a blot upon our civilization, and a stigma upon the Christianity we profess." Convicts, it reported, were "tortured out of all semblance to human beings; their sufferings are such that the realities of a brimstone Inferno would be a welcome relief." Humanity, said the Natchez *Democrat*, demanded a change. "There is a barbarism existing among us, as dark and shameful as ever disgraced a civilized people."[27] Statistics compiled for the years 1881-1885 showed an annual mortality rate among Mississippi convicts of more than 11 per cent. For the same period in New Hampshire, Ohio, Iowa, and Illinois it was slightly over 1 per cent.[28] At some periods the rate in Mississippi rose above 17 per cent and rarely dropped below 10 per cent. "This brutal system," concluded a historian of the subject, "left its trail of dishonor and of death which could only find a parallel in some of the persecutions of the Middle Ages."[29]

Reaction against the system resulted in the prohibition of further leases by the constitution of 1890.[30] A new system was soon evolved, however, to circumvent the constitutional ban. Under this system the state Penitentiary Board leased lands from individuals and worked them with convict labor The plantation owner was left, however, in direct violation of the constitution, to manage the leased lands, and in practice the scheme was the same as the former one. The big difference was in the amount of the state's profit. The new contracts provided for an equal division of profits between state and landowner. In 1896 one black county editor reported the new system no longer an "experiment," but on the contrary

[26]Report of Hinds County grand jury, quoted in Macon *Beacon*, July 16, 1887; Chickasaw *Messenger*, July 14, 1887; Jackson *Weekly Clarion*, July 12, 1887. See also Report of the House Committee to Investigate the State Penitentiary, in Mississippi, *House Journal*, 1888, Appendix.

[27]Chickasaw *Messenger*, Mar. 10, July 14, 21, Oct. 20, 1887; Natchez *Democrat*, Jan. 17, 1889.

[28]Chickasaw *Messenger*, Oct. 20, 1887.

[29]J. H. Jones, "History of the Measures Submitted to the Committee on Penitentiary in the Constitutional Convention of 1890," in Mississippi Historical Society, *Publications*, II (1899), 112.

[30]Mississippi Constitution, 1890, Art. X, Secs. 223-226.

"eminently successful." There were nearly a thousand convicts working on state-leased plantations, and the net profit to the state that year was more than $56,000. Two years later the state's share was reported at more than $150,000.[31]

As might be expected, competition soon developed among plantation owners for use of convicts on their lands, and political influence was used to win awards. "I want you to give Capt. Jenkins a talk for me before the Board of Control contracts to work the prisoners next year," wrote Governor McLaurin's brother to him. He wanted "about 250 of them" to work "our place on shares." Jenkins, he said, wanted the state to lease the land for cash and keep all the profits, but "I think it best for the state to work land on shares." He urged the governor to say nothing of the request "until I see you or until Walter or Sidney [other brothers of the governor] explains what I want." In order to avoid criticism he agreed to "fix them in [the] name of another party."[32]

If the state's profits increased under the new system, it is doubtful if the convicts' living conditions improved. Too frequently they were set to clearing malaria-infested swamps. A medical examiner visiting one of the Delta prison camps in 1896 reported finding seventeen emaciated consumptives who had been confined in the rude camp for weeks with malarial fever. The camp surroundings were, he reported, unsanitary and filthy.[33]

In 1902 criticism of the new system resulted in a legislative investigation. The report of the committee scored the handling of the penitentiary business by the Board of Control. This body was made up of the governor, the attorney-general, and the three railroad commissioners. The legislators reported the penitentiary books in such shape that it was impossible to ascertain with any degree of accuracy the results of the Board's operations. Some accounts were credited with sums "for labor of convicts," with no record of the number of convicts, the nature of the work, or with whom contracted. The books also, the report charged, failed to show payments for a very large proportion of the convicts' labor on the

[31]Macon *Beacon*, Feb. 15, 1896; Jackson *Clarion-Ledger*, Jan. 27, 1897, Feb. 3, 1898.

[32]H. J. McLaurin to A. J. McLaurin, Nov. 4, 1895, Letters of Governors, Series E, 99.

[33]Report of R. D. Farish, M. D., to Penitentiary Board of Control, May 23, 1896. Letters of Governors, Series E, 110.

various farms to which they were leased.[34] The evils complained
of, said the Vicksburg *Herald*, ran back to the end of the Stone
administration. The *Herald* thought the new revelations, however,
"the worst [scandal] in the history of the state." The practical con-
clusiveness of the report was apparent since all members of the
committee had signed it. "To all appearances," the newspaper said,
"the award of convicts has been pretty deep in Delta politics." There
were some significant changes of farm leases prior to the 1899 and
1900 campaigns—"changes that caused no little talk when followed
by election incidents and results that were thought to have been
thus influenced." The *Herald* suggested that convict awards were
"poisoned and perverted to promote the fortunes of faction leaders."
One of the wardens, grilled by the committee, admitted that politics
was involved in the making of leases.[35]

The *Clarion*, an administration paper, admitted that loose management and unbusinesslike methods were used and that it was
impossible to learn from the books what the Board's transactions
had been. "Large tracts of land," it said, "have been cleared by
convict labor for various parties with whom the board . . . had no . . .
contracts whatever, and in whose lands the state had no interest
whatever." The cashbook, supposed to contain all cash transactions
from 1896 to 1902, had only 110 pages. The *Herald* charged that
more than $400,000 had been stolen from the state during Mc-
Laurin's term as governor.[36] When Longino came to his defense,
he too was criticized.

Although the committee had made a unanimous report, the legislature refused to adopt it.[37] The 1904 legislature was still dominated by the McLaurin-Longino element, and it refused to act on
Vardaman's recommendation that the Board of Control be abolished
and that an entirely new system of penitentiary management be
instituted.

When the 1906 legislature convened Vardaman was in the midst
of a legal suit with the Board of Control, all of whom, excepting

[34]Report of joint legislative investigation committee, in Mississippi, *House Journal*,
1902, pp. 58-67.

[35]Vicksburg *Herald*, Jan. 9, 15, 22, 1902. See also committee report in Mississippi, *House Journal*, 1902, pp. 64-65.

[36]Jackson *Clarion-Ledger*, Jan. 16, Feb. 6, 20, 1902; Vicksburg *Herald*, July 7,
1907.

[37]Jackson *Clarion-Ledger*, Mar. 6, 1902; Vicksburg *Herald*, Jan. 6, 1904.

himself, were members of the McLaurin faction. The Board, over his protest, had leased State Senator H. J. McLaurin's Sandy Bayou plantation. When the attorney-general refused to file an injunction against the Board's execution of the contract, Vardaman brought suit himself. The lower court upheld Vardaman, but the state supreme court reversed the decision and dismissed the injunction. S. S. Calhoon and Jeff Truly, both McLaurin appointees to the court, gave the majority opinion, while A. H. Whitfield, Vardaman's appointee, dissented.[38]

Vardaman devoted a large part of his legislative message to the evils of the penitentiary system. He reviewed its history and rang the changes on all the evils that had grown out of it. He cited the folly of the state's neglecting its own valuable lands while contracting with a state senator to work his Delta plantation on shares. He used the report of the legislative investigating committee of 1902 to show instances where the state had in some cases paid in advance six dollars an acre a year; and in others had made money while dividing its profits with Delta plantation owners. "If the state can make money working a private individual's land and giving that . . . individual half of the [profit], it can . . . make more money working its own land and keeping the entire product," he said. He scored H. J. McLaurin, whose "fertile land, hypnotic power, political pull, and long enjoyment of a robust share of the revenue arising from convict labor, seems to have clothed him with the modern brand of divine right to the perpetuation of that special privilege."[39]

Vardaman seemed not as concerned with the economics of the system, however, as with its inhumanity. Money had been made in the past, it was true, but it had been "money coined out of the blood and tears of the unfortunate convicts." The prime purpose of the penitentiary, he said, had been overlooked by the Board of Control. Instead of being conducted for the benefit of the convicts—"a kind of moral hospital, where the moral cripples could be treated"—the question of money-making for the favored few had been the chief end. "I am more interested," he said, "in the salvation of men than I am in hoarding gold." What if the convict was

[38]Jackson *Clarion-Ledger*, Dec. 14, 21, 1905, Jan. 25, Mar. 8, 1906; Vicksburg *Herald*, Jan. 3, 31, 1906.

[39]Mississippi, *House Journal*, 1906, pp. 17-19.

a "low-bred, vulgar creature, congenitally corrupt, inured to physical and moral filth, brutal and inhuman treatment?" So much greater his need of "kindly treatment, a decent bed to sleep on, and sanitary surrounding." He was there to be improved and not degraded. Vardaman saw man as "the creature of heredity and environment." Man's acts, he said, were "often the result of influence set in motion by the unconscious deeds of some forgotten ancestor." He urged that this should be borne in mind and a more charitable attitude taken toward the moral derelicts.[40]

Vardaman did not think that the state's responsibility to the convict ended with improving conditions in the penitentiary. He pointed out the difficult and hopeless prospect which a released convict faced. "The brand is upon him, and the back of the world's hand is against him, even God's providence seems estranged." He urged setting aside portions of the products of the convict's toil, over and above the cost of conviction and keeping and maintaining him, for the use of his family or other dependents. If he had no dependents, Vardaman urged that the surplus be returned to the convict after he served his term. This might be the means of "giving him a start upward and of enabling him to become a useful citizen." Disclaiming sentimentalism or the seeking of Utopia for the convict, Vardaman insisted that "No man should be permitted to control or manage a convict, who is not an upright, honorable, intelligent and just man. . . . It is no place for the cheap, dingy demagogue and political striker. Partisan politics should be absolutely eliminated from penitentiary management." He recalled that the manifest purpose of every warden in the past decade had been "to serve himself or a few partisan or political friends." Too often the office had been given as a reward for political activity. As a result, incapable and brutal men, placed in charge of convicts, had perpetrated acts "rivalling in brutality and fiendishness, the atrocities of . . . Torquemada." At the same time "votes were controlled in conventions and nominations made with the sole end in view of leasing some political dictator's delta plantation."[41]

Meanwhile a joint committee of the legislature had been at work investigating once more the penitentiary conditions. Their report drove home the need for the reforms which Vardaman was advocat-

[40]*Ibid.*, 19-20.
[41]*Ibid.*, 20-22.

ing. The committee found shocking conditions at the state's Oakley Farm. E. E. Jackson, the sergeant in charge, was operating an adjoining farm of his own with the labor of the convicts. These convicts were supposed to be ill and had been sent to Oakley to recuperate. Through the connivance of the farm doctor, the convicts were retained after they were well and were worked by Jackson. When members of the Board defended Jackson it was shown that they, together with Anselm McLaurin, had received costly gifts from him. Although only thirty "patients" were at the farm, 12,740 morphine tablets and a barrel of whiskey were consumed every forty days at Oakley. In the huge shack used as an incurable ward where a dozen Negroes were in a dying condition, all window glass was broken out and the patients were exposed to the wintry weather.[42]

At the state's Rankin County farm the committee found conditions even worse than at Oakley. It was a "nest of cruelty and graft." A drunken guard had recently "forced a convict trusty to cruelly murder a prisoner." Wagonloads of supplies were weekly sent from the farm to a neighboring hotel owned by a relative of Sergeant Puckett, the warden of the farm, and Puckett's horses were fed on the farm provender. "For neither pork, beef, vegetables or horse feed did the state ever receive a cent."[43]

Spurred on by these revelations the legislature passed a bill eliminating the Board of Control and creating an elective commission of three, with a superintendent appointed by the governor. The legislature also prohibited the leasing of private lands for working the state convicts.[44]

Vardaman's appeals and the report of the legislative committees had succeeded in stirring the conscience of the people. Able administrators were chosen by Vardaman and his successors—men who seemed to see the penal institution as a hospital for the morally sick. Never again were Mississippi's convicts to be subjected to the pre-1906 conditions. The state farm system was given a laudatory report by a legislative committee in 1912.[45] Two years later a

[42]Report of legislative investigating committee, in Mississippi, *House Journal,* 1906, pp. 615-28, 916-18, 1328-29. For minority report of E. D. Cavette, see *ibid.,* 638-44.

[43]*Ibid.,* 916-18.

[44]Mississippi, *Laws,* 1906, Chap. CXXXVII; *Code,* 1906, pp. 1012-13

[45]Quoted in Jackson *Clarion-Ledger,* Feb. 8, 1912.

Memphis paper reported the state's profits from its convict farms as $313,087 for the 1913-1914 season. Not only was the new system proving profitable financially, but the convicts were being trained in scientific methods of farming. "Here," said the Memphis editor, "is a school within itself."[46]

Within a decade after the reform the system had won general praise. A Gulf Coast editor, after a tour of inspection of the state farms in 1916, wrote a glowing account of the happy circumstances attending them. He praised Vardaman for his "wisdom and humanity" in eliminating the leasing system and substituting the working of the state's prisoners on state farms. The 1,700 convicts were humanely cared for, and the state was reaping big financial returns. Ten years before, he said, the Parchman farm had been an unbroken wilderness in Sunflower County. Now its nearly 18,000 acres were valued at $1,500,000. The other state farms in Rankin, Hinds, and Holmes counties had been old plantations worn by excessive cultivation when the state purchased them. They had all been wonderfully improved and were worth several times what the state paid for them. Net profits for the year 1915 were $300,000,[47] and the next year they were estimated at double that amount.[48]

In summarizing Vardaman's administration it would be well to review both the legislation which was sponsored by him and that which he opposed. He urged and obtained the enactment of laws (1) ending the leasing of convicts and improving their conditions; (2) increasing common-school appropriations almost 20 per cent and teachers' salaries almost 30 per cent; (3) creating a state text-book commission which broke the monopoly of the American Book Company; and (4) regulating insurance companies, railroads, utilities, banks, manufacturers, and trusts. He opposed and vetoed measures (1) permitting corporations to hold $10,000,000 worth of real estate; (2) permitting a merger of the Southern Railroad with the Mobile and Ohio; and (3) permitting fire insurance companies to form a central bureau which would have resulted in monopolistic practices. In addition he advocated, but did not obtain at the time, (1) a reduction of the legal interest rate from 10 per cent to 8 per

[46]Memphis *Scimitar*, quoted, *ibid.*, June 23, 1914.
[47]Pass Christian *Coast Beacon*, July 22, 1916.
[48]Jackson *Clarion-Ledger*, Oct. 16, 1916.

cent; (2) the creation of a state highway commission; (3) aid to cripples and unfortunates; (4) laws governing child labor; and (5) the building of a state school for the deaf and dumb.[49]

A northern journalist touring Mississippi in 1908 to study the Negro's condition there reported that he heard "no one accuse [Vardaman] of corruption in any department of his administration." Some of the "best people," he said, were bitter in their opposition to him, but "on the whole, they said he had directed the business of the state with judgment." His own conclusion was that Vardaman had given the state the best administration it had ever had.[50] An admirer of Vardaman thought his administration was characterized by progressiveness and "great development in the state, a higher recognition of the rights of the individual, and greater service to the common man." It was also accompanied, he said, "by peace, honesty, and an increase of all those things which contribute to the happiness of the larger number of the people."[51] An examination of the contemporary press failed to discover any dissent from this estimation.

In his last message to the legislature Vardaman renewed his former request to submit to the voters a constitutional amendment on the school fund distribution. He also urged again a reapportionment of legislative representation; an elective judiciary; a child labor law; the establishment of state depositories; broader powers for the railroad commissioners; a further reduction in the interest rate; various public building improvements; and the establishment of a state charity hospital, an old women's home, an institute for feeble-minded children, and a normal school for teacher training.[52] The conservative editor of the Vicksburg *Herald* called the message a "Remarkable Document" and told Vardaman that "The whole state said to him, 'Well done, Thou good and faithful servant'."[53]

[49]Mississippi, *House Journal*, 1904, pp. 142-56; *ibid.*, 1906, pp. 13-39, 45-50, 1306-308; *ibid.*, 1908, pp. 79-81; Mississippi, *Laws*, 1904, Chaps. III-XVII, LXXIX, LXXX, LXXXI, LXXXVI, CIV, CVIII, CXI, CLXXXII; *Laws*, 1906, Chaps. IV-XI, CVII, CXXXVII, CXL; Heber A. Ladner, "James Kimble Vardaman, Governor of Mississippi, 1904-1908," in *Journal of Mississippi History*, II (1940), 185-95; Ray Stannard Baker, "The Negro in Politics," in *American Magazine*, LXVI (1908), 172-73.

[50]Baker, "The Negro in Politics," *loc. cit.*, 172-73.

[51]Watkins, Address, May 17, 1936, pp. 14-15, in Mississippi Department of Archives and History.

[52]Mississippi *Senate Journal*, 1908, pp. 11-56.

[53]Vicksburg *Herald*, Jan. 10, 1908.

John Sharp Williams, just elected to the United States Senate after a bitter struggle with Vardaman, praised his erstwhile opponent for "his good record as governor."[54]

With Vardaman's retirement from office the New Orleans *Times-Democrat* devoted a full-column editorial to a review of his administration. That administration had, it said, been distinguished by "honesty and unswerving devotion to the best interests of the state." Abuses had been corrected, evils eliminated, "greater liberality toward educational and other public institutions . . . consistently urged." Mob demonstrations had been sternly suppressed, and no governor had been "more prompt to invoke the military power of the state for the protection of imperilled prisoners, black or white."[55]

[54]*Ibid.*, Jan. 14, 1908.
[55]New Orleans *Times-Democrat*, quoted, *ibid.*, Jan. 23, 1908.

CHAPTER XV

THE ELECTION OF 1907

EARLY in Vardaman's administration Senator Money announced that he would not be a candidate for re-election in 1907, and speculation began at once as to his successor. Congressman John Sharp Williams had had senatorial ambitions for some time, and it was assumed that he would run. On the other hand, Vardaman was young, ambitious, and had won a remarkable victory over the McLaurin forces in 1903. The constitution would not permit his succeeding himself as governor. What more likely than that he should aspire to Money's seat? Disturbed over this prospect the Yazoo City *Herald*, admirer of both Vardaman and Williams, urged early in 1905 that one of them—it did not care which—take Money's seat in 1907 and the other run against McLaurin in 1912.[1]

The *Clarion*, never an admirer of Vardaman, replied that Mc-Laurin was, and had been for years, "the strongest man in public life . . . in Mississippi" and could have another nomination in 1912 if he wanted it, "with or without opposition."[2]

In any contest in which he was a candidate Vardaman would have the opposition of McLaurin. Enmity between them was of long standing, and Vardaman had intensified it in his fight for penitentiary reform. In his 1906 message to the legislature he had reflected on the personal integrity of all former penitentiary wardens. McLaurin's late brother, Walter, was one of these, and Anse swore undying vengeance on Vardaman.[3] The McLaurins, said the *Clarion*, "do not like Vardaman at best and now . . . they will esteem it a . . . brotherly duty, to bring together every influence possible at their command to rebuke the man who has put a stigma upon him whose lips are sealed in death."[4] In such circumstances it might have been wiser for Vardaman to wait until 1912 and oppose McLaurin himself. In that event he might have counted on Williams' support or at least his neutrality. But that was five years off, and many changes could occur in the political scene with Vardaman in

[1]Yazoo City *Herald*, quoted in Jackson *Clarion-Ledger*, Mar. 16, 1905.
[2]*Ibid.*, Mar. 16, Apr. 6, 1905.
[3]Brookhaven *Leader*, quoted, *ibid.*, Jan. 18, 1906.
[4]*Ibid.*, Jan. 11, 1906.

temporary retirement. Weighing all factors he decided to run against Williams.

The two men, though of different social backgrounds, were on the best of terms. Williams was an aristocratic Delta planter, while Vardaman was the son of a poor farmer who had migrated to Texas before the Civil War in search of economic opportunity, and back to Mississippi after the war when he failed to find it. Since 1897 Vardaman had been an admirer of Williams and had predicted that he would "one day rank with the great Senators of America."[5] Williams had supported Vardaman in the 1903 election and during his administration had praised him highly.[6]

Despite the intensity of the campaign that developed, nothing occurred to mar the pleasant relation between them, and the two men were warm personal friends at its conclusion. Neither side resorted to scurrilous character assaults. It was well known that Vardaman was a "teetotaler" and that Williams was "fond of his toddy." Yet Vardaman's committee refused to circulate the "malicious falsehood" that Williams was drunk while speaking at Hermanville and Clinton. On the other hand, Williams' committee refused to approve a vicious attack made on Vardaman by Frederick Palmer in *Collier's Weekly*. Five days before the primary the two committees agreed not to bring out new campaign material, and they called upon their friends to observe the agreement. The object of this was to avoid any last-minute surprises which the opposition would have no opportunity to answer. There was no complaint that this agreement was violated, and on the whole the campaign was reported as being "freer of acrimony and personality than any other senatorial fight in Mississippi within the past two decades."[7] Williams refused to extend any financial assistance to newspapers for their support, because it was "improper,"[8] and there is no evidence that Vardaman did either.

It would be wrong, however, to assume that the campaign was a gentle and mild affair. While avoiding personalities each candi-

[5]Greenwood *Commonwealth*, May 27, 1897; J. K. Vardaman to Charles C. Elliott, Sept. 25, 1903, quoted in Jackson *Clarion-Ledger*, July 18, 1907.

[6]"There is not a state in the Union," Williams was quoted as saying, "better governed [than Mississippi], not a state that has a more upright, honorable and conscientious executive." Natchez *Democrat*, June 16, 1904.

[7]*Ibid.*, July 23, 27, 1907; Vicksburg *Herald*, July 27, 1907.

[8]J. S. Williams to H. B. Wilson, June 10, 1907, Williams Papers.

date turned the full force of his oratory on the professional deficien-
cies of the other. Tom Watson, the Georgia Populist, wrote letters
to the Mississippi press saying that Williams' election would mean
that "the corporations would have just one more doodle-bug in the
United States Senate."[9] When Williams retorted that Vardaman's
backers were "the old Populite" following,[10] Vardaman charged that
Williams was supported by the trusts.

The two candidates engaged in a bitter controversy over government ownership of railroads, which Vardaman favored and Williams opposed.[11] Williams tried to confine the campaign to this and
other national questions such as trust regulation and the tariff, but
Vardaman refused to be thus hedged in. In a speech at Macon in
June he discussed imperialism, the tariff, and government ownership. Then he touched on the race question, and it was noted that
his remarks "struck a responsive chord in the hearts of his hearers,
and he was loudly and continuously applauded."[12] From then on
Vardaman knew no restraint. Luridly and graphically he related
instances of white women being raped by Negroes.[13] He was an
extremely emotional man, and he and his listeners seemed to have
been caught in a vicious whirlpool. His oratory stirred them, and
their response seemed to inspire him to fiercer attacks. He called
attention of the voters to the fact that Negroes outnumbered Mississippi whites by a quarter of a million; that Negro men outnumbered white men by 50,000; that the average vote cast in state elections was less than 60,000; and that thus there was danger of Negro
political supremacy. He pointed again to the 125,000 Negro children of school age in the state and to the nearly half-million dollars
which the state was annually appropriating to their education. He
urged the modification of the Fourteenth Amendment and the repeal of the Fifteenth as the only real safeguard for white supremacy in Mississippi. The Negroes, he charged, would regard his
defeat as a victory for them. In a speech at Columbus in July he

[9]George C. Osborn, "John Sharp Williams Becomes a United States Senator," in
Journal of Southern History, VI (1940), 233-34.

[10]Williams to H. C. Majure, June 10, 1907, Williams Papers.

[11]Jackson *Weekly Clarion-Ledger*, Feb. 7, 14, 28, 1907.

[12]Macon *Beacon*, June 22, 1907.

[13]New Orleans *Times-Picayune* and Jackson *Evening News*, quoted in Natchez
Democrat, July 5, 1907; Jackson *Clarion-Ledger*, July 11, 1907.

said that the Declaration of Independence did not apply to "wild animals and niggers."[14]

The opposition press again shouted "Demagogue" and chided Vardaman with having failed to do anything about the school funds when he was governor although that had been the main plank of his 1903 platform. "Mr. Vardaman didn't divide the school funds," said the *Dixie Press*, "nor did he make a persistent effort to do so. ... What was the cause of his favoring the division of ... school funds? Don't know, but it looks like it was done merely to catch votes."[15] Vardaman defended himself against this charge by citing his appeals to the legislature and attributed the latter's refusal to act to the McLaurinite majority in that body.[16]

Williams objected to injecting the race question into national politics. He agreed on the advisability of repealing the Reconstruction amendments if it could be done. "If the Fifteenth Amendment could be repealed," he said, "I would be as willing to do it as Governor Vardaman." Such, however, was impossible. On the contrary, any attempt to do so would only result in "The enforcement of the Fourteenth [and Fifteenth?] Amendment[s] and a stringent and drastic enforcement of [anti-]peonage [laws] to the detriment of Southern planting interests."[17] Thus it would seem that Williams' objection to Vardaman's program was, like Critz's and Noel's, not inspired by humanitarian interest in the Negro, but by expediency and by his fear that it would react "to the detriment of Southern planting interests." At the same time Williams, like Critz and Noel, was not anti-Negro in a positive sense as was Vardaman. Such anti-Negro statements as Williams, Noel, and Critz uttered seemed drawn from them as a defense against Vardaman's earlier and more vicious statements. To that extent their guilt may be less than his.

Williams, if reluctantly, made some capital of the racial issue. He predicted that government ownership of railroads would result in Negroes receiving important positions. He denied that he had

14Macon *Beacon*, July 6, 1907; Natchez *Democrat*, July 5, 1907; Jackson *Clarion-Ledger*, July 11, 1907, Mar. 17, 1910.

15West Point *Dixie Press*, quoted in Jackson *Evening News*, May 1, 1907.

16Natchez *Democrat*, July 12, 1907.

17Jackson *Clarion-Ledger*, July 11, 1907; Williams to Capt. Thomas Evans, June 10, 1907; Williams to Majure, June 10, 1907; Williams to J. F. Gray, Jan. 10, 1907; Williams to J. E. Warnock, Feb. 9, 1907; Williams to L. T. Carpenter, June 10, 1907, Williams Papers.

ever advocated an industrial training school for Negroes. "I think that is about the worst thing that could be given them," he said. "I mean," he added, ". . . the worst to the interest of white people. It brings them into competition with white mechanics and artisans." When the Vardaman faction spread a report that Williams had discharged his white servant because she refused to eat with the Negro servants, he published the fact that he had discharged her "because she would eat" with them.[18]

There were other charges and countercharges made during the campaign, but they seem to have been of minor importance. Some Vardaman people were urging the election of their candidate so as to keep both him and Williams in the public service. To counteract this Williams declared that he would interpret the election of Vardaman as a repudiation of himself and would retire from Congress. He was willing, he said, to let the Jeffersonian maxim "Is he competent; is he faithful; is he honest?" be the measure of the candidates. He would run on his congressional record and said he had opposed "every pretense of special privilege and of class legislation."[19]

Two months before the election Williams was disturbed over the fact that he did not have "much of an organization." Vardaman, on the other hand, had "a self-constituted organization composed of recipients of appointments to judgeships, trustees and militia 'gew-gaws'." Besides, Agricultural Commissioner Henry E. Blakeslee had managed it so that Vardaman was "uniformly invited to address the Farmers Union and I have never received a single invitation." Williams urged his followers to work among the farmers to offset this disadvantage while he went off to address the railroad workers at McComb City. Before doing so he sent an urgent request to his secretary to locate and forward to him his "card of membership in the Isthmian Canal Locomotive Engineers Union."[20] Williams was attacked for having voted in Congress for a pension for General Nelson A. Miles, the Union officer who had been Jefferson Davis' keeper and who had placed shackles on him while in prison.[21]

[18]Jackson *Clarion-Ledger*, Feb. 12, 1907; Williams to Charles E. Hooker, Jr., June 10, 1907; Williams to R. A. Barnett, May 27, 1907, Williams Papers.

[19]Williams to Thomas Spight, May 27, 1907; Williams to S. J. Creekmore, Feb. 12, 1907; Williams to John B. Taylor, Feb. 14, 1907, *ibid.*

[20]Williams to John Y. Murray, May 3, 1907; Williams to N. T. Currie, June 10, 1907; Williams to Robert Bowman, Jr., May 27, 1907, *ibid.*

[21]Jackson *Clarion-Ledger*, June 27, 1907.

Throughout the campaign Williams repeatedly challenged Vardaman to joint debates, which Vardaman as often declined. Vardaman seems to have been inept in the hurly-burly of debates requiring quick retorts, preferring rather to let his oratory soar in unrestricted generalities. Finally, however, he was persuaded to accept a challenge, and the two candidates faced each other at Meridian on July 4 for their only joint speaking of the campaign. More than fifteen thousand turned out to hear and see the two most popular men in the state. Vardaman again urged repeal of the Fifteenth Amendment and modification of the Fourteenth. Williams scoffed at this. Taking a copy of the federal Constitution and a pencil he tendered them to Vardaman and urged him to delete and add what he would. Vardaman ignored the challenge. Williams then bombarded Vardaman's position with ridicule. There was, he said, no issue between them on the race question. Vardaman knew as well as he, he said, that there was no possibility of amendment. Nor was it necessary, for the "white man ruled and ruled by law."[22]

Both state and national press echoed this latter sentiment. Pointing to the fact that less than two thousand Mississippi Negroes voted in the last presidential election, the Jackson *News* thought it "shilly-shally nonsense" to assert that they were interested in politics. The Macon *Beacon* said Vardaman was holding out only a chimerical hope to the people and that even if his plan were practical, he was poorly fitted to accomplish it. If repeal of the Reconstruction amendments should come, said the Washington (D. C.) *Post*, it would be as a concession by the North to men of Williams' type, rather than by demand of men like Vardaman. His radicalism was more likely to provoke passage of the Crumpacker Resolution decreasing the representation of southern states in Congress. "The fifteenth amendment is inoperative in Mississippi," said the *Post*. "The North knows it and acquiesces in it, but let Vardaman go to the Senate . . . and he will likely precipitate an issue that will do Mississippi little good. His eloquence tells [only] with the rednecks and hill billies."[23]

Vardaman seems to have gained the displeasure of two influen-

[22]Natchez *Democrat*, July 5, 1907; Jackson *Clarion-Ledger*, July 5, 1907.
[23]Jackson *Sunday News*, May 5, 1907; Macon *Beacon*, July 6, 13, 27, 1907; Washington *Post*, quoted, *ibid.*, July 27, 1907.

tial elements, the preachers and the ladies. In his Meridian speech he stated that the Jackson *News* could not tell the truth about him "with the assistance of a Methodist Conference and Baptist Association." The *News* shrieked against this "gratuitous insult that the Governor has handed to both these great denominations," and the cry was taken up by others. Also his "spectacular and vulgar argument with the negro as his premise" was said to be "out of place in a dignified white man's race for the Senate." It was charged that he was making speeches "no lady can afford to listen to." When Williams spoke at Natchez the ladies were "most cordially invited" to attend. They did so in large numbers and heard "not one word fall from the lips of the gifted speaker that could offend the most sensitive" of their sex.[24]

The primary was held on August 1. So close was the contest that not until eight days later was the result known. Finally, on August 9, after canvassing the returns, the State Democratic Executive Committee announced that Williams had won by 648 votes. Curiously, each candidate failed to carry his home county. The hill counties stood by Vardaman, although Williams took several of them. The Delta went largely for Williams. South Mississippi was divided.[25] It was estimated by Williams and admitted by Vardaman supporters that more than fifteen thousand of Vardaman's votes had come from Populists. Williams urged that something be done to insure that future nominations be made by "*bona fide* Democrats."[26]

"The reign of the demagogues is over," shouted the anti-Vardaman press with the news of Williams' victory. "Natural ability has won over egotism and assurance, and . . . Mississippi has again returned to sanity and reason." Passion and prejudice would no longer control the state. But the most bitter of all anti-Vardaman papers, the Jackson *News*, saw ominous portents in the closeness of the race. "To have run Williams nearly an even race in this indicates," it said, "that Governor Vardaman is a man of positive political strength in Mississippi." It saw future trouble. The Vicksburg

[24]Jackson *Daily News*, July 5, 1907; *ibid.*, quoting others; Sunflower *Tocsin*, quoted in Jackson *Clarion-Ledger*, July 25, 1907; Natchez *Democrat*, July 12, 14, 16, 1907.

[25]*Biennial Report of the Secretary of State to the Legislature, October 1, 1905-October 1, 1907* (Nashville, 1908); Macon *Beacon*, Aug. 10, 1907.

[26]Macon *Beacon*, Aug. 10, 1907; Natchez *Democrat*, Aug. 13, 1907; Coody, *James K. Vardaman*, 42.

Herald, Vardaman's staunchest supporter in 1903, remained neutral throughout the campaign. When Williams' victory was announced it retained its impartiality by praising both candidates. Williams would make an "eminent successor" to his illustrious predecessors. But Vardaman deserved a hand "for the lofty and manly manner" in which he "bows to the majority will."[27]

The gubernatorial election in 1907 was overshadowed by the senatorial race. Candidates for governor were Charles Scott of Bolivar, Earl Brewer of Coahoma, Jeff Truly of Jefferson, E. F. Noel of Holmes, E. N. Thomas of Washington, and T. W. Sisson of Montgomery. Scott at the outset seemed to have the advantage. He was a wealthy Delta planter and had the backing of the Vicksburg *Herald,* the Natchez *Democrat,* and Jackson *News,* three of the most influential of the daily papers. Attempts were made by other candidates to have him disqualified because he had, years before, sent a challenge to a duel, but nothing came of the move.[28]

Scott, an old enemy of McLaurin, charged that the clan's influence had entered both Truly and Brewer against him in an effort to re-establish their supremacy in state politics. The backers of Truly and Brewer, he said, were "pretending to be at outs with each other" but were really in a combine to defeat him. According to Scott, Anse and five of the brothers were backing Truly, the real candidate of the clan, while the other two brothers were backing Brewer. But Brewer, he said, was only in the campaign to draw votes from him. The McLaurins charged that Scott "belongs to the Y. and M. V. Railroad" and that that was the only reason the Vicksburg *Herald* was backing him.[29]

Scott's program called for a reduction of the interest rate so as to relieve borrowing farmers and to invite outside capital to invest in state industry. He also advocated the encouragement of Italian immigration into the state to help relieve the planter's dependence on Negro labor. This latter plan was jumped upon by Truly and his McLaurin backing who appealed to the nationalistic prejudice against Italians. Truly, however, was charged with playing a different tune in regions such as Natchez and Vicksburg where there

[27]Macon *Beacon,* Aug. 3, 1907; Jackson *Clarion-Ledger,* Aug. 1, 1907; Jackson *Daily News,* Aug. 3, 1907; Vicksburg *Herald,* Aug. 9, 1907.

[28]Jackson *Clarion-Ledger,* Apr. 4, 1907; Vicksburg *Herald,* Jan. 2, 3, 1906, June 4, 1907; *ibid.,* Jan. 3, 1906, quoting Jackson *News;* Natchez *Democrat,* July 30, 1907.

[29]Vicksburg *Herald,* June 4, 1907; Jackson *Clarion-Ledger,* July 25, 1907.

was already a considerable Italian element. But in eastern Mississippi where there was none he played up the "Mafia" crimes and said that Scott was proposing "to flood the state with black hand and criminal Italians."[30]

Truly, in addition to attacking the Delta planter's Italian immigration scheme, also attacked the school fund distribution which, he charged, borrowing a page from Vardaman, benefited the black counties at the expense of the white. The Jackson *Clarion*, which was backing Noel, admitted that this was true, but only in so far as the poll tax was concerned. In the general fund, it said, Warren, Washington, Jefferson, Claiborne, Bolivar, and Adams paid in $65,000 more than they drew out, while Benton, Calhoun, Choctaw, Covington, Itawamba, Lawrence, Neshoba, Perry, Smith, Tishomingo, Webster, and Winston, "all poor hill counties," paid in only $3,700 more than they drew.[31]

Noel, a wealthy lawyer, played up his youthful poverty and charged that Brewer, who was running on an anti-corporation platform, was really tainted with railroad support. Noel advocated heavier taxes on railroads and a more equitable apportionment of legislators.[32]

Brewer, too, advocated a more equitable distribution of the school funds, but his main attack was against the railroads. Railroads, he claimed, were taking an active part in the campaign and were actually subsidizing the opposition press. This was vehemently denied by the Macon *Beacon*, one of Brewer's critics, which pointed out that some of his most ardent supporters, J. N. Flowers, James H. Neville, C. C. Miller, George Q. May, and R. J. Powell, were prominent railroad attorneys. It dismissed his tirade against the railroads as blind but expressed some concern lest his school program would catch many votes. His method of division, it pointed out, would reduce Noxubee's share by $10,000 while increasing neighboring Kemper's by that amount.[33] The reason for all this clamor for reform in both legislative apportionment and in school fund distribution was, thought the *Beacon*, that south Mississippi

[30]Vicksburg *Herald*, July 24, 1907; Jackson *Clarion-Ledger*, July 25, 1907.
[31]Jackson *Clarion-Ledger*, July 23, 1907.
[32]*Ibid.*, Mar. 24, Aug. 22, 1907.
[33]*Ibid.*, Sept. 13, 1906, Mar. 21, Aug. 22, 1907; Macon *Beacon*, July 6, Aug. 17, 1907. For Editor Ferris' views eight years before see Macon *Beacon*, Nov. 18, 1899, Sept. 29, 1900.

was on the warpath and was demanding her rights. A fight was sure to develop in the next legislature on those issues, and the governor would have commanding influence. "If ever Noxubee County was interested in the governorship of Mississippi, now is the time."[34]

Scott's strength faded as the campaign progressed, and in the first primary he ran third behind Brewer and Noel.[35] The runoff primary between the two leaders was ordered for the last of August, and the two candidates launched themselves into the final campaign. Each charged that the other was the favorite of the railroads and corporations, but Noel was more specific and named a large list of corporate lawyers who were backing Brewer.[36] Vardaman supported Noel. It was later charged that the consideration for this support was Noel's promise that "he would not be a candidate for the United States Senate in 1911." Vardaman's influence, it was said, "was very subtly exerted, but it was sufficient nevertheless to defeat Brewer, who without it, very likely would have been elected."[37]

In a joint debate between the candidates at Jackson on August 17, Noel charged that Brewer was the candidate of the "saloon element." Brewer retorted that Noel had a saloonkeeper as his campaign manager in Quitman County. Pandemonium then broke loose. Both speakers were jeered and neither was permitted to be heard. When they finally gave up in despair, the audience resolved itself into a whooping mob of political partisans. It was, said the Natchez *Democrat*, "worse than a bull-fight."[38]

The runoff between Noel and Brewer was almost as close as the Williams-Vardaman contest in the first primary. Again there was uncertainty until the executive committee canvassed the returns. On August 29 the committee announced that Noel had won by 2,002 votes.[39]

There seems to have been an effort to see that the election of 1907 was conducted more fairly than had been customary in the past. Early in May the candidates in Lincoln County pledged themselves not to use money or liquor in the primary. They resolved

[34]Macon *Beacon*, Aug. 17, 1907.
[35]Jackson *Clarion-Ledger*, July 25, 1907; *Report of Secretary of State, 1905-1907*.
[36]Natchez *Democrat*, Aug. 16, 1907.
[37]Magnolia *Gazette*, Aug. 15, 1917.
[38]Jackson *Clarion-Ledger*, Aug. 22, 1907; Natchez *Democrat*, Aug. 20, 1907.
[39]Natchez *Democrat*, Aug. 30, 1907; *Report of Secretary of State, 1905-1907*.

further that they would not "lend" money when approached by voters. "All of us know," said their joint statement, "that in past years there has been some money and a good deal of liquor used." It was reported that the saloon faction, alarmed by the activities of prohibitionists, endeavored to register Negroes in local-option elections. But county registrars uniformly, it was said, refused to permit this.[40]

Despite such efforts, many candidates complained of irregularities in both the first and second primaries. Vardaman's followers charged that the Williams faction was trying to secure the registration of Negroes so as to help defeat Vardaman, but this was vehemently denied by Williams. "Somebody, somewhere," he said, "may have been trying to register some negroes," but "anybody who says that a negro had been registered at my instance or knowledge . . . is a liar. . . . I am no more in favor of voting negroes than Governor Vardaman."[41] Charles Scott later charged and produced affidavits showing that "wholesale registration [of voters] had been made in Pontotoc County to the number of 500 or more in direct violation of law." Some of these, he said, were made by "telephone and telegraph messages to the clerk, . . . some by proxy, and some of them in person on the day before election."[42]

The use of the Australian ballot made bribery difficult, but it seems to have been practiced nevertheless. Printers of ballots, said one editor, "are frequently so unscrupulous as to give out tickets in advance." These advance tickets, he explained, could then be taken and filled out by "heelers." The filled-out ticket would be given to the voter with instructions that he "drop it into the box, and bring back . . . the ticket which is given him by the commissioners at the box." This procedure was reported to be a common method employed to defeat the aims of the primary law. Then, too, said the same editor, it seemed impossible to prevent sore spots in close elections. It was most natural for many disqualified voters to attempt to vote. Indeed many of them were "good men" who were disqualified for failure to pay taxes on time and "from other accidents." Many delinquents, especially in the rural areas, were freely permitted to vote. Many others simply "slip through unchallenged."

[40]Jackson *Evening News*, May 2, 7, 1907.
[41]Williams to Hunter Sharp Walker, June 10, 1907, Williams Papers.
[42]Vicksburg *Herald*, June 28, 1911.

The remarkable size of the vote in 1907 led to the suspicion that "there is something rotten in the State of Denmark." More than 118,000 votes had been cast for the two senatorial candidates, which was considerably larger than the registration list. No official protests were made, however, and the Vicksburg *Herald* thought that the irregularities were practiced by all factions. It later surmised that knowledge of the part his followers had played kept Vardaman from demanding a recount.[43]

It was found too that the primary failed to eliminate the trading of candidates which had been one of the chief objections to the convention. In Jackson, it was said, "governors and United States Senators ... were traded for constables of the peace." The *Clarion*, at least, was convinced of the truth of the charge. It was alleged that Vardaman supporters in the northern counties "traded Scott right and left to get votes for ... Vardaman," despite the fact that Vardaman more than a year before had pledged his support to Scott. These trades, it was charged, had swung the balance and placed Brewer instead of Scott in the runoff with Noel.[44]

Listening to all the complaints of swindling, cheating, lying, and trading that were the aftermath of the campaign, the *Clarion* concluded that the primary law should be repealed and replaced by the old convention system. "It is believed," said Editor R. H. Henry, that "more evils occurred in the late primaries than in all the conventions ever held in the state."[45]

The charge may or may not have been true, but it was not the complaint of a disappointed supporter. The *Clarion* had backed both Williams and Noel to the hilt, and both had triumphed. Yet even in the moment of victory it seemed to Henry that the rules whereby that victory had been won were not conducive to good government. There was some truth in Henry's observations. The primary had not eliminated all the evils which had accompanied the convention system. Skilled politicians were to develop techniques of manipulation which sometimes might control primaries just as conventions had been controlled. But control of the primary by a favored few was more difficult of attainment. The mass of

43*Ibid.*, July 31, Aug. 7, 1907, June 28, 1911; Jackson *Clarion-Ledger*, Aug. 10, 1907.
44Jackson *Clarion-Ledger*, Oct. 10, 1907; Jackson *Daily News*, Aug. 5, 1907.
45Jackson *Clarion-Ledger*, Aug. 9, Sept. 12, 1907.

voters was too unwieldy and too unpredictable to be led and cajoled as the handful of convention delegates had been. More important still, the primary furnished the voters an invincible weapon with which to break the power of political bosses. The voters might not avail themselves of this weapon on all occasions. But it was there within their grasp whenever they should be stirred to reach for it.

CHAPTER XVI

THE SECRET CAUCUS

VARDAMAN accepted his defeat at the hands of Williams in good grace, and after his retirement from office in January, 1908, continued to make his home in Jackson, where he began publication of a newspaper called the *Issue*. Meanwhile Noel had been inaugurated governor, and Williams had taken his seat in the United States Senate as a colleague of Anse McLaurin. At Christmas time in 1909, McLaurin died suddenly at his home in Brandon, and the legislature soon to assemble would have the unexpected duty of choosing his successor.

United States senators were still chosen by the legislature, but since the introduction of the primary in Mississippi, candidates for that office were nominated in the same manner as all others. It thus was the duty of the Democratic legislature to choose the candidate who had been nominated by the party primary. McLaurin's term was not to expire until 1912, and accordingly the primary to name his successor would not have been held until 1911. His death, therefore, gave the legislature free choice in naming his successor, and a contest was precipitated which was to have tremendous consequences on the politics of the state.

Pending election by the legislature, Governor Noel was urged to appoint Vardaman. This would have committed the administration's support to Vardaman in the election and would have enhanced his prestige—perhaps enough to have insured his subsequent election. Despite the fact that Vardaman had supported him in the 1907 primary after Scott's defeat, Noel declined to appoint anyone, and the legislature convened with the office vacant.

The legislature of 1910 has been characterized by a friendly critic as not an "impressive" body of men. "Its members were not venal," he said, "but most of them were timid and third-rate."[1] A number of applicants appeared before the joint caucus and announced their candidacy. Prominent among them, in addition to Vardaman, were Leroy Percy of Washington County, C. H. Alexander, a wealthy lawyer of Jackson, Congressman Adam Byrd, F. A. Critz, Vardaman's opponent in the 1903 primary, State Senator W. D. Anderson, Representative J. C. Kyle, and Speaker H. M. Streit

[1]Percy, *Lanterns on the Levee*, 145.

of Meridian. All were allowed an opportunity to address the caucus. Vardaman reiterated his race views, favored an income tax, urged more stringent trust regulation, and favored state-wide and national prohibition. All the other candidates denounced Vardaman's racial program, and it soon became suspect that there was some sort of union among them directed at preventing Vardaman's nomination. Within a short time a host of followers of the several candidates had hurried up to Jackson to work in the interest of their favorite. It was conceded that Vardaman would have at least fifty-four votes from the outset. Eighty-five were needed for nomination by the caucus, and at least thirty members were uncommitted. It was thought that Governor Noel's influence would have a marked effect on the outcome, and it soon became obvious that his influence would not be used in Vardaman's behalf.[2]

Vardaman and Percy had been political allies back in the days when both were trying to break the grip of the McLaurin clan. "Mr. Percy is unquestionably a man of the highest order of talent," Vardaman had said in those days, "—he is a consummate lawyer and an advocate of great force and eloquence." On the other hand, Percy had given Vardaman his blessing in 1903—racial program and all— as had many others who were now to leave him. But they had broken when, in 1905, Vardaman had refused to appoint Percy's man to the Upper Levee Board.[3]

A sketch of Vardaman has been given by Percy's son who was active for his father both in the caucus and in the primary the following year. It was written years later, after both Percy and Vardaman had shuffled off the scene, but it is interesting as a picture of Vardaman by one of his most inveterate enemies. He describes Vardaman as

a kindly, vain demagogue unable to think, and given to emotions he considered noble. He was a handsome, flamboyant figure of a man, immaculately overdressed, wearing his black hair long to the shoulders, and crowned with a wide cowboy's hat. . . . He had made a good governor . . . and he craved public office because the spot-light was his passion and because, eternally in need of money, he abhorred work. . . .

[2]Natchez *Democrat*, Jan. 2, 5, 1910; Jackson *Clarion-Ledger*, Jan. 13, 1910; Magnolia *Gazette*, Aug. 15, 1917; Watkins, Address, May 17, 1936, p. 17, in Mississippi Department of Archives and History.

[3]Greenwood *Commonwealth*, May 20, 1897; Greenville *Times*, May 18, 1903; Jackson *Clarion-Ledger*, Dec. 14, 1905.

For political platform he advertised his love of the common people. . . .
He did love the common man after a fashion, as well he might. . . . He
stood for the poor white against the "nigger"—those were his qualifications as a statesman.[4]

Vardaman, he said, stood for all his father considered "vulgar
and dangerous," although he does not say when his father started
thinking thus. Yet, he continued, "Father rather liked Vardaman—
he was such a splendid ham actor, his inability to reason was so con-
tagious, it was so impossible to determine where his idealism ended
and his demagoguery began." Besides, Vardaman had "a charm and
a gift for the vivid, reckless phrase." He was not "a moral idiot of
genius . . . [but] merely an exhibitionist playing with fire."[5]

At the outset the question arose of whether the caucus should
be by open or secret ballot. Senator Leftwich, a leader of the Percy
faction, moved for a secret ballot, and it was carried over the Vardaman opposition by a vote of 101 to 69. The reason for the vote of
the majority, according to a Vardaman backer, was that "there are
quite a number of representatives who wish to oppose Mr. Vardaman and don't want their constituents to have knowledge of the
fact." The "Secret Caucus," as it became known, was not actually
closed to spectators. Attempts were made to clear the chamber of
all but legislators, but the hall leading to the chamber was so
jammed with men and women that efforts were given up and the
crowds remained. All newspaper men were admitted and the gal-
leries were open to all. Only the voting was secret.[6] This feature
of the caucus was much denounced then and later by Vardaman
and his supporters. It was pointed out, on the other hand, that
precedent had established the secret ballot. J. Z. George had been
nominated by secret ballot in the caucus of the 1880 legislature. So
had McLaurin in 1894 and Money in 1896. Speaker H. M. Streit,
who had been present at the caucus of 1894, reported that its proceedings were identical with that of 1910.[7]

Conditions were not the same in the two caucuses, however, as
the Vicksburg *Post* pointed out. In 1894 there was no combination

4William A. Percy, *Lanterns on the Levee* (New York, Alfred A. Knopf, 1941),
143-44.

5*Ibid.*, 144.

6Indianola *Enterprise*, quoted in Jackson *Issue*, Feb. 19, 1910; Natchez *Democrat*,
Jan. 8, 1910; Macon *Beacon*, July 1, 1910.

7Jackson *Clarion-Ledger*, Jan. 6, 1910; Natchez *Democrat*, July 5, 1916.

to defeat any particular candidate. The object of that caucus had been to consolidate the Democratic legislators in support of one candidate, so that the thirty Populist members could not act as a balance between the factions supporting Lowry or McLaurin. In 1910 there was no Populist party and the caucus was the same as the legislature. The only purpose of the secret ballot at the latter date was, said the *Post*, to prevent constituents from knowing how legislators voted.[8]

The suspicions of the Vardaman forces about an alliance against their candidate were soon confirmed. The Natchez *Democrat*, backing Percy, said that it was the field against Vardaman, and that "all the McLaurin influence is opposed" to him too. The Vicksburg *Herald*, which had supported Vardaman in 1903 but was now supporting Percy, also admitted that there was a combination against Vardaman and that the alliance was due to the race issue. Admitting that Vardaman had been a good governor, it now held that his position on the race question was dangerous. The *Herald* made no explanation of its conversion to this belief. As the caucus developed into a deadlock, it compared Vardaman's plight to that of Barksdale in 1892 and called on Vardaman to withdraw as Barksdale had done and "take his medicine like a man."[9]

Vardaman received 71 votes on the first ballot to 99 distributed among the other candidates. For the next six weeks of the caucus, his vote varied between 65 and 78, generally about 70. It was known that he had a sufficient number of votes pledged to him as second choice to insure his election should several of the opposition candidates withdraw. The strategy of the coalition, therefore, was to keep all candidates in the race until those second-choice votes could be won from Vardaman, then to center all its strength on one candidate. Vardaman's hope lay in discouraging candidates early so that they would withdraw, thus enabling him to gain a majority as second choice of the withdrawing candidates' supporters.[10]

By mid-January there were rumors afloat of the use of undue influence to obtain votes. It was reported that certain legislators had received letters promising aid for future political aspirations in exchange for their votes and warning of political ruin for them if

[8]Vicksburg *Post*, quoted in Jackson *Issue*, Sept. 2, 1910.
[9]Natchez *Democrat*, Jan. 7, 1910; Vicksburg *Herald*, Jan. 16, 30, 1910.
[10]Natchez *Democrat*, Feb. 23, 1910.

they did not accede. Vardaman charged that his vetoes while governor had aligned against him "Every railroad attorney, the representatives of the lumber trust, the whiskey trust, and every other trust that does business in Mississippi." He charged further that their agents were engaged in bribing and debauching the legislators in their effort to defeat him. Percy issued a statement denying this and calling on Vardaman to name names.[11] This Vardaman did not do.

Illegal use of patronage was also charged. In the midst of the caucus Attorney-General Stirling resigned and no successor was announced. Vardaman asserted that this empty office and others were being used by Noel to effect his defeat. "Legislators have been approached," he said, "with the proposition that if they 'would vote against Vardaman, . . . some of their friends would be appointed attorney-general, and others given the district attorneyship'."[12] Noel was accused, "and with apparent good reason," according to the Vicksburg *Post*, "of prostituting his appointive power by promising judgeships to members of the Legislature as a reward for their treason to the people of the State." While the caucus was in session a bill was passed creating the office of county attorney. "These [seventy-nine] places," said a Vardaman supporter, "were used to induce members of the Legislature to withdraw their support from Vardaman," and ultimately all were "given to men who voted or worked against Vardaman," some of whom, he added, "had started out as his friends." It was even alleged that President Taft had been persuaded to hold up the appointment of a federal district attorney for Mississippi so that the office might go to some legislator who voted against Vardaman.[13]

How many, if any, of these charges were true there is no way of knowing. That they were believed almost universally by Vardaman's supporters and by some of Percy's backers is amply evident. Within a week of the opening of the caucus one editor reported that in his section thousands of supporters had been won by Vardaman because they thought "an attempt is being made to crush him politically by the combined strength of the ring politicians, the leading corporation lawyers, interested newspapers, and others."[14]

Reports early began to circulate that at Percy headquarters in the Edwards House liquor was being freely dispensed to debauch legislators and to influence votes. A sensation was produced, however, when Representative Walter W. Robertson, of Copiah, a Vardaman supporter, issued a statement that he had been "poisoned with whiskey" in Vardaman's headquarters. Since Vardaman was a militant prohibitionist, this statement from one of his own followers would hurt him badly. After the caucus ended, Robertson repudiated the statement in such a way as to reflect on the Percy faction. In a signed statement he charged that he was put "in a certain state of mind when I was not myself" by the Percy faction in their headquarters and induced to sign the prepared statement. He denied having knowledge of the content of the statement he had been induced to sign and stated that "great pressure was brought to bear on me in several ways to get me to desert Governor Vardaman."[15] Another state senator charged in a signed statement that "whiskey, women, gubernatorial patronage, the influence of the Republican administration, money and an unholy alliance or combination" had been used by the opposition in an attempt to defeat Vardaman.[16]

Save for the Robertson statement which was later repudiated, there were no charges at the time of the use of whiskey by the Vardaman party. Perhaps they were not as well supplied as their opponents, but it was later revealed that they too had been more than generous in their hospitality to thirsty legislators. In the words of Speaker Streit, "The game of politics seems to have been played to a finish and as in all games some outclassed others."[17]

After six long weeks of balloting without a decision, the caucus voted to drop the low man on each ballot. Support for the resolution came from the coalition, and it was opposed by the Vardaman party. Apparently the strategy of the coalition had been perfected, or at least they were confident that it had. On February 23, on the fifty-eighth ballot, after all other candidates had been withdrawn,

14Yazoo *Sentinel*, quoted in Vicksburg *Herald*, Jan. 14, 1910.
15Brookhaven *Leader*, quoted in Jackson *Clarion-Ledger*, Feb. 3, 1910; Natchez *Democrat*, Feb. 2, 1910; Jackson *Issue*, June 9, 1910.
16Statement by Theodore G. Bilbo, in Jackson *Issue*, July 22, 1910.
17Macon *Beacon*, July 21, 1911.

Percy received 87 votes to Vardaman's 82. The Natchez *Democrat* conceded that Vardaman had made a remarkable fight, that the "brains of the state had been arrayed against him," and that his followers had stuck to him "closer than brothers."[18]

The Vardaman press did not take his defeat gracefully. The Aberdeen *Weekly*, while praising Percy's qualifications, observed that he was not the choice of the people. The Columbus *Dispatch* said that Vardaman's defeat was brought about by "a hundred men, representing their conflicting ambitions, the corporations of the state, the administration of the state, the money of the state." The Laurel *Ledger* thought it "scarcely necessary to discuss . . . the multiplicity of influences that culminated in [Vardaman's] defeat," and the *Democrat-Star* thought the caucus the "most disgraceful political farce [ever] enacted at our state capital."[19]

Immediately after the caucus Vardaman's followers held a mass meeting in Jackson and made plans for the 1911 primary when their leader would oppose Percy before the people for the full term of the Senate seat. Vardaman, speaking on that occasion, disclaimed any ill will toward Percy and wished him well. "Much has been said about corrupt methods—the use of money, whiskey, and the promise of office. . . . Whether or not there is truth in the charge I cannot say. But I am slow to believe that a white Mississippian would betray the people for money." A week later, however, he charged that his defeat had been brought about by the lumber and whiskey interests and insinuated that bribery had secured Percy's election.[20] Similar charges were rampant throughout the state, and the legislature was urged to investigate. When it hesitated, Judge Sam Cook charged the Hinds grand jury with investigation of the rumors.

On March 28 the grand jury returned an indictment against L. C. Dulaney, a planter and levee contractor of Issaquena County, charging that he had paid Senator Theodore G. Bilbo of Pearl River County $645 to obtain his vote for Percy. The senate thereupon ordered an investigation of the bribery charges. Meanwhile the legis-

---

[18]Jackson *Daily News*, June 8, 1911; Natchez *Democrat*, Feb. 23, 1910; Jackson *Clarion-Ledger*, Feb. 24, 1910.

[19]Quoted in Jackson *Issue*, Mar. 5, 12, 1910; Jackson *Clarion-Ledger*, Mar. 17, 26, 1910.

[20]Jackson *Issue*, Feb. 26, Mar. 5, 1910; Jackson *Clarion-Ledger*, Mar. 3, 8, 1910.

lature instructed its Joint Committee on Contingent Funds to investigate Vardaman's accounts while he was governor.[21]

Thus, in addition to the grand jury investigation, there were two legislative investigations—one by the Joint Committee on Contingent Funds investigating Vardaman's official accounts, the other a senate Committee of the Whole, investigating the bribery charges. "The fair name of the grand old state," moaned the *Clarion*, "is being dragged through the slime and mire."[22]

The contingent fund investigation dropped out of sight for a time, and attention was centered on the senate bribery investigation. "Nothing else is thought of or talked about in Jackson now," reported the *Clarion*. "It is the one absorbing theme, and is discussed on the streets, in the business houses, in offices, in workshops, in homes, around the hotels, at the capital, everywhere." Never, it said, had there been a greater sensation; never had people been so stirred; never had worse feeling been shown. And Jackson, it added, was merely the barometer of the state. "Whatever goes on here is echoed throughout the length and breadth of Mississippi." Violent trouble was expected at the capitol, where the senate was conducting its investigation behind closed doors. "If a search had been made," said one reporter, "dozens of guns could have been extracted from the hip-pockets of legislators, political lieutenants, and other persons who thronged the lobbies."[23]

Since a motion to expel Bilbo was pending, the senate investigation amounted to a trial. Two senators were appointed to prosecute and two to defend him. He testified that, disturbed by rumors of bribery, he suggested to some of his colleagues early in the caucus that a trap be laid to catch the guilty. Getting little encouragement from them he had then called a meeting of Vardaman's leaders in Agricultural Commissioner Blakeslee's office and suggested a plan whereby he and Representative J. O. Cowart act as detectives. They would, he proposed, accept a bribe, if offered, and then turn over the money and expose the bribers. Present at the meeting, in addition to himself and Cowart, were: J. Swep Taylor, a prominent Jackson businessman and later mayor of the city; T. P. Barr, a prominent Jackson merchant; Judge Wiley Potter; Ben Ward, editor of the

[21]Mississippi, *House Journal*, 1910, pp. 1472-1502; *Senate Journal*, 1910, p. 996; Jackson *Clarion-Ledger*, Mar. 3, 8, 20, 23, 24, 1910.
[22]Jackson *Clarion-Ledger*, Mar. 31, 1910; Natchez *Democrat*, Mar. 29, 1910.
[23]Jackson *Clarion-Ledger*, Mar. 31, 1910; Natchez *Democrat*, Mar. 29, 1910.

Union Advocate; and several others. There was some disagreement among witnesses over who the others were—there was even uncertainty whether or not Vardaman was present. All present agreed that Bilbo should pursue his plan, but Potter advised against exposing any bribery detected until after the election. "The lines," Bilbo quoted him as saying, "were drawn pretty tight and the friends of the other candidates would say it was a political trick [and it] would result in harm to Mr. Vardaman."[24] The others had then agreed with Potter, he said, and the final decision was against revealing the fraud during the caucus. It was believed that such a revelation would create "a great turmoil in the legislature, but . . . would do Vardaman no good."[25]

After this meeting, Bilbo stated, he was approached in the interest of Percy by two women, Mrs. C. J. Neil, a fellow boarder with him at the Lemon Hotel, and Mrs. Ruby Hall, wife of the proprietor of the Lemon. They told him, he said, that money was being paid for Percy votes, and urged him to accept some of it. Subsequently Mrs. Neil introduced him to Dulaney. After several meetings with Dulaney, he said, it was agreed that he was to receive $500 if he would switch his vote from Vardaman to Percy, and $500 additional if Percy was elected. He planned, he said, to accept the money before witnesses. To that end he had had the assistant chief of police of Jackson arrange a rendezvous at the assignation house of Mary Stamps, a mulatto, in south Jackson. Several witnesses were to be concealed to observe the transaction. The stage was set and the witnesses gathered, but at the last minute the plans fell through.[26]

Matters then cooled for a while, said Bilbo, but later Dulaney approached him again and a new series of meetings occurred in Dulaney's room in the Edwards House. At one of these meetings, he said, Dulaney had given him $150, and at another time $145. He had taken the money and shown it to S. B. Culpepper, president of Clark Memorial College, who was staying with him temporarily at the Lemon. The day after the election of Percy, he said, he had again called on Dulaney and was given $350 more. He had taken $500 of the money to his wife in Poplarville, he said, and kept the other $145 with him because he might need it. He had then re-

24*Investigation by the Senate of the State of Mississippi of the Charges of Bribery in the Election of a United States Senator* (Nashville, 1910), 29-36.

25*Ibid.,* 80, 83, 99.

26*Ibid.,* 80-99.

turned to Jackson, and when the grand jury met several weeks later, he went before it, told all he knew, and turned over the money.

Bilbo's testimony was corroborated in substance, if not in all details, by numerous other witnesses. Swep Taylor, Ben F. Ward, Judge Potter, T. P. Barr, and Cowart all testified to the meeting in Blakeslee's office where the plans were first laid. Potter disagreed on one detail. He said the sentiment at the meeting was unanimous for exposure of the bribery, if discovered, during the caucus. He had merely insisted, he said, that before any exposure was made definite evidence be secured implicating some responsible member of the opposition. Barr and others agreed with Bilbo that Potter had expressed the fear that exposure during the caucus would adversely affect Vardaman.[27] Culpepper testified that Bilbo had shown him $150 on one occasion and $145 on another and had told him that it came from the "Percy people" and that he was going to expose them. Senators J. A. Bailey, C. E. Franklin, S. J. Owens, and Representative J. L. Seawright stated that Bilbo had told them early in the caucus of his intention of trapping bribers. Owens testified that Bilbo told him ten days before Percy's election that "My scheme has worked all right. I have got the evidence and in good time I am going to expose it." Later, while the grand jury was in session, Owens said, Bilbo showed him a roll of money and said he was going to turn it over to the grand jury. Representative A. C. Anderson, a teller at the caucus, stated that he saw Bilbo's ballot on the last vote and that it was marked for Vardaman. Assistant Chief of Police J. L. Raney corroborated the proposed tryst at Mary Stamps' place. Representative E. J. Pollard of DeSoto testified that Bilbo had told him the week before the grand jury met that he had "a bomb up [his] sleeve that [would] give them a jar."[28]

Mrs. Hall had signed a statement to the effect that she had been given twenty dollars by Dulaney who told her to give it to Bilbo "to hold him in line." She later repudiated the statement and said she had been induced to sign it by District Attorney M. S. McNeill, a member of Vardaman's faction, on a promise that it would "keep her out of trouble." She testified that Bilbo had sought her out shortly before the grand jury met, told her he was in trouble, and asked her to lend him $280 for a short time. Later, she said, Bilbo

27Ibid., 29-35, 120-34, 151-58, 233-42.
28Ibid., 100-13, 297, 299-300, 243-57.

had again approached her and offered her $1,000 if she would go again before the grand jury and "make a clean breast" of all she knew.[29] The strategy of this testimony was two-edged. It purported to blacken Bilbo's character by insinuating both that if he had received a bribe he had spent it for his own use and that he had himself attempted to bribe a witness.

District Attorney McNeill refused to turn over the stenographic notes of the grand jury hearings to the senate. He testified before them, however, as did also the stenographer, R. S. Streit, that Mrs. Hall had stated before the jury that she had been given twenty dollars by Dulaney to give to Bilbo. McNeill denied that he had used any unfair tactics to get her to so testify. Bilbo denied offering her $1,000 or any amount to testify.[30]

Mrs. Neil's testimony corroborated Bilbo, although in giving it she blackened her own reputation. She gave her home as Chattanooga, Tennessee, and her business as "keeping books and working in real estate and trying to buy Mississippi Legislators." She stated that she was commissioned by Dulaney to solicit prospects for bribery and that she was go-between for Dulaney in his dealings with Bilbo and Cowart. She first had been persuaded to work in Percy's interest, she said, by J. G. Bennett of the Jackson *Daily News*. He had told her that Percy was sure to win because his crowd "had the money." She then, she said, had been asked by Dulaney to "feel the Senators and the Representatives, and secure as many weak ones, and those that liked money or enjoyment," and to introduce them to him. She presented Bilbo to Dulaney and arranged a private interview for them in a room at the Lemon. After the meeting, she said, Dulaney told her "There is nothing in the damned little rascal. He won't talk to me." Bilbo had told her, she said, that "Dulaney must take me for a fool. I am not going to talk plain." She said that after a few days she became convinced that Bilbo was "doing a little detective work." Mrs. Neil also testified that she had introduced Representative Cowart to Dulaney and that Dulaney had later told her that he could not seem to come to terms with Cowart. She quoted Dulaney as saying that he did not know whether Cowart "wanted money or that judgeship."[31]

29*Ibid.*, 80-85.
30*Ibid.*, 193, 195-98, 200-201, 204-205.
31*Ibid.*, 259-62, 266, 275.

Before the caucus ended, Mrs. Neil said, she had gone to Vicksburg. From there she went to New Orleans at Mardi Gras time to sell a story of the caucus to a newspaper. While she was there and on her return trip to Jackson, she said, she was shadowed by men wearing red ribbons in their lapels. One of them, R. S. Seay, who was admittedly working in the interest of the Percy faction, tried to induce her to remain in New Orleans, and when she refused the others threatened her.[32]

Representative Cowart not only corroborated Bilbo's testimony but brought forth startling revelations of his own. He stated that Dulaney had offered him $1,000 to induce him to vote for Percy but that he had not agreed. After that, he said, R. N. Miller, Wood Magee, and Will A. Percy, Leroy's brother, had offered him, in the presence of "Private" John Allen, official positions to secure his vote for Percy. Magee, he said, had tendered him a circuit judgeship. When this did not seem to move him, Miller and Will Percy had held out to him a United States judgeship or a foreign consulate. They had also offered, he said, if he would move to some town on the Y. and M. V. Railroad, to give him a "lucrative practice." They told him that "after Leroy was elected they could turn things bottom side upwards." Cowart said that he called on Governor Noel and attempted to tell him that illegal offers were being made in his name but that Noel had cut him short, telling him that he did not want to know anything about it as he had nothing to do with it. Miller admitted that he told Cowart "his chances [for a judgeship] would be improved by voting for some other candidate who was not so hostile to the administration of Governor Noel as . . . Vardaman was," but denied that he had actually tendered the offer as a bribe. Noel denied that Cowart had mentioned to him any matters concerning the attempted bribery. Cowart had charged that Will Percy was the representative of Secretary of War J. M. Dickinson who had promised, according to Cowart, federal patronage for Percy votes. Will Percy neither admitted nor denied this.[33]

Despite the sensations that were being revealed hourly, everyone was awaiting impatiently the appearance of Dulaney as a witness. He was summoned and gave his testimony. He said that he

[32]*Ibid.*, 276-96.
[33]*Ibid.*, 207-23, 227-31, 397, 460-63, 470-71.

had always been a supporter of McLaurin but that after the Senator's death he had come to Jackson to support Percy or anyone else against Vardaman. His opposition was based on Vardaman's Negro policy which had caused the Negroes "to move away from our county . . . by the hundreds into Arkansas. . . . It was detrimental to the interests of all of us where the negro labor was a factor." He denied that he had attempted to bribe anyone. He said that Mrs. Neil had sought him out once and told him that she could deliver nine votes for $2,000, but that he had repulsed her and had not seen or talked to her since. He said his only contacts with Bilbo had been several visits which Bilbo had made to his room. Bilbo, he said, would come to his room, have several drinks, and then depart, carrying out with him each time a bottle of whiskey. Once Bilbo had tried in vain to borrow $50 from him, he said. He branded Bilbo's statement that he had received $645 from him as "a most infamous, filthy lie," and he denied offering Cowart $1,000 for his vote.[34] Dulaney admitted giving Mrs. Hall $50 for entertaining friends of Percy.

Meanwhile the press of the state was giving the investigation full coverage. The Macon Beacon bemoaned the scandal, although it placed no credence in Bilbo's story. Percy's "high character and invincible integrity," it thought, ". . . put him above pollution by such a scandal," while "Everything [Bilbo] has done has been the act of a liar and a corrupt man." The Coast Beacon thought the investigation a waste of time. If there was any consideration extended or accepted, it said, neither the giver nor the receiver was "going to admit it, so the white wash brush may be applied at once." The Beacon agreed with "Private" John Allen that "There seems to have been several legislators running around Jackson holding out their hands seeking to be bribed." It urged that since none of those charged with accepting the bribes had voted for Percy, the investigation be dropped.[35] The Issue pertly remarked that the only Negro exodus from Dulaney's county during Vardaman's governorship "was the movement of about fifty or sixty convicts from his plantation, from whose toil for a number of years he had reaped a liberal profit."[36]

[34]Ibid., 301-20.

[35]Macon Beacon, Apr. 1, 8, 1910; Coast Beacon, quoted in Jackson Clarion-Ledger, Mar. 31, 1910.

[36]Jackson Issue, Apr. 16, 1910.

Despite Bilbo's explanation of his delay in revealing the alleged bribery, the press made much of the fact that he had waited several weeks after he claimed receiving the money before he had divulged the bribery. The Natchez *Democrat* thought this looked "exceedingly yellow." It pointed out that if he had exposed the bribery when he charged it occurred, it would have resulted in Vardaman's election. Thus, it said, Bilbo, "if his story is true, is a coward and a traitor to Vardaman." The two Jackson papers and the Vicksburg *Herald* agreed with the *Democrat*. The *Clarion* said Bilbo's story was "unreasonable and improbable and . . . is hatched up in order to becloud . . . the investigation into the contingent fund . . . and to give Vardaman an advantage in the Senate race next summer." If Bilbo had been "touched" as he claimed, "he certainly did Vardaman a very great injustice in sitting down like a clam and see[ing] him go to slaughter, when by a word he could have elected him." "Was there ever before," asked Editor Henry, "anything like it on this earth, the heavens above, or the water below?" The *Herald* thought Bilbo's failure to reveal the alleged bribery during the caucus "stamps the charge as libel and an after thought."[37]

But the *Issue* said it was a question of "damned if you do and damned if you don't." If Bilbo had made the exposure during the caucus, the same people who were now criticizing him for not doing so would have denounced him for perpetrating "a political trick" to elect Vardaman.[38] His further delay after the caucus was over, Bilbo said, was inspired by the fear that if the opposition got wind of the evidence before the jury was ready to act, they might succeed in preventing the indictment. "I knew," he said, "what would take place when the facts were out." Since the exposure, Jackson had been filled with "an effort to defeat the indictment and overcome it." That, he said, was the purpose "in keeping this thing a secret."[39]

In the investigation Bilbo's character and reputation were minutely examined. Witnesses from Bilbo's neighborhood in south Mississippi were produced by both sides, one group attacking Bilbo's character, the other defending it. Bilbo was able to show that some of the opposition witnesses were in the employ of the Gulf and

[37]Macon *Beacon*, Apr. 8, 1910; Natchez *Democrat*, Mar. 29, 30, 31, 1910; Jackson *Clarion-Ledger*, Mar. 31, 1910; Vicksburg *Herald*, Mar. 29, 1910.

[38]Jackson *Issue*, Apr. 9, 1910.

[39]*Senate Investigation*, 80, 83, 99.

Ship Island Railroad. This corporation was openly hostile to Vardaman and had been denounced by him as "always in [politics] . . . for its own interest as against the interests of the taxpayers."[40] One witness, Walter A. White, an attorney from Biloxi, testified that he had heard that a legislative bill redistricting judicial circuits in Harrison County had been defeated by Bilbo's influence. He investigated and learned of rumors of Bilbo's accepting bribes. He and Judge James Neville, chief counsel of the Gulf and Ship Island, attempted to set a trap for Bilbo by bribing him to support a dummy bill. They had engaged R. M. Moseley as their agent, and Moseley testified that Bilbo had promised to support the bill for $300. The plot, however, was not carried to execution. Bilbo denied the charge and was able to discredit it when he presented as a witness the man who had introduced Moseley to him on the occasion in question. This witness testified that Moseley was so drunk at the time that in his judgment he would not know what had transpired.[41] Other witnesses impeaching Bilbo were presented, but he was able to show in most cases that they were not impartial.[42]

An attempt was made to discredit Bilbo's story when it was revealed that three of the bank notes which he turned over to the grand jury had been issued by the National Bank of Poplarville. Bilbo explained this by the statement that his wife had deposited the money in the bank for safekeeping without requesting that the identical bills be preserved.[43]

The testimony did not seem to change any opinions. As the *Clarion* pointed out, the contest was political rather than judicial. "The Vardaman folks," it said, "are of the opinion that Bilbo is telling the truth . . . while the opposition . . . are of the opposite way of thinking."[44] The *Sea Coast Echo* remarked on the peculiar situation of "a majority of the legislature exhausting every means to break down the evidence of one of its own members given before a grand jury that returned a true bill against an alleged briber." It pointed out that the alleged briber was not a member of the legislature, yet that body was "making his cause the cause of the state . . . throwing every shield around and about the accused and

40*Ibid.*, 354, 367, 385-87; Jackson *Issue*, Feb. 22, 1908.
41*Senate Investigation*, 375-78, 348-62, 406; Natchez *Democrat*, Apr. 9, 10, 1910.
42*Senate Investigation*, 435-37, 443-45, 452-54, 476-78, 480.
43*Ibid.*, 437-38.
44Jackson *Clarion-Ledger*, Apr. 14, 1910.

stooping to the lowest depths to discredit its own member." The Yazoo *Sentinel* said the senate should, instead of attempting to impeach Bilbo, "tender him a vote of thanks for uncovering the rottenest piece of politics that has ever disgraced the name of Mississippi." The Columbus *Dispatch*, too, believed Bilbo's story, and the Vicksburg *Post* charged that the investigation was designed to discredit him as a witness in the Dulaney trial.[45]

At least one member of the opposition believed that Vardaman was beaten by unfair means. Writing several years later a cousin of John Sharp Williams revealed his belief that "from what I saw and knew . . . improper influences *were* used to defeat him."[46]

After the testimony was all in, the resolution to expel Bilbo was voted on. It received 28 votes to 15 against it, failing by one vote of the necessary two-thirds majority. Senators Anderson and Leftwich, the two prosecutors, then offered a resolution characterizing as "utterly unexplained and absolutely incredible" Bilbo's claim to have acted in good faith while failing to disclose "until weeks after the nomination had been made and a Senator elected" the information "alleged to have been obtained by him." It further resolved, because of these "unexplained inconsistencies and inherent improbabilities" in his testimony, as well as in his "established bad character and lack of credibility," that the senate condemn the charge "and the statement of the role played" by Bilbo as a "trumped up falsehood utterly unworthy of belief." It resolved further that Bilbo was "unfit to sit with honest upright men in a respectable legislative body" and called on him to resign. A dozen or more of Bilbo's supporters walked out before the vote, and the resolution carried 25 to 1. The senate then adopted, 28 to 0, a resolution stating that, in their belief, the conduct of every candidate in the senatorial contest had been "dignified, honorable, and upright," that no vote in the caucus was procured "by any improper means or corrupt influence," and that Percy's election was "free from any fraud or corruption."[47]

The Natchez *Democrat* called Bilbo's "escape" from expulsion

[45]Quoted in Jackson *Issue*, Apr. 9, 16, 1910.

[46]Garrard Harris to Williams, Jan. 25, 1916, Williams Papers.

[47]*Senate Investigation*, 7-9. The House passed a similar resolution. See Mississippi, *House Journal*, 1910, p. 1523. See also House minority report, *ibid.*, 1527-28, charging that "undue influence," "liquor," and "Executive influence" were used to effect Percy's election.

due "entirely to partisanship and sympathy," and the *Clarion* agreed. "It now remains," said the latter, "for Bilbo to resign, suppress himself, withdraw to the shades of private life, to which he will forever hereafter be retired."[48] But Bilbo did not resign. Instead he issued a militant statement branding the senate investigation as a "whitewash." It was, he said, "a bitter and disgraceful fight with the friends of the common people and clean government on the one side and the mercenary politicians and corporate interests on the other." The "interests," he said, when they failed to prevent Dulaney's indictment, "threw the whole affair into the state senate . . . for the professed purpose of investigation, but . . . the scheme was to secure the state's evidence, whitewash the guilty parties, defeat justice, confound the public as to the real facts, expel or condemn me and to recommend themselves powerfully." The corporations of south Mississippi, he said, had had him marked ever since he entered public life because he had "dared to oppose them in the interest of the people." They had "scoured south Mississippi as with a fine tooth comb" to discredit him. The same twenty-eight senators who voted to expel him, he said, were interested only in damning him and would have voted the same way before the investigation as they did afterward. The investigation he termed a "star chamber proceeding." Anderson and Leftwich, "who were supposed to represent the senate," were in daily conference with Dulaney and the Percy brothers and their attorneys. "People of Mississippi," he concluded, "the fight between the classes and the masses, between the corporate influences and the people is on, and it will be a fight to the finish."[49]

The trial of Dulaney on the indictment was delayed by a change of venue to Yazoo County. This change brought charges from the Vardaman press that the court was favoring the defense. The Percy press was distressed at this attitude and blamed it on Vardaman, who, it said, had "done more to lower the tone of politics in Mississippi . . . than any other [man] in the state's history."[50] The trial was held in November and December and charges of partiality were made by both factions. The Jackson *News* was shocked when the prosecuting attorney withdrew an embarrassing question he

[48]Natchez *Democrat*, Apr. 23, 1910; Jackson *Clarion-Ledger*, Apr. 21, 1910.
[49]Jackson *Clarion-Ledger*, Apr. 28, 1910; Jackson *Issue*, Apr. 30, 1910.
[50]Columbus *Dispatch*, quoted in Macon *Beacon*, Dec. 9, 1910.

had propounded to Bilbo. It charged the prosecution with "taking more care of Bilbo, looking after his interests with more energy . . . than any other feature of the case." Every move made, it alleged, had been with the view to bolstering up his testimony and protecting him from counsel for the defense. The sensational story, it said, told by "the miserable little moral pervert, Theodore G. Bilbo," was a cowardly political frame-up "hellishly conceived by the followers of Vardaman to bolster his waning political fortunes." The *News* scouted the idea that Bilbo left the trial before its conclusion because he feared he might meet with personal violence from Dulaney. The latter had said, according to Editor Fred Sullens, that he would not "soil his hands on the dirty pup."[51]

The jury acquitted Dulaney. It then issued a sworn statement to the public certifying that its verdict was unanimous and on the first ballot, and "was based upon the fact that each of us . . . believed Mr. Bilbo's statement to be untrue . . . and his charge to be a 'frame-up' and pure fabrication." This statement was made, the jurymen said, so the public might know that "we were not misled in any respect, nor Mr. Dulaney acquitted on any so called 'legal technicality', but upon the testimony as given by all the witnesses under oath." The jurors were polled as to their political affiliation, and six stated they had favored Vardaman for senator, four Percy, and two Alexander. Said E. S. Barksdale, one of the Vardaman men: "I was ready to bring in a verdict of not guilty when Bilbo had concluded his testimony." Another, W. B. Vaughan, said, "It did not take me long to make up my mind after I heard Bilbo testify." A third, J. J. Inge, said, "I think the entire jury was of one mind after hearing Bilbo's testimony."[52]

When the trial resulted in a repudiation of Bilbo the *Clarion* thought this should result in Vardaman's defeat in 1911. "Bilbo is Vardaman property," it said, "his by right of discovery, by virtue of the celebrated frame-up, the purpose of which was to destroy an honorable Senator . . . ruin a private citizen, and bring disgrace on the state."[53] Nor did the Jackson *News* see any further place for Bilbo in the Vardaman camp. "He has destroyed his usefulness

[51]Jackson *Daily News*, Nov. 23, 27, Dec. 2, 3, 1910.

[52]Jackson *Clarion-Ledger*, Jan. 5, 1911; Macon *Beacon*, July 28, 1911; Jackson *Daily News*, Dec. 3, 4, 1910.

[53]Jackson *Clarion-Ledger*, Dec. 8, 1910.

to The Ambitious One," it said after the trial. It suggested that the best thing to do with him was "to confine the malodorous creature in a small room with a dozen polecats until they stink each other to death."[54]

Sentiment was not so unanimous, however, throughout the state. The Osyka *Herald*, while having "not the least patience with Bilbo or men of his stripe," was convinced that "Dulaney gave him money and whiskey to influence his vote." The Ripley *Sentinel* discounted the claim that six of the jurors were Vardaman men. Perhaps, it said, "they were converted to his standard while on the job." The *Issue* charged that "Messrs. Percy and Williams . . . , the governor . . . with all . . . his . . . power, the administration at Washington, an unlimited amount of money . . . and the most sagacious, resourceful criminal lawyers in the state" were all employed to secure the acquittal. It had, it said, expected nothing else.[55]

But the effects of the Secret Caucus were not to end with the acquittal of Dulaney. Nor was Bilbo destined to be stunk to death by polecats. The reverberations of the sensational struggle were to be felt in every political contest for a decade, and Bilbo was to rise to power and even supplant the "White Chief" himself on the prestige which came to him as a result of the part he played. Lines were to be drawn more tightly and with more vindictiveness than ever before in the history of the state, and scarcely a man in politics but believed that he owed his success or his defeat to his stand on the question.

Whether Dulaney was guilty or whether, as he said, it was a charge trumped up by Bilbo, it is impossible to say. Bilbo told a convincing story, was corroborated by credible witnesses, and supplied other abundant proof to substantiate his charges. On the other hand, Dulaney denied the charge, and a jury of twelve men, six of whom claimed to be Vardaman followers, believed him. So far as our story is concerned it matters little whether Dulaney was guilty or not. The important thing was the bitterness which the incident created among the people of the state. The malice, ignor-

[54]Jackson *Daily News*, Dec. 4, 1910.

[55]Jackson *Issue*, Dec. 9, 1910; *ibid.*, Dec. 16, quoting Osyka *Herald*, Ripley *Sentinel*, Coahoma *Monitor*, Newton *Record*, Enterprise *Journal*, Crystal Springs *Meteor*, Carroll County *News*, and Columbus *Dispatch*; Jackson *Clarion-Ledger*, Dec. 15, 1910; Macon *Beacon*, Dec. 16, 1910.

ance, and thoughtlessness with which the factions carried on their fight convinced many good people that a great wrong had been perpetrated. The result was a great political upheaval and the bringing of the revolution, started by Vardaman in 1903, to complete fruition.

CHAPTER XVII

THE ELECTION OF 1911

IMMEDIATELY after the senate bribery investigation Percy proposed that he and Vardaman enter a joint canvass for a primary election to be held in November, 1910. If the election went against him, Percy said, he would resign when the legislature met in 1911. Vardaman accepted the proposal in principle but suggested several changes. The primary, he thought, should be held in August instead of November, Percy should resign "immediately" in case of an adverse vote, Governor Noel's agreement to appoint the winner should be obtained, and the loser should promise to support the winner in the regular 1911 primary for the full term. Percy insisted that the primary not be held before November and refused to ask Noel to appoint the winner. Vardaman then agreed to Percy's stipulations, and the Democratic state executive committee ordered the primary. The attorney-general, however, ruled that such an agreed primary would be illegal, and Noel let it be known that he would not appoint Vardaman even though he won the primary and Percy resigned. Thereupon the scheme was dropped, and each side accused the other of bad faith. Vardaman charged that Percy and Noel were in collusion, and the state executive committee charged that the affair had fallen through because Vardaman had not agreed to the terms prescribed by the committee. The Percy press charged that Vardaman had shown a "yellow streak" and that he had flatly declined to meet Percy in joint debate.[1]

With the proposed 1910 primary in the discard, Vardaman, Percy, and C. H. Alexander announced their candidacies for the full term in the primary to be held in August, 1911. Though that date was fifteen months off, canvassing began with political rallies in the spring of 1910 and continued through the spring and summer of the following year. At the same time Bilbo, aligning himself with Vardaman, announced his candidacy for lieutenant-governor.[2]

[1]Jackson *Clarion-Ledger*, Apr. 21, 28, May 12, 1910; Macon *Beacon*, Apr. 22, Aug. 19, 1910; Natchez *Democrat*, Apr. 16, 17, 19, May 1, 7, Aug. 23, 1910; Jackson *Daily News*, May 7, 1910; W. A. Percy to J. K. Vardaman, Apr. 15, 1910; Vardaman to Percy, Apr. 15, 1910, published in Jackson *Issue*, Apr. 16, 1910; *ibid.*, Apr. 30, 1910.

[2]Natchez *Democrat*, May 7, Aug. 23, 1910; Jackson *Clarion-Ledger*, July 7, 1910, Jan. 26, 1911.

Indications of a bitter and vindictive campaign were early seen by the Greenville *Democrat*. With Vardaman and his "partisan press" upholding Bilbo and "cussing out" the governor, legislature, and executive committee, the *Democrat* thought a campaign "on what is termed a 'high plane'" an impossibility. In a speech at God-bold Wells on July 4, 1910, Percy, heckled by an audience with shouts of "Hurrah for Vardaman!" "Hurrah for Bilbo!" "Hurrah for Mary Stamps!" became angered and called them "cattle" and "red-necks." These names were adopted by the Vardaman following, and wherever Vardaman went to speak he was greeted by crowds of men wearing red neckties and was carried in wagons drawn by oxen. This accentuated the class division in the struggle.[3]

Vardaman charged that Percy had been unfairly elected by the caucus. Percy challenged Vardaman to meet him in open debate, but this Vardaman would not do. "If you can substantiate that charge," said Percy, ". . . then that legislature should be branded with disapproval and the man who sought to profit by that corruption should be driven in shame out of public life." On the other hand, if Vardaman could not substantiate it, then he stood "convicted of having slandered the legislature . . . for political profit, and [was] unworthy of any honors at the hands of the people." The feeling between the two men had become personal. When they met in public "Neither showed the slightest sign of recognition. They passed each other without a nod."[4]

Most of the "old line" politicians in the state were backing Percy or Alexander. McLaurin's three surviving brothers, his only son, and the remnants of his organization were aligned with his old enemy, Percy, against his greater enemy, Vardaman. Sidney McLaurin thought this called for an explanation, and he gave it. Admitting that bad blood had existed at one time between his brother and Percy, Sidney said that at the time of Anse's death they were personally and politically on the best of terms. On the other hand, Vardaman's opposition to McLaurin had been "bitter, vindictive, and malicious, from the time he first thought Senator McLaurin was in his way politically."[5] John Sharp Williams was backing

[3]Greenville *Democrat* and Raymond *Gazette*, quoted in Jackson *Clarion-Ledger*, June 2, 9, 1910; *ibid.*, June 16, July 7, Aug. 18, 1910; Vicksburg *Post*, July 6, 1910.

[4]Vicksburg *Herald*, June 1, 1911; Jackson *Daily News*, June 10, 1911.

[5]Sidney L. McLaurin to Editor, Brandon *News*, June 22, 1911, published in Jackson *Clarion-Ledger*, June 29, 1911.

Percy, whom he termed "one of the most intelligent, brainy, and efficient men in the United States—and a gentleman every inch of him." He later said that he staked his own political future in backing Percy, because it was "plain at the time" that, "owing to some local conditions," Percy would be defeated.[6] Governor Noel, of course, was actively canvassing for Percy. The daily press of the state, with the lone exception of the Vicksburg *Post,* was backing either Percy or Alexander, or both.[7]

By May, 1911, political news was crowding all other off the front pages of the papers. A dispatch from Wesson to a New Orleans paper said that not even the closing down of the great mills there "has caused business in Wesson to suffer so much as the present senatorial campaign." From early morning until late at night men "spend their time on the streets and in the stores, post office, depot, and livery stables, discussing who is going to be United States Senator." Business, it said, "has been lost sight of."[8]

Although the Secret Caucus and class divisions were to be the decisive issues in the campaign, every attempt was made to win support on other issues. Vardaman and Bilbo had long been advocates of school fund reform and a reapportionment of legislative representatives for the benefit of south Mississippi.[9] To counteract these issues, Noel, himself a "liberal" at heart, advocated legislative reapportionment which would "give each county its proper voice in . . . lawmaking"; modernization of the tax system to make burdens "borne by the different counties just . . . and equitable"; and modification of the school tax to let counties able to bear their own burden do so and to use state funds only "for counties unable to educate properly their own children."[10]

All three candidates claimed they were being opposed by the trusts. Ross Collins, a Vardaman supporter and candidate for attorney-general, charged that his opponent, S. S. Hudson, running for re-election, had accepted money from the Hines Lumber Company to have an antitrust indictment against it quashed. Hines was a Chicago concern and both Vardaman and Bilbo were bitter in

[6]J. S. Williams to President Woodrow Wilson, Nov. 17, 1916, Apr. 24, 1917, Williams Papers.

[7]Natchez *Democrat,* July 4, 1911; Jackson *Clarion-Ledger,* July 20, 1911.

[8]New Orleans *Times-Democrat,* quoted in Jackson *Clarion-Ledger,* May 25, 1911.

[9]*Senate Investigation,* 92; Jackson *Issue,* Feb. 1, 1908.

[10]Jackson *Clarion-Ledger,* July 6, 1911.

their denunciation of it. Allegedly it was sponsor of the landholding bill which Vardaman had vetoed as governor. Vardaman charged that Hines was interested in electing a legislature which would pass and a governor who would approve a new bill. "He [Hines] does not own quite all the timber lands in South Mississippi yet," said Vardaman, "he wants them all." Vardaman also declared against a protective tariff on lumber, which Percy had not done.[11]

In his message to the legislature in 1908 Vardaman had urged extensive powers for the railroad commission enabling it to fix rates, supervise roadbeds and rolling stock, prevent dividends on watered stock, and prohibit overworking of conductors, engineers, and telegraph operators. He had vetoed the merger of the Southern and the Mobile and Ohio railroads, which, he said, had gained him the undying enmity of those two lines. In 1911 he was urging stricter enforcement of railroad regulation as the only alternative to government ownership.[12]

As the campaign progressed classes were arrayed against masses, and country against town. The contest between capital and labor, said Vardaman, was inevitable. The laboring man "was not given an equal chance . . . under our . . . *unjust* and *partial* laws." "If labor would survive it must organize for its own protection and see to it that men are sent to the legislature and to congress who will enact laws that vouchsafe to every citizen an equal chance in the race of life." He said the contest was for supremacy "between the man whose toil produces the wealth of the country, and the favored few who reap the profit of that toil." He did not, he said, favor persecution of corporations. He believed they should enjoy the same rights and opportunities accorded to individuals, but no more. Capital, he said, should be taxed at the same rate as labor. Vardaman was commended and Percy condemned by the *Mississippi Labor Journal.*[13]

The Percy and Alexander supporters cried out against these "populistic, socialistic . . . and anarchistic utterances," and said they left Vardaman's "democracy under the very gravest suspicions."

[11]Jackson *Issue* and Aberdeen *Examiner,* quoted in Macon *Beacon,* July 15, 1910; Jackson *Clarion-Ledger,* July 20, 1911; Jackson *Issue,* June 16, 1911.

[12]Mississippi, *House Journal,* 1908, pp. 50-52; *ibid.,* 1906, pp. 45-50.

[13]Jackson *Issue,* May 27, 1910, May 5, 1911; Jackson *Clarion-Ledger,* Aug. 3, 1911.

The conservative and thoughtful people in the state, they said, would consider his election a great tragedy. They denounced his appeals "to ignorance and prejudice" and taunted him because a railroad attorney was campaigning for him. They condemned his "notorious profanity" and his use of whiskey and wine during the caucus "while loudly proclaiming loyalty to prohibition." They estimated that 98 per cent of the preachers of the state were opposed to Vardaman, and when the Reverend Stephen Archer upheld from the pulpit Percy's "high character" he was praised by the anti-Vardaman press.[14]

The opposition charged that Vardaman had accepted and used a pass on the Gulf and Ship Island Railroad in violation of the law. Vardaman, admitting that his memory might be defective, denied any knowledge of ever having used a pass and called on his accusers to produce it. If they did, he promised to have a cut made of it and publish it in his paper. Thereupon Will Crump, Percy's campaign manager, produced pass number 864, issued by the Gulf and Ship Island to Vardaman. Vardaman kept his promise and printed a cut of the pass in his paper but denied that the pass was ever in his possession or used by him. It was, he said, issued as a compliment to trustees of the Old Soldiers' Home. The whole affair, he said, was merely an attempt by the railroad to destroy him.[15]

Meanwhile the contingent fund committee of the Secret Caucus legislature had investigated Vardaman's accounts while governor and reported that they failed to find vouchers for expenditures amounting to $1,700. In addition they charged that he made private use of a campaign fund raised for Bryan in 1904 and did not return it until after he had left office; that his trips investigating state institutions were paid for twice—once by the institution he was inspecting and once out of the contingent fund; that he failed to account for approximately $1,000 which he claimed he spent for relief of Meridian cyclone sufferers; and that he had misappropriated funds raised to purchase a silver service for the new battleship,

14Jackson Clarion-Ledger, July 27, 1911; Macon Beacon, July 28, 1911; Greenville Democrat and West Point Leader, quoted, ibid., July 15, 22, 1910; Natchez Democrat, July 2, 1911; Southern Sentinel and Jackson Daily News, quoted in Macon Beacon, June 2, 1911.

15Jackson Issue, Apr. 30, 1910, Feb. 24, 1911; Jackson Clarion-Ledger, Mar. 2, 1911.

Mississippi. In all, the alleged shortages amounted to $2,721.27.[16] At first Vardaman ignored the charges; then he denied them in a general manner rather than categorically. The opposition press leaped to the attack.

The Jackson *Daily News* said Vardaman's explanations were entirely unsatisfactory and called for more light on the subject. The *Clarion* had editorials almost daily on the shortages, and the Aberdeen *Examiner* said Vardaman stood convicted of the charges since he failed to prosecute his accusers for libel. When C. M. Williamson, "one of the exceedingly few members of [the legal] profession in high standing who is supporting Vardaman," admitted that he had signed a note for Vardaman just a few days before the former governor turned the battleship fund over to the commissioners, the *News* called on Vardaman to disprove the allegations or "shut up."[17]

Vardaman replied that vouchers and accounts of all expenditures were in his office when his term expired. The committee of the 1908 legislature had been invited to inspect them, he said, but apparently had failed to do so. He charged that later they had been removed from the files by his enemies in order to embarrass him. His statement was supported by Senator Clayton D. Potter, a member of the 1908 committee. According to Potter, Vardaman informed the committee before the expiration of his term that all vouchers and accounts were in his office ready for inspection. "Through an oversight," he said, "we failed to check over and approve same. The fault was ours, not his." All but $65 of the missing vouchers were for expenditures between 1904 and 1906. George Edwards, the current state treasurer, had been Vardaman's secretary during that period. He stated to the committee that the vouchers had been made and kept by him for all expenditures, and that all were in the file when he left Vardaman's service in 1906.[18]

[16]Mississippi, *House Journal*, 1910, pp. 222-25, 595-99, 1455-72; Jackson *Clarion-Ledger*, Mar. 10, 24, Apr. 19, 1910; Koscuisko *Courier*, quoted in Macon *Beacon*, July 21, 1911.

[17]Natchez *Democrat*, May 2, 1911; Macon *Beacon*, July 8, 1910, June 2, 16, 1911; Jackson *Clarion-Ledger*, Aug. 18, Sept. 1, 8, 1910; Aberdeen *Examiner*, quoted in Macon *Beacon*, July 21, 1911; Jackson *Daily News*, May 4, 9, 1910, June 5, 1911; Vicksburg *Herald*, June 6, 11, 1911.

[18]Testimony before Senate and House Joint Committee to investigate expenditures of Contingent Fund, in Mississippi, *House Journal*, 1910, pp. 1472-1502. For Potter's report see *ibid.*, 1455. Also see Vicksburg *Post*, Apr. 1, 1910; Jackson *Issue*, May 7, 1910.

Noel denied that the vouchers had been removed by him, and the opposition renewed the attack. Finally the legislature employed an accountant, Charles J. Moore, to investigate the charges against Vardaman. Moore subpoenaed Vardaman to appear before him. Vardaman went, but refused to answer Moore's questions. "The papers, vouchers, and memoranda . . . ," he said, "have all been out of my hands for nearly four years, and in the hands of . . . my bitterest political enemies . . . who are now, I think, resorting to this investigation solely for political purposes."[19] Moore then subpoenaed Vardaman's private account from the Mississippi Bank and Trust Company. The bank refused to honor the summons and was fined fifty dollars for contempt. It then obtained an injunction against Moore restraining him from issuing another subpoena until after the election. Before that event the bank went into receivership—forced, it said, through "politics."[20]

The issue was not settled then, nor was it ever to the satisfaction of everyone. Throughout the campaign opposition speakers and papers played on this tune as though it were the refrain of their campaign melody. "When the people asked for facts he [Vardaman] gave them poetry," said the Macon *Beacon* a few days before the election, "and when they asked to see the records, he replied with verbal tributes to their sovereignty."[21]

Bilbo played a colorful, if undignified, part in the campaign and drew much of the fire of the opposition. The large crowds which he drew were dismissed by one editor as the result of idle curiosity. "He is attractive," said the editor, "in the same way that freaks of nature are regarded." The *Clarion*, too, directed much of its attack throughout the campaign at Bilbo, whom it termed a "discredited and repudiated man" with "no reputation to protect." He used, it said, "language that would shock a fishwoman." They taxed their ingenuity for terms to express their contempt of him. Vardaman was condemned for associating with such "a thorough rascal" and for trying to win the senatorship with the aid of "the whelp Bilbo." The *Daily News* professed to be horrified when Vardaman referred to Bilbo as "that excellent gentleman." Bilbo was denounced as

---

[19]Jackson *Clarion-Ledger*, May 26, 1910, May 11, 1911; Jackson *Daily News*, May 25, 1910; Jackson *Issue*, May 19, 1911.

[20]Jackson *Daily News*, July 10, 1911; Natchez *Democrat*, July 14, 15, 22, 1911.

[21]Macon *Beacon*, June 2, 16, July 28, 1911; Vicksburg *Herald*, June 11, 1911.

"a self-confessed bribe-taker," a "frequenter of lewd houses," and a "pimp." He was accused of having formerly introduced bills in the legislature injurious to certain interests and then accepting bribes to defeat them. He was even accused of having stolen money from a sleeping companion.[22] But Bilbo was to pay the opposition back with interest and demonstrate that in the art of using invective language he had no peer in Mississippi.

Immediately after the senate investigation was completed in the spring of 1910 Bilbo had thrown himself into the campaign. In May, in a speech in Pike County, he "worked on the passion and prejudice of his hearers to such an extent," it was reported, that he was frequently interrupted with shouts of "We are the low-brows, we are the red-necks, rah for Vardaman!" Two months later at Newton, refused permission to speak from the same platform with Alexander, he had a temporary platform erected hard by, and when Alexander began speaking so did Bilbo. Bilbo was caned and knocked down on the streets of Yazoo City by Major W. D. Gibbs after Bilbo had referred to him in a speech as "a renegade Confederate soldier."[23] Some months later, speaking at Blue Mountain College, Bilbo called J. J. Henry, former penitentiary warden of ill repute,[24] "a cross between a hyena and a mongrel." "He was," said Bilbo, "begotten in a nigger graveyard at midnight, suckled by a sow and educated by a fool." Even some of the Vardaman press repudiated such scurrility. The New Orleans *States* said "Nothing like it has ever been heard before anywhere or in any political campaign on earth, and it wrote down the man guilty of its use as an unspeakable wretch, who should be barred from all association with decent people." The Memphis *Commercial Appeal*, also a Vardaman supporter, called Bilbo's remarks "horribly repulsive, disgusting and shocking." It was charged that five ladies left the audience while Bilbo was denouncing Henry, but the five ladies published a statement denying that that was the cause of their departure. They had left, they said, because of the late hour and

[22]Macon *Beacon,* July 8, Aug. 5, 1910; Vicksburg *Herald,* Aug. 3, 1910; Jackson *Clarion-Ledger,* July 7, Dec. 22, 29, 1910, Jan. 26, 1911; Jackson *Daily News,* May 12, 1910; Natchez *Democrat,* May 7, Aug. 23, 1910.

[23]Jackson *Clarion-Ledger,* May 25, June 2, Aug. 4, 1910.

[24]See Report of House Committee on Penitentiary, in Mississippi, *House Journal,* 1906, pp. 615-28.

the call of their "domestic duties," and "not because of anything Senator Bilbo said."[25]

Henry swore personal vengeance on Bilbo. On July 6 he entered a train at Starkville on which Bilbo was a passenger, made his way to the coach where Bilbo was seated with Ross Collins, and beat him into insensibility with a pistol. It was thought at first that Bilbo was seriously wounded, but when his train arrived in Jackson he was able to walk from it. The brutal attack was denounced by the Vardaman press, which predicted that it would result in a tremendous change of sentiment toward Bilbo and that he would be elected by a majority of tens of thousands of votes.[26]

Bilbo's denunciation of Henry produced a slight split in the Vardaman-Bilbo lines. Judge Robert C. Blount and C. M. Williamson, two eminent members of the Mississippi bar who were supporting Vardaman, openly repudiated Bilbo. This brought glee to the opposition press. Blount and Williamson were, said the Jackson *News*, "excellent gentlemen" and were supporting Vardaman only because of "some mistaken sense of gratitude" toward him. At least they were trying to preserve "some self-respect." The *News* tried to widen the breach by charging that a vote for Vardaman was a vote for Bilbo. "Vardaman loves Bilbo," it said, "and Bilbo loves Vardaman." The two were in the same political boat, and it did not see how one could vote for one and not for the other.[27]

The fury of the attack on Bilbo increased. State Senator Cunningham, debating with Bilbo at Iuka, charged that Bilbo had the reputation of a "crook" in the state senate; that he devoted his time to presenting nuisance bills which he would later kill for a bribe; that he kept a young girl in an assignation house run by a Negro woman in Jackson; and that he had defrauded a client out of a legal judgment and, when sued by the client, gave him a check which was protested by the bank. He said that if Bilbo disputed the charges, he would make another appointment with him at a later date and at the same place and produce documentary evi-

[25]Jackson *Clarion-Ledger*, July 13, 1911; New Orleans *Daily States*, quoted, *ibid.*; Natchez *Daily-Democrat*, July 7, 1911, quoting Memphis *Commercial Appeal*; Jackson *Issue*, July 7, 1911.

[26]Jackson *Issue*, July 7, 1911.

[27]Vicksburg *Herald*, June 6, 7, 1911; Jackson *Clarion-Ledger*, June 3, 1911; Jackson *Daily News*, June 7, 1911.

dence. Bilbo did dispute him, but there seems to have been no later meeting between them.[28]

The most devastating verbal lashing which Bilbo received was from the tongue of Leroy Percy. He, like Alexander, had consistently refused to speak from the same platform with Bilbo. Percy was scheduled to speak at Lauderdale Springs on July 4, and "two or three thrifty fellows," according to the *Clarion,* in order "to sell dinners, pop, soda water, etc.," invited Bilbo to appear, but did not inform Percy. When he arrived and found that Bilbo was to debate with him, Percy contemplated leaving, but was prevailed upon to remain and speak. Bilbo spoke first. His remarks were interpreted by a hostile reporter as "on a par with his low, depraved nature, seasoned with coarse expressions, strained efforts at rude wit, saturated with profanity, ribald jests . . . and slanderous remarks about his superiors."[29]

Percy's few local supporters had advised him that the crowd was in a threatening mood and that he had best not mention Vardaman or his henchmen in his speech, but confine his remarks to innocuous subjects, such as the tariff. According to his son, he agreed to do so. When he arose to speak his voice was drowned out by hisses and by shouts for Vardaman. All the while, Bilbo "sat smiling on the porch at his immediate left." When the crowd refused to subside, Percy became enraged. "Burning-cold insults poured from his lips, he jeered them as cowards afraid to listen, and dared them to keep on." Finally, says his son, "He cowed them by sheer will-power and lashed them into silence by leaping invective." Abandoning then his earlier resolution, he launched into a scathing denunciation of Vardaman and all he stood for.[30]

Finishing with Vardaman, he turned to Bilbo. He denounced him as "an informer who should be shunned by all decent and respectable people, a miserable, contemptible creature, who, if his tale be true, should be doing service for the state." Bilbo was, he continued, "a low-flung scullion, who disgraces the form of man," a "vile degenerate," and a "moral leper." If Bilbo was unfit "to sit with honest, upright men in a respectable legislative body," said

[28] Jackson *Clarion-Ledger,* Sept. 15, 1910, May 25, 1911; *ibid.,* July 13, 1911, quoting New Orleans *Daily States.*
[29] Jackson *Clarion-Ledger,* July 7, 1910, July 30, 1915.
[30] Percy, *Lanterns on the Levee,* 150-51.

Percy, he was also unfit to speak to an audience of decent, honest people from a platform with honest men. At the end of the senate investigation, he said, there was left standing on the stage, "a mark for the scorn and contempt of all honest men, only one figure, a characterless man, a self-confessed liar, a self-confessed bribe taker; and for his only ally, a poor, broken-down, shameless woman of the streets." It was not unusual for people to assemble, "out of idle curiosity," to view an unusual dwarf, a three-legged man, or a two-headed calf. Such exhibitions of physical monstrosities had no elevating effect; but the "exhibition of a moral monstrosity," such as was made in the person of Bilbo that day, "has a debasing and degrading effect." Percy predicted that if Vardaman attempted to foist upon the people of Mississippi "this creature, this bribe-taker, this liar, this consorter with lewd women and frequenter of assignation houses; this man whose sole claim to prominence, is the infamy to which he has attained," that long before the campaign was over Vardaman, "with pallid lips, will be praying to his God: Oh God! deliver me from this body of death." Turning then from Bilbo to the audience, Percy said he felt like the man who, picking a yellow-striped caterpillar out of the dust and swallowing it, said, "It is not my regular diet, I just wanted to see how strong my stomach was."[31]

The anti-Vardaman press at the time hailed the Percy diatribe with glee. Scarcely one of them failed to publish his speech in full, with the portions castigating Bilbo italicized. Weeks and even months later they were quoting and requoting the pithy phrases he had used, and "the striped caterpillar" became a name commonly applied to Bilbo. A few years later at least one of them had come to doubt the wisdom of the attack. The debate caused, said the *Clarion* at that time, more bitter feeling than any event ever before produced in the state and set the whole country talking. "Some of the things said," it added, ". . . some of the figures and comparisons used, will never be forgotten and are frequently referred to even to this very day." At the time, however, the *Clarion* with the rest applauded Percy. Simultaneously it condemned the Vardaman press for publishing "the most offensive and insulting articles about those with whom they happen to differ." It predicted that such a course, if not checked, would "sooner or later result in bloodshed."[32]

[31]*Ibid.;* Jackson *Clarion-Ledger,* July 7, 1910; Vicksburg *Herald,* July 5, 1910.
[32]Jackson *Clarion-Ledger,* July 30, 1915, Sept. 22, 1910.

Rowdyism there was, but considering the example set for them by the "decent" and "respectable" press, the crowds were remarkably restrained in their violence. When John Allen, debating with Judge Blount at Winona, stated he was for Percy, the Vardaman supporters in the audience howled him down and refused to let him talk. Then Blount was served in like manner by the Percy supporters, and the meeting broke up without either being heard. At Bentonia, in Yazoo County, a campaigner for Alexander was drowned out by shouts of "Hurrah for Vardaman!" Finally the sheriff arrested one heckler for disturbing the peace. The Vardaman supporters were enraged at this, and it was thought that violence was only avoided by a hasty adjournment to a barbecue dinner. After dinner Allen was permitted to speak, but was interrupted throughout by a Vardaman follower.[33]

The only recorded incident of spectator violence occurred at Rose Hill in Jasper County. Percy was speaking there when he was heckled by "four hoodlums." He offered to let them speak from the platform, but they preferred the places they held. When a deputy sheriff attempted to quiet them, a fight developed in which the deputy was seriously cut. The anti-Vardaman press made much of the fact that the officer was "stabbed in the back while performing his duty," and Percy charged that Vardaman himself was "morally responsible," because he "incited his followers to violence."[34]

Past records were dug up and brought into the campaign. After John Allen had become active in Percy's interest three Vardaman editors published charges that Allen, thirty-one years before, had broken into a mill and stolen a jug of whiskey and the only reason he had not been arrested was that he had skipped the country for a time and could not be found. For this charge Allen had all three editors indicted for criminal libel. They were acquitted.[35] When Percy spoke at Marion in June, Vardaman's friends propounded a series of prepared questions to him. They asked if he had ever been fined for gambling; if he had ever represented as counsel the Negro Knights of Pythias against a white man's lodge; if he had

[33]*Ibid.*, June 1, July 6, 27, 1911.

[34]*Ibid.*, July 20, 1911; Natchez *Democrat*, June 25, 28, 1911; Vicksburg *Herald*, June 25, 1911.

[35]Corinth *Corinthian*, Aberdeen *Weekly*, and Meridian *Dispatch*, quoted in Jackson *Clarion-Ledger*, June 29, 1911, and in Natchez *Democrat*, June 27, July 4, 1911.

violated the Sabbath by hunting or fishing; if he had paid board
bills of legislators during the Secret Caucus session; if he had obtained votes from legislators by use of money, whiskey, and "women
of faded reputation"; if he was presently subsidizing the Jackson
Daily News; if he had made a "deal" with Alexander during the
Secret Caucus; if he had solicited corporate support; and if he was
legal counsel for the whiskey interests. Percy, in answer, admitted
having once paid a fine for card-playing on Sunday, of having shot
birds on Sunday, and of having represented the Pythians but denied
all other charges.[36]

The charge of press subsidization was frequently made against
Percy. It was indignantly denied by his editor friends, but at least
one Vardaman editor seemed to discount the denial. He privately
offered to change his allegiance for a consideration. "If you want
the support of this paper during this campaign," he wrote Percy's
manager, "and are willing to stand for the amount of my loss from
the Vardaman followers discontinuing their subscriptions, you may
have it."[37]

It was as difficult to find substantial charges against Vardaman's
private life as it was that of Percy, but the attempt was made.
Finally a farmer was found who claimed Vardaman owed him $27
for a cow purchased fifteen years before; a tinner was found who
claimed he had done $195 worth of work on Vardaman's house
twenty years before and never been paid; and a representative of a
lyceum bureau was unearthed who charged that Vardaman had
collected and failed to turn over to the bureau its share of receipts
amounting to $200 for a lecture tour he had made. The farmer's
claim for the cow was given some authenticity when Vardaman's
friends chipped in $27 and sent it to him. There is no record that
the tinner or the lyceum man were ever the richer for their contribution to the Percy cause.[38] The anti-Vardaman press did not
accuse Vardaman of dishonesty in regard to these debts. Rather
they cited them as instances proving his ineptness as a manager of

[36]Macon *Beacon,* June 23, 1911.

[37]*Ibid.;* Louis C. Barber to William Crump, Aug. 20, 1910, published in Jackson
Clarion-Ledger, Aug 20, 1910.

[38]William N. McCaula, J. D. Gunther, and R. A. Carson to Editor, Vicksburg
Herald, published in Jackson *Clarion-Ledger,* June 13, 15, 1911; Macon *Beacon,*
June 23, 1911.

business affairs. And this was the case in regard to the alleged contingent fund shortage, too.

It was notorious that Vardaman was penniless, and it was a common saying by friend and foe that he never had sufficient funds or provisions laid up to take care of his family's basic needs for thirty days. His campaign expenses seem to have been defrayed by petty contributions from thousands of admirers. His only paid advertisements were pleas from his campaign committees urging his followers to send in contributions of twenty-five or fifty cents, or any amount they could afford. His improvidence was extolled as a virtue by his supporters and denounced as a vice by his antagonists. The latter cited his "failure" both as a lawyer and as an editor. He was charged with having dissipated a $50,000 estate which had been entrusted to his management. His enemies said that when he left Greenwood to take office as governor, "he left nothing save debts. ... The house was sold to satisfy a mortgage, and the circuit clerk's record showed over $2,500 in judgments pending against him—and they are still unsatisfied." Nor had his condition improved since. "In the city of Jackson today," said a hostile editor during the campaign, "... James K. Vardaman has the lowest possible rating on the books of the Retail Merchant's Association."[39]

These and other trivialities and irrelevancies were brought out, and they must have played a considerable part in the result, if not always in the way they were designed. But the big issue was the race question, and most attention was paid to it. Vardaman's advocacy of repeal of the Reconstruction amendments was defended because, he said, the question had become national and only Congress could correct the situation. Many Negroes, he said, had qualified for voting and more would "if they are stirred up." The situation prior to 1890 would then be repeated, he said, and fraud and violence would be necessary to retain white supremacy.[40]

Both Alexander and Percy pointed out that there was no threat to white supremacy, and that to urge the unsympathetic North to

[39]Macon *Beacon*, June 23, 1911; Jackson *Issue*, files 1910-1911; Jackson *Daily News*, June 10, 1911.

[40]Jackson *Issue*, June 2, 1911. Vardaman's racial prejudice did not extend to Jews. Decrying persecution of Jews in Europe, he said there were "bad Jews" just as there were "bad Gentiles," but that, as a race, "there is no class of citizens that are more public spirited and more deserving of the good opinion of mankind." *Ibid.*, Mar. 3, 1911.

modify the Fourteenth and Fifteenth amendments might lead to greater strictures. They charged Vardaman with insincerity; that he had obtained the governorship by pledging to divide the school fund between the races according to the taxes paid by each, but that as governor he had not redeemed that pledge. The charge was unjust but was repeated by others. John Allen called Vardaman the "most irresponsible demagogue the State had ever known." The Macon *Beacon* said Vardaman had never, in any of his campaigns, run on a "fair, square, honest, and real principle." He had always dealt in false and specious issues. The bases of his appeal to the voters, it said, were "Some vast, vague, and indefinable good which he will accomplish by some vague and undefined means, flattery and abuse and false cry of fraud." The *Beacon* admitted that Vardaman had been a good governor but opposed him for fear his election would agitate the race question.

The Vicksburg *Herald* shortly before had praised Vardaman's stand on the race question. "Those who go to hear [Vardaman] expecting 'hatred, hypocricy [*sic*], or demagogy,'" said the *Herald* at that time, "will be disillusioned." Pointing out that Vardaman had made the state "a courageous, honest, conservative" executive, the *Herald* had also defended his racial position. "He never failed to speak out for the protection of the negro in his . . . person and property. It was due to him that the grafting convict leasing system, under which the negro prisoners were cruelly abused . . . was broken up root and branch." Ten months later the *Herald* condemned the same stand as "pettifogging" and the "brutal boast of a mission of encouraging race prejudice . . . odious to reason and justice." "The only part the negro plays in our political affairs," said the Natchez *Democrat*, "is that of furnishing tricky, calculating politicians an opportunity of getting up and venting their alleged animosity against the race." "The agitation of the race question here, where we are all of one mind," said the *Clarion*, "can only be carried on . . . in order to get . . . votes."[41]

One feature of the campaign which the opposition press was unable to understand was the large and enthusiastic audiences

41Jackson *Clarion-Ledger*, June 5, July 7, 1910, Apr. 20, July 6, 16, 1911; Macon *Beacon*, July 8, 1910, June 23, 1911, Natchez *Democrat*, July 4, 1911; Vicksburg *Herald*, Sept. 29, 1909, July 17, 1910, Jan. 5, 1912; Jackson *Issue*, July 22, 1910; Aberdeen *Examiner*, quoted in Macon *Beacon*, July 28, 1911.

which Vardaman drew whenever he spoke. At first the *Clarion* questioned the authenticity of reports and suggested that the Vardaman press photographers were "blowing up" pictures of his crowds and "reducing" pictures of opposition crowds. A few months later it admitted that his Jackson rally was "a large affair." The *Clarion* was impressed as well as puzzled with the extraordinary hold which Vardaman had on his following. They seemed to be "for him against the world, the flesh, and the devil, and would stand out in the cold, in the rain, or . . . even in a snowstorm, to hear him speak." His power was the less explicable because he seemed to defy all conventions, and "while posing as a commoner, looks and acts the part of an aristocrat." There was nothing about Vardaman, thought the *Clarion*, that would appear to attract the common man, "for he is always dressed like a dandy, and moves around with a stilted, imperious air." No other man could dress and do as he did and receive much consideration at the hands of the people. But his "airs, graces, and good looks" did not seem to injure him; rather they drew men to him. Studying his style and his platform technique, Editor Henry concluded that he was "an odd man, a dilettante who seems able to say what he pleases, abuse anybody he dislikes, curse out those who oppose him, and still hold his following, to grapple them to him with hoops of steel." Yet, observed Henry, Vardaman was not always a firebrand. With all his show and mannerisms, "he is always gracious and polite to those he likes, and is able to get down on a level with everyone, and make himself agreeable." Ere long Henry himself was almost captivated. "The attractive and picturesque . . . Vardaman," he said, ". . . as an orator . . . rather puts it over his distinguished competitors, neither of whom has his voice, his splendid gestures, or forensic tread." "He has winning ways," he added, "is a capital mixer, and knows how to please his followers."[42]

Editor McNeily of the Vicksburg *Herald*, Vardaman's erstwhile friend and supporter, was similarly puzzled. Commenting on a dispatch telling of Vardaman's being carried on the shoulders of the people and of his hat being cut to ribbons and distributed among the crowd, McNeily was unable to account for such idolatry. "It never occurred in Mississippi," he complained, "before this Vardaman and Bilbo craze broke out." Commenting again on a state-

[42]Jackson *Clarion-Ledger*, Dec. 29, 1910, Mar. 2, Apr. 6, 1911.

ment of an admirer comparing Vardaman to Moses, Ahab, Jeremiah, and Christ as an agitator in the interest of the masses, McNeily observed that "the ordinary hero-worshipper" would have been content to compare his "agitator" with Patrick Henry, John Hancock, Pym, or Hampden. "But they are not exalted enough for Vardaman," he added. McNeily was even more perplexed at a letter which a Vardaman supporter in Pontotoc County wrote to a critical editor. "You had just as well," said the Vardaman enthusiast, "go to church anywhere in Pontotoc . . . get up in the pulpit and tell the people that Jesus Christ is a bastard as to say anything against . . . Vardaman to the people here." It was too much for McNeily. "His followers," he concluded, "look on him as sanctified—his proven and uncontradicted offenses against moral and civil law do not diminish their adulation."[43]

Concern was expressed by Vardaman over the action of the state board of election commissioners in the appointment of county election commissioners. As has been explained, these county commissioners were empowered to purge the registration books. Alleging that Percy and Alexander were in a "combine" against him, Vardaman argued that he should have as many of his party on each board as the other two combined. His plea was overruled and each candidate was given one representative on each county board. This gave the opposition, Vardaman complained, a majority in every county, and it was possible for them "to take every advantage of every pretext and technicality . . . to . . . strike from the registration rolls every known supporter of [mine] it is possible to eliminate." It was even reported to Vardaman that one of the men high up in the counsels of the opposition had said that "if Vardaman gets the votes he will be counted out."[44]

At the same time the opposition press started a campaign to purge the rolls. The *Daily News*, estimating that 50,000 whites delinquent in their poll tax payments had been participating in recent primaries, called on Governor Noel to enforce the law. The *Clarion*, estimating that the delinquents were between 40,000 and 60,000, admitted that in practice the requirement of presenting tax receipts

[43]Vicksburg *Herald*, June 25, 27, 1911; *ibid.*, quoting Pontotoc *Advance* and Jackson *Issue*.

[44]Jackson *Issue*, May 5, 1911; Dr. G. W. Luster to J. K. Vardaman, May 8, 1911, published, *ibid.*, May 12, 1911; Jackson *Clarion-Ledger*, Sept. 1, 8, 1910, July 27, 1911.

at primary polls was rarely complied with, but thought it should be.[45] The *Clarion* also credited rumors that sheriffs in some counties were issuing antedated receipts for taxes paid after the February 1 deadline to the partisans of their choice for senator. If the county commissioners all did their duty, said the *Clarion*, the list of voters would be cut in half.[46]

Vardaman urged that every white Democratic voter in the state who was a bona fide resident be allowed to vote regardless of the poll tax requirement. He charged that the sudden zeal to enforce the requirement was aimed only at injuring him. The purpose of the law originally, he argued, was to eliminate Negroes from politics, and since the white primary did this there was no necessity for the provision, at least in the primary itself. He warned the country voters that the opposition was going after them because they were, as a rule, for him, and he urged them to register in time. When the county commissioners began their purge he attacked them savagely, charging them with specially construing the laws to cut off his votes. This charge was denied by his own member of the board in Adams County, but one of his followers in Jones threatened to lead an armed mob at his precinct to see "that all white Democrats are permitted to vote, whether on the poll books or not."[47]

The Secret Caucus was even made the issue in the legislative campaigns. The *Clarion* argued that this was improper and unnecessary. Months before the primary the *Clarion* had publicly expressed the fear that Vardaman would win the senatorial nomination, and it was, perhaps, bent on saving what it could from the wreckage which it anticipated. The legislators, regardless of their individual preferences, it said, would be bound by the results of the senatorial primary and must elect the winning candidate. But Vardaman, not willing again to trust his election to the honor of the legislature, had candidates in every legislative district and urged his followers to vote for them. He even had a congressional candidate in each district.[48]

[45]This was a reversal of the *Clarion's* views of a few years before. See p. 221.

[46]Jackson *Daily News*, May 1, 1910; Jackson *Clarion-Ledger*, May 12, 1910, Jan. 26, Mar. 30, Apr. 13, 20, 27, 1911; Brookhaven *Leader*, quoted, *ibid.*, Apr. 20, 1911.

[47]Jackson *Issue*, Feb. 24, Apr. 21, 1911; Vicksburg *Herald*, June 2, 1911; Jackson *Clarion-Ledger*, July 27, 1911; Natchez *Democrat*, July 22, 23, 1911.

[48]Jackson *Issue*, May 26, 1911; Jackson *Clarion-Ledger*, Aug. 25, 1910, Mar. 30, 1911.

All the opposition, even Percy and Alexander, admitted that
Vardaman would get a plurality, but not a majority, in the first primary. There was, therefore, some interest as to which of the opposition candidates—Percy or Alexander—would run second and
thus fight it out with Vardaman in the second primary. Many people
believed that Alexander was merely the tail to Percy's kite and that
if Percy should pull the string as he did in the caucus, Alexander
would immediately drop out of the race. Vardaman played up this
theme at first, much to Alexander's annoyance, who threatened to
"make revelations that would turn Vardaman's headquarters inside
out" unless such underhanded attacks on him ceased. Later Vardaman predicted that Alexander would run ahead of Percy. It was
suspected that this was part of Vardaman's strategy, that he felt
Alexander would be easier to defeat in a runoff than Percy and accordingly was trying to build him up at Percy's expense.[49]

On the eve of the election Alexander's headquarters predicted
that their candidate would lead Percy in the first primary and have
an easy victory over Vardaman in the second. The *Clarion*, though
not very hopeful, expressed some pride in its favorite, Alexander.
"He has," it said, "developed into a mixer . . . and handshaker the
equal of the lamented Anse McLaurin." The Vardaman forces expressed confidence throughout that their candidate would obtain a
clear majority in the first primary.[50]

The vote was the largest cast in Mississippi up to that time, and
the result was an overwhelming Vardaman victory. His total was
more than 76,000, while the combined vote of his two opponents
was little more than 50,000. Percy's vote was almost 10,000 short of
Alexander's. Vardaman also succeeded in placing an overwhelming
majority of his followers in the legislature. He had been at work,
too, to regain control of the various committees of the party, state
and local, and succeeded in doing so. "Those fellows," regretfully
wrote a Percy supporter, "can weild [sic] a very great power."
Bilbo's vote was almost as large as Vardaman's.[51]

[49]Jackson *Clarion-Ledger*, June 1, July 6, 13, 1911; Macon *Beacon*, July 21, 1911.
[50]Jackson *Clarion-Ledger*, July 13, 20, 27, 1911.
[51]*Biennial Report of the Secretary of State to the Legislature of Mississippi from
October 1, 1909 to October 1, 1911* (Nashville, 1911); Jackson *Clarion-Ledger*,
Aug. 17, 1911; Natchez *Democrat*, Aug. 3, 5, 1911; Sargeant Prentiss Knut to Williams, May 8, July 22, 1915, Williams Papers.

Earl Brewer of Coahoma County was the only candidate for governor and had accordingly been declared the nominee of the party by the state Democratic executive committee a few weeks before. It was reported to be the first time in the history of the state that the gubernatorial nomination had been uncontested.[52]

The size of Vardaman's majority stunned the opposition papers. It was unbelievable that their favorites could have been so routed by "upstarts" like Vardaman and Bilbo. Pondering the result for more than two weeks, the *Clarion* concluded that the Secret Caucus had been the decisive factor in Vardaman's victory. The people, it thought, had "gotten the idea into their heads that . . . the caucus was a most infamous affair, and no amount of argument or reason could remove that impression." It was unable to explain Bilbo's victory. The Natchez *Democrat* attributed the result to the systematic manner in which the "horny sons of toil" had been arrayed against men of wealth. This same conclusion was reached by an active Percy campaigner. He said he had often heard people say of Percy, "he is an aristocrat," "he is a man of great wealth, feels himself above you voters, does not need or care for your support or endorsement, etc., etc." The Daily *News*, admitting that Vardaman was "The People's Choice," contended that his selection did not represent "the best thought" of the state. "Wisdom, sanity and conservatism," it said, "have been swept aside, and passion, prejudice, and hysteria are triumphant." The New Orleans *Picayune* regretfully observed that Mississippians were "putting the foot down firmly on all that remains of the old aristocracy . . . and they are choosing their representatives among the new generation."[53]

Immediately after the primary the candidates reported the sums they had spent on the campaign. Alexander listed an expenditure of $25,000; Percy $20,000; and Vardaman only $2,000. No charge was made that Vardaman had expended more than he reported. Thus the fear formerly expressed that a primary nomination could only be won after a huge expenditure of money found no support in this race. The two losing candidates spent together more than twenty-two times as much as the winner. Each of them had spent

[52]Natchez *Democrat*, July 18, 1911; Jackson *Clarion-Ledger*, July 20, 1911.

[53]Jackson *Clarion-Ledger*, Aug. 17, 1911; *ibid.*, Aug. 10, 1911, quoting New Orleans *Picayune*; Natchez *Democrat*, Aug. 5, 1911; Jackson *Daily News*, Aug. 2, 1911; John P. Mayo to Williams, Sept. 27, 1915, Williams Papers.

almost a dollar, on the average, for each vote received. Vardaman's unit cost had been less than three cents. The election seems to have been particularly free from fraud. The only complaint of dishonesty came from Lincoln County where indictments for vote buying were returned against several of the "very best citizens."[54]

A week after the election a gala celebration was held in Jackson by the Vardaman party. Crowds poured into the city from near and far, some in wagons, some riding mules, some on special excursion trains made up for the occasion. "The oldest inhabitant" was reported as saying, "It was the greatest demonstration in years." The *Clarion* estimated that six thousand slept in the streets the night before the big celebration. A tremendous parade, starting at the Vardaman headquarters on Capitol Street opposite the Edwards House, wound its way through town to the capitol. Bilbo shared honors with Vardaman and rode with him in the parade. Men on horseback, clothed in white and with red neckties, rode beside them as a guard of honor. Arriving at the capitol Vardaman addressed the throngs that overflowed the grounds into the neighboring streets and perched in trees, in windows, and on housetops. He wanted, he said, the government "returned to you, the people of my state." He wanted the white people to rule, and he was going to Washington to see that they did, and to "strike at predatory wealth."[55]

Either it was an impressive occasion, or else Editor Henry was again enchanted by the Vardaman personality. He praised the speech, and expressed regret that Vardaman during the campaign had "been more severely criticized, more terribly abused, and . . . more savagely persecuted, than any other man offering for public office in the history of Mississippi." He was not so captivated by Bilbo. That selection was, he thought, "the saddest thing in . . . the election, the most humilating event in the history of the state." It showed, he concluded, how completely Bilbo had fooled the people "with his fluent tongue and tale of woe."[56]

54Natchez *Democrat*, Aug. 3, 1911; Jackson *Clarion-Ledger*, Sept. 28, 1911.
55Jackson *Clarion-Ledger*, Aug. 10, 1911.
56*Ibid.*

CHAPTER XVIII

OLD AND NEW FACTIONS

ALTHOUGH routed in the election of 1911, the anti-Vardaman wing of the party did not give up the struggle. A few weeks after the election the Noel administration filed suit against Vardaman to make him account for all contingent funds he handled while governor. Rankled by the repudiation of the people, Percy publicly invited Vardaman to join him in requesting an investigation of the Secret Caucus by the United States Senate. If Vardaman's charges were true, he said, he, Percy, should be in prison. If they were false, Vardaman was unworthy to serve in the Senate. Percy's motive in this move is not quite clear. Despite the vindication of Dulaney by the jury, it is doubtful if Percy hoped for a clean bill of health from such an investigation. So much was known of irregularities by both sides in that contest that perhaps he hoped, like Samson, to pull down the temple and to destroy Vardaman with himself. But Vardaman brushed the invitation aside. The people of Mississippi had already investigated, he said, and returned their verdict.[1]

Instead of contesting the suit filed against him, Vardaman secured an injunction against Attorney-General Hudson staying proceedings. The Nashville *Banner*, admitting it knew nothing of the facts, thought it strange that Vardaman would fight charges of graft with "technicalities seeking avoidance and delay," instead of insisting on a trial in chancery.[2] But Vardaman's motive soon unfolded itself. Within a few weeks the newly elected officials would come into office. While Governor-elect Brewer was not identified with Vardaman's faction, Attorney-General-elect Ross Collins was, as was also an overwhelming majority of the new legislature.

The Vardaman strategy proved effective. Immediately after his induction, the new attorney-general offered to dismiss the suit if Vardaman would permit an examination of his bank account. Vardaman agreed, and Collins entered a dismissal decree. This was called by the opposition "a clearance without trial and upon suppression of evidence."[3]

---

[1]Jackson *Clarion-Ledger*, Nov. 23, Dec. 14, 1911.

[2]Nashville *Banner*, quoted in Vicksburg *Herald*, Jan. 9, 1912.

[3]Jackson *Clarion-Ledger*, Dec. 28, 1911, Mar. 2, 1912; Vicksburg *Herald*, Feb. 18, 1912.

Meanwhile the new legislature[4] had convened, and Vardaman wrote Frank Burkitt, chairman of the joint committee on contingent funds, requesting a legislative investigation of the charges against him. He was, he said, the victim of much persecution and the target of all manner of obloquy and slander. The committee held extensive hearings, calling before it Vardaman, former Governor Noel, the accountant, C. J. Moore, and Vardaman's two former secretaries. Its report completely vindicated Vardaman. It pointed out that both former secretaries, one of whom had also served as Noel's secretary, testified that they had taken vouchers for every expenditure save ten dollars paid for postage stamps during Vardaman's administration. Evidence also showed that the metal case in which the vouchers were kept was not locked and that any person desiring to do so might have had access to them. Also it was learned that the legislative committee of 1906 had checked the contingent fund item by item for 1904 and 1905 and found it correct. That Accountant Moore had later found vouchers missing for those years proved, the report said, that "some of the vouchers examined by the committee on April 19, 1906, were afterwards lost, mislaid, or have been abstracted." The committee thought it "rational to conclude that neither Vardaman nor any friend of his abstracted them from the file," and it "acquitted the Governor [Vardaman] of any and all charges concerning them."[5]

Accountant Moore called the report a "whitewash," and the Vicksburg *Herald* called its authors "accessories after the fact" and a "packed jury." The Nashville *Banner* said Vardaman had obtained a "political acquittal" by insisting on an investigation by a legislature which was composed overwhelmingly of his friends.[6]

The report was adopted by the legislature and a resolution was offered to send a copy of it to John Sharp Williams with a request that he present it to the United States Senate. Thereupon the anti-Vardaman group threatened to send a minority resolution condemning the report and charging that the investigation was not complete

[4]Of the eighty-seven legislators who had voted for Percy in the Secret Caucus, only five were in the new body. George Creel, "The Carnival of Corruption in Mississippi," in *Cosmopolitan Magazine*, LI (1911), 735.

[5]Vicksburg *Herald*, Jan. 9, 13, 1912; Natchez *Democrat*, Jan. 13, 1912; Jackson *Clarion-Ledger*, Jan. 25, 1912.

[6]Jackson *Clarion-Ledger*, Feb. 27, 1912; Natchez *Democrat*, Jan. 13, 16, 1912; Vicksburg *Herald*, Jan. 13, 16, 1912; *ibid.*, Jan. 9, 1912, quoting Nashville *Banner*.

or thorough. The Vardamanites retaliated by threatening that if such action were taken, they would pass a resolution denouncing the methods by which Percy was elected by the legislature of 1910 and demanding his resignation. Such a resolution, thought a neutral observer, would have passed by a majority of sixty-three in the house and fifteen in the senate.

Governor Brewer was able to bring about a temporary peace, but before the end of the session open warfare had broken out between the factions. On March 5 the legislature passed, by a vote of 66 to 39 in the house and 26 to 13 in the senate, the threatened resolution demanding Percy's resignation. The minority offered a resolution requesting the United States Senate to investigate the charges of fraud and corruption incident to Percy's election in 1910. They felt confident that Vardaman would oppose it as likely to open up charges against him. Their object was to put the Vardaman majority on record as unalterably opposed to an investigation of its own charges. Their belief seemed justified, for the resolution was voted down.[7]

Percy had stated after his election by the Secret Caucus that if it was shown in the primary that he did not enjoy the confidence of the people, he would resign without awaiting expiration of his term. After the primary it was reported that he intended doing so but that he was being urged by his friends to serve out the term. The passage of the resolution demanding his resignation revived "all the pent-up hatred, political animosity, and factional bitterness" which had begun to die down, and Percy flatly refused. Even some of the Vardaman papers were doubtful of the propriety of the resolution. The Yazoo *Sentinel* thought it a mistake. The Crystal Springs *Meteor* thought, "in the interest of harmony and coalescing of the factions," the resolution should not have been presented.[8] Undoubtedly they were right. No useful purpose was served; Percy did not resign; no investigation of the Secret Caucus was made; and the whole affair served only to aggravate the bitter factional feeling.

[7]New Orleans *Picayune,* quoted in Vicksburg *Herald,* Jan. 21, 1912; *ibid.,* Mar. 6, 1912; Jackson *Clarion-Ledger,* Jan. 25, Mar. 14, 1912; Natchez *Democrat,* Jan. 23, Mar. 8, 1912.

[8]*Ibid.,* Mar. 6, 8, 10, 1912; *ibid.,* quoting Yazoo *Sentinel* and Crystal Springs *Meteor;* Vicksburg *Herald,* Mar. 6, 10, 1912.

The election of 1911 had left Vardaman in complete control of the political machinery of the state. The Democratic state executive committee, the mainspring of that machinery, was revised to accord with his wishes. Even T. G. Heard, the only member who had supported Vardaman, was dropped, according to the Macon *Beacon*, because he was a "man of substance and a man of affairs. Mr. Vardaman wants men who have no stake in the state's welfare other than a political stake." Vardaman dominated the state convention called in May to enunciate a program and to choose delegates to the national convention. John Sharp Williams and others wished to commit the delegates to Woodrow Wilson, but Vardaman swung the convention to a declaration for Oscar W. Underwood. A platform was adopted embodying all the planks which Vardaman had for years been advocating. These included: submission of an amendment to the people for repeal of the Fifteenth Amendment to the federal Constitution; election of United States senators by direct vote; new legislative apportionment as a matter of justice to south Mississippi; and the building of good roads in the state.[9]

In the legislature Vardaman's control was as complete. When a bill was proposed creating two separate court districts in Covington County, its senator pleaded with the senate not to "steam roller" his county. Claiming to be a strong Vardaman man himself, he said the Vardaman machine had voted for his bill previously, but later certain senators told him they could not do so again because they had been "called" and "had to line up with the Vardaman machine or lose their scalps." "No one has thought," said the Vicksburg *Herald*, ". . . of questioning the supremacy of Vardamanism in our state politics." Reviewing the work of the legislature after its adjournment, the Macon *Beacon* acknowledged that "Vardaman is now Boss of Mississippi." It was a familiar sight when the legislature was in session, it said, to see him "talking to some member as a teacher talks to a whipped boy or a master lectures a servant." His domination was complete. "He orders and commands and his henchmen obey."[10]

It was feared that the legislature elected in 1911 would be a "radical" one and would "overturn the existing order of things . . . leaving a trackage of debris . . . behind it." When the new mem-

[9]Macon *Beacon*, May 16, 17, 1912; Jackson *Clarion-Ledger*, May 23, 1912.
[10]Vicksburg *Herald*, Jan. 28, Mar. 13, 19, 1912; Macon *Beacon*, May 17, 1912.

bers came up to Jackson in January, however, it was found that "they looked like any other." Measures of a "liberal" nature were passed, but nothing "radical." Bilbo, now lieutenant-governor, sponsored a bill requiring a privilege tax of twenty cents an acre on all firms or corporations owning or holding more than 1,000 acres of land. He explained that the bill affected south Mississippi where the holding of timber lands for speculation was a recognized business and was retarding development. The bill, amended to apply only to holdings in excess of 5,000 acres, was passed. In an effort to induce lower interest rates an act exempted money lent at 6 per cent or less from taxation. Even the Vicksburg *Herald,* admitting that similar bills had been defeated eight years before by Longino's veto and four years before "by banker influence," called the measure "good sound business sense." Bills levying an income tax, outlawing poolrooms, and making landlords responsible for illegal use of their property were also passed. The south Mississippi delegation introduced a resolution calling for relief of their section from the constitutional restrictions placed on its number of representatives. The delegates from the other sections, combining under the leadership of Frank Burkitt, repelled the attempt. By the end of the session the legislature was drawing praise from such conservative journals as the Vicksburg *Herald* and the *Clarion.* Instead of proving "revolutionary" it had actually been, said the *Clarion,* "a conservative force."[11]

But Governor Brewer's administration was not destined to serve out its term in peace and harmony. Antagonisms—new and old, personal, factional, and sectional—were at work, awaiting the spark that would ignite them into open hostility. In the spring of 1913 the Delta was clamoring for a special session of the legislature. The levee boards had already spent next year's anticipated revenue and $20,000 besides and were demanding that more funds be provided for levee work. South Mississippi, chagrined at its rebuff the previous year, was threatening to "hold up" the Delta and not to give relief unless more representatives and school funds were allotted to it. Nor was all harmony within the Delta. Factionalism still divided that section, and Representative Ed Franklin of Sun-

[11] Jackson *Clarion-Ledger,* Jan. 11, Feb. 8, 15, Mar. 14, 1912; Vicksburg *Herald,* Jan. 12, 28, Mar. 14, 19, 1912; Natchez *Democrat,* Feb. 8, Mar. 17, 1912; Macon *Beacon,* July 21, 28, 1912.

flower was determined to offer a constitutional amendment, if the special session were called, taking the appointment of levee board members from the governor and having them elected by direct vote of the people.[12]

Brewer, a Delta resident himself, called a special session to meet June 10, but before that date a financial scandal had been unearthed in the office of the state prison board. Early in May, Lawrence Yerger, secretary of the board, confessed to embezzling $30,000 of the prison board's funds. The governor then decided to examine all affairs of the prison board, but a controversy arose between him and the trustees whether he or they should conduct the investigation.[13]

When the legislature met in special session to relieve the levee boards, the controversy was at its height. Now the legislature split —the house taking the side of the governor, the senate that of the trustees. The house authorized the governor to spend $10,000 investigating penitentiary affairs, but the senate refused to sanction the bill. Instead it passed the so-called "Norwood Resolution" providing for a joint legislative investigation of all departments of the state government. It was reported that the senate move was inspired by Bilbo, who wanted to embarrass the governor's penitentiary investigation and to "whitewash" his friends, the trustees. This was vigorously denied by Bilbo. The house refused to concur in the "Norwood Resolution," adding an amendment excluding the prison from the legislative investigation. In the regular session the following January, however, the house concurred in a senate resolution for a legislative investigation of the penitentiary.[14]

Brewer had suspected for some time that all was not well with the penitentiary management and had hired detectives to investigate. He revealed that Boyce and Company, a Memphis exporter, had bought practically all the cotton from the state's prison farms for the past four years without competitive bidding. It was reported that Boyce's profit had been excessive, and Brewer charged that there was collusion between Boyce and Yerger. Boyce explained his

12Macon *Beacon*, May 30, June 27, Dec. 12, 1913.

13Jackson *Clarion-Ledger*, May 7, 18, 1913; Natchez *Democrat*, May 7, 1913; Macon *Beacon*, May 30, June 27, 1913.

14Mississippi, *Senate Journal*, 1913, pp. 17, 30, 34, 36, 37, 865; Jackson *Clarion-Ledger*, June 12, 1913; Natchez *Democrat*, June 15, 1913.

huge profits as well as his monopoly of the state's crop by the fact that he was a pioneer in shipping direct from the producer to the English spinning mills and could eliminate costs which others could not. Brewer had made a trip to England to investigate Boyce's dealings there and apparently was not satisfied that Boyce had revealed all the advantages which he had over other buyers.[15] He attempted to make Boyce produce his books, but he had to threaten to attach all his property in the state to get him to do so. When Boyce produced some books, Brewer said they were not genuine but were copies "recently made" which would not establish his real dealings with the state.[16]

Yerger was indicted shortly after his confession. He refused to involve others, claiming that his was the only guilt. It was rumored that a "deal" had been made between him and Bilbo promising a pardon for him by the next governor if he would "take the rap." The only indictments which Brewer was able to secure for all his pains were for comparatively trivial offenses. C. C. Smith, president of the prison board, was charged with perpetration of a petty fraud in regard to a secondhand automobile which he sold to the board for a sum alleged to be several hundred dollars in excess of its value. He was sentenced to five years in prison, but Brewer commuted the sentence to a $500 fine when physicians testified that Smith's health would preclude his outliving the sentence. The *Clarion*, still anti-Vardaman and anti-Bilbo, called this commutation a "crime" and speculated on the "hue and cry" that would have been raised if Bilbo had, while acting as governor, pardoned Smith.[17] The Macon *Beacon*, however, praised Brewer's "absolute courage," "unwavering firmness of character," and his "playing no favorites . . . despite the charges of some of the accused ones." He was, it said, wholly free from rancor or vindictiveness toward any person.[18]

Indictments were also secured against W. B. Gowdy, a Jackson

[15]Jackson *Clarion-Ledger*, June 19, 21, 24, 1913; Macon *Beacon*, May 30, 1913; Natchez *Democrat*, June 26, 1913.

[16]For statement of Boyce's denial see Report of joint legislative investigating committee, in Mississippi, *Senate Journal*, 1914, pp. 1290-99; Jackson *Clarion-Ledger*, June 19, 21, 27, 1913, Mar. 20, 24, 1914; Natchez *Democrat*, June 26, 1913.

[17]Natchez *Democrat*, June 26, 1913; Jackson *Clarion-Ledger*, June 27, July 10, 17, 18, 1913, Mar. 7, 1914.

[18]Macon *Beacon*, July 4, 11, 1913.

oilman, A. C. Davis, shipping clerk at the Parchman farm, and W. A. Montgomery, another trustee. Montgomery was fined $100 and removed from the board because of negligence in performance of his duties. Davis and Gowdy were acquitted. Of the five men indicted, Davis and Smith were said to be Vardaman supporters, the other three anti-Vardaman.[19]

Meanwhile the senate investigation was proceeding. The insane asylum at Jackson proved to be its most fertile field. As a result of its disclosures six indictments were returned against asylum officials, charging that the institution was run for the benefit of private interests rather than for care of the inmates. W. S. Hamilton, a trustee, was indicted for being a stockholder in a firm doing business with the asylum, but no crime could be proved against him and he was discharged. Of the other five only two were convicted; one of these was merely fined, but the other was sentenced to the penitentiary. Of the six indicted, only one was said to be a Vardaman supporter, and even he had not been an active participant in Vardaman's campaigns.[20]

It was obvious that the several investigations were the manifestation of a new and bitter rivalry that had sprung up between Brewer and Bilbo. The *Issue,* which after the departure of Vardaman for the Senate had passed into the control of Bilbo, had from the first discouraged the penitentiary investigation as a political maneuver on the part of the governor and had urged instead an investigation of Brewer. It was joined by other papers identified in previous campaigns with Vardaman, some of which predicted that Brewer was laying plans to oppose Vardaman four years later.[21] Brewer was defended, in general, by the anti-Vardaman press and by a resolution of the house of representatives upholding his conduct of the prison investigation. This resolution was passed by a vote of 49 to 39, indicating the division in that branch of the legislature.[22] Since Vardaman had an overwhelming majority there it

[19]Jackson *Clarion-Ledger,* June 27, July 10, 17, 18, 1913.

[20]See Report of joint legislative investigating committee, in Mississippi, *Senate Journal,* 1914, pp. 211-15; Jackson *Clarion-Ledger,* July 19, 23, 24, Aug. 9, 1913, Feb. 6, 1914.

[21]Jackson *Issue,* files summer 1913, especially Aug. 10; *Hinds County Gazette,* Yazoo *Sentinel,* and McComb City *Journal,* quoted in Jackson *Clarion-Ledger,* Aug. 3, 10, 12, 16, 31, 1913.

[22]Mississippi, *Senate Journal,* 1914, p. 121; Natchez *Democrat,* Mar. 28, 1914.

would seem that he was not directly aligned in the battle being waged between the governor and lieutenant-governor.

The legislature elected with Vardaman in 1911 convened for its last session in January, 1914. It was reported that a "third house" embracing "every calling and interest" swarmed through the lobbies, intent on looking to its own multifarious interests. Bankers were there opposing a bank guaranty bill; lumbermen were urging a law to permit laborers to work eleven hours under contract; office-holders were fighting fee reduction bills; officials of state institutions were working for increased appropriations; "radical" prohibitionists were supporting the anti-liquor bill; "conservative" prohibitionists were opposing it; representatives of railroads and telegraph companies were watching legislation inimical to their interests; and female suffragists were hoping to secure an amendment permitting women to vote. Bills of every nature and description were presented. "Our policy in sending our wisest statesmen to this great deliberative body," said one editor sarcastically, "safeguards us against the lack of regulation of anything which humanity is heir to." Another thought that what the state needed more than anything else was a law to safeguard it from its legislature, to regulate it so that it would confine its activities to considering just as few bills as possible and so wording those that their provisions would be easy of enforcement.[23]

The legislature adjourned March 28, having appropriated $922,000 more than any of its predecessors. The largest increase was for the common schools, a total of $3,318,100 being set aside for their support during the next two years.[24] The conservative press did not protest against this large increase. Perhaps Vardaman had been able to awaken a social consciousness in the people, or perhaps the result was much better than had been anticipated. Even the Vicksburg *Herald* was not displeased. Said Editor McNeily, "Taken altogether . . . this legislature . . . has brought its session to a close with credit."[25] The dire predictions of the wreckage which it would leave in its wake had not come to pass.

[23]New Orleans *Times-Democrat*, quoted in Vicksburg *Herald*, Jan. 20, 1914; Jackson *Clarion-Ledger*, Mar. 26, 1914; *ibid.*, quoting Neshoba *Democrat*.

[24]Natchez *Democrat*, Mar. 29, 1914.

[25]Vicksburg *Herald*, Mar. 29, 1914.

CHAPTER XIX

THE RISE OF BILBO

THE CONTROVERSY between Brewer and Bilbo over the investigation of the penitentiary was but the opening salvo of a violent struggle to be fought between them in the courts, in the legislative halls, in the press, and at the polls. Their feud was to accentuate class antagonisms which had been dividing the state since the advent of Vardaman into high office a decade before. Factional and partisan politics were to be introduced into all public questions. The period was to be marked by an utter abandonment of restraint and a complete absence of dignity in the settlement of disputes.

From the time of his exposure of the alleged bribery in the Secret Caucus Bilbo had been a marked man in Mississippi politics —marked for destruction by his foes and for greater honors by his adherents. His character seems to have lacked some of the complexity of Vardaman's—at least in the opinion of his enemies, who generally were the same as those who were opposed to Vardaman. But whereas they were free to confess that there was some idealism and statesmanship intermixed with Vardaman's "demagoguery," they failed to observe any of these elements in Bilbo's conduct. To them he was evil incarnate, and they were never able to understand the hold which he gained on the people of the state.

Bilbo had gone to McComb City on May 31, 1910, to launch his campaign for lieutenant-governor. Fresh from the rough handling he had received from the Percy majority of the senate in the investigation of his charges against Dulaney, he seems at first to have been uncertain how to proceed. Four thousand had turned out there to hear him, mainly to find out if he "were fool or knave or both." Bilbo started slowly and seemed embarrassed. Gradually he warmed to his subject. He found that when he denounced Noel or praised Vardaman the crowd responded enthusiastically, and he played that tune until he was exhausted. It was reported that the crowd "was thoroughly 'Bilboed'," and many leading county politicians present promised to back him for governor if he would run. "Mr. Bilbo has made," said an observer, "the greatest hit in this county ever made by [a] stranger within its borders."[1]

[1] New Orleans *Picayune*, quoted in Jackson *Issue*, June 3, 1910.

Discriminatory methods used by the opposition to suppress him proved ineffective. The circuit judge adjourned court at Corinth to permit Earl Brewer to open his campaign for governor, but he refused to let Bilbo speak after him. Bilbo then spoke at the opera house and was greeted by an overflow crowd. "Many went there," it was reported, "antagonistic to him, but left believing he was simply telling the truth and the facts."[2] Attempts of the opposition to drown him with invective only served as fuel to his fire. It was hard for the people to believe that any man could be such a monster as he was portrayed. The bitterness and extremity of opposition denunciations caused the people to rise up about him and sweep everything before him. "Instead of building up opposition," said Vardaman, "they are arousing sympathy, and sowing a more elaborate destruction for their own candidates."[3]

But the opposition aggressively went on denouncing Bilbo. Nor did they ever show signs of stopping. Writing in 1941, one of them described him as "a pert little monster, glib and shameless, with a sort of cunning common to criminals which passes for intelligence." For years the opposition thought Bilbo was "fooling" the people, but one of them, at least, thought otherwise. The people loved him, he concluded, not because they were deceived in him, "but because they understood him thoroughly; they said of him proudly, 'He's a slick little bastard.' He was one of them and he had risen from obscurity to the fame of glittering infamy—it was as if they themselves had crashed the headlines."[4]

Whether that be true or not, certain it is that Bilbo's popularity among the people rose overnight so that it almost rivaled that of Vardaman. With the passing of the "Great White Chief" from state to national politics, Bilbo found an open door to leadership of the masses in state affairs.

The climax of the Brewer-Bilbo feud came in the winter of 1913-1914. Almost two years before, in February, 1912, a bill had been introduced in the legislature to create a new county in the Delta from portions of Washington, Yazoo, Leflore, Sunflower, Holmes, Sharkey, and Issaquena counties. Representatives from the Delta counties opposed the bill, and when rumors insinuated that money

---

[2]Vicksburg *Post*, quoted in Jackson *Issue*, July 22, 1910.
[3]Jackson *Issue*, Sept. 2, 1910.
[4]Percy, *Lanterns on the Levee*, 148.

was being used to win support for the bill the subcommittee in charge gave an unfavorable report and the bill was killed. The committee was composed of Senators Bond, Nabors, Burrows, Donald, and Hobbs, and later it was shown that Bilbo had persuaded them to stop the bill because of the rumors afloat.[5]

The matter lay dormant for almost two years; then suddenly, on December 1, 1913, a grand jury in Warren County brought indictments against Senator G. A. Hobbs and Lieutenant-Governor Bilbo. The first count of the indictment charged them with soliciting a bribe of $2,000 from Steve Castleman, a large property holder in Belzoni, the proposed seat of the proposed county, to procure passage of the bill in the next session of the legislature. The second count charged them with actually receiving $200 from Castleman as a bribe.[7] Both Hobbs and Bilbo protested their innocence. Bilbo called it "political piracy." He said it was merely a plot on the part of Brewer to ruin him politically. Hobbs stated, and later testified, that Brewer had called him in a few days before the indictment and offered him immunity if he would confess and testify against Bilbo. Brewer called this statement "a lie out of the whole cloth," but he remained ominously silent as to everything else. "Let the facts [at the trial] speak for themselves," he said.[6]

Even the anti-Bilbo press was taken too much by surprise to form judgments. The *Clarion* contented itself with the obvious conclusion that "Either most unscrupulous men have been exalted to high position . . . or false charges are being preferred against them." The Jackson *Daily News* regretted to see "even Hobbs and Bilbo in a trouble of this sort . . . not because of the individuals themselves . . . , but because of the unenviable notoriety . . . to our commonwealth." The Natchez *Democrat* wisely observed that Bilbo's adherents would believe in his innocence "until the cows come home" and feared that unless his guilt could be established beyond any doubt he would "advance several pegs in the political life of the state."[7]

[5]Speech of Judge Pat Henry, in *Bilbo-Hobbs Trial, Jury Speeches in Full* (Jackson, Miss., n.d.), 30-31; Jackson *Clarion-Ledger*, Feb. 22, 1912; G. A. Hobbs, *Bilbo, Brewer, and Bribery* (n.p., 1917), 117-34; Macon *Beacon*, Dec. 12, 1913.

[6]Jackson *Clarion-Ledger*, Dec. 2, 3, 1913; Macon *Beacon*, Dec. 12, 1915; Vicksburg *Herald*, Dec. 2, 1913; Natchez *Democrat*, Dec. 3, 4, 5, 1913; Jackson *Daily News*, Dec. 3, 1913.

[7]Jackson *Clarion-Ledger*, Dec. 3, 1913; Jackson *Daily News*, Dec. 3, 1913; Natchez *Democrat*, Dec. 4, 1913.

The first move of the defense was to quash the indictment, charging that court officials in Warren had hand-picked the grand jury which indicted them. This motion was overruled. They then moved for a change of venue on the ground that the inflamed state of the public mind in Warren and the fact that Lieutenant-Governor Bilbo's integrity had been made an issue precluded a fair trial there. This, too, was overruled. One hostile editor observed that Warren was no exception to the other counties of the state. "In all of them there exists 'an inflamed condition of the public mind' and there are very few, if any, in which . . . Bilbo's integrity has not been questioned."[8]

It was suspected that the defense was using delaying tactics in an attempt to prolong the trial until the legislature should meet in January. It was pointed out that if this could be done Bilbo might tie up all judicial appointments and thus disorganize the criminal courts, or have a two-thirds majority in the legislature to impeach Brewer. In the latter event he would himself become governor and could appoint a judge to the Warren circuit who would dismiss the case.[9]

When the venue motion was overruled the state moved for separate trials of Hobbs and Bilbo and the trial of Hobbs proceeded. The state had attempted to employ as special prosecutor Judge Pat Henry of Vicksburg, the outstanding criminal lawyer of the state and a bitter opponent of both Vardaman and Bilbo. Strangely, Henry declined. He confounded the administration by becoming counsel for the defense and represented them ably. The trial, he said, was a "political game," and he wished to be "on the side of the people."[10]

The chief witness for the state was Castleman. He was, he stated, interested in procuring the new county because it would enhance the value of his property in Belzoni. In the spring of 1912, he said, after the legislature had adjourned without creating the new county, he had received a telephone call in Belzoni from Hobbs in Jackson. Hobbs, he said, refused to tell him his business over the phone, but urged him to meet him in Jackson where, he promised,

[8]Jackson *Clarion-Ledger*, Dec. 8, 11, 1913; Natchez *Democrat*, Dec. 9, 10, 13, 1913; Macon *Beacon*, Dec. 19, 1913.
[9]Jackson *Clarion-Ledger*, Dec. 12, 14, 1913.
[10]Henry's Speech, in *Bilbo-Hobbs Trial*, 22, 23.

he would offer a proposition which would interest him. At Vicksburg on the way to meet Hobbs, he ran into Brewer, whom he told about the mysterious call. Brewer urged him to proceed to his rendezvous, which he did. In Jackson, according to Castleman, Hobbs had proposed that for $2,000 he and Bilbo could secure the passage of his bill. He had, he said, replied noncommittally to Hobbs, and on the way back to Belzoni had again encountered Brewer, this time at Morehead. He told the governor of his meeting with Hobbs, and Brewer urged him to "string along" Hobbs and to "try to catch others" who were working with him.

Castleman declared that he proceeded to blow hot, then cold, keeping Hobbs guessing as to his intentions. In the course of the next few months Hobbs made several trips from his home in Brookhaven to meet Castleman—twice in Jackson and once in Belzoni. On each occasion, Castleman said, Hobbs had urged him to agree to the $2,000 payment. Meanwhile Brewer had employed Burns detectives from New Orleans to aid in the plot to catch Hobbs and the "others." Finally in October, 1912, Castleman succeeded in luring Hobbs to Vicksburg under the impression, it seems, that Bilbo would accompany Hobbs. He secured room 214 in the National Park Hotel there, and the detectives, hiding detectaphones in the room, waited in the room above and took notes of the conversation between Castleman and Hobbs.

Hobbs seemed to suspect nothing, even when Castleman roared at him in a raucous voice. Castleman, who was insuring that the faulty detectaphones would record the conversation, explained to Hobbs that he could not lower his voice since he was accustomed to "hollowing at mules, cows, and pigs." Hobbs again agreed to secure the passage of the bill for the consideration and insisted that Bilbo "understands everything" and that he and Bilbo "controlled the legislature." Castleman later testified in court that he had previously given Hobbs $100 on account and that together they went from his room to the lobby where he cashed a draft for $100 and gave it to Hobbs there. Two subsequent meetings between Hobbs and Castleman were held at the Royal Hotel in Jackson. On both occasions the room was again wired with detectaphones in the hope that Bilbo would be present also, but he did not appear.

Governor Brewer testified that he had employed the detectives after Castleman told him he had been approached by Hobbs. He also testified that Hobbs had come to him a few days before the indictment, confessed his guilt, and pleaded for clemency. This was corroborated by Mattie Plunkett, the state librarian. She testified that Hobbs had come to her in a desperate mood, begged her to get an interview for him with the governor, and showed a pistol with which she thought he meant to kill the governor. She stated that she was present at the interview between Hobbs and Brewer and that Hobbs broke down and confessed his guilt. She also testified that the first call which Hobbs made to Castleman at Belzoni had been put through in her office at Hobbs' request.

The stenographic notes of the detectives bore out the testimony of Castleman. The detectives also testified that Hobbs' voice was heard through the device saying that Bilbo was thoroughly acquainted with the proposition and would assist on the bill. The sheriff of Hinds County testified that he heard Hobbs in the Royal Hotel in Jackson "whining and pleading" with Castleman for payment of the money.

Hobbs himself corroborated most of Castleman's testimony. He admitted meeting Castleman at Belzoni, Jackson, and Vicksburg, and urging him to pay $2,000 to secure passage of the county bill. His purpose, however, was "patriotic." Learning of rumors of bribery in the 1912 legislature, he, Bilbo, Swep Taylor, mayor of Jackson, and others had decided to turn "detectives" and catch the guilty. It was agreed among them, he said, that he should pursue Castleman, who rumor had it had offered Mrs. Turnage, postmistress of the legislature, $2,500 to secure passage of his bill. He denied that Castleman had actually paid him $200, or any amount. He said, further, that he had not solicited an interview with the governor. Miss Plunkett, he said, had asked him to see the governor and had told him that if he did not insist that she testify, she would get the governor to leave him alone. Miss Plunkett, said Hobbs, while posing as his friend, had actually "sprung the trap" for Brewer to destroy him.

Hobbs' testimony was corroborated by Bilbo and Swep Taylor. Taylor testified that Hobbs had been selected by him and the others to trap Castleman. He stated that Mrs. Turnage had told him that Castleman had made the bribe offer to her, but this was denied by Mrs. Turnage. Much was made by the defense of the fact that, although two "detectaphone" meetings were held after the alleged

$200 had been paid, neither Castleman's nor Hobbs' voice had been recorded as mentioning the payments. Much was also made of the fact that Brewer testified that he had enough evidence to convict Hobbs in October, 1912, fourteen months before. This, they said, proved that Brewer was merely plotting to involve Bilbo. Pat Henry's presence among defense counsel gave much credence to this belief.

The trial lasted throughout the month of December. The jury was locked up and kept from their homes even on Christmas Day. The case went to the jury at 9:00 P. M. on December 30, and the following morning at 10:00 it returned a verdict of not guilty.[11]

Brewer and others expressed astonishment at Hobbs' acquittal. It seemed to them that the Vardaman-Bilbo faction was in a majority in almost every county in the state, and it would be impossible to secure a conviction of any of them "where a jury verdict rules." The Natchez *Democrat* said the case was not tried on its merits and that "an extremely ugly state of affairs is working incalculable injury to the state." Since Castleman was never indicted or tried, the jury must have concluded, thought the *Democrat*, that both parties were "patriots" and stumbled into each other's arms. The Aberdeen *Weekly*, professing neutrality, thought there was too much smoke in the affair for there not to be some fire. Without naming names the *Weekly* contrasted "present leaders" with "old time patriots." The Memphis *Commercial-Appeal*, too, was forced to conclude that "those who are dead and gone were either terribly overrated or . . . the standards of the measurement of men have changed." Predictions were freely made that when the legislature convened shortly Bilbo would institute impeachment proceedings against Brewer.[12]

Perhaps Bilbo would have done so if he could have controlled the house as he did the senate. Certainly he did what he could

[11]The above account is taken from Hobbs, *Bilbo, Brewer, and Bribery; Bilbo-Hobbs Trial, Jury Speeches in Full;* the files of the Jackson *Clarion-Ledger* for December, 1913, especially Dec. 2, 4, 24, 28; files of Macon *Beacon* for December, 1913, especially Dec. 5, 12; files of Jackson *Daily News* for December, 1913, especially Dec. 3, 28, 29, 30; files of Natchez *Democrat* for December, 1913, especially Dec. 13, 18, 20, 21, 23, 24, 27, 28, 31, Jan. 1, 1914.

[12]Aberdeen *Weekly*, Jan. 9, 1914; Memphis *Commercial Appeal*, quoted in Jackson *Clarion-Ledger*, Jan. 2, 1914; Vicksburg *Herald*, Jan. 1, 1914; Jackson *Daily News*, Dec. 29, 1913; Natchez *Democrat*, Jan. 1, 1914.

to embarrass the governor in the latter body. When the legislature convened Bilbo took the floor in the senate, called for peace, and urged the forgetting of factionalism in the interest of the state's business.[13] Despite this it soon became apparent that all anti-administration bills were originating in the senate, and it was charged that Bilbo and Hobbs openly lobbied in the house for their passage. Together they fostered a bill, aimed at Brewer, making all vacant offices elective instead of appointive. It passed the senate but was defeated in the house. By early March there was no longer any doubt, said the *Clarion*, that politics was being played in the legislature and that the "schemes are being hatched in the Senate." The political lines between the governor and lieutenant-governor were being drawn taut, and "The members of the Legislature are lining up either on one side or the other." Soon a bitter exchange was indulged in by Brewer and Bilbo, each charging the other with bad faith and with injuring the state. The governor claimed that while the senate was pretending to carry on the people's business, it was actually smothering it in committee rooms where appropriation bills were being held up. All of this, he said, was at the direction of Bilbo, who was in league with "crooks and grafters" who had been indicted or convicted of "pillaging" the state.[14]

An impasse developed over an appropriation to pay expenses incurred by Brewer in his investigation of the penitentiary and of the Hobbs case. In the special session held in the summer of 1913 the house had passed a resolution authorizing the governor to spend $10,000 of his contingent fund for the penitentiary investigation. Brewer had done so. Bilbo now attempted to prevent an appropriation for this item, but even his own senate would not follow him thus far and passed the bill by a narrow margin. He then attempted, with more success, to prevent payment to the Burns Detective Agency for its detectaphone work in the Hobbs case. The bill was hung up in committee in the senate, and a resolution was passed by that body requiring a two-thirds vote to consider a bill given an adverse committee report. For this he was denounced by Brewer as "the most crooked man who has ever done business in the State."

[13]Mississippi, *Senate Journal*, 1914, pp. 4-5.
[14]*Ibid.*, 620-21, 725, 922, 1035, 1066; Natchez *Democrat*, Jan. 5, Mar. 6, 11, 1914; Jackson *Clarion-Ledger*, Mar. 1, 6, 1914.

When a resolution was offered in the senate to bring the Burns appropriation from committee, it was defeated by a vote of 20 to 13. The house then authorized the governor to pay the detectives out of money collected as a result of the penitentiary investigation, but the senate refused to consider this bill.[15]

As the session dragged on, with the senate frequently not sitting for lack of a quorum, it was charged that Bilbo was purposely prolonging the session so as to avoid his trial. Venue had been changed to Hinds County, and the spring term there would expire in early summer. While the legislature was in session, of course, Bilbo was immune. It was also rumored that certain senators, friends of Bilbo, had made an offer to Brewer that his appropriations would be approved if he would nol-pros Bilbo's indictment. Bilbo denied emphatically that anybody was authorized by him to make a proposal of any nature to Brewer, and a senate resolution called on Brewer to furnish it with the names of those who had made the offer. In response Brewer named Senators J. M. Arnold of Hattiesburg and Sidney McLaurin of Brandon. Both admitted the charge but stated that their activities were wholly in the interest of peace and had been made only after consultation with other senators and with Swep Taylor and J. M. McBeath, chairman of the Democratic state executive committee.[16]

Meanwhile preparations were going forward for Bilbo's trial. Bilbo asked that the case be sent back to Warren County, charging that special Judge Teat would not give him a fair trial and that Brewer had stacked the jury panel. Teat had been assigned to the Hinds circuit when Bilbo had objected to being tried by the regular judge, E. L. Brien. Brewer denounced the charge of stacking the panel as "false as hell," and the Jackson *News* dismissed the charge against Teat as delaying tactics. Bilbo, it said, did not want a fair trial. It pointed to the numerous motions of the defense as evidence that it wanted to avoid the trial on technicalities, if possible. These, it said, were not "the acts of an innocent man . . . who wants to prove to the world that he is innocent." The *News* also charged that copies of qualified jurors in Hinds were surreptitiously prepared

15Mississippi, *Senate Journal*, 1914, pp. 888, 1187, 1324; Jackson *Clarion-Ledger*, Mar. 1, 6, 10, 11, 15, 1914; Natchez *Democrat*, Mar. 21, 24, 25, 1914.

16Mississippi, *Senate Journal*, 1914, pp. 853-56, 1376-83; Natchez *Democrat*, Mar. 15, 19, 21, 27, 1914; Vicksburg *Herald*, Mar. 5, 17, 27, 1914; Jackson *Clarion-Ledger*, Mar. 27, 1914.

and turned over to Bilbo so that he might poll them and disqualify those who were not his political supporters. It warned the people to refrain from expressing themselves on the merits of the case. At the same time the Hinds grand jury was investigating a charge of bribery in connection with the creation of Walthall County by the legislature in 1910. It was rumored that Bilbo had received a bribe of $1,500 from sponsors of the new county to push the bill through the legislature. Bilbo's supporters charged that this and other moves were designed to "railroad" Bilbo, and it was reported that plans were being made to bring a trainload of his followers from Pearl River County to see that he got a "fair trial."[17]

Bilbo came to trial in mid-June. A sensation was created when the defense presented an affidavit of a member of the Warren grand jury which had indicted Hobbs and Bilbo. This affidavit stated that the jury had intended to indict Hobbs but not Bilbo and that Bilbo's indictment had come as a result of pressure by the district attorney. In a subsequent statement the juror claimed that the affidavit had been secured by Bilbo's attorneys through false representation, but the affidavit's original effect was not entirely destroyed. The state's case was further crippled by the failure of Mattie Plunkett to appear. It was insinuated that Bilbo had caused her absence, but this was never proved. The most damaging evidence to Bilbo's reputation concerned a matter completely extraneous to the issue presented by the indictment. Ira W. Sample, a Chicago lawyer who had been Brewer's "guest" at the mansion for two years, testified that Hobbs had proposed that Sample should induce the Hines Lumber Company to settle a case which the state had against it. "The Attorney-general . . . runs that," Hobbs was alleged to have said, "and . . . Bilbo controls the attorney-general. If an arrangement can be made by which Mr. Hines is willing to pay for it, that suit can be dismissed." According to Sample, $35,000 was the price which Hobbs asked. Of this, $5,000 was to go to the attorney-general, Ross Collins, and $20,000 to Hobbs and Bilbo. The remainder was to be split among various other officials. Ross Collins testified that Bilbo had approached him suggesting such a settlement.[18]

[17]Jackson *Issue,* quoted in Jackson *Clarion-Ledger,* June 6, 13, 1914; Macon *Beacon,* July 3, 1914; Jackson *Daily News,* Apr. 5, 16, 20, June 19, 28, 1914.

[18]Jackson *Clarion-Ledger,* July 7, 10, Sept. 5, 1914; Natchez *Democrat,* June 27, July 7, 1914.

After twelve hours deliberation, the jury returned a verdict of not guilty. One juror later stated that on the first ballot seven voted for conviction but later changed. The anti-Bilbo press was undoubtedly prepared for this verdict, but professed shock nevertheless. The Natchez *Democrat* resignedly admitted that "Today it is almost impossible to convict a man of . . . influence." It predicted that the people would render a different verdict at the polls the following year, when Bilbo would be a candidate for governor. The *News* thought the verdict only illustrated the limitless possibilities for escape from justice when shrewd lawyers employed technical pleas. It blamed the state's attorney for not making a better case and admitted that the testimony did not connect Bilbo with the transaction in a conclusive manner. The Macon *Beacon* wanted to add to Solomon's three wonders the way of a petit jury with a criminal. "What will the end be?" it asked. "God alone knows," it replied. "Never before in the history of the State have Mississippians been put to such shame."[19]

The trial indicated that even the courts were considered by the people to have been aligned in the factional fight, and their prestige suffered as a result. Before the trial the Hickory *Middle Buster* advocated electing Bilbo governor "even if he's guilty" and advised the people to "take him out of the pen" if sent there. After Bilbo's acquittal a jubilation meeting was held in Smith Park in Jackson. Senator Hal Sanders of Tallahatchie, speaking on the occasion, was quoted as saying that if Bilbo had been convicted, "Tallahatchie County would have sent 750 men armed with muskets, rifles and revolvers" to rescue him from the law.[20]

Before the trial had started the campaign for the gubernatorial nomination in 1915 had begun. From the start it was admitted by experienced observers that the nomination would come from the Vardaman ranks. "No man of ordinary sense," said the *Clarion*, "doubts Vardaman's ability to name the next Governor of Mississippi if he so wills; and as a rule he is by no means modest in asserting his power." It only hoped that Vardaman would name a man whose character was "above reproach."[21]

[19]Jackson *Clarion-Ledger*, July 10, 1914; Natchez *Democrat*, July 10, 1914; Jackson *Daily News*, July 10, 1914; Macon *Beacon*, July 17, 1914.

[20]Hickory *Middle Buster* and New Orleans *Times-Picayune*, quoted in Jackson *Clarion-Ledger*, Dec. 16, 1913, July 14, 1914.

[21]*Ibid.*, June 24, 1914.

Four candidates besides Bilbo were in the field: W. M. Reily of Natchez, P. S. Stovall and H. M. Quinn of Jackson, and J. R. Tally of Hattiesburg. It was obvious from the start that it was a case of the field against Bilbo. All kept challenging him to joint debates, and, departing from Vardaman's practice, he agreed to meet them one at a time. Shortly before the election, however, it was reported that no joint debates "worthy of the name" had taken place, although two of the candidates had made more than "600 speeches each."[22]

Repeated attempts were made to effect a breach between Vardaman and Bilbo. Judge Robert Powell claimed that Bilbo had told him in 1913 that he was considering forming a political alliance with Brewer to defeat Vardaman. The anti-Vardaman-Bilbo press played up the failure of Bilbo to expose the alleged bribery in the Secret Caucus in time to elect Vardaman then. This was cited by them as an example of Bilbo's "treachery" even to his own leader, Vardaman, and as justification for Vardaman's abandoning Bilbo now if he should choose to do so. Warnings were also issued to Vardaman that he had best scotch Bilbo now if he wanted to retain control of his own forces. If Bilbo should be elected governor in 1915, suggested the *Clarion*, and, "with the shrewdness and ability he is known to possess in dealing with the public," become a popular governor, "he might . . . become quite a formidable opponent of Senator Vardaman" in the senatorial election of 1918. The Natchez *News* repeatedly accused Bilbo of attempting to "knife" Vardaman and thought the only reason he did not make an open break was that he wanted the Vardaman votes. "But elect him," said the *News*, "and watch him take off the mask. . . . He never has played fair and there is no indication he will now."[23]

The plotters seemed to think their scheme was working. Judge Powell stated that Vardaman "had never had any use for [Bilbo] since he claimed he had been bribed by Dulaney." The Vicksburg *Herald* alleged that the bribery charge was a "hoax" and was known as such by Vardaman, who profited from it. Nevertheless it thought that a rift had occurred between Bilbo and Vardaman and that the latter's followers were using this charge of "treachery" to defeat

[22]Jackson *Clarion-Ledger*, Mar. 9, July 11, 1915.
[23]Jackson *Daily News*, Dec. 28, 1913; Vicksburg *Herald*, Feb. 1, 1914; Jackson *Clarion-Ledger*, Mar. 1, 1914; Natchez *News*, Aug. 1, 1914.

Bilbo's gubernatorial aspirations.[24] It was made to appear that there was a vast gulf separating the idealism of the two men. "If Vardaman really stands for anything in Mississippi," said the Senatobia *Democrat,* "Bilbo stands for the opposite, and merely because they have mutual enemies they should not be classed together." The same sentiment was expressed by the Clarion.[25]

Furthermore, good relations between Brewer and Vardaman were supposed to have been promoted by Brewer's commuting the sentence of C. C. Smith, the convicted penitentiary trustee. It was even thought that the pardon had come as a result of a request from Vardaman, and there were rumors of a "line-up" of Brewer and Vardaman against Bilbo. When Bilbo's law partner was defeated in a judicial primary by Judge Teat, who presided at Bilbo's trial and against whom Bilbo campaigned vigorously, it was taken as an indication of a Vardaman-Bilbo split, and the *Clarion* gloated over Bilbo's "waning influence." Shortly thereafter, Brewer attempted to persuade Vardaman openly to oppose Bilbo's candidacy. When Vardaman refused, Brewer became enraged and attacked him viciously. He charged that "Senator Vardaman knows as well as I do that Bilbo is a crook but . . . he fears that . . . Bilbo . . . will go right after his position in the Senate."[26]

Despite Bilbo's close association with Vardaman he did not, during the campaign or later as governor, resort to the anti-Negro tirades which characterized Vardaman's political campaigns. His technique was of a different kind. He appealed to the voters as an exposer of oligarchic corruption and as a victim of oligarchic persecution. Like Vardaman he appealed to them on a broad program of governmental and social reform.

A concerted campaign was waged by the anti-Bilbo press to discourage the farmers from voting in the election. Mississippi, it was said, had been suffering "from a surplus of politics and a scarcity of grain crops." The farmers had been neglecting their work for politics long enough. "The people of Mississippi have about come to the conclusion," said the *Clarion,* "that there are other

24Jackson *Daily News,* Dec. 28, 1913; Vicksburg *Herald,* Feb. 1, 1914.

25Senatobia *Democrat,* Jan. 8, 1914, in Vardaman scrapbook, Mississippi Department of Archives and History; Jackson *Clarion-Ledger,* June 21, 1914.

26Macon *Beacon,* Mar. 13, 1914; Jackson *Clarion-Ledger,* Aug. 20, 21, Oct. 4, 6, 1914; Greenwood *Enterprise,* Sept. 18, 1914, and Senatobia *Democrat,* Oct. 1, 1914, in Vardaman scrapbook.

things more profitable than the cultivation of the political crop."
It promised that henceforth the papers would devote more space
to agriculture and less to politics. With the primary less than a
month off the farmer was advised to tend to his crops "and leave
the politicians to hoe their own row."[27]

There were large issues, which will be discussed in the next
chapter, but they seem to have been obscured by petty bickerings
and personalities. Reily had a Catholic wife, and this was an issue,
but only a *sub rosa* one. It was charged that W. P. Holland, president
of the Planter's Bank of Clarksdale, had contributed $500 to Bilbo's
campaign. His object was supposed to be the controlling of the
levee board, which handled a half million dollars annually and
which the new governor would appoint. The Vicksburg *Herald*
was fair enough to admit that if true it was doubtful if "the interest
of the people will thereby be worsted or changed." Holland controlled the board under the present administration, it said, and
only wanted to continue to do so. Bilbo's backing by Frank Burkitt
brought charges that he was aligned with the former Populists,
which was probably true, and that he planned to revive the Populist party, which was false. Bilbo promised to take "politics" out of
the schools and named G. M. Hightower, president of the Agricultural and Mechanical College and a Brewer appointee, as the first
who would go.[28]

Brewer, interested only in defeating Bilbo, was vigorously
campaigning for Reily. Congressman B. G. Humphreys and John
Sharp Williams were secretly supporting Reily and applauded
Brewer's work. Most of Brewer's speeches were attacks on Bilbo's
record, from his attempt to hamstring the penitentiary investigation,
through the Hobbs trial and his part in holding up legislative business for his own interest, to his own trial for bribery. He charged
him with having committed "numerous other frauds and crimes"
which had never been exposed.[29] He charged that Bilbo and state

[27]Jackson *Clarion-Ledger*, Dec. 15, 1914, Apr. 6, May 21, June 1, July 10,
1915; *ibid.*, May 21, quoting Madison County *Herald*; Natchez *Democrat*, July 4,
23, 1915; Green County *Herald*, July 10, 1915.
[28]Vicksburg *Herald*, Jan. 25, 1914, June 19, 1915; *ibid.*, quoting Grenada
Sentinel; Macon *Beacon*, June 25, 1915; Jackson *Daily News*, Apr. 30, 1914.
[29]Jackson *Clarion-Ledger*, Apr. 20, May 2, 1915; Greenwood *Commonwealth*,
quoted in Macon *Beacon*, June 25, 1915; B. G. Humphreys to J. S. Williams, May 29,
1915; Williams to Earl Brewer, June 2, 1915, Williams Papers.

Senator Lee Russell, who was campaigning for lieutenant-governor on Bilbo's slate, had formed "a cabal . . . for securing political advantage for a faction through a dirty intrigue." "Never before in the State," said he, "was political depravity so open and bold and defiant in asserting itself." The Macon *Beacon*, professing to believe all Brewer's charges, was horrified at the "low moral tone" to which Mississippi politics had descended when men like Bilbo and Russell could aspire to office by appeals to "the uninformed class of people who are ignorant of the facts." "Self-confession of immorality—of bribery, and lying about it—no longer seems," it said, " . . . to deter a man from offering for high office or to prevent voters from flocking to his standard."[30]

It is difficult to understand why Bilbo's opponents kept calling him "a self-confessed bribe taker." Whether or not Bilbo was a "bribe taker" was certainly an issue in Mississippi politics. But never at any time did he confess that he was. He admitted receiving money from Dulaney during the Secret Caucus of 1910. He charged that Dulaney had given him the money to influence his vote, but he denied that his vote had been so influenced and, on the contrary, claimed that his only purpose in accepting it had been to trap and expose Dulaney. Since intent is a necessary ingredient in such a crime, the mere fact that he accepted money, without intending to be influenced by it, could not constitute bribery. To charge that he "confessed" to have been bribed, when his whole political career thus far had been based on repeated and categorical denials of it, was a gross misrepresentation of fact.

Of course Bilbo and Russell paid Brewer back in kind, sometimes with interest. In a joint debate between Russell and Brewer at Wesson on July 14, Russell charged that Brewer had stolen a pending bill from the legislative hopper. Again Brewer let his temper get out of control and threatened to cut Russell's throat "from ear to ear" if he ever repeated the accusation. Bilbo publicized the fact that Brewer had been sued by the husband of Adele Blood, the actress, for alienation of his wife's affections.[31]

The opposition to Bilbo received two strong stimulants during the last months of the campaign. In May, in a speech at Pontotoc,

[30]Macon *Beacon*, July 30, 1915.

[31]Jackson *Clarion-Ledger*, July 19, 1914, July 20, 1915; Natchez *Democrat*, July 17, 1915; Jackson *Daily News*, July 15, 1915.

Vardaman denounced "bribetakers." This was universally interpreted as a blow at Bilbo. It "was a bitter pill for Bilbo's friends," said the Jones County *News*, and could only mean that Vardaman wanted his friends to vote "against Bilbo and the corporate alignments he has made." Vardaman subsequently denied that he had aimed the remark at Bilbo and claimed that he was "neutral" in the governor's race since all five candidates were his friends.[32]

Two months later John W. Armstrong, a former Vardaman supporter, exploded a bomb. In a letter to B. F. Jones of Hernando he stated that during the Secret Caucus he was approached by Bilbo who told him that "the other side" was offering to pay his room and board bill and give him "money to spend" if he would help them. Bilbo, he said, told him that he "controlled seven votes" and that if Armstrong could get him $100 he would "stay put." According to Armstrong, he related the incident to Vardaman and his advisers so that Vardaman "would not become entangled with Bilbo." Dr. Ben F. Ward, Vardaman's political mentor, admitted that Armstrong at the time had told him of the incident, but that he did not then, nor did he now, believe Armstrong. Vaughan Watkins, Vardaman's campaign manager in 1911, admitted writing a check at the time for $100, marking it "For God Knows What," and giving it to Armstrong who told him it was for Bilbo. Bilbo denounced Armstrong as a "liar," and charged that he was expelled from the Elks Club and the Country Club at Jackson for cheating at cards. Armstrong denied this and submitted affidavits to prove otherwise. The Jackson *News* had no doubt Armstrong's story was true, but said it had been revealed too late to do any good. Had it come five years before, it said, "it would have changed the entire course of Mississippi's political history." Nor did the *News* think that was the only money used by the Vardaman crowd in the Secret Caucus. "It took a large bunch of greenbacks to keep that crowd together," it said, "and they were distributed freely whenever and wherever needed."[33]

Whether Vardaman credited the story is not definitely known, but obviously it was not news to him. He issued no statement,

[32]Vicksburg *Herald*, May 19, 1915; *ibid.*, quoting Jones County *News*.

[33]Macon *Beacon*, July 23, 1915; Vicksburg *Herald*, July 23, 28, 1915; Jackson *Clarion-Ledger*, July 26, 1915; Jones County *News*, July 29, 1915; Jackson *Daily News*, July 25, 1915.

announcing merely that he was coming home to vote. This was interpreted as indicating that Bilbo had his support.[34]

On the eve of the election the Natchez *Democrat* called on the voters to "repel the invasion" of an "arrogant political ring." The election, it said, was "a battle to rescue the fair name of Mississippi from the slums of political rottenness." Reports were spread of the circulation through the state of a "Bilbo line-up ticket" as a suggestion to voters. Bilbo denied that he had any commitments to other candidates and stated that the ticket was a trick of his opponents to gain for him the enmity of those candidates left off the list.[35]

A record vote of 140,000 was cast. Of these Bilbo received 74,573, a majority of nearly 9,000 over all his opponents, and more than 25,000 in excess of his nearest rival, Reily. He carried all but three white counties, but received less than 35 per cent of the vote in the Delta counties.[36] There was evidence of some ballot-box stuffing, particularly in Pontotoc. There it was shown that the vote far exceeded the registration; that Bilbo received 700 more votes there than were counted for all candidates in 1911, and 730 more than Lee Russell, winning candidate for lieutenant-governor who was allied with him. Editor Fred Sullens asked for an investigation, but this was refused by the state executive committee and Bilbo was declared the nominee.

Subsequently it was alleged and proved by each side that Negroes were voted in the primary. In Harrison County at the McHenry precinct, it was shown that thirty-five Negro mill hands were voted by one faction. Similar charges were made and proved concerning Pike, Lamar, Lincoln, and Pearl River counties. In these counties there were factional struggles for local control, and it was not thought that the gubernatorial candidates were involved in the irregularities, although they may have profited or been injured by them.[37]

Fred Sullens' chagrin knew no bounds after it became known that Bilbo was nominated. He petulantly maintained that Bilbo

[34]Vicksburg *Herald*, July 28, 1915.

[35]Natchez *Democrat*, Aug. 1, 1915; Jackson *Clarion-Ledger*, Aug. 1, 2, 3, 1915.

[36]*Biennial Report of the Secretary of State to the Legislature, July 1, 1913-July 1, 1915* (Memphis, 1915).

[37]Natchez *Democrat*, Aug. 11, 1915; Jackson *Clarion-Ledger*, Aug. 5, 6, 7, 1915; Jackson *Daily News*, Aug. 6, 1915; Macon *Beacon*, Feb. 18, 1916.

would be governor for "but little more than one half the people of Mississippi." The robe of office, he said, could not hide "the bar sinister across his forehead." It was "an unhappy day for Mississippi" and there were to be "more unhappy days ahead." "He stands for nothing that is high or constructive, he represents nothing save passion, prejudice, and hatred, he advocates nothing that is worthy." His nomination had only transpired, Sullens said, because "a majority of the voters, fooled, deluded, blinded, lost to all reason, have said . . . that they would rather wallow in filth than walk on clean ground." He suggested substituting "a carrion crow" for the eagle on the state seal and removing the eagle from the dome of the capitol and replacing it with "a puking buzzard." Bilbo was and would remain "a self-accused bribe taker, a self-confessed grafter, a foul tongued slanderer, an unmitigated liar and contemptible crook."[38]

The Macon *Beacon* agreed with Sullens on everything except his explanation of why the people voted for Bilbo. It did not think they preferred "to wallow in filth." Rather it thought they "disbelieved the statements of facts made by the *News,* the *Beacon,* by Governor Brewer, and by that contained in the [senate] resolution of April 15, 1910." The Newton *Record,* too, thought that Bilbo's large vote was a reaction to Brewer's vigorous campaign against him. The Vicksburg *Herald* agreed, observing that "Brewer's petroleum was . . . feeding instead of extinguishing the baleful Bilbo flame." The *Clarion* simply gave up trying to explain "the freakish caprice of the voter." Frequently, it said, the slightest thing would influence his action, and at other times it was impossible to change his views. It thought the voter, as a rule, acted on his own initiative when he entered the voting booth. "Away from the crowd and the appeals of the candidates, he makes up his mind to vote for somebody, vote against somebody, or not to vote for this or that man for reasons of his own."[39] While more complex, this guess was probably as good as the others.

[38] Jackson *Daily News,* Aug. 8, 1915.

[39] Macon *Beacon,* Aug. 13, 1915; Vicksburg *Herald,* Aug. 8, 1915; *ibid.,* quoting Newton *Record;* Jackson *Clarion-Ledger,* Aug. 8, 1915.

CHAPTER XX

REFORM – AND SCANDAL

THE LEGISLATURE which met in January, 1916, contained only forty veterans of the previous session. A contest for the speakership developed between Oscar Johnston of Coahoma, Joseph E. Norwood of Pike, and M. S. Conner of Covington. Bilbo was known to be opposed to Johnston and a warm friend of Conner's father. Johnston was from the Delta but seemed to lack the united support of that section. Affairs of the Yazoo Delta Levee Board had provoked a factional quarrel that was said to be responsible for Johnston's poor showing in the election of a speaker. Conner was chosen on the fourth ballot. He was the youngest man ever to hold the office, and his attaining the distinction was said to be due to "the powers that be." Norwood was made chairman of the important judiciary committee.[1]

Brewer refused to attend the inaugural exercises because Bilbo objected to his speaking. He issued a farewell statement, however, which did more to clarify the issues between him and Bilbo than all his campaign oratory. He explained the hostility between them as owing to sectional interests. Bilbo, he said, favored a constitutional convention, and he did not. The purpose of such a convention would be to effect a reduction of taxes in south Mississippi and an increase in other sections and to increase legislative representation in south Mississippi at the expense of north and west Mississippi.[2]

In his message to the legislature Bilbo advocated a constitutional convention to revise legislative apportionment; a revision of tax laws to equalize assessments in the several counties; a pardoning board to relieve the governor of the arduous duty of examining clemency appeals; the establishment of a state highway department to build and unify a system of state roads; the building of a hospital for the treatment of pellagra; and the issuing of $1,200,000 in bonds for permanent improvements in the state hospitals.[3] Not content

[1]Jackson *Clarion-Ledger*, Jan. 5, 7, 10, 1916; Natchez *News Democrat*, Jan. 5, 6, 9, 1916.

[2]Mississippi, *Senate Journal*, 1916, pp. 149-51; Natchez *Democrat*, Jan. 19, 1916; Jackson *Clarion-Ledger*, Jan. 19, 1916.

[3]Mississippi, *Senate Journal*, 1916, pp. 106-32.

with advocating these measures, Bilbo openly lobbied for them. It was frequently reported that he was spending a good deal of time on the floors of both houses "mingling with the members and urging the passage" of bills he recommended.[4]

It soon became apparent that there was disunity between the senate, which was said to be under Bilbo's influence, and the house, controlled by the antiadministration forces. The senate seemed to favor greater spending for welfare agencies, while the house was intent on cutting expenditures. Nevertheless the legislature passed many bills Bilbo favored, and also passed several he opposed over his veto—four in one evening. Upon one occasion he went on the floor of the house and spoke in defense of his veto of a measure only to have it overridden by a vote of 82-33.[5]

When the legislature showed no disposition to call a convention, Bilbo sent letters to outstanding citizens asking their opinions and published answers of those who favored a convention. The needs most commonly stressed in these answers were: more equitable distribution of school funds, more representation for southern counties, and equalization of assessments of real estate values. Some of these, for instance the school-fund distribution and the tax-equalization scheme, might appeal to counties in sections other than south Mississippi, but the legislative apportionment would restrict the influence of all north and west Mississippi, both Delta and the Hills. No convention bill was passed.[6]

Before the legislature adjourned it was reported that Bilbo had lost all control over it. This was not displeasing to the conservative press, which praised the legislature as "liberal, yet conservative." Although petty jealousy, "peanut politics," and other evils had seemed to thrive in the legislature, it did, they said, "accomplish much for the good of the state" and had "protected the interests of the people." The biennial appropriation was more than $9,000,000, an excess of $300,000 over the 1914 appropriation.[7]

The legislature had, nevertheless, gone along with Bilbo on

[4]Natchez News Democrat, Mar. 14, 1916; Jackson Clarion-Ledger, Mar. 31, 1916.
[5]Jackson Clarion-Ledger, Mar. 31, 1916; Natchez News Democrat, Feb. 11, Mar. 14, 1916.
[6]Macon Beacon, Feb. 18, Mar. 24, 1916; Vicksburg Herald, Feb. 20, 1916.
[7]Jackson Clarion-Ledger, Mar. 31, Apr. 9, 1916; Natchez Democrat, Apr. 11, 1916.

several important measures; among these was the tax-equalization scheme. Bilbo had advocated this during the campaign more vigorously than any other issue, and the legislature embodied his program in the Kyle Law. To understand its significance it will be necessary to review briefly some of the state's fiscal history.

Mississippi had emerged from the Reconstruction period unburdened by the huge debt which most of the southern states were carrying. The experience of the Planter's Bank bonds in the 1840's, when the state had pledged its credit to enhance the market value of the bank's bonds only to repudiate them when the bank failed, seemed to have made a lasting impression on the people of the state. Forthwith, a provision was written into the fundamental law forbidding the state to pledge its credit in any private or corporate venture, and this feature had been incorporated in the constitutions of 1868 and 1890. Consequently, when "Radical" rule was overthrown in 1876, the state's indebtedness was only $830,750, with a carrying charge of $45,000.[8] But unwise policies increased this debt in the next decades. Taxing power was vested in both legislature and county boards of supervisors. The legislature could fix the tax rate, but it was left to each of the seventy-odd boards of supervisors to assess the value of property in its county. Moreover, the board of supervisors was empowered to levy separate taxes in its county for local administration. Thus a sort of game developed among the counties to see which could, by lowering its property valuations, pay least taxes into the state treasury. At the same time the county could take care of its local needs by raising the county levy.[9]

The viciousness of this scheme was obvious, but no one seemed to know what to do about it. As the state levy went up, property assessments went down, and the state deficit grew. In addition, several extraordinary occurrences had added to the state's embarrassment. In 1890 the state treasurer had embezzled over $315,000, a sum far in excess of any peculation charged against any official of the Reconstruction regime. To take care of this the legislature authorized the sale of $400,000 of 4 per cent bonds at 95 per cent

[8]Mississippi Constitution, 1868, Sec. 5; ibid., 1890, Sec. 258; Charles M. Brough, "History of Taxation in Mississippi," in Mississippi Historical Society, Publications, II (1899), 124.

[9]See Governor Bilbo's message to legislature, in Mississippi, Senate Journal, 1916, pp. 106-11.

of their face value. Governor Stone objected to selling state bonds at less than par, and none was sold. The state was thus simply "in arrears," and warrants had to be issued to carry on the ordinary business of the state. The expense of the constitutional convention that year added another $60,000 to the state's debt. Prior to 1892 only about $400,000 per year was paid out of the treasury for the support of the common schools. The constitution of 1890, however, required a school term of at least four months in every county and school district. This would require an outlay of over $900,000 annually. In 1892 a fire at the lunatic asylum necessitated an expenditure of $125,000 for repairs. Failure to collect the poll tax and the inroads of local prohibition, which were cutting down liquor licenses, added to the distress. Governor Stone in 1894 reported over $425,000 of disbursements in excess of receipts for the fiscal year, and in 1896 the deficit was almost $390,000. The state levy had been increased from 2½ mills in 1876 to 6 mills in 1896.[10] Despite this, the treasury was bare, and state warrants were selling at a discount.

When McLaurin became governor in January, 1896, he approved a bill authorizing $400,000 of 5 per cent bonds to meet the running expenses of the government. But this only added to the debt. It put off the day of reckoning but made no preparation for meeting that day. By 1897, despite increased tax levies of almost 300 per cent, the state debt had grown to $1,106,000, and the deficit that year was another $400,000.[11] Some of the conservative papers were advocating a reduction in the school appropriation as the only alternative to increased taxes which would be "too heavy a burden upon the people."[12]

Year after year the deficit was passed, like a hot iron, from one legislature to the next; and year after year the county boards fixed their assessments, deliberately lowering them to deprive the state of revenue. Throughout the period the Delta counties seem to have been the worst offenders in this respect. They were incomparably the richest counties of the state, but it was frequently complained

[10]Mississippi, *House Journal*, 1894, p. 18; *ibid.*, 1896, p. 18; Brough, "History of Taxation," *loc. cit.*, 113-24; Macon *Beacon*, Jan. 23, 1897; Rowland, *History of Mississippi*, II, 352.

[11]Mississippi, *House Journal*, 1897, p. 8; Brough, "History of Taxation," *loc. cit.*, 124; Macon *Beacon*, Jan. 23, 1897.

[12]Natchez *Democrat*, quoted in Macon *Beacon*, Jan. 23, 1897.

that they were not paying their share. "Can anyone explain why," a Jackson editor asked in 1894, "Copiah, a piney woods county, should be the second county in tax paying . . . property in the state . . . ahead of all the river and prairie counties?" How was it, he wanted to know, that little piney woods Lincoln should stand tenth on the list, "ahead of all the river counties except Adams, Warren, and Washington," each of which had a large city. "Tell us why," he continued, "Jones, the typical piney woods county, should be ahead of Carroll, Chickasaw, Clay, Grenada, Jefferson, Lafayette, Leflore, Monroe, Montgomery, Oktibbeha, et al." "It would appear," he sarcastically concluded, "that the piney woods is the best part of the state."[13]

By 1916 finances were in a chaotic state. The state debt had grown to $2,500,000, and the state levy was raised to nine mills. Still the low valuation placed on lands by county boards rendered the increase useless. A legislator complained that this was particularly prevalent in "the rich Delta counties," where the planters objected to paying their "just proportion of the State's obligations." In one county there, he said, three-fourths of the land was valued at one dollar an acre.[14]

The purpose of the Kyle Law was to remedy this injustice, as well as to bring order out of chaos. The law created a central board of equalization, with power to revise assessments of any county which it felt did not correspond to actual property values. It was rather an arbitrary power and provoked considerable protest. It had been a general custom of county supervisors to fix assessments at 50 per cent of the estimated value of property. Since the new state board had no base from which to start, it fixed the assessment at 100 per cent of estimated values. This was coupled with a promise that the next legislature would reduce the tax levy to two mills. This brought howls of protest from the Delta where low assessments on realty were coupled with leniency toward corporations.[15]

Within a year of its creation the commission accomplished radical revisions in assessed valuation. Railroad and public service cor-

[13]Natchez *News Democrat*, Jan. 11, 1916; Vicksburg *Herald*, Feb. 12, 1916; Jackson *Clarion-Ledger*, Nov. 8, 1894.

[14]Natchez *News Democrat*, Jan. 11, 1916; Vicksburg *Herald*, Feb. 12, 1916; Jan. 14, 1922; Macon *Beacon*, July 27, Sept. 27, 1917, Jan. 18, 1918.

[15]Mississippi,*Laws*, 1916, Chap. XCVIII, 95-100; Macon *Beacon*, July 27, 1917, Jan. 18, 1918; Jackson *Clarion-Ledger*, Sept. 27, 1917.

poration assessments were increased $40,000,000.[16] Assessments in sixty-five of the poor counties were generally reduced. On the other hand, assessments in Bolivar, Coahoma, and Washington, three of the richest counties, were increased 463.7 per cent, 433.5 per cent, and 234 per cent respectively.[17] Pearl River County, where Bilbo lived, also paid more under the new scheme than it had under the old, as did several other south Mississippi counties.[18] This would indicate that the new system was not being used merely as a punitive measure against counties which were opposed to the administration. Bilbo was strong in his home county and had carried the southern counties whose assessments were increased.

Naturally the commission came in for much criticism. The *Clarion* reported that complaints were coming in "from all parts of the state." Never, it said, had taxes been so high. "Every county in the state feels that it has been outraged if not raped by the Tax Commission." It predicted that the Kyle Law would be repealed by the next legislature.[19]

To meet the objections of taxpayers, Bilbo called the legislature into special session in September, 1917. He pointed out that tax receipts under the new valuations would not only bring in excess revenues, but would be an undue hardship. He urged reduction of the levy. The legislature complied and adopted a four-mill levy. This proved insufficient to balance the increased appropriations of the 1918 legislature, and a new deficit appeared.[20] Subsequently, when the levy was once more raised to six mills, the budget was balanced, and the value of the equalization board made manifest. Writing in 1930, the outstanding authority on the subject called it "the very cornerstone" of Mississippi's fiscal machinery.[21]

It had been predicted by Bilbo's enemies that he would use his appointive power, reckless of qualifications, to build up his political

[16]Jackson *Clarion-Ledger*, Sept. 27, Dec. 13, 1917.

[17]Mississippi, *Senate Journal*, 1918, pp. 37-38; M. C. Rhodes, *History of Taxation in Mississippi, 1798-1929* (Nashville, 1930), 98.

[18]Mississippi, *Senate Journal*, 1918, p. 38; Vicksburg *Herald*, Jan. 11, 1918.

[19]Jackson *Daily News*, Nov. 16, 1917; Jackson *Clarion-Ledger*, Nov. 25, 28, Dec. 12, 13, 1917, Jan. 12, 13, 1918.

[20]Mississippi, *Laws*, 1917, Chap. XXII, Sec. 1, p. 13; Mississippi, *House Journal*, 1917, pp. 28-30; Vicksburg *Herald*, Jan. 11, 1918, Jan. 14, 1922; Macon *Beacon*, Mar. 1, 1918.

[21]Rhodes, *History of Taxation*, 94-97.

following in the state. His record on this score is confused, as some of his appointments drew blame and others praise from his enemies. The first few months of his term he was severely criticized for "showing a disposition to act the boss." He ousted many officials of the various state institutions, frequently over the protest of trustees, and refused to recognize an opinion of the state supreme court in regard to the term of office of the state factory inspector. The *Clarion* called him the most "interfering, bossy governor the state has ever had." Six months after his inauguration the *Clarion* was convinced that the state was "so permeated with politics that nothing goes except by political preference." A man's qualifications, it thought, counted for naught "unless his politics are on straight, and if his politics are of the right stamp his qualifications can be overlooked." Bilbo was charged with forcing levee board members and institutional trustees to swear to appoint his henchmen to places of profit which they controlled.[22]

Yet at almost the same time another enemy, in a confidential letter, was expressing "astonishment that Governor Bilbo is making so many good appointments." It almost seemed to him that Bilbo had "seen a light, and turned from ways of sin into righteousness." Another bitter enemy lauded the appointment of Professor P. P. Garner as commissioner of agriculture. Garner, said the *Beacon*, was "the best fitted man" and the "best appointment possible."[23]

Other features of Bilbo's administration drew praise from his enemies. When he succeeded in negotiating a state loan of more than $1,300,000 on favorable terms, the *Beacon* published a laudatory article headed "Governor Bilbo Good Financier."[24] Bilbo appointed a commission to investigate and recommend a remedy for illiteracy in Mississippi. The commission found more than 30,000 white illiterates, of whom almost 12,000 were males of voting age. It at once started voluntary night schools for them, and these were regularly attended. This drew universal praise, as also did other educational improvements. Manual training and farm mechanics were introduced into the curricula of rural schools, and 2,000 white and 500 Negro teachers pledged themselves to prepare to teach

[22]Jackson *Clarion-Ledger*, June 1, 6, 15, 1916; Macon *Beacon*, June 9, 1916.
[23]Lloyd L. Gilkey to J. S. Williams, May 6, 1916, Williams Papers; Macon *Beacon*, July 21, 1916.
[24]Macon *Beacon*, Aug. 11, 1916.

those subjects. Even the *Daily News* praised the work being done for the betterment of Mississippi's school system and credited Bilbo for instituting the reforms.[25]

In his message to the legislature in 1918 Bilbo staggered conservative editors by submitting a budget calling for appropriations totaling over $12,500,000. This represented an increase of almost $2,275,000 over the previous budget. Permanent improvements were to receive $1,765,000, and the remainder was to go in increased appropriations to schools and hospitals. Specific recommendations included: purchase of 5,000 acres of land for prison farms; a law empowering county school boards to employ superintendents instead of requiring that they be elected; free textbooks for indigent children; a uniform warehouse receipts act to save farmers from "middleman" charges; sale of the governor's mansion and acquisition of one "more in harmony with democratic standards of simplicity and unpretentious dignity"; enlargement of the state industrial training school for delinquent children; larger appropriations for the state Board of Health; a million-dollar bond issue for the state's four colleges; and the building of four new state hospitals. The message also called for ratification of the Eighteenth Amendment, a state constitutional amendment to equalize school funds among white children, compulsory vaccination of hogs to prevent cholera, and conservation of the state's dwindling timber resources.[26]

The message drew applause from the bitterest of Bilbo's enemies. The *Daily News* called the proposed legislation "constructive" and urged its adoption. It called particular attention to the good work which the Board of Health had been doing and urged particularly that the governor's school proposals be adopted. The *Clarion*, too, approved of much of the message and benignly noted that the governor had "broadened out more along financial lines than any man who has ever held public office in this state."[27]

It must not be supposed that everything in Bilbo's administration met with such approval. Charges were made from time to time of various misfeasances on his part—the pardoning of a convict for

[25]*Ibid.*, Aug. 18, Oct. 6, 1916; Mississippi, *Laws*, 1916, Chap. CX, 148-49; Jackson *Daily News*, Nov. 1, 1917.

[26]Mississippi, *Senate Journal*, 1918, pp. 11-41.

[27]Jackson *Daily News*, Jan. 8, 24, 1918; Jackson *Clarion-Ledger*, Jan. 3, 8, 1918.

political reasons, the using of state funds for "junketing" trips about the country, and of scandalous relations between him and a female nurse at the Confederate Veteran's Home at Beauvoir.[28]

The most sensational charge concerned affairs of the state insane hospital at Jackson. For some time before the legislature met in January, 1918, rumors had been circulating in Jackson of gross immorality in the conduct of attendants at the insane hospital. It was rumored that an unmarried nurse had just given birth to a child and that two women had been "spirited away" to prevent their talking. "High officials of government" were said to be involved. Bilbo had recently removed the superintendent of the hospital and had replaced him with a personal friend, Dr. R. M. Butler. Shortly after its convocation, the house, still containing an antiadministration majority, appointed a committee to investigate conditions there. Thereupon the Bilbo-controlled senate appointed a committee of its own to investigate. It was generally understood that the purpose of this committee was to "white wash" any charges brought by the house committee.[29]

The house committee held closed hearings, but juicy bits of scandal leaked out and were published in the press after each day's hearing. Testimony was said to reveal that Butler had "taken no notice of immoral conditions surrounding the institution" and that Butler himself had "been too free and intimate with the young female nurses." The *Clarion*, shocked at the revelations, denounced the administration. "Let it be borne in mind," it said, "that those who are responsible . . . are a part and parcel of the state administration; that they are the political allies, personal friends, and official creatures of the Governor."[30]

The house committee made its report on February 6. It revealed distressing conditions among the inmates. A defective hot-water system would not permit the patients to get even one bath a week. Their incapacity to take care of their natural physiological functions made this particularly revolting. The report further indicated that

---

[28]Jackson *Clarion-Ledger*, Nov. 23, 1916; Vicksburg *Herald*, Jan. 3, 1918, May 2, June 12, 1919; Jackson *Issue*, Apr. 4, 1918.

[29]Mississippi, *House Journal*, 1918, p. 87; *Senate Journal*, 1918, p. 142; Jackson *Daily News*, Jan. 13, 19, 1918; Jackson *Clarion-Ledger*, Jan. 17, Feb. 3, 1918; Vicksburg *Herald*, Jan. 25, 1918.

[30]Jackson *Clarion-Ledger*, Feb. 5, 7, 1918.

patients did not get sufficient food, while Dr. Butler used provisions intended for them for his own use. Sleeping rooms for the patients had no heat, and the patients had insufficient clothing and bed covering. The committee even reported cases of cruelty practiced on the patients by the attendants. Most of the report concerned the misconduct of the attendants. The immorality of the nurses, said the report, "was a scandal that had covered . . . Jackson . . . for more than twelve months." The place, it said, was commonly referred to by neighbors as "the assignation house." Female nurses, as well as male, drank whiskey on the premises and "were frequently drunk and profane." The female nurses "went into rooms of male nurses at night for immoral purposes." There were several cases of pregnancy of nurses, and at least one abortion had been performed there. The report called for the impeachment of Butler.[31]

Throughout the investigation Bilbo remained steadfastly loyal to Butler. It was reported that he had refused to accept Butler's proffered resignation, and had stated that if Butler resigned he would reappoint him. On the night after the legislative report Bilbo called a "secret caucus" at the executive mansion to consider means of Butler's salvation. His old stand-by, Swep Taylor, had parted company with him over the scandal, but Clayton Potter, George Butler, and James Cassidy, all prominent lawyers, were present. An attempt was made that night, it was reported, to get those members of the hospital staff unscathed by the report to endorse Butler, but it failed.[32]

Although the anti-Bilbo press was making much of the affair,[33] it had become clear to at least one of their number that "the investigation has assumed the aspect of a partisan political fight." The Natchez News Democrat was convinced that both sides were moved by political reasons rather than a desire to get to the bottom of the evils and correct them. "The public has learned during the past several years," it said, "that when partisan politics starts anything . . . exaggeration is the first requisite." It predicted that if Butler were impeached by the house he would not be convicted by the senate. Many were advocating impeachment of Bilbo as well as Butler. The Jackson Daily News opposed this because, it thought,

[31]Mississippi, House Journal, 1918, pp. 435-42.
[32]Jackson Clarion-Ledger, Feb. 7, 8, 1918; Jackson Daily News, Feb. 7, 1918.
[33]See quotations in Jackson Clarion-Ledger, Feb. 10, 1918.

such action would furnish Bilbo with the necessary ammunition to insure his further political success. It pointed out that he had been elected lieutenant-governor as a result of his cry of "persecution" in the Dulaney bribery affair and had been elected governor on the issue of his indictment in the Delta County bribery scandal. It urged leaving "his fate in the hands of the Lord."[34]

The house started impeachment proceedings against Butler. Thereupon he resigned and Bilbo appointed Dr. Mitchell of Pontotoc as his successor. In view of this Representative Howerton of Tate moved withdrawal of the impeachment. Johnson of Coahoma objected, pointing out that it was reported Bilbo had said he would reappoint Butler unless he were convicted on impeachment. He offered a resolution demanding a message from Bilbo promising never again to appoint Butler to a public office. During these proceedings Bilbo was sitting beside Speaker Conner, "prompting his leaders by sending tips to them." At the same time the senate notified the house that it had received notice of Butler's resignation. But the house stood pat. The Howerton resolution was laid on the table by a vote of 80 to 9, and then the Johnson resolution was passed, 72 to 18. Bilbo then had his secretary bring to the house Butler's letter of resignation together with an official copy of Mitchell's appointment. But the house, now aroused to obstinance, still refused to pass the Howerton resolution, leaving to the senate the chore of dismissing the impeachment charges. The senate did so.[35]

Bilbo maintained that there was nothing wrong or immoral in his conduct "in connection with the political investigation at the asylum" and asserted that anyone who intimated otherwise "is a dirty, infamous, and slanderous liar." The "political conspirators," he said, "with a stacked committee, and the state resources at their command," worked day and night for months to establish something against him. In the end, however, they "had to admit their failure so to do."[36]

[34]Natchez *News Democrat*, Feb. 12, 1918; Jackson *Daily News*, quoted in Macon *Beacon*, Feb. 22, 1918.

[35]Mississippi, *House Journal*, 1918, pp. 645-49; *Senate Journal*, 1918, p. 557; letter of Representative E. D. Cavette of Noxubee to Editor, Macon *Beacon*, published in *Beacon*, Mar. 1, 1918.

[36]Vicksburg *Herald*, July 30, 1919.

Thus ended the most scandalous of the many charges against Bilbo while he was governor. There was nothing in the nature of the affair that could redound to his political prestige. All he could do was defend himself from the innuendoes that he himself was a participant in the orgies that were alleged to have been held at the asylum. He could not assert, as he had in other affairs, that he was performing a patriotic duty, seeking to entrap those who would prostitute the interests of the people. Further, he was placed in a disadvantageous position by his staunch loyalty to Butler whose notorious misconduct seems to have been well established and generally believed. In the end Bilbo had been forced to surrender ignominiously. "How the mighty have fallen," said the *Beacon*, when his message was sent to the house in accord with the Johnson resolution.[37]

Bilbo's last legislative message, in January, 1920, called for a budget of over $20,000,000, almost double the previous one, necessitating an increase in the state levy to seven and a half mills. The largest increases went to education and to eleemosynary institutions. Specifically the message called for enlargement of the Industrial Training School at Columbus; establishment of a school for the crippled and feeble-minded; more liberal appropriations for the Board of Health; enlargement of all state charity hospitals and more liberal appropriations for them; creation of new hospitals in the eastern, northern, and Delta sections; a more liberal appropriation for the tuberculosis sanitorium, which had been compelled to turn away a thousand patients during the year; appropriations for the common schools large enough to insure better pay for teachers, and other improvements in the system; retention of the Board of Pardons and the State Tax Commission; laws to conserve timber and to provide reforestation; increased salaries for state officials; abolition of the Prison Board and the vesting of entire control in the superintendent; a law requiring candidates for office to file sworn statements of campaign expenses two weeks before election; the establishment of a state electric light plant to service the public buildings at Jackson; appropriations to offer educational opportunities for 300,000 adult illiterates, the vast majority of whom were Negroes; creation of a sinking and insurance fund to replace state property

[37]Macon *Beacon*, Mar. 1, 1918.

destroyed by fire and storm; sale of the governor's mansion and provision for a simpler home for the governor; floating of a $25,000,000 bond issue to build a system of modern highways touching every county of the state and a $5,000,000 bond issue for new buildings for colleges and eleemosynary institutions.[38]

The message denounced those who opposed the League of Nations, "which is built upon the tears and blood of the teeming millions who died for the sake of humanity." It urged the dedication and consecration of the League to "the peace of the world, the brotherhood of mankind, and the freedom of the people of the earth." It denounced war profiteers and "money lords," who "would coin the tears and heartaches of those who gave their loved ones in the supreme sacrifice into filthy dollars to fill their yawning coffers that they might continue to live in luxurious ease."[39]

Although Bilbo's term of office expired, the administration that succeeded him—Lee Russell's—had been hand-picked by him and promoted his program. The "high pressure," or progressive, sentiment was overwhelming in the legislature, and the "low pressure" members submittted gracefully. Final appropriations totaled $18,600,000, and the hospital bond issues requested by Bilbo were passed. The need for the appropriations seems to have been recognized even by Bilbo's worst enemies. The arch-conservative and aging J. S. McNeily, still at the helm of the Vicksburg *Herald*, called the legislature, after its adjournment, "the most progressive . . . in twenty-five years."[40]

Upon retiring from office Bilbo could point with pride to several notable improvements which he had promoted in the state's affairs. He claimed and it was admitted by his enemies that he had contributed greatly to: the establishment of the State Tax Commission, adding $300,000,000 of property to the tax rolls; the establishment of a new state tubercular sanitorium; the erection of a state charity hospital at Laurel and provision for three additional ones; a statewide dipping law for the eradication of cattle ticks, and a hog vaccination law for the elimination of cholera; the creation of a state highway commission with projected plans for a network of modern roads; creation of a Board of Pardons which in four years had re-

[38]Mississippi, *House Journal*, 1920, pp. 38-72.
[39]*Ibid.*, 33-35.
[40]Vicksburg *Herald*, Apr. 8, 1920; Mississippi, *Laws*, 1920, Chaps. I-XC, 1-95.

duced pardons from 2,200 to 800; passage of a uniform negotiable instrument act; abolition of the fee system in county offices; creation of a state Board of Legal Examiners; enactment of a blue sky law to prevent the marketing of worthless stocks; establishment of two lime-crushing plants where farmers could get crushed limestone at cost; enactment of an antilobbying law; restoration of the old capitol; and the abolition of public hangings.[41]

A month before his term expired the *Clarion*, which had been one of Bilbo's greatest critics, protested against a suggested disposal of future offices which did not include Bilbo. Admitting that it had "sometimes disagreed" with the governor and was not then in his "private counsels," it argued "in the name of justice . . . against the side-tracking of Bilbo in this manner. He has done the state some service and should not be thrown into the discard in the days of his young manhood."[42] Such is the consistency of politics.

[41]Mississippi, *Laws*, 1916, Chaps. XCVIII, CVIII, CLXVII, CLXVIII, CVI, CCXLIV, CII, CVII, XCVII, CXII, CV, CCXVIII; *ibid.*, 1918, Chap. CCXLIII; Mississippi, *House Journal*, 1920, pp. 36-38; Vicksburg *Herald*, Jan. 8, 1920; Jackson *Clarion-Ledger*, Jan 8, 1920.

[42]Jackson *Clarion-Ledger*, quoted in *Vardaman's Weekly*, Dec. 4, 1919.

CHAPTER XXI

THE FACTION DIVIDES

WHEN Vardaman joined John Sharp Williams in the Senate in 1913 there were signs that a truce might be reached between the two senators,[1] but this went aground on the rocks of federal patronage and government policy. Under an old patronage agreement representatives were to name, with certain exceptions, postmasters in their districts, while senators had the allotment of judicial and treasury officials. Vardaman and Williams at first could not come to terms on a division of their share, but eventually an arrangement was made whereby Vardaman was to have the naming of the marshals and their deputies, while Williams was to name the attorneys and their assistants.[2]

For a time this worked well, but within two years Williams was complaining that terms of the agreements were not being complied with. Vardaman, he claimed, seemed to be getting a slice of the postal patronage pie; for postmasters were being appointed who were "the strongest supporters of Senator Vardaman." Williams himself seems not to have been observing the agreement rigidly; for the basis of his complaint was that the Vardaman postmasters "put out my friends and put in friends of the opposite political faction." Obviously some arrangement had been made between each of the senators and those congressmen friendly to him on a division of these spoils. But Williams complained that Vardaman was hitting below the belt in another respect. Williams and his associated congressmen were put "in the fiery furnace" by the Vardamanites through "campaign lies" charging they had "retained a nigger postmaster at Muldrow . . . and refused to give the office to a white man." The facts of the case were, wrote Congressman E. S. Candler to Williams, that the Negro had received the office by default since no white man lived in the locality. Subsequently a white man moved to the community and sought the job, but in the meantime

[1] The Vicksburg *Post* and the Magnolia *Gazette*, both Vardaman papers, recommended in the spring of 1913 that T. V. Session, a Vardaman supporter, not oppose Williams in the contest for Williams' successor in 1916. Quoted in Jackson *Clarion-Ledger*, Apr. 10, 1913.

[2] J. S. Williams to Gilbert J. Wood, Jan. 14, 1916; Williams to Wood, Jan. 14, 1916; Williams to President Wilson, Oct. 8, 1915, Williams Papers.

the Negro had been placed under civil service and could not be removed without cause. While Candler was seeking a "cause" for the Negro's removal he urged Williams to get the postmaster-general to write letters to their constituents explaining that they were not responsible for the Negro's appointment or retention. "I hope to get the nigger out," wrote Candler, "and give the place to the white man."[3] The plight of the Mississippi Negro can be appreciated when it is realized that Candler and Williams were leaders of the faction denouncing Vardaman's racial program.

Williams objected, too, to Vardaman's manner of exercising his "legitimate" patronage. Although under the agreement each senator had the exclusive right to name certain officials, political etiquette called for them to appoint no one who was "personally obnoxious" to the other. Vardaman, he said, was disregarding this propriety and was appointing marshals "who have been without exception . . . shouting for Bilbo and working for him against me." Finally, when Williams' choice for the assistant district attorneyship at Jackson was turned down and a Vardaman supporter given the place, Williams could bear no more. He would, he wrote the President, retire from politics at the end of his term. He would retire at once, he said, save for the fact that he had "served the public so long and myself so badly that I need the salary."[4]

Before this incident occurred Williams and Vardaman had reached the point of open rupture. The occasion was precipitated by a newspaper interview in which Vardaman denounced as "pusilanimous [sic]" and "treacherous" all who voted for repeal of the clause of the Panama Canal Act exempting coastwise steamers from the payment of canal tolls. Shortly afterward, he denied in the Senate that he had ever "uttered an unkind word" about any of his colleagues. Williams then arose and read the account of the interview. Thereafter Vardaman refused to speak to Williams, and it was reported that he had said he would "see to it" that Williams was not re-elected.[5]

No doubt Vardaman did toy with the idea of replacing Williams

[3]H. C. Metzger and J. A. Gibson to Williams, Jan. 22, 1915; Williams to Albert S. Burleson, Apr. 26, 29, 1915; E. S. Candler to Williams, Aug. 9, 1916, ibid.
[4]Williams to President Wilson, Aug. 2, 11, Oct. 8, 1915; President Wilson to Williams, Aug. 17, 1915, ibid.
[5]Williams to W. H. Maybin, Jan. 11, 1915, ibid.

with one of his own faction. As early as the summer of 1914 rumors that he had given the nod to state Senator Hebron had Williams' friends worried and Williams resigned to his defeat. Later there was open speculation that Vardaman might run Bilbo or Swep Taylor against Williams.[6] But Hebron's kite would not fly. By the fall of 1914 Williams was being told by his friends that "things were looking mighty good for you" and that "most everyone looks upon Hebron's race against you as a joke." More reassuring still, men associated with Vardaman's organization were writing Williams assuring him of their support. One, who claimed to have "followed the political fortunes" of Vardaman "with a loyalty that never once failed or faltered," wrote to Williams that he would not follow Vardaman "if it is his purpose . . . to oppose your re-election." "Father and I have always supported him [Vardaman]," wrote another, but "We will support Senator Williams in 1916." "I hear on all sides, wherever I go," wrote Congressman Humphreys, "that many if not most of the Vardaman men throughout the Delta are strong for you."[7]

Perhaps some explanation of this can be found in Williams' changed attitude toward Bilbo. He wrote early in 1916 that he and Bilbo had not "up to date belonged to the same political faction in Mississippi." Yet, he wrote five months before, "There are some very violent Bilbo men that are almost equally violent Williams men." He could not explain how it had come about, but it seemed to be "undoubtedly true and it seems to be also beyond dispute that there are a very great number of them." Williams' opinion of Bilbo had been "rather emphatically uttered in the Percy campaign," yet he remained strangely quiet in the gubernatorial race of 1915. He would not, he said at that time, take the stump "in behalf of or against anybody." He would content himself with aiding candidates for minor office "on the dead quiet, of course," he wrote, and with "taking a turn at the county committees." By May, 1915, he was told by a competent observer that he was "stronger today than you have ever been" and that all he had to do to win was to "keep out

6John M. Dabney to Williams, July 29, 1914; Williams to Dabney, Aug. 5, 1914, *ibid.*; Jackson *Clarion-Ledger*, Apr. 11, Aug. 8, 1915.

7G. L. Donald to Williams, Nov. 13, 1914; Maybin to Williams, Jan. 5, 1915; B. Lampton Crawford to Percy Quin, Oct. 2, 1915; B. G. Humphreys to Williams, May 8, 1915, Williams Papers.

of the factional fight that is embroiling the state." After Bilbo's nomination he was assured that "Bilbo has sense enough to see that the thing for him to do is to back you . . . next year, and then go against Vardaman next time."[8]

One further obstacle in the person of former Governor Earl Brewer still stood in Williams' path. At Brewer's inaugural in 1912, he had promised a friend of Williams that he would not be a candidate against Williams in 1916. A few months later, however, Brewer "had weakened." If the "Bilbo crowd" attacked him, he said, he might "need election to the Senate to show the world he was not what [they] said he was." "It is as plain as day to me," wrote a friend to Williams in the spring of 1915, "that Brewer is right . . . now moving heaven and earth to get your place." His rout a few months later at the hands of Bilbo may have changed Brewer's mind. At any rate Brewer was not a candidate for Williams' seat. "I am for John Sharp Williams," he wrote the following spring, "for anything from President down."[9] It is doubtful if either his support or opposition at that time was a factor to weigh with any candidate for office in Mississippi.

Six months before the election all opposition had been swept aside and the coast was clear. "In my opinion," wrote Williams, "all I have got to do . . . is to ask for renomination and reelection and get it." But Williams forgot to announce his candidacy officially, and on the eve of the deadline it was "whispered around" that the state executive committee would declare Hebron the nominee by default. Learning of this, Williams hastily filed notice of his candidacy and forwarded his checks to the various county chairmen for his assessments.[10]

At the last minute Hebron withdrew and Williams went into the primary unopposed. The vote, in contrast to recent ones, was light.

    [8]Williams to Robert R. Read, Feb. 29, 1916; Williams to V. P. Whitaker, Sept. 22, 1915; Williams to B. P. Harrison, May 13, 1915; Williams to Humphreys, May 22, 1915; Sargeant Prentiss Knut to Williams, Nov. 17, 1915; Harrison to Williams, May 13, 1915; Williams to Harrison, May 21, 1915; Knut to Williams, Nov. 17, 1915, *ibid.*

    [9]Knut to Williams, May 8, 1915; Earl Brewer to Humphreys, June 20, 1916, *ibid.*

    [10]Williams to President Wilson, Feb. 7, 1916; O. F. Lawrence to Williams, July 7, 1916; Williams to Joseph E. Norwood, July 13, 1916; Williams to Robert Lewis, July 13, 1916, *ibid.*

"Not more than half the voters of the state, or perhaps not more than a third," said the *Clarion*, "attended . . . and some . . . forgot to fill out their ticket."[11]

Williams was "intensely gratified" over his unopposed election. He had not, he boasted, made "the slightest effort to be re-nominated." He had not, he said, published "for distribution a single speech," nor had he written "a single letter to a single man to ask his support." He did not feel that he owed the unanimity of his election "to the magnanimity of my enemies." There was quite a combined effort, he said, to defeat him, but it had "gone to pieces. They couldn't get any votes behind it." His enemies would, he said, "have fought if they had dared." He was chiefly glad he had won "because it kept some fellow of a different ilk, belonging to that crowd I don't like . . . from winning out." He was growing tired of the "drudgery" and "insincerities" of politics and was determined to retire at the end of his new term. Perhaps, too, his pecuniary condition had improved. He would not have run in 1916, he said, if anybody had been mentioned to succeed him "that I thought could have worthily represented the state of Lamar, George, and Walthall, and Jefferson Davis."[12]

The next state-wide election would be in 1918 to choose a successor to Vardaman, and interest began to center on that. Vardaman seems to have struck the zenith of his political influence in the period from 1911 to 1915. Thereafter, his course in national politics together with new factional alignments in Mississippi produced a change and his fortunes went into decline. Long before the election of 1918 there was grave doubt that he could be re-elected.

Early in his senatorial career Vardaman joined the liberal bloc headed by Robert M. La Follette of Wisconsin and George W. Norris of Nebraska. Along with them he supported the proposed Child Labor Amendment, the Underwood Tariff, the Income Tax Amendment, and voted for confirmation of Louis D. Brandeis as an associate justice of the Supreme Court. For these and other

11Jackson *Clarion-Ledger*, Aug. 15, 17, 1916.

12Williams to Edward H. Woods, Aug. 14, 1916; Williams to John Richards, Feb. 15, 1917; Williams to Mrs. Lizette McF. Blakemore, Aug. 25, 1916; Williams to D. D. Colcock, Jan. 12, 1917; Williams to C. J. Money, Feb. 13, 1917, Williams Papers; Jackson *Clarion-Ledger*, Dec. 21, 1916, Aug. 4, 1917.

stands Vardaman drew generous praise from the Mississippi press.[13] This praise was tempered, however, with hostile attacks. When he spoke in the Senate in complimentary terms of the old Populist program,[14] and when Tom Watson, "the notorious Georgia Populist," approved his stand on the Panama Canal tolls question, he was denounced as a Populist. "James K. Vardaman," said the *Daily News*, "is not . . . [and] never has been a Democrat." When he failed to make the national headlines four months after going to Washington, the Macon *Beacon* attributed it to the "inferiority" which made him incapable of dealing with the "brilliant" men there. "As the barnyard cock's influence and prowess is greatest when he crows upon his own dunghill," said the *Beacon*, "so is that of the White Chief at its maximum . . . when indulging demogogic appeals to mislead the masses of his own state."[15]

Vardaman early incurred the enmity of the Wilson administration through his independent stand on the Income Tax, the Panama Canal Tolls Bill, and the Ship Purchase Bill. He and his liberal bloc felt that the income tax rates proposed by the administration were not high enough. Vardaman refused to be bound to the administration proposal by the party caucus, and he and his colleagues succeeded in materially increasing the rates.[16] When President Wilson, after his inauguration, reversed his campaign pledge and urged Congress to repeal the law exempting coastal trading ships from paying the canal tolls, Vardaman refused to go along with the Senate majority. He denounced Wilson for repudiating his campaign commitments and surrendering to British demands.[17] After the outbreak of the World War the administration urged Congress to empower it to purchase the German ships interned in American ports.

[13]*Congressional Record*, 63 Cong., 2 Sess., 14315, 14318, 14517, 14588, 14589, 14593, 16154, 16170; *ibid.*, 64 Cong., 1 Sess., 12138, 12220; Jackson *Clarion-Ledger*, June 16, Dec. 22, 1916; Hattiesburg *News*, Jan. 16, 1916; Jackson *Issue*, Apr. 25, 1918; Scott County *News*, quoted in *Clarion-Ledger*, Oct. 14, 1915; Memphis *Commercial Appeal*, quoted in Jackson *Issue*, July 25, 1918.

[14]*Congressional Record*, 63 Cong., 2 Sess., 2159.

[15]Jackson *Daily News*, May 1, 1914; Macon *Beacon*, July 10, 1914.

[16]Wiley R. Huddleston, "The Senatorial Career of James Kimble Vardaman, Mississippi's 'White Chief'" (M.A. thesis, Louisiana State University, 1935), 52-76.

[17]*Congressional Record*, 63 Cong., 2 Sess., 8823, 8824, 9526, 9723-26, 10160, 10170, 10171, 10235-40; Jackson *Clarion-Ledger*, June 14, 1914.

Vardaman opposed this as a government subsidy to the "shipping trust."[18]

But it was Vardaman's opposition to the administration's general policy through the period of neutrality—private and government loans to Allied nations, preparedness, the arming of merchant vessels, the severance of diplomatic relations with Germany, and finally the declaration of war itself—which brought a complete rupture between him and the administration, and which helped to end his political career.[19] Throughout the period of neutrality Vardaman expressed his personal sympathy with the Allied cause. He maintained, however, that American interests could only be served by maintaining "an attitude of perfect neutrality,"[20] and this, he charged, the administration was not doing. He approved Secretary of State William J. Bryan's stand in resigning in protest against the dispatch of the *Lusitania* note in the summer of 1915. He toured the country that fall, urging peace, talking against preparedness, and charging that the administration was partial to the Allies. He became one of "the little group of wilful men" who, the President charged, were responsible for rendering the United States "helpless and contemptible before the world."[21] "I will not," said Vardaman, "delegate to the President . . . the power to execute a trust . . . when I believe the delegation of such a trust . . . would in all probability bring on war." After the declaration of war he opposed some of the administration policies for waging it, such as the draft and the Food Control Bill.[22]

Vardaman could not have been unaware that his opposition to the administration both before and after the war declaration was losing him friends in Mississippi. His continuation of his opposition

18*Congressional Record*, 63 Cong., 3 Sess., 1921, 1922, 1935, 1937; Jackson *Clarion-Ledger*, Feb. 14, 1915.

19*Congressional Record*, 64 Cong., 1 Sess., 1311, 3478-80, 3484, 3486, 3846, 4105, 5417, 5570, 5571; *ibid.*, 64 Cong., 2 Sess., 2734, 4777; *ibid.*, 65 Cong., 1 Sess., 5, 6; Huddleston, "James K. Vardaman," 76-83; Jackson *Clarion-Ledger*, July 4, Nov. 13, 1915, July 20, Aug. 11, 1916, Feb. 8, Mar. 3, 6, 7, Apr. 26, 27, 29, 1917.

20Columbus *Dispatch*, Sept. 29, 1915.

21*Ibid.*, Sept. 29, 1915, Mar. 6, 7, 1917; Jackson *Clarion-Ledger*, July 4, Nov. 13, 1915.

22*Congressional Record*, 65 Cong., 1 Sess., 5-6, 933, 1000, 1085, 1174, 1312-14, 1320-22, 1464, 1471, 1483, 1494, 2645-47, 2986, 3039, 3777, 3919-22, 3934, 4064, 4066-67, 4070, 4216, 4453-54, 4474, 4477-78, 4591, 4593-94, 4831, 44838, 4937 4955, 5261.

despite this seems to belie the charge of demagoguery, at least in this instance. A policy of benevolent neutrality toward the Allies in the early stages of the war and an all-out backing of the administration in its war policies after the United States had entered were popular in Mississippi, and Vardaman knew it. On the eve of the declaration of war Judge Winston Houston of Aberdeen made a special trip to Washington to urge Vardaman to vote for the war resolution. Vardaman acknowledged, according to Houston, that his failure to do so would probably end his political career. Nevertheless, he said, he could not conscientiously vote for the declaration.[23] A somewhat similar mission was undertaken shortly thereafter by a group of Vardaman's friends. This time the meeting was in the Roosevelt Hotel in New Orleans, where Vardaman had gone to speak. A graphic account of the interview was later given by one of the participants.

We informed Senator Vardaman of the change in sentiment in Mississippi from peace to war . . . and told him that we felt his attitude would cost him his seat in the Senate.

He replied that his position on the war was the result of extensive investigation, great study and mature deliberation, and that he would not in conscience change it and that his loss of his seat in the United States Senate was nothing as compared with the loss of lives and liberty and opportunities which would follow such a war.

We reminded him that if he lost his seat in the Senate that his great work on the negro question would not be carried on. He walked over to the window . . . and stood there a few minutes silently, with his hands behind his back, and turning came over to us and said: "I appreciate your coming down here to see me today. Some one else will carry on my work if I am defeated. I have an abiding faith in the people of the United States doing the right thing when they have an opportunity to think clearly. Even if it should cost me my life I cannot do what you now think you want me to do."[24]

Evidence that Vardaman was losing political control was appearing before this. In 1915 it had been freely admitted by the opposition that he could name any candidate for office in Mississippi. Yet in a special congressional election in January, 1916, his candi-

[23]Statement of A. S. Coody of Jackson, Mississippi, to author, Aug. 17, 1946. Coody said Houston told him the story.

[24]Watkins, Address, May 17, 1936, p. 27, in Mississippi Department of Archives and History.

date, J. H. Joyner, was defeated by Judge Webb Venable, a friend of Williams.[25] Reports that the state executive committee had been wrested from Vardaman's control were substantiated when a contest developed over the chairmanship of the 1916 state Democratic convention. The Vardaman faction was said to be urging Speaker Conner for the chair, but the opposition was backing Congressman Pat Harrison. A "compromise" had to be made. Conner was elected temporary chairman, but Harrison received the permanent chairmanship. In the fourth district congressional primary a few months later, T. U. Sisson, an anti-Vardaman candidate, defeated W. C. Ward, the son of Dr. B. F. Ward, "the High Priest of the cult of Vardaman." Sisson carried every county by a large majority.[26]

When Vardaman addressed the state legislature in the fall of 1917, it was reported in the Jackson press that he received a "chilly reception." The following day the legislature adopted a resolution sternly censuring the press for saying so. It was noted, however, that the legislature also adopted a resolution pledging loyalty to the federal government, which nine Vardaman legislators opposed. "No doubt," said the *Daily News*, "the Junior Senator is beginning to be convinced that his official actions do not meet with the approval of the people of Mississippi."[27]

He was attacked on all sides. Some wanted to read him out of the party. Frequently he was referred to as "Herr Von Vardaman," an "arch traitor and super demagogue," and "the Kaiser's Newest Friend." When he voted against entry into the war, the Macon *Beacon* published a front-page article entitled "Vardaman Earning the Kaiser's Iron Cross." When he voted against conscription the *Clarion* called him "a Kaiser-loving betrayer of the American people" and said it placed him "in the army of slackers." It urged the Senate to expel him.[28]

[25]Marcus D. Herring to Williams, Jan. 14, 1916, Williams Papers; Yazoo *Sentinel,* Jan. 20, 1916.

[26]Jackson *Clarion-Ledger,* May 1, 18, 19, June 8, 1916; Macon *Beacon,* Aug. 25, 1916.

[27]Mississippi, *House Journal,* 1917, pp. 222-23; Jackson *Clarion-Ledger,* Oct. 4, 13, 1917; Jackson *Daily News,* Oct. 13, 1917.

[28]Yazoo *Sentinel,* Feb. 18, 1914; Macon *Beacon,* Feb. 5, Mar. 5, 1915, Aug. 17, 1917; Vicksburg *Herald,* Aug. 15, 1917; Jackson *Daily News,* Aug. 4, 1917; Jackson *Clarion-Ledger,* Aug. 14, Oct. 3, 1917.

Nor did such attacks come only from his old enemies. Many of them were from former friends and supporters. The Newton *Record,* Mayerville *Spectator,* Woodville *Republican,* Biloxi *Herald,* and many other papers openly repudiated him. The *Herald* wanted to know what Mississippi had done that she should be plagued with a man of his type. The *Republican,* after his vote against conscription, said he had "gone the limit." J. G. Spenser of Port Gibson, claiming to have been a loyal Vardaman supporter for twenty years, announced that he had parted company with him.[29] In vain did Vardaman point out the inconsistent motives given for American entry into the war. First, he said, it was to protect American rights on the seas; next it was a war "to make the world safe for democracy"; finally it was urged that if we did not fight Germany then we would have to do so later alone and when she was much stronger. The real reason, he thought, was "interference on the part of Germany with commerce between New York and London." Every statement he made was twisted by his enemies and given an unpatriotic interpretation which his statement had not warranted. John Sharp Williams charged that his statements "graze the very edge of treason" and reported that there was "almost universal condemnation" of his course in Mississippi.[30]

To be sure not all of Vardaman's old friends left him, and a few new ones even rallied to his support.[31] These were but feeble props to bolster him against the withering attacks launched upon him by the overwhelming majority of the Mississippi press.

Vardaman's position was further embarrassed by a coolness that had developed between him and Bilbo. The reasons for this change in their relations are as complex as the personalities of the two men. In general they both had the support of the lower-level economic classes, but it is probably true that the Vardaman people "believed they were a higher grade party than the Bilbo party."[32] Too, a sort

[29]Biloxi *Herald,* quoted in Jackson *Clarion-Ledger,* July 25, 1917; Newton *Record,* Woodville *Republican,* and Mayersville *Spectator,* quoted in Natchez *News Democrat,* Aug. 19, 21, 1917; Jackson *Daily News,* Nov. 5, 1917.

[30]Vicksburg *Herald,* quoted in Macon *Beacon,* Aug. 17, 1917; Issac D. Wall to Williams, Mar. 5, 1917; Williams to R. S. Buck, Mar. 10, 1917; Williams to President Wilson, Aug. 16, 1917, Williams Papers.

[31]Scott County *News,* Aug. 14, 1917; Jackson *Issue,* Nov. 29, 1917; Hattiesburg *News,* Aug. 25, 1917, in Vardaman scrapbook.

[32]Rowland, *History of Mississippi,* II, 346.

of jealousy seemed to grow between them after the election of 1911 over who had contributed most to the success of the other. By the summer of 1915 the breach had grown to such an extent that there were rumors that Bilbo would oppose Vardaman for the Senate seat in 1918.[33]

The opposition did what it could to fan the flames. During Bilbo's administration some Negro guards were employed at the state penitentiary farms. On one occasion it was reported that they had cursed and whipped some white prisoners. This was denounced by the opposition, who pointed out that such conditions could not have existed under Vardaman. "No negro guards were allowed to serve on our state farms . . . during the Vardaman administration," they said.[34]

Supporters of both Vardaman and Bilbo suspected that the opposition was attempting to split their faction. Any talk of pitting Bilbo against Vardaman, said the Columbus *Dispatch*, was a plot of the enemies of both "to stake these gentlemen against each other in a race, knowing that one or the other of them would be eliminated." But the *Dispatch* believed there was even "a deeper laid conspiracy." The plan, it thought, was to divide the Vardaman-Bilbo forces, "and then enter a third man and defeat them both."[35] The Tupelo *Herald* agreed with the *Dispatch's* diagnosis. "There can be no doubt," it said, "that the enemies of Vardaman and Bilbo are at work to create a split between the two leaders." "They are seeking to bring this about," it added, "by feeding the vanity of Bilbo in assuring him that he can defeat Senator Vardaman for the Senate." Their only object, it warned, was to "split the dominant faction in Mississippi politics and thus secure control of the state themselves." Both the *Dispatch* and the *Herald* dismissed the possibility of the scheme succeeding. Neither did much to assuage Bilbo's vanity. One ascribed his success to Vardaman's support; the other said he had "no more chance of beating Senator Vardaman than he has of being elected Sultan of Turkey."[36] The Yazoo *Sentinel* claimed to have it

[33]Macon *Beacon*, July 10, 1914; Columbus *Dispatch*, May 10, 1916, in Vardaman scrapbook; Jackson *Clarion-Ledger*, Aug. 25, 1915.

[34]Laurel *Times*, May 11, 1916, in Vardaman scrapbook.

[35]Columbus *Dispatch*, May 10, 1916, in Vardaman scrapbook.

[36]Tupelo *Herald*, May 20, 1916, in Vardaman scrapbook.

direct from "a leading member of the anti-Vardaman-Bilbo faction" that such was their scheme.[37]

Whether this was true or not it was evident that the two leaders were not as close as they had formerly been. When Bilbo went to Washington it was remarked that he was seen much with Congressman Pat Harrison and little with Senator Vardaman. After America's entry into the war Bilbo was an enthusiastic supporter of the Wilson administration's policies, and the cleavage seemed more pronounced. By the summer of 1917 it was "believed by many that the erstwhile good friends and political comrades in arms Vardaman and Bilbo, are now separated by an impassable gulf."[38]

In August there was a "current rumor" that an alliance had been made between Harrison, Bilbo, and Russell. According to this rumor Bilbo was to be a candidate for Congress in Harrison's district, the sixth. He was to have Harrison's support in exchange for his support of Harrison for the Senate. Russell was to receive the support of both for the governorship. He, it was thought, could give Harrison much aid in north Mississippi, where he lived.[39]

On August 23 Harrison announced his candidacy at the Neshoba County Fair. His platform was one of "Loyalty to the President and to the country." He called on the spirits of Washington and John Paul Jones to inspire America. He attacked Vardaman's lack of patriotism and charged him with "giving aid and comfort to the enemies of the government." Seated on the platform giving "aid and comfort" to him was the incongruous trio, Bilbo, Brewer, and Fred Sullens.[40] The incongruity did not pass unnoticed. "What potent and irresistible influence," asked the Magnolia *Gazette*, "brought these . . . heretofore fiercely antagonistic Mississippi politicians into such delightful harmony?" The spectacle of "the lion and the lamb lying down . . . placidly on the . . . hustings" drove it to sarcastic rhapsodies. "Blessed are the peacemakers," it said, "—for to them, peradventure, shall be given the dispensation of federal patronage in Mississippi." The Calhoun *Monitor* remarked, too, on the "strange

[37]Yazoo *Sentinel*, quoted in Jackson *Clarion-Ledger*, June 6, 1916.

[38]Jackson *Clarion-Ledger*, Sept. 5, 1916, July 1, Aug. 2, 1917.

[39]*Ibid.*, Aug. 2, 16, 1917, quoting New Orleans *Times-Picayune* and Magnolia *Gazette*; Ripley *Southern Sentinel*, Aug. 17, 1917; Senatobia *Democrat*, Aug. 16, 1917; Magnolia *Gazette*, Aug. 25, 1917, in Vardaman scrapbook.

[40]Jackson *Clarion-Ledger*, Aug. 24, 1917; Vicksburg *Post*, Aug. 25, 1917, in Vardaman scrapbook.

bedfellows," and the Kemper *Herald-Star* was outraged. "The new firm is now styled Brewer, Bilbo, Fred Sullens, Pat Harrison & Company," it said. It predicted that the voters would make short shrift of "that bunch of rotten political shysters." The McComb City *Journal* blamed the alliance on Bilbo. He, it said, had pushed Harrison into the race so that when the time came for selecting a successor to Williams, he would have Vardaman, Harrison, and Williams all out of the way. "Pretty smooth!" was its laconic conclusion.[41]

Former Governor Noel announced also as a candidate for Vardaman's seat. This was seen by some as a complicating factor for Harrison, as any votes Noel would get would supposedly detract from his. Since Bilbo had already announced for Harrison's seat in Congress, retreat for Harrison was cut off in that direction. He must go on. It soon became apparent, however, that Noel would not be much of a factor.[42]

Harrison challenged Vardaman to joint debates, but Vardaman disregarded the challenge as he had those of previous opponents. Vardaman remained in Washington until shortly before the election. Most of his campaign was waged through that portion of the press which remained loyal to him. Harrison toured the state in early spring, 1918, for the alleged purpose of promoting war bond sales. He was able to intersperse his patriotic with political speeches. He attacked Vardaman's record of "consistent" opposition to President Wilson. He charged that in his opposition to the Ship Purchase Bill, Vardaman had actually "sold out" to the shipping interests, who, Harrison said, opposed the bill. "Many a bottle of champagne was opened . . . by the shipping trust" the night before the final vote, he charged.[43] Most of his attack was centered on the charge of Vardaman's "disloyalty." Throughout the spring and summer of 1918 the Harrison press was filled with editorials and news stories impugning Vardaman's patriotism. He was denounced as "pro-German" and "anti-Wilson." Again and again it was pointed out that he had opposed the bill for arming merchant ships, the war resolution, the con-

41Magnolia *Gazette*, Aug. 29, 1917; Calhoun *Monitor*, Aug. 30, 1917; Kemper *Herald-Star*, Aug. 24, 1917; McComb City *Journal*, n. d., in Vardaman scrapbook.

42Vicksburg *Post*, Aug. 22, 25, 1917; Jackson *Clarion-Ledger*, Aug. 12, 16, 1917; Aberdeen *Weekly*, n. d., in Vardaman scrapbook.

43Eupora *Progress-Warden*, July 25, 1918, in Vardaman scrapbook; Jackson *Clarion-Ledger*, Nov. 29, 1917.

scription bill, and the espionage bill. His record, the papers said, was "indefensible," and his re-election would be an "indictment" of the "character and patriotism of Mississippi."[44]

Vardaman's statements were shaded and twisted to give them an unpatriotic tenor. When he spoke at Meridian shortly before the election, a man arose in the audience and propounded to him a series of questions the answers to which might clarify his position. Vardaman replied by reading from the *Congressional Record* in an attempt to prove that he was misquoted. One of the accusations, often repeated, was that he had said the United States by declaring war was "stabbing Germany in the back." Vardaman denied that he had made such a statement. The expression, he admitted, had been used by him, but only in an allegorical sense. He was trying, he said, to show the inconsistency of the administration's neutrality policy and was only illustrating what others might say. But his explanation failed to satisfy his enemies. They continued their attack and published statements of former Vardaman supporters who said they did not want "a senator who believes we are stabbing Germany in the back while England and France have her down." When Mississippi citizens were arrested for draft-dodging or for disloyalty, the opposition was quick to charge that they were Vardaman supporters. They did this too quickly on one occasion. They charged that such a citizen of Greenville was a Vardaman man but a Vardaman paper obtained and published a statement from him that he intended to vote for Noel.[45]

When Harrison first announced, Vardaman had attempted to wither him with scorn. He called Harrison "a peculiar species of embryonic statesmen," "the spawn and product of the slime-covered pools of war," "the evolution from the human microbe which found its origin in the troubled womb of abnormality." This "insignificant creature," he said, was "incubating an ambition to serve his country, or rather himself, in the halls of state."[46] By the following spring, however, Vardaman had gone on the defensive, fighting for his political life. The small portion of the press which remained loyal to

[44]Good examples are the Macon *Beacon*, Aug. 2, 9, 16, 1918; Vicksburg *Herald*, June 11, 23, 1918.

[45]Woodville *Republican*, July 20, 1918, in Vardaman scrapbook; Macon *Beacon*, Aug. 9, 1918; Jackson *Issue*, Jan. 10, July 25, 1918.

[46]Yazoo City *Sentinel*, Aug. 22, 1917, in Vardaman scrapbook.

him devoted issue after issue to a defense of his patriotism. His record as a volunteer in the Spanish-American War was broadcast. It was pointed out that he had, after war was declared on Germany, offered to resign and raise a regiment for the battlefield, but had been turned down. It was pointed out that he had two sons in the service. It was denied that there was any issue between him and the President. Harrison was attacked as an enemy of labor and for being backed by the same crowd which had backed Percy. The charge of disloyalty, Vardaman's friends said, was merely "part of a scheme worked out by his enemies to encompass his defeat." It was pointed out that Harrison, although comparatively a young man, had made no motion to volunteer for service. Harrison was also criticized for leaving his post in Washington at such a critical time to mend his political fences in Mississippi.[47]

Some attempt was made by Vardaman to draw the campaign into other issues. He charged that the opposition to him was sponsored by big business because of his curbing of their predatory "activities while he was governor, because of his part in having the income tax rates raised from three to seven per cent, and because of his exposure of excess profits and graft in the procurement of war contracts." He pointed out that he had supported the administration on the Woman's Suffrage Amendment, while Harrison had opposed it. But the Harrison forces would not be led astray. "The issue is clearcut," said the Macon *Beacon*. "No attempt to muddy the waters can avail. It is not a question of class against class. It is not a question of trusts against the people. . . . It is purely a question of whether or not Mississippians shall show by their votes that they are loyal to this government."[48]

At a meeting of the state Democratic executive committee prior to the election it was apparent that Vardaman had completely lost control. The secretary of the committee was absent, and Chairman Mullins, a Vardaman supporter, attempted to appoint a temporary substitute for him. The anti-Vardaman members revolted and passed

[47]Jackson *Issue*, spring and summer of 1918, especially July 4, 18, 25; Ripley *Sentinel*, quoted in Vicksburg *Herald*, July 28, 1911; Yazoo *Sentinel*, Mar. 30, 1918; Vicksburg *Post*, Aug. 30, 1917, in Vardaman scrapbook.

[48]Jackson *Issue*, Aug. 15, 1918; Yazoo *Sentinel*, July 17, 1918; Brookhaven *Leader*, Jan. 16, 1918; Jackson *Issue*, July 25, 1918, in Vardaman scrapbook; Macon *Beacon*, Aug. 16, 1916.

a resolution by a vote of 13 to 9 depriving the chairman of appointive power. Judge Harmon Thompson, an anti-Vardamanite, was then elected acting secretary by the same vote. Judge Robert Mayes, a Vardaman man, offered what was called a "mild" resolution endorsing the Wilson administration. W. Calvin Wells, Harrison's campaign manager, then offered a substitute resolution bitterly denouncing Vardaman. The substitute was adopted.[49]

Despite expressions of confidence by some of the Vardaman press, it was believed by both sides that the race would be close. The Columbus *Dispatch*, a Vardaman paper, admitted that Vardaman had "lost strength in the cities" but hoped he had "gained votes in the country where he has always been strong." It refused to predict the outcome.[50] On the other hand, some of the opposition were feeling none too sanguine. "Vardaman has laid his last egg," wrote a friend to John Sharp Williams a year before the election. The people "are not speaking of the long haired man in very complimentary terms," wrote another. Yet there was "no telling what those red-necks will do (east of the I. C.)." A month before the election Williams was worried and was urging the President to see "that we get a fair representation of the soldier vote." The "Williams-Pat Harrison men in Mississippi are nearly all in the army," he wrote. Their side was "in a pretty bad fix" because "the slackers and skulkers who are supporting the other side" had stayed at home.[51]

An important factor in the election was a letter which the President wrote to M. S. McNeil, a Harrison backer. The letter was in answer to an inquiry of McNeil's about the President's attitude in the race. "If the voters . . . should again choose him [Vardaman] to represent them," said Wilson, " . . . I should be obliged to accept their action as a condemnation of my administration." This letter was blazed across the front pages of the anti-Vardaman papers throughout Mississippi. It brought forth renewed appeals from

[49]Jackson *News*, quoted in Vicksburg *Herald*, Aug. 10, 1918.

[50]Oxford *Eagle*, Feb. 14, 1918; McComb City *Enterprise*, Mar. 7, 1918; Yazoo *Sentinel*, July 20, 1918; Brookhaven *Leader*, Aug. 10, 1918, in Vardaman scrapbook; Columbus *Dispatch*, Aug. 18, 1918.

[51]James E. Hall to Williams, Mar. 12, 1917; L. C. Johnson to Williams, Mar. 21, 1917; Williams to President Wilson, June 24, 1918, Williams Papers.

them to the voters to "stand by" the President and to "remain loyal" to the government. It was denounced by Vardaman as "unwarranted interference" in state affairs by the President. It was, moreover, he said, unjust, since he had "supported the administration 99 times where I have opposed it once."[52]

In the election Harrison received 56,715 votes, Vardaman 44,154, and Noel 6,730.[53] The total was considerably lower than others in recent years, but that can probably be accounted for by the absence of so many men of voting age in the armed services. Harrison's majority over both Vardaman and Noel was almost 6,000, and he was thus the winner in the first primary. It was reported that the word had been passed down by the anti-Vardaman forces not only "to beat Vardaman but to drown all the pups," and defeated candidates for minor offices attributed their setbacks to their having been associated with Vardaman in the past.[54]

The usual post-mortems were indulged in by observers when the election results were known. Friends of Vardaman seemed grief-stricken. They looked upon his defeat as a blow to democracy. He was, they said, "the only true friend" and "the ablest advocate" the people of Mississippi ever had. Most of them attributed his defeat to the charge of "disloyalty," although some attributed it to "the splendid Harrison organization and the money they spent." Most of them denied that the "real wishes" of a "majority of the white voters" had been voiced. Percy Maer, editor of the Columbus *Dispatch* and a Vardaman supporter, thought his defeat due to his stubborn defense of his unpopular course. Had he admitted error, thought Maer, and promised to change, the people would have forgiven him.[55]

The hostile Vicksburg *Herald* agreed with Maer's analysis. At a time when "conciliation and consideration for the sentiments and opinions . . . of his friends and former supporters was called for," it said, Vardaman "roamed and rampaged over the state,"

[52]Vicksburg *Herald*, Aug. 11, 1918; Macon *Beacon*, Aug. 16, 1918; Magnolia *Gazette*, Aug. 15, 1918, in Vardaman scrapbook.

[53]*Biennial Report of the Secretary of State to the Legislature*, in *Mississippi Official and Statistical Register, 1920-24*, p. 345.

[54]Macon *Beacon*, Aug. 22, 1918.

[55]Kosciusko *Herald*, Sept. 27, 1918; Ripley *Sentinel*, Dec. 12, 1918; Oxford *Eagle*, Aug. 22, 1918, in Vardaman scrapbook; Columbus *Dispatch*, quoted in Macon *Beacon*, Aug. 30, 1918.

denouncing his opposition, and giving the impression that he would "do it again" if the people should send him back to Washington. "No other man living or dead," said the *Herald*, "held a stronger hold on the state . . . and no other man was ever so trusted, and forgiven for offenses that would have blasted others." The ease with which he distanced "better and abler men in the competition for public favor," said Editor McNeily, "turned his shallow head and led to his undoing." All admitted that Wilson's letter had done much to effect Vardaman's defeat. Vardaman and the Brookhaven *Leader* thought it was the decisive factor. Up to the time of the publication of the letter, said the *Leader*, "Vardaman's success at the polls was a matter only of counting the votes." It was convinced, it said, that "the issue made by President Wilson . . . brought about the defeat of Mr. Vardaman." Vardaman was equally emphatic. He denied that Harrison's popularity had prevailed over him or that the voters believed him disloyal. "The controlling influence was Woodrow Wilson."[56]

Undoubtedly both Vardaman's stubborn behavior and Wilson's letter were factors in Vardaman's undoing. Perhaps if Vardaman had been more conciliatory in his campaign, he might have won despite Wilson's letter. Perhaps if Wilson had not written the letter, Vardaman might have pursued the same course and won. A third factor, of much greater significance to Mississippi politics, seems to have been overlooked by contemporary observers in the smoke of battle. That was Vardaman's split with Bilbo. Had the two former allies held together it is doubtful that either of them could have been defeated. As it was both went down in defeat.

Bilbo attempted to carry water on both shoulders during the campaign by issuing denials that he was supporting either candidate.[57] He mortgaged his farm in Pearl River County for enough money to buy an automobile and toured the sixth district in an extensive campaign for Congress.[58] He ran second in the first primary and was snowed under in the runoff.[59]

[56]Vicksburg *Herald*, Aug. 21, 1918; Brookhaven *Leader*, Aug. 21, 1918, in Vardaman scrapbook; *Vardaman's Weekly*, Oct. 9, 1919.

[57]Vicksburg *Evening Post*, Aug. 28, 1917; Stone County *Enterprise*, Sept. 1, 1917, in Vardaman scrapbook.

[58]Jackson *Daily News*, Dec. 20, 1917.

[59]*Report of Secretary of State*, in *Official and Statistical Register. 1920-24*, pp. 346-48.

Thus, the faction which had dominated Mississippi politics for a decade had been divided and conquered. Both leaders were stripped of all power, relegated to private life, and their followings disorganized. For Vardaman, the eclipse was to be permanent. Perhaps the illness which was soon to remove him from an active participation in affairs was already upon him. Throughout the campaign, dispatches from even friendly papers remarked on his "changed appearance," his "lack of fire," his "broken voice," and his "prematurely aged appearance."[60] Certainly, his speeches lacked the pungency and the flair for showmanship which were characteristic of an earlier period. It could not have been due to age. He was still in the prime of life. As for Bilbo, his eclipse was temporary. After a decade he was to make a comeback. Never again, however, was he to have the overwhelming influence which he and Vardaman shared in the period from 1910 to 1918.

[60]Quoted in Vicksburg *Herald,* July 26, 1918.

CHAPTER XXII

EXIT VARDAMAN

EARLY in Bilbo's administration jockeying began within the old Vardaman-Bilbo faction for the succession to the governorship. Chief aspirants for the faction's support were Ross Collins, the attorney-general; H. E. Blakeslee, the commissioner of agriculture; and Lee Russell, the lieutenant-governor, who had Bilbo's support. By the spring of 1916 it was noted that Bilbo and Collins, who had been close friends for eight years, were no longer so and that Bilbo was consulting Judge Robert Mayes on state legal business instead of the attorney-general. It was rumored that Collins had refused to step aside in Russell's favor and was resolved to run despite Bilbo's wishes. Blakeslee was more amenable and accepted a three-year appointment as director general of the Mississippi Centennial Exposition. This method of disposing of him was extravagantly termed by the *Clarion* the "most gigantic political deal ever put over in Mississippi."[1]

Collins' determination to run against Russell might have had disastrous results for the remnants of the Vardaman-Bilbo machine, save for the fact that the opposition too was divided. It had early been agreed by the latter that Oscar Johnston, antiadministration Delta planter in the state senate, should be its standard-bearer. Belatedly, former Governor Longino had announced that he would be a candidate. His candidacy would detract from Johnston's following, just as Collins' would injure Russell's.

There were issues of real importance, but they were almost lost sight of in the character attacks made on the several candidates. Russell, running on the record of the Bilbo administration, upheld the state tax commission. He also stood for the preservation of the pardon board, arguing that without it too much of the governor's time would be taken up with the study of clemency petitions. Johnston urged the abolition of the tax commission and the pardon board. He argued both that the tax commission's authority was autocratic and that its legality was questionable. Longino, gentlemanly but innocuous as always, spent much of his time deny-

[1]Jackson *Clarion-Ledger*, June 8, July 16, 1916.

ing that he had used convict labor on his farm and that he had, while governor, pardoned a Negro condemned for rape. Collins, bitter after his break with his old comrades, pitched his campaign on the charge that Russell, if elected, would appoint Bilbo president of the Industrial Institute and College for Women at Columbus.[2]

Controversy over this charge seems to have featured the campaign. "Bilbo ... has some experience with school girls boarding at schools taught by him," said Collins, "and the story of what happened during this period would make an interesting story if a certain ... educator ... could be induced to tell the story." The Vicksburg *Herald*, crediting the charge, thought the mere suggestion of placing "the defender and alleged participant in the insane asylum ... scandal of lust at the head of the State Female College" was enough to make any prospective Russell voter "blush with shame." The *Daily News*, also eager to believe the charge, shuddered to think what would happen if "this combination of Don Juan and gay young Lothario" should be placed at the head of the college. "No father or mother," it said, "who cherishes the chastity of their [*sic*] daughter would care to send the girl to Columbus. It would be practically the same as sending her into the red light district."[3]

Bilbo denied that he was an applicant for or would accept the post if offered him. Roguishly he suggested that he might announce that if Russell "was not elected" he might ask for the appointment. Then he could "announce that every vote against Russell would be construed as an endorsement of my application." Walter Dent, assistant attorney-general, produced and Collins read to an audience at Carrollton what purported to be a letter from Bilbo to one of the trustees of the college asking for the appointment. Bilbo challenged the authenticity of the letter, and it was later admitted to be spurious. Bilbo then issued a statement attacking the characters of Collins and Dent, and for this he was kicked and knocked down in the streets of Jackson by Dent.[4]

[2]Jackson *Daily News*, Aug. 3, July 23, 1919; Vicksburg *Herald*, July 15, 19, Aug. 2, 3, 19, 24, 1919; Macon *Beacon*, Aug. 22, 1919; Natchez *Democrat*, Aug. 9, 1919.

[3]Vicksburg *Herald*, July 19, Aug. 3, 1919; *ibid.*, Aug. 22, 1919, quoting Jackson *Daily News*.

[4]Vicksburg *Herald*, July 31, Aug. 19, 24, 1919; Jackson *Daily News*, July 23, 1919; Macon *Beacon*, Aug. 22, 1919; Natchez *Democrat*, Aug. 9, 1919.

Many discharged soldiers had returned to the state after the February 1 deadline for the payment of poll taxes. The Democratic state executive committee had directed that the poll tax requirement should be waived in their cases. Despite the equity of such a ruling its legality seems questionable. When some of the county committees, allegedly supporting Russell, seemed reluctant to comply with this directive, it was cited as "proof positive" that Russell feared "the soldier vote."[5]

The campaign was said to be the "dullest" in the history of the state. The lethargy of voters was remarked generally and was said to be unprecedented. Political rallies were drawing hundreds where formerly they drew thousands. This was attributed to the fact that farmers were "too busy trying to save their crops from grass and boll weevils" and to a "tired feeling" resulting from "the lowered political standard culminating in the present administration in scandalous and abusive events."[6]

Despite this lethargy almost 150,000 votes were cast in the first primary. Russell led with 48,000; Johnston was second with 39,000; and Longino and Collins ran third and fourth respectively with about 30,000 votes each.[7] The latter two were thus eliminated, and Russell and Johnston fought it out in the second primary.

The tempo of the campaign increased in the second primary. The anti-Vardaman-Bilbo press called on Johnston, Longino, and Collins to "ground arms, get together, pool their forces, and get ready to make the greatest three weeks canvass," in order to rid the state of the final vestige of "Vardamanism and Bilboism" in the person of Russell. Longino's campaign manager and Collins at once announced their support of Johnston. It was claimed that Longino had pledged himself for Johnston, but this Longino denied. For more than two weeks he remained strangely silent and then, on the eve of the election, announced that he would support neither candidate. Reliable information had come to him, he said, that some of Johnston's "close friends" had announced before the first primary that if Russell were in the runoff with Longino, they would support Russell. Thus, if they thought Russell fit to be governor

[5]Jackson *Daily News*, July 28, 1919.
[6]Vicksburg *Herald*, July 6, 9, Aug. 5, 1919; Natchez *Democrat*, Aug. 1, 1919.
[7]*Report of Secretary of State*, in *Official and Statistical Register, 1920-24*, p. 369.

then, with his Vardaman and Bilbo "predilections," they were estopped from demanding support for him now "because of [his] factional alignment."[8]

Meanwhile Vardaman, who seemed reluctant to choose between Russell and Collins in the first primary, came out strongly for Russell in the second. He urged support of Russell largely on the grounds of his poverty. "No man," he said, "who has not known the hardships of the poor people is able to sympathize with them." Russell, he said, was one of the "common people." He had come from the "humbler walks of life" and was able to understand the poor. It was the same eternal struggle, said Vardaman, the rich against the poor. Lies and deception had been practiced on Russell in the first primary, and large sums had been spent to defeat him.[9]

Following the former practices of Vardaman and Bilbo, Russell issued appeals to his friends to send in small contributions "to meet the legitimate expenses of the campaign." This was denounced by the opposition as "demagoguery." Johnston was denounced as an enemy of labor and of the small farmer. He was pictured as a rich planter living in a river county. The issue, said Russell supporters, was "whether the entire citizenship . . . should have a square deal." The rich Delta section and the large timber interests, they said, "had long escaped paying their just proportion of our state taxes." Now they were spending huge sums in an attempt to defeat Russell and repeal the tax equalization law. This argument was denounced by the Johnston forces as a "Hill Billy" appeal to "passion, prejudice, and narrowmindedness." But it had telling effect. It was, said Johnston's manager, "the hardest proposition I have to meet."[10]

He did the best he could. Russell, he charged, had opposed a bill introduced by Johnston in the last legislature to increase the age of consent for females from ten to fourteen years. Russell, he charged, "in order to keep a few negroes from getting their just

[8]Vicksburg *Herald*, Aug. 7, 1919; Jackson *Clarion-Ledger*, Aug. 7, 1919; Natchez *Democrat*, Aug. 8, 1919; Macon *Beacon*, Aug. 8, 22, 1918; Jackson *Daily News*, Aug. 8, 9, 1919; Memphis *Commercial Appeal*, quoted in Vicksburg *Herald*, Aug. 21, 1919.

[9]*Vardaman's Weekly*, Aug. 7, 1919.

[10]Vicksburg *Herald*, Aug. 17, 1919; Ripley *Sentinel* and Hinds County *Gazette*, quoted in Vicksburg *Herald*, Aug. 26, 31, 1919; Macon *Beacon*, Aug. 19, 22, 1919.

deserts," was unwilling "to protect the white girls of Mississippi."[11]
Thus again the opposition to Vardaman and Bilbo made use of the
much despised and demagogic tools when it served their purpose.

The results of the election showed that, despite the defeats of
Bilbo and Vardaman the preceding year, united they were still the
strongest force in Mississippi politics. Russell received 77,427
votes to Johnston's 69,565.[12] Despite pre-election warnings by both
sides that the enemy intended to use fraud, no charges were made.
Johnston's defeat was attributed by his followers to the failure of
the Longino forces to support their candidate. Russell, they said,
was not elected by the Democrats, but by the "Bolshevists, the
I. W. W.'s, the Socialists, the ignorant, the illiterate, the riff-raff,
the rag-tag, and the bobtail of creation." "Don't blame God or the
Democratic party," they said. The Jackson *Daily News* called
Russell "a common little bounder and character assassin," a "shameful liar and contemptible slanderer."[13]

When the legislature met in January, 1920, it soon became
evident that the new governor was to have a rocky road. A fight
developed at once over the speakership. Conner, who had been
elected speaker in 1916 with Bilbo's support, had split with him
and Russell. He had campaigned against Bilbo in 1918 and against
Russell the following year. Despite their opposition, however, Conner was chosen speaker.[14]

A fight next developed over appropriations. The "low pressure" element had grown stronger, and there was much talk of
economy. Speaker Conner insisted that there was little chance of
retrenchment. Most of the revenue was expended on education and
eleemosynary institutions, and even the most radical of the "low
pressure" members did not dare insist on a cut in these items. The
house of representatives voted down an early resolution pledging
a reduction in the tax levy and a trimming of appropriations by
$5,000,000. Governor Russell's message called for an increase in
appropriations for the department of labor, for a new department
of forestry conservation, an increase for the highway department,

---

[11]Natchez *Democrat*, Aug. 19, 1919.

[12]*Report of Secretary of State*, in *Official and Statistical Register, 1920-24*, p. 369.

[13]Jackson *Daily News*, Aug. 25, 28, 1919.

[14]Mississippi, *House Journal*, 1920, pp. 22-23; Natchez *Democrat*, Jan. 2, 7,
1920.

a new home for the aged and infirm, and for creation of a public utilities commission. He also urged employment of a state purchasing agent, retention of the existing scale of state salaries, and a new anti-lobbying bill.[15] Little was accomplished, however, and the session ended without much constructive legislation.

During the next session, in 1922, a fight was again raging in the Delta counties over control of the Yazoo-Mississippi Delta Levee Board. Walter Sillers, son of Anse McLaurin's old henchman, was sponsoring a new bill to take the appointive power of board members away from the governor and make them elective. Russell and the board were, of course, opposing the bill. A legislative investigating committee was appointed after it was charged that the levee board had renegotiated with a contractor and paid him 78 per cent more for work than his contract called for. The contractor, it was charged, "was a strong political supporter" of Russell and had "contributed to his campaign fund." When the board's engineer justified the transaction because of the increased costs after the contract had been made, the committee approved. It, however, censured the board in its report, and the legislature passed Sillers' bill over the governor's veto.[16]

In the midst of the session Miss Frances Birkhead, a former secretary of Russell, filed suit against him in federal court for $100,000. She alleged that he had seduced her repeatedly under promise of marriage as soon as he could secure a divorce from his wife. She alleged further that he had arranged for the performing of an abortion on her which had left her an invalid for life.[17]

Russell called the suit "the most damnable blackmail conspiracy in the history of Mississippi" and attributed it "to malicious attempts of [my] enemies to blacken my character."[18] He had the year before instituted an antitrust suit against a group of old-line fire insurance companies, as a result of which they had withdrawn from the state. He charged that they had concocted the damage suit against him. The anti-Russell faction in the house then passed, over Russell's opposition, a resolution calling for him to submit what evidence he had to substantiate his charges against the insurance companies.

[15]Mississippi, *House Journal*, 1920, pp. 195-228, 1472.
[16]*Ibid.*, 1922, pp. 941-55, 2156.
[17]Natchez *Democrat*, Feb. 7, 1922.
[18]Mississippi, *House Journal*, 1922, pp. 924-28.

Russell attempted to get the house to reconsider the resolution but failed. He then dispatched a letter to the house, declining to appear before it but stating that the information on which he based the charge had come from the state revenue agent. The revenue agent was called by the house, and he testified that the evidence was hearsay told him by several people. These latter when called were unable to verify, of their personal knowledge, any of the facts alleged by Russell. Thereupon the house adopted by a vote of 61 to 20 a resolution branding Russell's charges "groundless and unwarranted."[19]

The suit was removed from Jackson for lack of jurisdiction to the northern district, and was tried at Oxford, Russell's home, the following December. At the trial Miss Birkhead was completely discredited, and the jury acquitted Russell after only twenty-five minutes' deliberation.[20]

A feature of the case was the conduct of Bilbo. He had split with Russell before the suit was filed and was subpoenaed by the prosecution to testify against Russell. He had frequently stated that he knew much and when the time came he would tell it. Yet he refused to answer the summons and was not found and brought before the court until after the verdict had been rendered. When he was found, he explained that his refusal to testify was on the ground that he had been Russell's attorney and had obtained evidence in confidence which he was not at liberty to disclose. This was a weak excuse, as he could have answered the summons and been excused from testifying. It was alleged that his real reason for not appearing was quite otherwise: that he had been implicated in the plot to injure Russell; that he had discovered the absence of certain letters from his files that would disclose this; that he suspected that Russell had obtained these letters and was prepared to incriminate him if he should appear. Under such circumstances, said one observer, "thirty days in jail looked far preferable to thirty minutes on the witness stand subject to cross examination."[21] Bilbo was found in contempt of court and sentenced to ten days in jail, which he served.

[19]*Ibid.*, 928-30, 956, 962-64, 978-79, 1345-46, 1895-1910, 1912; Natchez *Democrat*, Feb. 24, 25, 28, Mar. 10, Apr. 2, 1922.

[20]*Ibid.*, Dec. 12, 1922.

[21]*Vardaman's Weekly*, Aug. 2, 1923.

The affair left a nauseating stench in the nostrils of many Mississippians. Several editors compared the recent political leaders with those of the generation before and found the modern generation falling short of the standard set by their predecessors. "Whether true or not," said the Newton *Record* of the charge against Russell, "can one imagine such a charge being brought against Stone, Lowry, McLaurin, and other governors on whom no such suspicion has ever rested?" Another editor thought the recent governors, "excepting Noel," had gone Nero, Claudius, and Caligula, "one better." Another, unfriendly to Russell, suspected that his charge of a "frame-up" was not groundless. "It's time that Mississippians got together," he said, "called a halt on such horrible conditions, and brought the old ship of state back to the moorings of honor and common decency."[22]

After his defeat by Harrison, Vardaman returned to Mississippi, took up the publication of a new journal, *Vardaman's Weekly*, and began a campaign to secure John Sharp Williams' senatorial seat in 1922. Williams had announced that he would not be a candidate to succeed himself, but whether inspired by distrust of this statement or of revenge for the part Williams had played in his 1918 defeat, Vardaman centered his attack on him. Much of this was in the form of charges of insobriety on the part of Williams. The Carroll *News* was glad to note that Williams had "sobered up sufficiently to support the administration's . . . shipping lobby."[23] The Vaiden *News* in successive issues in January, 1919, alleged that Williams was "drinking himself to death."[24] Six months later Vardaman himself remarked that "The poor old fellow [Williams] has been drunk for thirty years" and was "well-nigh a mental and physical wreck." He charged that Williams' mind "like most alcoholics' . . . moves around in a circle," and that he had not made a logical argument in ten years. Williams, he said, had tied himself to President Wilson because of expediency. He was undergoing "mental and physical decay" and presented "a pitiful spectacle." A month later he characterized a Senate speech by Williams as "drunken"

22Newton *Record*, Sunflower *Tocsin*, and Yazoo *Sentinel*, quoted in Natchez *Democrat*, Feb. 7, 1922.

23Carroll *News*, Feb. 12, 1919, quoted, *ibid.*

24Vaiden *News*, Jan. 9, 17, 1919, in Vardaman scrapbook.

and "nasty."[25] He published a dispatch from a New York paper in which fellow senators had charged that Williams was drunk when he made an "incoherent and rambling" speech and that Senator Boies Penrose had protested against Williams' sleeping in Penrose's seat and had had him removed.[26] Vardaman even charged that Williams' victory over him in 1907 had been because of "the many votes he and some of his managers defrauded me of."[27]

Vardaman did not neglect his old enemies, the trusts. It was they, he said, who had pictured him as pro-German and Williams as a super-patriot. The reason for this was that he had "voted to tax the big profiteer and multimillionaires, while Williams wanted to be light on them." He upheld the cause of labor against capital. Labor, he said, had done a good job during the war. Some unusually high wages had been paid, but compared to the profits of big business they were nothing. "The man who says 'Labor is a menace to the peace of the country' is both a fool and a liar," he said. "I should like to know," he added, "how long the capitalists would enjoy the luxuries of life if it were not for the products of the hands that toil."[28]

Large sums, he said, had been spent by trusts to defeat him in 1911 and 1918, and he had no doubt that "the plutocratic thieves that exploited Hog Island," together with the railroad interest, would contribute again to a campaign against him. He published a list of corporate executives, many of whom represented lumber interests of south Mississippi, who were actively opposing his election and who were "commanding" their employees to vote against him. He was alarmed, he said, because so much of the press was controlled by wealthy interests. Free government, he said, could not exist without "free speech, freedom of action, and the utmost freedom of thought." He appealed to his readers to obtain subscriptions for the *Weekly*. Otherwise, he said, he could not continue its publication.[29]

Vardaman claimed much credit for the passage of the Flood Control Bill of 1918, whereby the federal government took over

[25]*Vardaman's Weekly*, July 10, Aug. 14, 1919.
[26]New York *American*, quoted, *ibid.*, Oct. 23, 1919.
[27]*Vardaman's Weekly*, Jan. 5, 1922.
[28]Jackson *Issue*, Jan. 9, 1919; *Vardaman's Weekly*, May 8, 1919, Feb. 12, 1920.
[29]*Vardaman's Weekly*, Apr. 24, May 8, 1919, June 16, Aug. 24, 1922.

the financing of levee building in the Mississippi Valley. This was very popular in the Delta and gained him some support in that section. Attempts were made by the opposition to discredit this claim, but Vardaman was able to publish statements from Delta citizens, received by him at the time of the bill's passage, commending him for his "most valiant and effective work" in behalf of the legislation.[30]

Vardaman's opponent in 1922, Hubert D. Stephens, made an active campaign, but it was admitted by his friends that he was "not an orator." His lack of color, together with Vardaman's absence from the stump, tended to make the campaign another lethargic one. A novel feature was the presence in the race of a woman, Miss Belle Kearney of Flora. It was the first time a woman had ever been a candidate for office in Mississippi. She was conceded not even an outside chance to win, but it was thought she might draw enough votes from the recently enfranchised women to prevent either of the male candidates from getting a majority in the first primary.[31]

Most of Stephens' campaign was given over to a denunciation of Vardaman's "radical" backing and to the old charge of disloyalty. He accused Vardaman of having said that "Lenin and Trotsky are two of the world's greatest statesmen, and the principles of Bolshevism are right and should prevail the world over." Vardaman's only supporters, he charged, were "I. W. W.'s, Communists, Bolshevists, radical-Socialists, pro-Germans, men who refused to subscribe to Liberty Loan drives, draft obstructors, and confidants of Lenin and Trotsky." He admitted that Vardaman had made a good record as governor, but charged that his Senate record "gave more aid and comfort to the Kaiser than any other man in America excepting Messrs. [Eugene V.] Debs and Lafollette."[32]

It was known that Vardaman's absence from the stump was due to mental illness. Occasionally he would sit on the platform while another spoke for him. It was said that he could not talk coherently on any subject for more than five minutes and that he

---

[30]See clippings in Vardaman scrapbook, especially Memphis *Commercial Appeal*, Aug. 19, 1922; Cleveland *Enterprise*, Aug. 15, 1918; also *Vardaman's Weekly*, July 3, 1919; Vicksburg *Herald*, Aug. 15, 23, 1922.

[31]Vicksburg *Herald*, June 16, 1922.

[32]*Ibid.*, Aug. 10, 31, 1922.

seemed to take "but little interest in what was going on." Late in the campaign he made one pathetic attempt to speak to an audience. After speaking for twenty minutes in a very low and feeble voice that could scarcely be heard, he sat down abruptly. His condition was openly remarked on by the press and was urged as further reason to defeat him. "It would be just as sensible," said the *Daily News*, "to go out to the Mississippi Insane Hospital, pick out one of the unfortunate inmates . . . , and adorn him with a Senatorial toga."[33]

In this extremity Bilbo came to his aid and stumped the state vigorously in his behalf. This was hailed by the Stephens forces as a sign of desperation on the part of Vardaman. They claimed that he "thoroughly despised and detested" Bilbo and pointed to the fact that Bilbo had not spoken until late in the campaign. Now, they said, Vardaman had "surrendered" to him "in a last desperate attempt to stem the tide." It was said that Bilbo's aid was not popular with many of Vardaman's supporters and that a division in their ranks would result.[34]

In the first primary a record vote of 158,838 was cast. When it is considered that the list of eligible voters should have been doubled by the advent of woman's suffrage, this was in reality a light vote. Vardaman received 74,573, Stephens, 65,980, and Miss Kearney, 18,285. In the second primary Stephens received 95,351 votes to Vardaman's 86,853.[35] This was 23,000 more than had been cast in the primary three weeks before. The Vardaman forces charged that it was due to a disregard of the registration laws and the poll tax requirement. Registration books, they said, were in some places actually taken to the polls, voters were registered, their poll taxes paid, and their votes cast all on the same day.[36] There was no substantiation of this charge, but the great increase in such a short period of time was unprecedented in Mississippi elections.

Vardaman's defeat was explained by his followers in still other

[33]*Ibid.*, June 16, Aug. 15, 1922; Jackson *Daily News*, July 27, 1922; *Vardaman's Weekly*, Aug. 18, 1922.

[34]Vicksburg *Herald*, July 28, 1922; Jackson *Daily News*, July 29, Aug. 3, 1922.

[35]*Biennial Report of the Secretary of State to the Legislature, October 1, 1923-October 1, 1925* (n.d., n.p.).

[36]*Vardaman's Weekly*, Sept. 7, 1922.

ways. Country women, they said, were for Vardaman and had failed to register. City women, who were opposed to him, had done so.[37] In many counties, they charged, new registrations were ordered and "so handled that the voters were not freely permitted to register, even when their taxes were paid." In Newton County a registration had been made the year before, but a new one was ordered nevertheless. Many Vardaman voters, they said, thinking their previous registration was sufficient, neglected to register the second time and were disqualified. In still other counties poll books were purged between the two primaries, "a thing wholly illegal," and it was alleged that many Vardaman voters were disqualified in this way.[38]

Save for one significant statement which Vardaman issued the following year, the election was his last act of participation in Mississippi politics. He was taken to the home of a daughter in Birmingham, Alabama, where he spent the remaining years of his life secluded and perhaps unconscious of his and his faction's disintegration.

Upon Bilbo's release from the Oxford jail where he had served a term for contempt of court, he made a speech from the jail steps announcing his candidacy for governor. The move seemed to be unpremeditated, for the campaign was already well under way. Four candidates—Henry L. Whitfield, Percy Bell, Lester C. Franklin, and M. S. Conner—each with an organized backing, had been in the field for many months. All four had formerly been intimately associated with Vardaman. Franklin was supposed to have the backing of the old Vardaman following, while Conner and Whitfield seemed to have support of the Vardaman opposition. Bell appeared to have support of parts of each group. Bilbo had the backing of nothing that could be termed a faction. Whitfield, running on a platform of reduced taxes, was embarrassed by the fact that as state superintendent of education he had been an advocate of

[37]The state constitution had been amended to require the payment of the poll tax by women, but the question arose as to whether women against whom no levy had been made could register and vote in the primary. Attorney-General Clayton Potter ruled that they could, but the state executive committee ruled otherwise. A year later the Vicksburg *Herald*, June 22, 1923, an anti-Vardaman paper, admitted that had Potter's ruling been followed the year before Vardaman would have been elected.

[38]*Vardaman's Weekly*, Sept. 7, 1922.

high taxes. Conner advocated more lenient treatment of corporations and, after Bilbo's entry, spent much time in defending himself against Bilbo's charge that he was a "slacker" during the war.[39] Bilbo also attacked Franklin, a Delta farmer who had Russell's backing, charging that he and Conner both had "trust" backing.

Bilbo had the most interesting program. He urged a state purchasing board, payments of convicts' earnings to their dependents, a radical change in road building by utilizing convict labor to make brick for the roads, and erection of a state printing plant to print textbooks for all school children. He made an appeal for the entire female vote by advocating the appointment of women members to all state boards and erection of a home for "fallen women." His entry into the race changed the tenor of the campaign. In June the Vicksburg *Herald* had noted an absence of "name-calling" and thought the state "after several years of indulgence in violent politics" was "turning the other way." By August it expressed its regret that the early indication had not been borne out. The last month, it said, had brought forth "as much mud-slinging and filthy politics as our state has ever witnessed." Most name calling was among Bilbo, Conner, and Franklin, and it was believed that whoever of them advanced into the second primary would be defeated by the opposition of the two eliminated.[40]

Many women had registered since the preceding campaign. There were reported to be 65,000 of them prepared to cast their votes, and it was expected by some that politics would be improved and "there will be a better order through and through."[41]

In the first primary more than 250,000 votes were cast, which was an increase of almost 100,000 since 1919, when women had not been permitted to vote. Whitfield had a plurality with 85,000. Bilbo, to the amazement of almost everyone, was second with 65,000. Conner was third, and Franklin fourth. Bell polled over 17,000 votes, which was said to be a "personal tribute," since he was "ground between the upper and nether millstones of factionalism."[42]

[39]Natchez *Democrat*, July 12, 13, 26, Aug. 10, 1923; Vicksburg *Herald*, June 13, July 3, 10, 1923.

[40]Natchez *Democrat*, July 13, 1923; Vicksburg *Herald*, June 10, July 20, Aug. 1, 1923.

[41]Natchez *Democrat*, July 26, 1923.

[42]*Report of Secretary of State, 1921-1923*; Jackson *Daily News*, Aug. 8, 1923.

After the first primary, Franklin, contrary to prediction, effected a settlement with Bilbo and pledged his support. It was feared Conner might do so too. He remained ominously silent for awhile, but finally declared for Whitfield, as also did Bell. Senators Williams and Stephens were also backing Whitfield.[43]

It was conceded that in the second primary south Mississippi would go for Bilbo, while the Delta and the central part of the state would go for Whitfield. The northeastern section would be the battleground and would decide the issue. This was a region where Vardaman had always been strong, and a great effort was made by both candidates to win support of Vardaman's old following. A week before the election State Senator Jeff Bell made a pilgrimage to Birmingham to see the White Chief. He spent the week end with him, and on his return made a speech in Polkville, in Smith County. He had been told by Vardaman, he said, that Bilbo had not been loyal to Vardaman and was "neither his personal nor political friend." On the other hand, Bell quoted him as saying, "Whitfield is a clean, decent man and should be elected Governor."[44] The message was headlined on the front page of all anti-Bilbo papers. Its authenticity, despite the absence of verification, was not questioned even by Bilbo. He took his medicine like a man, not even issuing a retaliatory statement against Vardaman.

In the election Whitfield received 134,715 votes to Bilbo's 118,143. Bilbo carried thirty counties, all of which were white. Large majorities were piled up against him in the black counties, in not one of which did he receive as much as 35 per cent of the vote.[45] Whitfield's majority was more than 16,000. This was sufficient to nominate him even if the votes of Coahoma, where eight ballot boxes had been destroyed, were thrown out. The Vicksburg *Herald* credited the victory to the vote of the women and praised them for having "made possible the redemption of Mississippi from the hands of the demagogues."[46]

The only other state-wide election of the period was that of 1924 when Earl Brewer made an ill-timed effort to stage a come-

[43]Natchez *Democrat*, Aug. 16, 1923.

[44]*Ibid.*, Aug. 26, 1923; Vicksburg *Herald*, Aug. 26, 1923; Jackson *Daily News,* Aug. 26, 1923.

[45]*Report of Secretary of State, 1921-1923.*

[46]Jackson *Daily News*, Aug. 30, 1923; Vicksburg *Herald*, Aug. 30, 31, 1923.

back by unseating Harrison. His effort was abortive, however, and the campaign passed almost unnoticed by the state press. Harrison won without extending himself, 80,371 to 17,496.[47] This was a decline of more than 150,000 in the vote cast the preceding year.

Thus, the period closed with the complete rout of the forces represented in the persons of Vardaman and Bilbo. If the latter part of this story has seemed heavily weighted with the personalities and doings of those two men, it is because they exercised a greater influence over their fellows, both friend and foe, than did any others of their time. In personality and character, as well as in appearance, they were radically different. In many ways they effected a revolution in the state, socially, politically, and economically. While no attempt has been made to judge the merits of the numerous and scandalous charges made against Bilbo—for none of which was he ever convicted—it is remarkable that, excepting the contingent fund affair, no question of Vardaman's integrity or morality was ever raised. For a politician active in a period when charges against other men were flying thick and fast, and loved and hated as few men before or since, this is indeed a tribute.

[47]*Report of Secretary of State, 1923-1925.*

CHAPTER XXIII

CONCLUSION

THROUGHOUT the period from 1876 to 1925 the central thread in Mississippi politics is a struggle between economic classes, interspersed with the personal struggles of ambitious men. Before the Civil War agriculture had been the dominant influence in Mississippi society. Industry was almost a negligible quantity. Almost everyone was engaged in agricultural pursuits, and leaders in thought and society were representatives of the agricultural class. Despite social differences existing between small farmer and big planter, there was a remarkable similarity in their economic interests.

The Civil War had effected great changes in economic conditions. The political and economic dominance of the rich planters was broken. Following in the wake of the war, industrialization, banking, and merchandising entered the state and complicated the former relatively simple agrarian society. The new interests engaged but a small fraction of the people, and the overwhelming majority of the population continued to be employed in agriculture. But greater profits were to be made in the new businesses than in the old. Many former political leaders, quick to see and take advantage of this, began to subordinate their agricultural interests to money lending, merchandising, and railroad promotion. This produced an economic cleavage between them and the dirt farmers.

The picture was further complicated by the presence of the Negro. His active participation in government caused a reaction among a large majority of white men, and all classes of them united to drive him out of the halls of state. W. E. B. Du Bois, a distinguished Negro historian, pictures this as a counterrevolutionary movement directed by the new business interests against the economic democracy which the Reconstruction governments were on the verge of establishing.[1] Such an interpretation may be questioned. It is doubtful if the new economic interests thrived any the less under Republican rule than they did under Democratic. Rather, it would seem, the class most endangered by the so-called "black domination" was composed of the large landowners. The ascendancy of the Negroes both in politics and in the social scale

[1] W. E. B. Du Bois, *Black Reconstruction* (New York, 1935).

was a disturbing factor in the labor market and rendered large holdings a burden rather than an asset. Regardless of its origin, there can be no doubt that the movement to overthrow the Reconstruction government was joined in heartily by all classes of whites, rich and poor, large and small farmer, banker and merchant.

Nor can there be much doubt that in the government established after 1876 representatives of the new interests were in complete control. Lamar, George, Walthall, and Lowry, the four who with Stone held an unshakable grip on the state's government until the end of the century, were all lawyers and represented ably the new business interests. George and Walthall, together with George's law partner, Wiley P. Harris, were the leading members of the Mississippi bar and were reputed to have the largest corporate practices in the state. Stone, while not a lawyer, was a devoted disciple of Lamar, and both were admittedly partial to railroad interests.

These men were not evil tyrants bent upon despoiling the masses. They were probably no better or worse men than those who tried to unseat them, though they were probably shrewder and more capable political manipulators. They were doubtless sincere in the belief that they were representing the best interests of their constituents, and they may have been. But in succeeding decades when agriculture was undergoing the pangs of depression while business was thriving, vast numbers of farmers came to feel that their interests were not being served. Their leaders, they felt, had abandoned them and had allied themselves with banks, railroads, and merchants, who had banded together to despoil the farmer. Generally, however, the farmers, because of the alleged threat of "negro supremacy," were loyal to the political leaders who had seized control at the end of the Reconstruction period.

Presence of the Negro soon came to be a great asset to the leaders in power. They used him unsparingly to crush all incipient revolts against their authority. Did the people wish to return to the horrors of black rule? they asked. If not, they must support their present rulers. Only thus could a division be presented which would inevitably result in "black domination." Only by "white solidarity," by a meek submission to dictates of the reigning oligarchy, could such a catastrophe be averted. Furthermore, deals could be made with Negro leaders to keep the masses of Negroes from joining it is the consensus of opinion in the State at the present time [1902], that the number of negroes who are being qualified under the educational conditions of the suffrage by the school facilities . . . will continue to increase, and that it may be only a question of time when there will again be a majority of qualified negro voters in the State.[6]

Such an opinion, while it may not excuse Vardaman from the charge of "demagoguery," at least might indicate his sincerity.

But it must not be forgotten that there was much more to Vardaman's program than its racial feature. For decades there had been a crying need for social reform, but the old-style politician went blindly on his way, paying lip service to the majesty of the people but doing nothing to alleviate their lot. There was convincing evidence that the state was controlled by political "rings" rotten to the core. Huge treasury deficits were discovered in 1890 and again in 1901.[7] Moreover, the "rings" seemed to be in an alliance with the new business interests, which the farmers regarded as the source of all their troubles. In 1882 new railroads and manufactures had been exempted from taxes for a term of ten years. This had been, the farmers thought, but an opening wedge for newer and greater concessions later. It had become customary for politicians to rant against corporations, but little action had been taken to allay their monopolistic grip. Finally, in 1900 at his inaugural, Longino was honest, bold, or stupid enough to express an open friendship for them. He hoped, he said, that "no more sentimental or prejudicial opposition to railroads or other corporate enterprises will find favor with the legislature."[8] Two years later he was pleased to report that "there exists . . . a becoming liberality of sentiment by the masses toward the corporate and other investments of money in our midst."[9]

Vardaman and other "demagogues" did not think so. It was against these interests, as well as against the Negro, that they directed their campaigns. Since they were fighting these interests,

[6]Johnston, "Suffrage and Reconstruction," loc. cit., 241.
[7]Annual Cyclopedia, New Series, XV (1890), 559; 3rd Series, VIII (1902), -52.
[8]Mississippi, House Journal, 1900, pp. 95-96.
[9]Ibid., 1902, p. 49.

such revolts. Should these efforts fail and the Negro masses refuse to follow their leaders, the opposition could be branded as controlled by Negroes, and enough whites could be rallied to prevent, by violence or fraud or both, success of such a movement.

Despite these well-laid plans the period was one of almost incessant agrarian revolt. Greenback, Grange, Alliance, and Populist movements were tangible evidence of discontent. At the same time, the ambitions of individuals who felt that they had not been properly rewarded for the part they had played in overthrowing Republicanism furnished leadership to the movement. Ethelbert Barksdale was the outstanding leader of the rebels during the 1880's, just as Frank Burkitt was to be during the 1890's, and Vardaman after the turn of the century. To a large extent they seem to have been motivated by a certain amount of idealism as well as personal ambition. James R. Chalmers, on the other hand, seems to have been almost altogether intent upon gaining revenge upon Lamar and in gratifying his own ego. Both he and Burkitt committed the "unforgivable crime" of leading their followers out of the Democratic party. Barksdale and Vardaman, although partial to much of the Populist program, thought it wiser to seek reform from within the party.

Programs advocated by the rebels were generally popular and would have won had the political machinery operated on more democratic principles. But political control under the convention system was in the hands of a few who ruled with or without support of the masses. Whoever they chose must be elected by the people. The alternative, the people were told and believed, was "black domination." With legal disfranchisement of the Negro effected by the constitution of 1890, this threat was less imminent, and revolting movements, particularly in county elections, became more prevalent. But the old convention system of nominating was still used, and the small farmers who had urged the constitutional convention found that political control was as far as ever from their grasp. Too, the poll tax had disfranchised thousands of white men who would have voted with the malcontents. It was not until the primary was instituted after the turn of the century that the rebels had any chance of success. Then, with anything like a "free ballot and a fair count," success was almost assured.

It is doubtful if Vardaman won because he was a more capable leader than Barksdale. He had tried twice for the gubernatorial nomination before the convention and failed, just as he was to fail again in the Secret Caucus of 1910. On the other hand, the first time he went before the people in a popular election he won, as he also won by an overwhelming majority in the election of 1911, a year after his defeat by the "convention-like" legislature.

It has been contended frequently that Vardaman was the first of the "demagogues" in Mississippi. If he was a "demagogue"—and certainly it must be conceded that he appealed to "passion and prejudice"—he cannot have been the first one. It is not reasonable to assume "that a race which for a hundred years had produced outstanding men in the field of government and politics, went suddenly 'moronic.'"[2] "Demagogues" had been active in Mississippi since 1876, and probably before. The pleas for "white solidarity," so insistently urged by all leaders, from Lamar through George, Walthall, Stone, Lowry, McLaurin, Percy, and Williams, were nothing but appeals "to prejudice and passion," just as Vardaman's crusade was. They urged exclusion of the Negroes from the polls as the only salvation for their society. Vardaman urged exclusion of the Negroes from the schools in order to make sure that they did not qualify for polls and as the only salvation for an impoverished school system. As to which of them was less sincere in his motives it is impossible to decide. Each of them climbed to power and maintained himself there by appeals to racial prejudice. Nor did Vardaman's opponents in later years, even Williams himself, hesitate to vie with him in competing for the Negro-hating vote.

The cry of "demagogue" was sometimes thrown at Lamar, George, Lowry, and McLaurin. More often it was hurled at Barksdale and Burkitt, and later at Vardaman and Bilbo. The reason for this is that the latter group more frequently appealed to the "prejudice and passion" of their followers. As a general rule the former group did not have to make such appeals. Generally, their appeals were directed to small and select groups—to executive committees and such. It was unnecessary to appeal to the passions of these men. There were closer and dearer interests that could be touched. Only

[2]Daniel M. Robison, "From Tillman to Long: Some Striking Leaders of the Rural South," in *Journal of Southern History*, III (1937), 309.

when an opposition ticket was in the field, and the voters had freedom of choice between candidates, did the existing leaders have to make appeals to the voters. Whenever these occasions arose the threat of "negro domination" was painted in such lurid colors that even the most illiterate might read. True, Vardaman was more violent and savage in his attacks upon the Negro than George, Lamar, and their followers had been. On the other hand, Bilbo in this period, and Barksdale and Burkitt in an earlier one, rarely appealed to racial prejudice. Yet they were denounced, as strongly as was Vardaman, as "demagogues."

Barksdale, Burkitt, Vardaman, and Bilbo, as representatives of the opposition, had to rely for success upon appeals to the discontented masses. They knew, just as Lamar and George knew, what appeals were strongest with these masses. That they did not hesitate to stoop to such appeals is regrettable. It should not, however, serve to set them apart from the so-called "better elements." It must be borne in mind that Vardaman's appeals were directed voters whose general educational level was not high. They understood little other than what they saw around them, and perhaps all of that. There was little friction between Negroes and well-to-do whites. But there were relatively few well-to-do whites in Mississippi in the period under consideration. On the other hand, between the poor whites and the Negroes "there is likely to be and there is very sure to be suspicion."[3] Vardaman's appeal emotional one. He campaigned in 1903 largely in the pine and "hill-billy" sections where poor whites abounded, mob violence and free rein to lynchers. Results were that he had not miscalculated. He carried counties with farmer percentages and lost those where tenant farmer paratively few.[4]

It would be unfair to assume that Vardaman was in expressed fear of "negro domination" if radical measures taken. Certainly there were many intelligent men Vardaman's following who urged his racial program necessity.[5] A Mississippi scholar wrote just a year man's first state-wide campaign:

[3]Murphy, *Problems of the South*, 156.
[4]Ladner, "J. K. Vardaman in Mississippi Politics," *loc.* White, "Anti-Racial Agitation," in *Journal of Mississippi Hist*
[5]Watkins, Address, May 17, 1936, p. 16, in Mississippi and History.

the chief publicity agency, the press, was opposed to them. Suffering under this handicap they had to resort to vivid and dramatic campaign tactics in order to publicize themselves. Their appeal was directed to poor as against rich, to farmer as against townsman, to the "common man" as against the aristocrat. Poverty, as A. B. Moore observes, seems to make the masses "susceptible to demagogic appeals." Frequently, he says, "people have turned . . . for relief to the so-called demagogues."[10] But it is too easy for those who control agencies of publicity to condemn their opponents as "demagogues." "Whether one is to be classed as a demagogue or a statesman seems to depend quite often upon the respectability of his followers and upon the agencies of propaganda which support or oppose him."[11] Thus, Burkitt was denounced as a "demagogue" when he allegedly advocated Negro voting, and Vardaman was similarly denounced when he advocated greater safeguards against Negro voting. It is a remarkable coincidence that, despite their radical differences on the Negro question, Vardaman inherited Burkitt's following.[12] This would tend to belie the charge that Vardaman's success was due to his Negro baiting alone.

"A demagogue," says Gerald W. Johnson, "is objectionable for a vast number of reasons, but he has at least the virtue of being alive; and when the choice lies between a demagogue and a political corpse," the voters must choose the former.[13] The old "respectable" Democratic leaders recognized no social responsibility other than the negative one of preventing "negro domination." That provided, they considered their duty done. Generally their rule was honest but selfish. Its gentility was enjoyed at the cost of the neglect of the social welfare of the masses of the population. It was not until the "demagogues" Vardaman and Bilbo awakened the social consciousness of the people that any constructive social legislation was enacted in Mississippi. Vardaman started the ball rolling with his crusade against unspeakable conditions existing in the penitentiary and other state institutions. Bilbo carried it further with his commission to eliminate adult illiteracy, a law to curb the textbook

[10]A. B. Moore, "One Hundred Years of Reconstruction," in *Journal of Southern History*, IX (1943), 174.

[11]Robison, "From Tillman to Long," *loc. cit.*, 298.

[12]McCain, "The Populist Party," 60.

[13]Johnson, "Live Demagogues or Dead Gentlemen," *loc. cit.*, 14.

trust, the furnishing of transportation for children in the rural con-
solidated schools, and the passage of a compulsory school-attend-
ance law. Under his administration, too, laws were passed curbing
the activities of corporations and the sale of bogus stocks, regulating
public utilities, and breaking the insurance trust. He sponsored the
building of hospitals and institutions for the subnormal, game and
fish laws, temperance, laws to eradicate ticks and tuberculosis from
cattle, estate and inheritance taxes, a tax-equalization commission,
antilobbying laws, and the elimination of public hangings.[14]

   These accomplishments may not establish Vardaman and Bilbo
as great statesmen, but they should tend to offset the charge of
"demagoguery" which has been so generally hurled at them by the
"respectable" press. If these reforms were effected by corrupt
means, as was so generally charged of Bilbo, that is merely the price
that has to be paid when reforms are neglected until a man of
Bilbo's type comes to power. The astonishing thing, as Gerald
Johnson points out, was the conservatism of the programs of these
"wild men" and the bitterness and hatred which the "wild men"
provoked in the "respectable" people. Instead of turning the affairs
of state into chaos, as was freely predicted, all they advocated and
gained was what was generally regarded in other sections "as the
merest routine of good government. Roads, schools, public health
service, the imposition of taxes on those best able to pay."[15] The
success of both Vardaman and Bilbo is proof of the inadequacy of
the kind of government in Mississippi before them. "Call these men
demagogues if you will," says Ray Stannard Baker speaking of
southern "demagogues" in general, ". . . they yet represent a genuine movement for a more democratic government in the South."[16]

   As for the Negro, whose presence in such large numbers in Mississippi has given such a distinctive influence to its politics, his lot
did not change throughout the period. No one thought of him save
to hold him down. No one sought to improve him. Whether race
baiters like Vardaman were in power, or whether "respectable"
politicians governed, he fared the same—no better, no worse. He
was and is the neglected man in Mississippi, though not the forgotten man.

   [14]Mississippi, *Laws*, 1916, Chaps. CX, CLXXX, XCII, XCV, CC, CCI, CCII,
CCIII, CCIV, CCV, CCVI, L, LXVII, LXVIII, CVIII; *ibid*, 1918, CCLVIII.
   [15]Johnson, "Live Demagogues or Dead Gentlemen," *loc. cit.*, 12.
   [16]Ray S. Baker, "The Negro in Politics," *loc. cit.*, 180.

CRITICAL ESSAY ON AUTHORITIES

The most fruitful source of manuscript material used in the preparation of this book was the Letters of Governors Series in the Mississippi Department of Archives and History at Jackson, Mississippi. Voluminous correspondence of the period up to 1899 is chronologically arranged in several hundred boxes. Practically all of the material in this collection is incoming mail to the governor's office. Much of it is routine correspondence—petitions for jobs and pardons. Yet scattered here and there are letters from local henchmen of the governor revealing matters of utmost secrecy and import and giving some insight into the actual working of a political organization at its core.

The John Sharp Williams Papers in the Division of Manuscripts of the Library of Congress contain more than two hundred boxes, chronologically arranged, of Williams' correspondence. The collection contains both outgoing and incoming mail. Most of the items are concerned with the period after Williams went to the Senate in 1909. One letter of Williams to President Cleveland, written in December, 1892, throws some light on the Populist movement in Mississippi. There are several items in the period 1915-1917 which help explain the behind-the-scenes break between Williams and Vardaman and also the Vardaman-Bilbo split.

The Henry L. Burkitt Diaries, 1875-1897, and the Frank Burkitt Diary for 1907, both in the possession of Mrs. Ruth Burkitt Gaskin of Paris, Tennessee, are most disappointing, containing almost no reference whatsoever to politics. The same is true of the James L. Alcorn Papers in the Southern Historical Collection of the University of North Carolina and the James T. Harrison Papers in the Stephen D. Lee Collection in the same institution. There were a few items of interest in the small Charlton N. Clark Collection and the George Wilson Humphrey Collection, both in the Mississippi Department of Archives and History. The James Z. George Papers and L. Q. C. Lamar Letterbooks in the same depository are small collections and reveal little of the great influence which both men executed on Mississippi politics.

Of slight value to the student of the period are the Henry Patrick Papers at Duke University, the L. P. Reynolds Papers in the Mississippi Department of Archives and History, the Lamar and Mayes Papers in the Daniel Manning Collection, Division of Manuscripts, Library of Congress, and the Grover Cleveland Papers in the Library of Congress.

PUBLIC DOCUMENTS

Mississippi *House Journals,* 1876-1924 (Jackson, 1876-   ) and Mississippi *Senate Journals,* 1876-1924 (Jackson, 1876-   ) were used for the identification of legislative activities, for governors' messages, and for special investigating committee reports. Mississippi, Secretary of State, *Biennial Report to Legislature,* 1896-1924 (Jackson, 1896-   ), contains the annual reports of the several executive departments. Mississippi *Laws,* 1870-1924 (Jackson, 1870-   ) contain the legislation enacted by the state legislature. The Mississippi constitutions of 1868 and 1890 are printed in Francis N. Thorpe (ed.), *The Federal and State Constitutions, Colonial Charters, and Other Organic Laws of the States, Territories, and Colonies Now or Heretofore Forming the United States of America,* 7 vols. (Washington, 1909), IV. The *Journal of the Proceedings of the Constitutional Convention of the State of Mississippi Begun at the City of Jackson on August 12, 1890 and Concluded November 1, 1890* (Jackson, 1890) contains the proceedings of the convention but not the debates. *Investigation by the Senate of the State of Mississippi of the Charges of Bribery in the Election of a United States Senator* (Nashville, 1910) gives a complete transcript of testimony in the investigation following the Secret Caucus.

The United States *Census,* 1880-1910, is the source for all population statistics used. The *Congressional Record,* 63rd Congress, 64th Congress, and 65th Congress, is used for an evaluation of Vardaman's activities in the United States Senate.

NEWSPAPERS AND PERIODICALS

The newspaper with the largest state circulation for the period was the Jackson *Clarion* and its successor the *Clarion-Ledger.* Next in importance to it were probably the Jackson *News,* the Natchez *Democrat,* and the Vicksburg *Herald.* They constituted the "big-city" press in contrast to the rural or "county" papers and were generally to be found defending the conservative side of all political issues and parties. An exception to this generality was the Vicksburg *Herald's* advocacy of Vardaman's cause from 1903 to 1909. A complete file of the *Clarion-Ledger* is in the possession of the Mississippi Department of Archives and History. The Department has numerous issues of the others, but a more complete file of each is in the newspaper collection of the Library of Congress. Between the two collections the student can find all but a few issues in the period. Closely akin to the above in its editorial slant is the Macon *Beacon,* a very extensive file of which is in the Duke University Library. More liberal in policy were the Vicksburg *Post* and the Vicksburg *Democrat-Commercial,* numerous files of which are either in the Mississippi Department of Archives and History or in the Library of Congress.

Papers edited by James K. Vardaman were the Greenwood *Enterprise* (1891-1893) and the Greenwood *Commonwealth* (1894-1902). Files for these years are in the courthouse in Greenwood. Vardaman later edited the Jackson *Issue* and *Vardaman's Weekly.* Files of these latter two are in the Mississippi Department of Archives and History.

Scattering issues of county papers examined were the Aberdeen *Examiner,* the Aberdeen *Weekly,* the Brookhaven *Leader,* the Carroll *News,* the *Jones County News,* the Oxford *Eagle,* the Senatobia *Democrat,* the Tunica *Independent,* and the Yazoo *Sentinel.* A few issues of Frank Burkitt's Okolona *Chickasaw Messenger* are in the possession of Mrs. Ruth Burkitt Gaskin of Paris, Tennessee.

In the Library of Congress are scattered issues of several Negro papers published in Mississippi. Among these are the Jackson *Weekly Pilot,* the Vicksburg *Golden Rule,* and the Vicksburg *Light.* The Jackson *Daily Times* was a Republican paper which continued publication for only a few years after the revolution of 1875.

Out-of-state papers of wide circulation in Mississippi were the Memphis *Appeal* and its successor the *Commercial Appeal,* the New Orleans *Daily News,* the New Orleans *Daily Picayune* and its successor the *Times-Picayune,* and the New Orleans *Sunday States.*

The following periodicals published articles pertinent to this study: *Outlook; American Magazine; Christian Century; Congressional Digest; Cosmopolitan; South Atlantic Quarterly; New Republic; Scholastic; Atlantic Monthly; North American Review; Harper's Weekly; Virginia Quarterly Review; Journal of Negro History; Independent; Nation; American Political Science Review; Review of Reviews;* and *Survey Graphic.*

STUDIES IN MISSISSIPPI HISTORY

The most significant recent publication concerning Mississippi history is Vernon L. Wharton's *The Negro in Mississippi, 1865-1890* (Chapel Hill, 1947). Mr. Wharton traces all phases of the Negro's career in the early decades after emancipation. His chapters pertaining to the Negro's participation in politics and the devious methods used to disfranchise him are a valuable contribution to an understanding of the period. An earlier work of value is James W. Garner, *Reconstruction in Mississippi* (New York and London, 1901).

Mississippi's most prolific historian, Dunbar Rowland, gathered voluminous data on the history of the state, but many of his interpretations are questionable. Of great value for this period are his *History of Mississippi, the Heart of the South*, 2 vols. (Chicago and Jackson, 1925) and *Encyclopedia of Mississippi History*, 2 vols. (Madison, Wis., 1907). He also contributed a chapter in Volume II of *The South in the Building of the Nation*, 12 vols. (Richmond, 1909-1913). He also edited *The Official and Statistical Register of the State of Mississippi*, 6 vols. (1904-1928). This latter is a compendium of Mississippi political history with brief biographical sketches of many officials.

Of considerable value to the student of fiscal affairs is M. C. Rhodes, *History of Taxation in Mississippi, 1798-1929* (Nashville, 1930). A monograph of equal importance is Stuart G. Noble, *Forty Years of the Public Schools in Mississippi* (New York, 1918).

William D. McCain's "The Populist Party in Mississippi" (M. A. thesis, University of Mississippi, 1931) has valuable interpretive material on Mississippi's excursion into populism.

The Mississippi Historical Society's *Publications*, 14 vols. (Oxford, 1898-1914), and Centenary Series, 5 vols. (Jackson, 1916-1921), contain many articles of considerable value by contemporaries and students. Among the better are: Charles B. Brough, "History of Taxation in Mississippi," II, 113-124; Alfred Benjamin Butts, "Public Administration in Mississippi," Centenary Series, III, entire volume; S. S. Calhoon, "Causes and Events that Led to the Constitutional Convention of 1890," VI, 105-111; Frank A. Johnston, "The Conference of October 15, 1875, Between General George and Governor Ames," VI, 65-77; Frank A. Johnston, "Suffrage and Reconstruction in Mississippi," VI, 141-244; J. H. Jones, "History of the Measures Submitted to the Committee on Penitentiary in the Constitutional Convention of 1890," VI, 111-128; J. S. McNeily, "Climax and Collapse of Reconstruction in Mississippi, 1874-1876," XII, 283-474; J. S. McNeily, "History of Measures Submitted to the Committee on Elective Franchise, Apportionment, and Election in the Constitutional Convention of 1890," VI, 129-140; Edmond F. Noel, "Mississippi's Primary Election Laws," VIII, 239-251; and R. H. Thompson, "Suffrage in Mississippi," I, 25-49.

Miss Willie D. Halsell has made some valuable contributions to an understanding of the so-called Bourbon period of Mississippi politics in articles published in the *Journal of Mississippi History*, II (1940), 123-125, and in the *Journal of Southern History*, VII (1941), 84-101, and X (1944), 37-58. Other articles in the *Journal of Southern History* are: William A. Mabry, "Disfranchisement of the Negro in Mississippi," IV, 318-333; A. B. Moore, "One Hundred Years of Reconstruction," IX, 153-183; and Daniel M. Robison, "From Tillman to Long: Some Striking Leaders of the Rural South," III, 289-310.

The conclusions of Alfred Holt Stone in "The Basis of White Political Control in Mississippi," in the *Journal of Mississippi History*, VI (1944), 225-236, are conventional but not to be trusted. Ray Stannard Baker published a series of articles analyzing the racial problem in the South. They may be found in *American Magazine*, LXVI (1908), and LXIII (1907).

BIOGRAPHICAL MATERIALS ON MISSISSIPPI

Full-length biographies of L. Q. C. Lamar by Edward Mayes and by Wirt A. Cate throw considerable light on the earlier decades of this period. George Osborn's *John Sharp Williams* (Baton Rouge, 1943) does the same for the later decades. From a literary point of view the best book ever written about Mississippi is William Alexander Percy's *Lanterns on the Levee* (New York, 1941). Its particular significance to the student is its reflection of the anti-Vardaman point of view during the period of reform in the early decades of this century.

Practically all of the material on Vardaman was written by devoted followers of the "Great White Chief" and is not unbiased. A. S. Coody's *Biographical Sketches of James Kimble Vardaman*

(Jackson, 1922) is completely untrustworthy. Of somewhat more scholarly quality are: Wiley Rufus Huddleston, "The Senatorial Campaign of James Kimble Vardaman, Mississippi's 'White Chief'" (M. A. thesis, Louisiana State University, 1935); and Heber A. Ladner, "J. K. Vardaman in Mississippi Politics" (M. A. thesis, Duke University, 1938).

No full-length biographical studies have been made of other Mississippians of the period, but articles concerning them are: Mary Virginia Duval, "The Chevalier Bayard of Mississippi; Edward Cary Walthall," in Mississippi Historical Society, *Publications*, IV, 401-413; James W. Garner, "Senatorial Career of J. Z. George," in Mississippi Historical Society, *Publications*, VIII, 201-226; and Garrard Harris, "A Defense of Governor Vardaman," in *Harper's Weekly*, XLIX (1905), 236-238.

Works Not Especially Concerned with Mississippi

The background for agrarian discontent is related in Emory Q. Hawk, *Economic History of the South* (New York, 1934); Julian A. C. Chandler and others, *The South in the Building of the Nation*, 12 vols. (Richmond, 1909-1913); and Solon J. Buck, *The Granger Movement: A Study of Agricultural Organizations and its Political, Economic, and Social Manifestations, 1870-1880* (Cambridge, 1913). Buck traces the course of the movement in *The Agrarian Crusade* (New Haven, 1921). Good studies of the movement in other southern states are given in C. Vann Woodward, *Tom Watson: Agrarian Rebel* (New York, 1938), and in Francis Butler Simkins, *Pitchfork Ben Tillman: South Carolinian* (Baton Rouge, 1944).

An able study of the resulting Negro problem in the South is Paul Lewinson, *Race, Class, and Party* (London and New York, 1932).

NOTE TO THE TORCHBOOK EDITION

Books written since publication of this work which throw light on Mississippi politics of the period are:

Thomas D. Clark, *The Emerging South* (New York, 1961); John S. Ezell, *The South Since 1865* (New York, 1963); E. Franklin Frazier, *The Negro in the United States* (New York, 1949); Dewey W. Grantham, Jr., *The Democratic South* (Athens, Georgia, 1963); V. O. Key, Jr., *Southern Politics in State and Nation* (New York, 1949); C. Vann Woodward, *Origins of the New South* (Baton Rouge, 1951).

INDEX

harper ✦ torchbooks

HUMANITIES AND SOCIAL SCIENCES

American Studies: General

THOMAS C. COCHRAN: The Inner Revolution: *Essays on the Social Sciences in History*   TB/1140

EDWARD S. CORWIN: American Constitutional History. *Essays edited by Alpheus T. Mason and Gerald Garvey*   TB/1136

A. HUNTER DUPREE: Science in the Federal Government: *A History of Policies and Activities to 1940*   TB/573

OSCAR HANDLIN, Ed.: This Was America: *As Recorded by European Travelers in the Eighteenth, Nineteenth and Twentieth Centuries. Illus.*   TB/1119

MARCUS LEE HANSEN: The Atlantic Migration: 1607-1860. *Edited by Arthur M. Schlesinger; Introduction by Oscar Handlin*   TB/1052

MARCUS LEE HANSEN: The Immigrant in American History. *Edited with a Foreword by Arthur M. Schlesinger*   TB/1120

JOHN HIGHAM, Ed.: The Reconstruction of American History   TB/1068

ROBERT H. JACKSON: The Supreme Court in the American System of Government   TB/1106

JOHN F. KENNEDY: A Nation of Immigrants. *Illus. Revised and Enlarged. Introduction by Robert F. Kennedy*   TB/1118

RALPH BARTON PERRY: Puritanism and Democracy   TB/1138

ARNOLD ROSE: The Negro in America: *The Condensed Version of Gunnar Myrdal's An American Dilemma*   TB/3048

MAURICE R. STEIN: The Eclipse of Community: *An Interpretation of American Studies*   TB/1128

W. LLOYD WARNER and Associates: Democracy in Jonesville: *A Study in Quality and Inequality* ‖   TB/1129

W. LLOYD WARNER: Social Class in America: *The Evaluation of Status*   TB/1013

American Studies: Colonial

BERNARD BAILYN, Ed.: The Apologia of Robert Keayne: *Self-Portrait of a Puritan Merchant*   TB/1201

BERNARD BAILYN: The New England Merchants in the Seventeenth Century   TB/1149

JOSEPH CHARLES: The Origins of the American Party System   TB/1049

LAWRENCE HENRY GIPSON: The Coming of the Revolution: 1763-1775. † *Illus.*   TB/3007

LEONARD W. LEVY: Freedom of Speech and Press in Early American History: *Legacy of Suppression*   TB/1109

PERRY MILLER: Errand Into the Wilderness   TB/1139

PERRY MILLER & T. H. JOHNSON, Eds.: The Puritans: *A Sourcebook of Their Writings*
Vol. I TB/1093; Vol. II TB/1094

KENNETH B. MURDOCK: Literature and Theology in Colonial New England   TB/99

WALLACE NOTESTEIN: The English People on the Eve of Colonization: 1603-1630. † *Illus.*   TB/3006

LOUIS B. WRIGHT: The Cultural Life of the American Colonies: 1607-1763. † *Illus.*   TB/3005

American Studies: From the Revolution to the Civil War

JOHN R. ALDEN: The American Revolution: 1775-1783. † *Illus.*   TB/3011

RAY A. BILLINGTON: The Far Western Frontier: 1830-1860. † *Illus.*   TB/3012

GEORGE DANGERFIELD: The Awakening of American Nationalism: 1815-1828. † *Illus.*   TB/3061

CLEMENT EATON: The Freedom-of-Thought Struggle in the Old South. *Revised and Enlarged. Illus.*   TB/1150

CLEMENT EATON: The Growth of Southern Civilization: 1790-1860. † *Illus.*   TB/3040

LOUIS FILLER: The Crusade Against Slavery: 1830-1860. † *Illus.*   TB/3029

DIXON RYAN FOX: The Decline of Aristocracy in the Politics of New York: 1801-1840. ‡ *Edited by Robert V. Remini*   TB/3064

FELIX GILBERT: The Beginnings of American Foreign Policy: *To the Farewell Address*   TB/1200

FRANCIS J. GRUND: Aristocracy in America: *Social Class in the Formative Years of the New Nation*   TB/1001

ALEXANDER HAMILTON: The Reports of Alexander Hamilton. ‡ *Edited by Jacob E. Cooke*   TB/3060

DANIEL R. HUNDLEY: Social Relations in Our Southern States. ‡ *Edited by William R. Taylor*   TB/3058

THOMAS JEFFERSON: Notes on the State of Virginia. ‡ *Edited by Thomas P. Abernethy*   TB/3052

BERNARD MAYO: Myths and Men: *Patrick Henry, George Washington, Thomas Jefferson*   TB/1108

JOHN C. MILLER: Alexander Hamilton and the Growth of the New Nation   TB/3057

RICHARD B. MORRIS, Ed.: The Era of the American Revolution   TB/1180

† The New American Nation Series, edited by Henry Steele Commager and Richard B. Morris.

‡ American Perspectives series, edited by Bernard Wishy and William E. Leuchtenburg.

* The Rise of Modern Europe series, edited by William L. Langer.

‖ Researches in the Social, Cultural, and Behavioral Sciences, edited by Benjamin Nelson.

§ The Library of Religion and Culture, edited by Benjamin Nelson.

Σ Harper Modern Science Series, edited by James R. Newman.

º Not for sale in Canada.

GILBERT BURCK & EDITORS OF FORTUNE: The Computer Age TB/1179

THOMAS C. COCHRAN: The American Business System: A Historical Perspective, 1900-1955 TB/1080

THOMAS C. COCHRAN: The Inner Revolution: Essays on the Social Sciences in History TB/1140

THOMAS C. COCHRAN & WILLIAM MILLER: The Age of Enterprise: A Social History of Industrial America TB/1054

ROBERT DAHL & CHARLES E. LINDBLOM: Politics, Economics, and Welfare: Planning and Politico-Economic Systems Resolved into Basic Social Processes TB/3037

PETER F. DRUCKER: The New Society: The Anatomy of Industrial Order TB/1082

EDITORS OF FORTUNE: America in the Sixties: The Economy and the Society TB/1015

ROBERT L. HEILBRONER: The Great Ascent: The Struggle for Economic Development in Our Time TB/3030

FRANK H. KNIGHT: The Economic Organization TB/1214

FRANK H. KNIGHT: Risk, Uncertainty and Profit TB/1215

ABBA P. LERNER: Everybody's Business: Current Assumptions in Economics and Public Policy TB/3051

ROBERT GREEN MCCLOSKEY: American Conservatism in the Age of Enterprise, 1865-1910 TB/1137

PAUL MANTOUX: The Industrial Revolution in the Eighteenth Century: The Beginnings of the Modern Factory System in England ° TB/1079

WILLIAM MILLER, Ed.: Men in Business: Essays on the Historical Role of the Entrepreneur TB/1081

PERRIN STRYKER: The Character of the Executive: Eleven Studies in Managerial Qualities TB/1041

PIERRE URI: Partnership for Progress: A Program for Transatlantic Action TB/3036

Contemporary Culture

JACQUES BARZUN: The House of Intellect TB/1051

JOHN U. NEF: Cultural Foundations of Industrial Civilization TB/1024

NATHAN M. PUSEY: The Age of the Scholar: Observations on Education in a Troubled Decade TB/1157

PAUL VALÉRY: The Outlook for Intelligence TB/2016

Historiography & Philosophy of History

ISAIAH BERLIN et al.: History and Theory: Studies in the Philosophy of History. Edited by George H. Nadel TB/1208

JACOB BURCKHARDT: On History and Historians. Introduction by H. R. Trevor-Roper TB/1216

WILHELM DILTHEY: Pattern and Meaning in History: Thoughts on History and Society. ° Edited with an Introduction by H. P. Rickman TB/1075

H. STUART HUGHES: History as Art and as Science: Twin Vistas on the Past TB/1207

RAYMOND KLIBANSKY & H. J. PATON, Eds.: Philosophy and History: The Ernst Cassirer Festschrift. Illus. TB/1115

MILTON C. NAHM: Genius and Creativity: An Essay in the History of Ideas TB/1196

JOSE ORTEGA Y GASSET: The Modern Theme. Introduction by Jose Ferrater Mora TB/1038

SIR KARL R. POPPER: The Poverty of Historicism ° TB/1126

G. J. RENIER: History: Its Purpose and Method TB/1209

W. H. WALSH: Philosophy of History: An Introduction TB/1020

History: General

L. CARRINGTON GOODRICH: A Short History of the Chinese People. Illus. TB/3015

DAN N. JACOBS & HANS H. BAERWALD: Chinese Communism: Selected Documents TB/3031

BERNARD LEWIS: The Arabs in History TB/1029

SIR PERCY SYKES: A History of Exploration. ° Introduction by John K. Wright TB/1046

History: Ancient and Medieval

A. ANDREWES: The Greek Tyrants TB/1103

P. BOISSONNADE: Life and Work in Medieval Europe: The Evolution of the Medieval Economy, the Fifth to the Fifteenth Centuries. ° Preface by Lynn White, Jr. TB/1141

HELEN CAM: England before Elizabeth TB/1026

NORMAN COHN: The Pursuit of the Millennium: Revolutionary Messianism in Medieval and Reformation Europe and its Bearing on Modern Leftist and Rightist Totalitarian Movements TB/1037

G. G. COULTON: Medieval Village, Manor, and Monastery TB/1022

HEINRICH FICHTENAU: The Carolingian Empire: The Age of Charlemagne TB/1142

F. L. GANSHOF: Feudalism TB/1058

EDWARD GIBBON: The Triumph of Christendom in the Roman Empire (Chaps. XV-XX of "Decline and Fall," J. B. Bury edition). § Illus. TB/46

MICHAEL GRANT: Ancient History ° TB/1190

W. O. HASSALL, Ed.: England 55 B.C.-1485 A.D.: As Viewed by Contemporaries TB/1205

DENYS HAY: The Medieval Centuries ° TB/1192

J. M. HUSSEY: The Byzantine World TB/1057

SAMUEL NOAH KRAMER: Sumerian Mythology ° TB/1055

FERDINAND LOT: The End of the Ancient World and the Beginnings of the Middle Ages. Introduction by Glanville Downey TB/1044

G. MOLLATT: The Popes at Avignon: 1305-1378 TB/308

CHARLES PETIT-DUTAILLIS: The Feudal Monarchy in France and England: From the Tenth to the Thirteenth Century ° TB/1165

HENRI PIERENNE: Early Democracies in the Low Countries: Urban Society and Political Conflict in the Middle Ages and the Renaissance. Introduction by John H. Mundy TB/1110

STEVEN RUNCIMAN: A History of the Crusades. Volume I: The First Crusade and the Foundation of the Kingdom of Jerusalem. Illus. TB/1143

FERDINAND SCHEVILL: Siena: The History of a Medieval Commune. Introduction by William M. Bowsky TB/1164

SULPICIUS SEVERUS et al.: The Western Fathers: Being the Lives of Martin of Tours, Ambrose, Augustine of Hippo, Honoratus of Arles and Germanus of Auxerre. Edited and translated by F. O. Hoare TB/309

HENRY OSBORN TAYLOR: The Classical Heritage of the Middle Ages. Foreword and Biblio. by Kenneth M. Setton TB/1117

F. VAN DER MEER: Augustine The Bishop: Church and Society at the Dawn of the Middle Ages TB/304

J. M. WALLACE-HADRILL: The Barbarian West: The Early Middle Ages, A.D. 400-1000 TB/1061

History: Renaissance & Reformation

JACOB BURCKHARDT: The Civilization of the Renaissance in Italy. Introduction by Benjamin Nelson and Charles Trinkaus. Illus.
Vol. I TB/40; Vol. II TB/41

ERNST CASSIRER: The Individual and the Cosmos in Renaissance Philosophy. *Translated with an Introduction by Mario Domandi* TB/1097

FEDERICO CHABOD: Machiavelli and the Renaissance TB/1193

EDWARD P. CHEYNEY: The Dawn of a New Era, 1250-1453. * *Illus.* TB/3002

R. TREVOR DAVIES: The Golden Century of Spain, 1501-1621 ° TB/1194

DESIDERIUS ERASMUS: Christian Humanism and the Reformation: *Selected Writings. Edited and translated by John C. Olin* TB/1166

WALLACE K. FERGUSON et al.: Facets of the Renaissance TB/1098

WALLACE K. FERGUSON et al.: The Renaissance: *Six Essays. Illus.* TB/1084

JOHN NEVILLE FIGGIS: The Divine Right of Kings. *Introduction by G. R. Elton* TB/1191

JOHN NEVILLE FIGGIS: Political Thought from Gerson to Grotius: 1414-1625: *Seven Studies. Introduction by Garrett Mattingly* TB/1032

MYRON P. GILMORE: The World of Humanism, 1453-1517.* *Illus.* TB/3003

FRANCESCO GUICCIARDINI: Maxims and Reflections of a Renaissance Statesman (Ricordi). *Trans. by Mario Domandi. Intro. by Nicolai Rubinstein* TB/1160

J. H. HEXTER: More's Utopia: *The Biography of an Idea* TB/1195

JOHAN HUIZINGA: Erasmus and the Age of Reformation. *Illus.* TB/19

ULRICH VON HUTTEN et al.: On the Eve of the Reformation: "Letters of Obscure Men." *Introduction by Hajo Holborn* TB/1124

PAUL O. KRISTELLER: Renaissance Thought: *The Classic, Scholastic, and Humanist Strains* TB/1048

PAUL O. KRISTELLER: Renaissance Thought II: *Papers on Humanism and the Arts* TB/1163

NICCOLÒ MACHIAVELLI: History of Florence and of the Affairs of Italy: *from the earliest times to the death of Lorenzo the Magnificent. Introduction by Felix Gilbert* TB/1027

ALFRED VON MARTIN: Sociology of the Renaissance. *Introduction by Wallace K. Ferguson* TB/1099

GARRETT MATTINGLY et al.: Renaissance Profiles. *Edited by J. H. Plumb* TB/1162

MILLARD MEISS: Painting in Florence and Siena after the Black Death: *The Arts, Religion and Society in the Mid-Fourteenth Century. 169 illus.* TB/1148

J. E. NEALE: The Age of Catherine de Medici ° TB/1085

ERWIN PANOFSKY: Studies in Iconology: *Humanistic Themes in the Art of the Renaissance. 180 illustrations* TB/1077

J. H. PARRY: The Establishment of the European Hegemony: 1415-1715: *Trade and Exploration in the Age of the Renaissance* TB/1045

J. H. PLUMB: The Italian Renaissance: *A Concise Survey of Its History and Culture* TB/1161

CECIL ROTH: The Jews in the Renaissance. *Illus.* TB/834

GORDON RUPP: Luther's Progress to the Diet of Worms ° TB/120

FERDINAND SCHEVILL: The Medici. *Illus.* TB/1010

FERDINAND SCHEVILL: Medieval and Renaissance Florence. *Illus.* Volume I: *Medieval Florence* TB/1090 Volume II: *The Coming of Humanism and the Age of the Medici* TB/1091

G. M. TREVELYAN: England in the Age of Wycliffe, 1368-1520 ° TB/1112

VESPASIANO: Renaissance Princes, Popes, and Prelates: *The Vespasiano Memoirs: Lives of Illustrious Men of the XVth Century. Introduction by Myron P. Gilmore* TB/1111

History: Modern European

FREDERICK B. ARTZ: Reaction and Revolution, 1815-1832. * *Illus.* TB/3034

MAX BELOFF: The Age of Absolutism, 1660-1815 TB/1062

ROBERT C. BINKLEY: Realism and Nationalism, 1852-1871. * *Illus.* TB/3038

ASA BRIGGS: The Making of Modern England, 1784-1867: *The Age of Improvement* ° TB/1203

CRANE BRINTON: A Decade of Revolution, 1789-1799. * *Illus.* TB/3018

J. BRONOWSKI & BRUCE MAZLISH: The Western Intellectual Tradition: *From Leonardo to Hegel* TB/3001

GEOFFREY BRUUN: Europe and the French Imperium, 1799-1814. * *Illus.* TB/3033

ALAN BULLOCK: Hitler, A Study in Tyranny. ° *Illus.* TB/1123

E. H. CARR: The Twenty Years' Crisis, 1919-1939: *An Introduction to the Study of International Relations* ° TB/1122

GORDON A. CRAIG: From Bismarck to Adenauer: *Aspects of German Statecraft. Revised Edition* TB/1171

WALTER L. DORN: Competition for Empire, 1740-1763. * *Illus.* TB/3032

CARL J. FRIEDRICH: The Age of the Baroque, 1610-1660. * *Illus.* TB/3004

RENÉ FUELOEP-MILLER: The Mind and Face of Bolshevism: *An Examination of Cultural Life in Soviet Russia. New Epilogue by the Author* TB/1188

M. DOROTHY GEORGE: London Life in the Eighteenth Century TB/1182

LEO GERSHOY: From Despotism to Revolution, 1763-1789. * *Illus.* TB/3017

C. C. GILLISPIE: Genesis and Geology: *The Decades before Darwin* § TB/51

ALBERT GOODWIN: The French Revolution TB/1064

ALBERT GUERARD: France in the Classical Age: *The Life and Death of an Ideal* TB/1183

CARLTON J. H. HAYES: A Generation of Materialism, 1871-1900. * *Illus.* TB/3039

J. H. HEXTER: Reappraisals in History: *New Views on History and Society in Early Modern Europe* TB/1100

A. R. HUMPHREYS: The Augustan World: *Society, Thought, and Letters in Eighteenth Century England* TB/1105

ALDOUS HUXLEY: The Devils of Loudun: *A Study in the Psychology of Power Politics and Mystical Religion in the France of Cardinal Richelieu* § ° TB/60

DAN N. JACOBS, Ed.: The New Communist Manifesto and Related Documents. *Third edition, revised* TB/1078

HANS KOHN: The Mind of Germany: *The Education of a Nation* TB/1204

HANS KOHN, Ed.: The Mind of Modern Russia: *Historical and Political Thought of Russia's Great Age* TB/1065

KINGSLEY MARTIN: French Liberal Thought in the Eighteenth Century: *A Study of Political Ideas from Bayle to Condorcet* TB/1114

SIR LEWIS NAMIER: Personalities and Powers: *Selected Essays* TB/1186

SIR LEWIS NAMIER: Vanished Supremacies: *Essays on European History, 1812-1918* ° TB/1088

JOHN U. NEF: Western Civilization Since the Renaissance: *Peace, War, Industry, and the Arts* TB/1113

FREDERICK L. NUSSBAUM: The Triumph of Science and Reason, 1660-1685. * *Illus.* TB/3009

JOHN PLAMENATZ: German Marxism and Russian Communism. ° *New Preface by the Author* TB/1189

RAYMOND W. POSTGATE, Ed.: Revolution from 1789 to 1906: Selected Documents TB/1063

PENFIELD ROBERTS: The Quest for Security, 1715-1740. * Illus. TB/3016

PRISCILLA ROBERTSON: Revolutions of 1848: A Social History TB/1025

ALBERT SOREL: Europe Under the Old Regime. Translated by Francis H. Herrick TB/1121

N. N. SUKHANOV: The Russian Revolution, 1917: Eyewitness Account. Edited by Joel Carmichael
Vol. I TB/1066; Vol. II TB/1067

A. J. P. TAYLOR: The Habsburg Monarch, 1809-1918: A History of the Austrian Empire and Austria-Hungary ° TB/1187

JOHN B. WOLF: The Emergence of the Great Powers, 1685-1715. * Illus. TB/3010

JOHN B. WOLF: France: 1814-1919: The Rise of a Liberal-Democratic Society TB/3019

Intellectual History

HERSCHEL BAKER: The Image of Man: A Study of the Idea of Human Dignity in Classical Antiquity, the Middle Ages, and the Renaissance TB/1047

R. R. BOLGAR: The Classical Heritage and Its Beneficiaries: From the Carolingian Age to the End of the Renaissance TB/1125

J. BRONOWSKI & BRUCE MAZLISH: The Western Intellectual Tradition: From Leonardo to Hegel TB/3001

ERNST CASSIRER: The Individual and the Cosmos in Renaissance Philosophy. Translated with an Introduction by Mario Domandi TB/1097

NORMAN COHN: The Pursuit of the Millennium: Revolutionary Messianism in medieval and Reformation Europe and its bearing on modern Leftist and Rightist totalitarian movements TB/1037

G. RACHEL LEVY: Religious Conceptions of the Stone Age and Their Influence upon European Thought. Illus. Introduction by Henri Frankfort TB/106

ARTHUR O. LOVEJOY: The Great Chain of Being: A Study of the History of an Idea TB/1009

MILTON C. NAHM: Genius and Creativity: An Essay in the History of Ideas TB/1196

ROBERT PAYNE: Hubris: A Study of Pride. Foreword by Sir Herbert Read TB/1031

RALPH BARTON PERRY: The Thought and Character of William James: Briefer Version TB/1156

BRUNO SNELL: The Discovery of the Mind: The Greek Origins of European Thought TB/1018

PAGET TOYNBEE: Dante Alighieri: His Life and Works. Introduction by Charles S. Singleton TB/1206

ERNEST LEE TUVESON: Millennium and Utopia: A Study in the Background of the Idea of Progress. | New Preface by the Author TB/1134

PAUL VALÉRY: The Outlook for Intelligence TB/2016

PHILIP P. WIENER: Evolution and the Founders of Pragmatism. Foreword by John Dewey TB/1212

Literature, Poetry, The Novel & Criticism

JAMES BAIRD: Ishmael: The Art of Melville in the Contexts of International Primitivism TB/1023

JACQUES BARZUN: The House of Intellect TB/1051

W. J. BATE: From Classic to Romantic: Premises of Taste in Eighteenth Century England TB/1036

RACHEL BESPALOFF: On the Iliad TB/2006

R. P. BLACKMUR et al.: Lectures in Criticism. Introduction by Huntington Cairns TB/2003

RANDOLPH S. BOURNE: War and the Intellectuals: Collected Essays, 1915-1919. ‡ Edited by Carl Resek TB/3043

ABRAHAM CAHAN: The Rise of David Levinsky: a documentary novel of social mobility in early twentieth century America. Introduction by John Higham TB/1028

ERNST R. CURTIUS: European Literature and the Latin Middle Ages TB/2015

GEORGE ELIOT: Daniel Deronda: a novel. Introduction by F. R. Leavis TB/1039

ETIENNE GILSON: Dante and Philosophy TB/1089

ALFRED HARBAGE: As They Liked It: A Study of Shakespeare's Moral Artistry TB/1035

STANLEY R. HOPPER, Ed.: Spiritual Problems in Contemporary Literature § TB/21

A. R. HUMPHREYS: The Augustan World: Society, Thought and Letters in Eighteenth Century England ° TB/1105

ALDOUS HUXLEY: Antic Hay & The Giaconda Smile. ° Introduction by Martin Green TB/3503

ALDOUS HUXLEY: Brave New World & Brave New World Revisited. ° Introduction by Martin Green TB/3501

HENRY JAMES: Roderick Hudson: a novel. Introduction by Leon Edel TB/1016

HENRY JAMES: The Tragic Muse: a novel. Introduction by Leon Edel TB/1017

ARNOLD KETTLE: An Introduction to the English Novel.
Volume I: Defoe to George Eliot TB/1011
Volume II: Henry James to the Present TB/1012

ROGER SHERMAN LOOMIS: The Development of Arthurian Romance TB/1167

JOHN STUART MILL: On Bentham and Coleridge. Introduction by F. R. Leavis TB/1070

PERRY MILLER & T. H. JOHNSON, Editors: The Puritans: A Sourcebook of Their Writings
Vol. I TB/1093; Vol. II TB/1094

KENNETH B. MURDOCK: Literature and Theology in Colonial New England TB/99

SAMUEL PEPYS: The Diary of Samuel Pepys. ° Edited by O. F. Morshead. Illus. by Ernest Shepard TB/1007

ST.-JOHN PERSE: Seamarks TB/2002

GEORGE SANTAYANA: Interpretations of Poetry and Religion § TB/9

C. P. SNOW: Time of Hope: a novel TB/1040

HEINRICH STRAUMANN: American Literature in the Twentieth Century. Third Edition, Revised TB/1168

PAGET TOYNBEE: Dante Alighieri: His Life and Works. Introduction by Charles S. Singleton TB/1206

DOROTHY VAN GHENT: The English Novel: Form and Function TB/1050

E. B. WHITE: One Man's Meat. Introduction by Walter Blair TB/3505

MORTON DAUWEN ZABEL, Editor: Literary Opinion in America Vol. I TB/3013; Vol. II TB/3014

Myth, Symbol & Folklore

JOSEPH CAMPBELL, Editor: Pagan and Christian Mysteries Illus. TB/2013

MIRCEA ELIADE: Cosmos and History: The Myth of the Eternal Return § TB/2050

C. G. JUNG & C. KERÉNYI: Essays on a Science of Mythology: The Myths of the Divine Child and the Divine Maiden TB/2014

DORA & ERWIN PANOFSKY: Pandora's Box: The Changing Aspects of a Mythical Symbol. Revised Edition. Illus. TB/2021

ERWIN PANOFSKY: Studies in Iconology: Humanistic Themes in the Art of the Renaissance. 180 illustrations TB/1077

5

HERBERT FINGARETTE: The Self in Transformation: *Psychoanalysis, Philosophy and the Life of the Spirit.* ||
TB/1177

SIGMUND FREUD: On Creativity and the Unconscious: *Papers on the Psychology of Art, Literature, Love, Religion.* § Intro. by Benjamin Nelson   TB/45

C. JUDSON HERRICK: The Evolution of Human Nature
TB/545

WILLIAM JAMES: Psychology: *The Briefer Course.* Edited with an Intro. by Gordon Allport   TB/1034

C. G. JUNG: Psychological Reflections   TB/2001

C. G. JUNG: Symbols of Transformation: *An Analysis of the Prelude to a Case of Schizophrenia. Illus.*
Vol. I: TB/2009; Vol. II TB/2010

C. G. JUNG & C. KERÉNYI: Essays on a Science of Mythology: *The Myths of the Divine Child and the Divine Maiden*   TB/2014

JOHN T. MC NEILL: A History of the Cure of Souls
TB/126

KARL MENNINGER: Theory of Psychoanalytic Technique
TB/1144

ERICH NEUMANN: Amor and Psyche: *The Psychic Development of the Feminine*   TB/2012

ERICH NEUMANN: The Archetypal World of Henry Moore. *107 illus.*   TB/2020

ERICH NEUMANN: The Origins and History of Consciousness   Vol. I *Illus.* TB/2007; Vol. II TB/2008

C. P. OBERNDORF: A History of Psychoanalysis in America
TB/1147

RALPH BARTON PERRY: The Thought and Character of William James: *Briefer Version*   TB/1156

JEAN PIAGET, BÄRBEL INHELDER, & ALINA SZEMINSKA: The Child's Conception of Geometry °   TB/1146

JOHN H. SCHAAR: Escape from Authority: *The Perspectives of Erich Fromm*   TB/1155

Sociology

JACQUES BARZUN: Race: *A Study in Superstition.* Revised Edition   TB/1172

BERNARD BERELSON, Ed.: The Behavioral Sciences Today
TB/1127

ABRAHAM CAHAN: The Rise of David Levinsky: *A documentary novel of social mobility in early twentieth century America.* Intro. by John Higham   TB/1028

THOMAS C. COCHRAN: The Inner Revolution: *Essays on the Social Sciences in History*   TB/1140

ALLISON DAVIS & JOHN DOLLARD: Children of Bondage: *The Personality Development of Negro Youth in the Urban South* || TB/3049

ST. CLAIR DRAKE & HORACE R. CAYTON: Black Metropolis: *A Study of Negro Life in a Northern City.* Revised and Enlarged. Intro. by Everett C. Hughes
Vol. I TB/1086; Vol. II TB/1087

EMILE DURKHEIM et al.: Essays on Sociology and Philosophy: *With Analyses of Durkheim's Life and Work.* || Edited by Kurt H. Wolff   TB/1151

LEON FESTINGER, HENRY W. RIECKEN & STANLEY SCHACHTER: When Prophecy Fails: *A Social and Psychological Account of a Modern Group that Predicted the Destruction of the World* || TB/1132

ALVIN W. GOULDNER: Wildcat Strike: *A Study in Worker-Management Relationships* || TB/1176

FRANCIS J. GRUND: Aristocracy in America: *Social Class in the Formative Years of the New Nation*   TB/1001

KURT LEWIN: Field Theory in Social Science: *Selected Theoretical Papers.* || *Edited with a Foreword by Dorwin Cartwright*   TB/1135

R. M. MAC IVER: Social Causation   TB/1153

ROBERT K. MERTON, LEONARD BROOM, LEONARD S. COTTRELL, JR., Editors: Sociology Today: *Problems and Prospects* || Vol. I TB/1173; Vol. II TB/1174

TALCOTT PARSONS & EDWARD A. SHILS, Editors: Toward a General Theory of Action: *Theoretical Foundations for the Social Sciences*   TB/1083

JOHN H. ROHRER & MUNRO S. EDMONSON, Eds.: The Eighth Generation Grows Up: *Cultures and Personalities of New Orleans Negroes* || TB/3050

ARNOLD ROSE: The Negro in America: *The Condensed Version of Gunnar Myrdal's An American Dilemma*
TB/3048

KURT SAMUELSSON: Religion and Economic Action: *A Critique of Max Weber's The Protestant Ethic and the Spirit of Capitalism.* || ° *Trans. by E. G. French; Ed. with Intro. by D. C. Coleman*   TB/1131

PITIRIM A. SOROKIN: Contemporary Sociological Theories. *Through the First Quarter of the 20th Century* TB/3046

MAURICE R. STEIN: The Eclipse of Community: *An Interpretation of American Studies*   TB/1128

FERDINAND TÖNNIES: Community and Society: *Gemeinschaft und Gesellschaft.* Translated and edited by Charles P. Loomis   TB/1116

W. LLOYD WARNER & Associates: Democracy in Jonesville: *A Study in Quality and Inequality*   TB/1129

W. LLOYD WARNER: Social Class in America: *The Evaluation of Status*   TB/1013

RELIGION

Ancient & Classical

J. H. BREASTED: Development of Religion and Thought in Ancient Egypt. Introduction by John A. Wilson
TB/57

HENRI FRANKFORT: Ancient Egyptian Religion: *An Interpretation*   TB/77

G. RACHEL LEVY: Religious Conceptions of the Stone Age and their Influence upon European Thought. *Illus.* Introduction by Henri Frankfort   TB/106

MARTIN P. NILSSON: Greek Folk Religion. Foreword by Arthur Darby Nock   TB/78

ALEXANDRE PIANKOFF: The Shrines of Tut-Ankh-Amon. Edited by N. Rambova. *117 illus.*   TB/2011

H. J. ROSE: Religion in Greece and Rome   TB/55

Biblical Thought & Literature

W. F. ALBRIGHT: The Biblical Period from Abraham to Ezra   TB/102

C. K. BARRETT, Ed.: The New Testament Background: *Selected Documents*   TB/86

C. H. DODD: The Authority of the Bible   TB/43

M. S. ENSLIN: Christian Beginnings   TB/5

M. S. ENSLIN: The Literature of the Christian Movement
TB/6

JOHN GRAY: Archaeology and the Old Testament World. *Illus.*   TB/127

H. H. ROWLEY: The Growth of the Old Testament
TB/107

D. WINTON THOMAS, Ed.: Documents from Old Testament Times   TB/85

The Judaic Tradition

MARTIN BUBER: Eclipse of God: *Studies in the Relation Between Religion and Philosophy*   TB/12

MARTIN BUBER: Moses: *The Revelation and the Covenant*   TB/27

MARTIN BUBER: Pointing the Way. Introduction by Maurice S. Friedman   TB/103

NATURAL SCIENCES AND MATHEMATICS